D1460364

LOGO DESIGN

Volume 2

Ed. JULIUS
WIEDEMANN

LOGO DESIGN

Volume 2

TASCHEN

FOREWORD/ INTRO/CASES

Foreword: ULI MAYER-JOHANSSEN   006
Brands & Identity

Introduction: WALLY OLINS   010
What Branding is All About Today

Case 01: METADESIGN   016
The Most Beautiful French Come from New York: Exhibition ID

Case 02: SASHA VIDAKOVIC (SVIDESIGN)   026
Big & Small, East & West: How Design Can Improve Brands

Case 03: MIKE JOHN OTTO (BLACKBELTMONKEY)   034
The Core Elements of a Design Studio Corporate Identity

Case 04: DAVE KINSEY (BLK/MRKT)   042
The Making of Burton Outwear Fall/Winter 2007

Case 05: STEFAN SAGMEISTER (SAGMEISTER INC.)   054
Logo Generator for a Music Centre: Interview with Stefan Sagmeister

Case 06: MICHEL DE BOER & TOM DORRESTEIJN (STUDIO DUMBAR)   064
The National Chinese TV Competition Identity

Case 07: MARTA DI FRANCESCO (MTV EUROPE)   078
Electro Folk: MTV's New Visual Language for Emerging Markets

Case 08: ATELIER TÉLESCOPIQUE   088
Identity in the Digital Era: Pictomato for Mobile

Case 09: DEAN DI SIMONE (TENDER)   096
Exploring the Sundance Channel Identity Online

Case 10: JACOB BENBUNAN (SAFFRON BRAND CONSULTANTS)   104
Vueling: Low Cost, High Style in the Skies above Barcelona

Case 11: JOOST PERIK (BSUR AMSTERDAM)   114
Rejuvenating Wrangler with Communicative Design and Designed Communications

Case 12: JEFF KNOWLES (RESEARCH STUDIOS)   126
Xindao: the Redesign of a Sports Brand from China

Case 13: FRIDA LARIOS (IDEAS FRESCAS)   138
The Heritage of the Maya: Redesigning an Ancient Identity

LOGO COLLECTIONS

CREATIVE INDUSTRY   146
Advertising Agencies, Architects & Architecture offices, Artists,
Branding Companies, Designers & Design Offices, Film Production studios,
Illustrators, Industrial & Product Designers, Photographers

EVENTS & ENTERTAINMENT   174
Championships, Contests, Exhibitions, Fairs, Festivals, Shows, Theatre Co.

FASHION & APPAREL   198
Clothing, Eyewear, Footwear, Accessories

INSTITUTIONS, GOVERNMENT & REGIONAL   220
Associations, Churches, Cities, Clubs, Colleges, Communities, Countries,
Foundations, Institutions, Museums, Organisations, Universities, Schools

MEDIA   246
Books, Campaigns, Films, Magazines, Newspapers, Portals, Publishers,
Radio, TV, Websites

MUSIC   270
Artists, Bands, Concerts, DJs, Music Festivals, Music Websites, Record Labels

RETAILERS & FOOD OUTLETS   292
Bars, Cafés, Markets, Shopping Malls, Restaurants, Stores

SERVICE & BUSINESS   318
Banking, Catering, Consulting, Hotels, Insurance, Logistic, Telecommunication,
Transportation, Printing Service, Spas, Yoga Studios

MISCELLANEOUS   340
Beverage, Electronics, Food, Sports, Transport

INDEX/LOGOS   372

INDEX/STUDIOS   378

ULI MAYER-JOHANSSEN

BRANDS & IDENTITY

We live in a world brimming with stimuli and information, surrounded by thousands of interchangeable messages about brands and products that focus less and less on quality differentiation. There is a daily struggle to capture the customer's attention – everywhere, at all times, and on all channels. New, often soulless products are constantly being brought on to the market and all this with no end in sight. As a customer, you are lost in a maze of diversity and choice, searching for clear criteria to help you decide from among a variety of products.

The consequence for companies is that they increasingly need to think about their core characteristics, i.e. what makes them stand out and how they differ from other companies. This is often the only yardstick to help the customer decide on a particular company and its products. To differentiate themselves in the market, companies require credible packaging closely allied to their identity – something that also applies to their products. The methods a company uses to communicate

Wir leben in einer Welt der völligen Reiz- und Informationsüberflutung, umgeben von tausenden, austauschbaren Botschaften zu Marken und Produkten, die immer weniger eine Differenzierung über die Qualität zulassen. Tag für Tag wird um die Aufmerksamkeit der Käufer gerungen – überall, jederzeit und auf allen Kanälen. Immer neue, oft seelenlose Produkte werden auf den Markt geworfen. Kein Ende ist in Sicht. Vielfalt und Auswahl sind so unübersichtlich, dass uns als Kunden jegliche Orientierung verloren geht. Wir suchen nach klaren Entscheidungskriterien, die uns die Produktauswahl erleichtern.

Das hat zur Konsequenz, dass sich die Unternehmen zunehmend auf das besinnen müssen, was sie im Kern ausmacht, wodurch sie unverwechselbar sind und was sie von anderen unterscheidet. Denn das ist häufig der einzige Weg, der den Kunden hilft, sich für das jeweilige Unternehmen und damit für dessen Angebote zu entscheiden. Um sich im Markt zu differenzieren, brauchen die Unternehmen eine glaub-

Nous vivons dans un monde peuplé de signaux et d'informations, assiégés par des centaines de messages interchangeables à propos de marques et de produits, messages qui sont de moins en moins axés sur la différence de qualité. Une bataille quotidienne se livre pour capter l'attention du consommateur – partout, à tout instant et sur toutes les chaînes. De nouveaux produits, souvent dépourvus d'âme, sont constamment mis sur le marché, et la chose n'est pas près de prendre fin. En tant que consommateur, on se sent perdu dans un labyrinthe de diversité et de choix, en quête d'un critère clair qui vous aiderait à décider parmi une telle variété de produits.

Pour les sociétés, la conséquence est un besoin croissant de réfléchir à leurs caractéristiques fondamentales, autrement dit à ce qui les particularise et les différencie de leurs concurrentes. C'est bien souvent la seule aune dont peut se valoir le consommateur avant de porter son choix sur une société donnée et ses produits. Pour se différencier sur le marché, les sociétés requièrent un emballage crédible étroite-

BY **ULI MAYER-JOHANSSEN**

its brand have to match the company's individuality, which in turn must adequately convey its values and therefore be able to carry the brand.

Market identity must follow corporate identity – not the other way round.

Products and brands that only pander to short-lived market needs and which are brought into being purely because of marketing decisions have no one to fight for them, no one who believes in them or who will be responsible for their continuity. Good design can cover up missing substance and identity for a while, but it cannot replace them. Nothing is more disillusioning than unfulfilled expectations – that applies not only to relationships between people but also to relationships with brands of products, services, and companies. If the communicated expectations a company generates are taken seriously by the public, brands can grasp their chance and act strategically within the context of their identity to deliver untold

würdige, aus ihrer Identität abgeleitete Geschichte – auch für ihre Produkte. Die Art und Weise ihrer Markenkommunikation muss zu ihrer Unternehmenspersönlichkeit passen, deren Werte adäquat übersetzen und damit die Marke tragen.

Die Markenidentität muss der Unternehmensidentität folgen – nicht umgekehrt.

Produkte und Marken, die ausschließlich kurzlebigen Marktbedürfnissen folgen und aufgrund von Entscheidungen geboren wurden, die rein vom Marketing getrieben sind, haben im Zweifelsfalle keinen, der um sie kämpft, der an sie glaubt und für ihr Überleben einsteht. Diesen Mangel an Substanz und Identität kann gutes Design gewiss für eine Weile kaschieren, aber nicht beseitigen. Und nichts ist so ernüchternd wie enttäuschte Erwartungen; das ist nicht nur in zwischenmenschlichen Beziehungen so, sondern betrifft auch die Beziehung zu Produkt-, Dienstleistungs- oder Firmenmarken. Nimmt ein Unternehmen die von ihm kommunikativ

ment lié à leur identité – ce qui s'applique également à leurs produits. Les méthodes qu'emploie une société pour communiquer sur sa marque doivent être en harmonie avec la personnalité corporative, laquelle doit à son tour véhiculer adroitement ces valeurs et, par conséquent, être en mesure de soutenir la marque.

L'identité de marché doit suivre l'identité corporative – et non l'inverse.

Les produits et les marques qui répondent exclusivement à des besoins de courte durée du marché, et dont le lancement est purement le fruit de décisions de mercatique, n'ont personne pour lutter pour eux : personne ne croit en eux et personne n'est chargé de leur continuité. Un bon design peut dissimuler quelque temps l'absence de substance et d'identité, mais il ne saurait les remplacer. Rien n'est plus décevant qu'une attente non comblée – et ceci s'applique non seulement aux relations interpersonnelles mais encore aux rapports avec les marques de produits, les

possibilities. Nothing is more reliable than a promise that is honoured.

Brands that communicate an idea, a purpose, and a clear promise together with technical and rational aspects almost always have something in common with the values and attitudes people have.

They can be likened to a genetic code. Design has the task of making this code noticeable in a branded world. In an ideal scenario, a logo brings this identity together in a concentrated form. As anyone who has worked with companies on the further development of an identity-based house-brand knows, the strongest component of the corporate design that employees associate with the identity of their company is symbolised by the logo. Any changes made in this area are closely scrutinised for their rationality and eligibility, and for good reason. An over-hasty, voguish adaptation of this individual emblem can herald the collapse of a company's personality.

It is therefore a pleasure to see a number of brands collected in this second volume of *Logo Design* whose formation and further development take into account the question of tradition, the resulting present and possible future not as a side issue but as a central theme. "Building the Future on Tradition" is the title of an essay by Odo Marquard. I cannot but agree with him.

geweckten Erwartungen allerdings ernst und ergreift die Chance, strategisch im Kontext seiner Identität zu agieren, ergeben sich ungeahnte Möglichkeiten. Nichts ist glaubwürdiger als ein eingelöstes Versprechen.

Marken, die eine Idee, ein Ziel und ein klares Versprechen vermitteln, haben neben den technischen und rationalen Aspekten fast immer etwas mit den Werten und der Haltung der Menschen zu tun.

Marken tragen dies wie einen genetischen Code in sich. Design hat die Aufgabe, diesen genetischen Code in der Marken-welt spürbar werden zu lassen. Und im Logo wird diese Identität im Idealfall in konzentrierter Form auf den Punkt gebracht. Jeder, der mit Unternehmen an einer identitätsbasierten Weiterent-wicklung der eigenen Marke gearbeitet hat, weiß: Stärker als alle anderen Bestand-teile des Corporate Designs wird für die Mitarbeiter die Identität ihres Unter-nehmens durch das Logo symbolisiert. Veränderungen werden hier besonders kritisch auf ihren Hintergrund und ihre Berechtigung hinterfragt. Und das zu Recht, denn mit vorschnellen modischen Anpassungen dieses individuellen Zeichens droht die Erosion der eigenen Unter-nehmenspersönlichkeit.

Um so schöner ist es, auch in diesem zweiten Band von *Logo Design* wieder einige Marken versammelt zu sehen, bei deren Entstehung und Weiterentwicklung die Frage nach der Herkunft, der daraus resultierenden Gegenwart und der dadurch möglichen Zukunft nicht am Rande, sondern im Zentrum des Prozesses standen. „Zukunft braucht Herkunft", so lautet der Titel eines Essays von Odo Marquard. Dem kann ich mich nur anschließen.

services et les sociétés. Si les expectatives de communication qu'une société suscite sont prises au sérieux par le public, les marques peuvent saisir leur chance et agir stratégiquement dans le contexte de leur identité, pour offrir des possibilités inédites. Rien n'est plus crédible qu'une promesse qui a été tenue.

Les marques qui, outre des aspects techniques et rationnels, communiquent une idée, un propos et un engagement lisible, ont presque toujours quelque chose en commun avec les valeurs et les comportements des gens.

On peut les identifier à un code génétique. Le design a pour mission de mettre ce code en évidence dans un monde de marques. Idéalement, un logo met en relation sous forme concentrée tous les éléments de cette identité. Comme le sait quiconque a travaillé avec l'entreprise au développement futur d'une marque de distributeur reposant sur l'identité, la composante-clé du design corporatif que les personnels associent avec l'identité de leur société est symbolisée par le logo. La rationalité et l'à-propos d'une quelconque modification dans ce domaine sont examinés minutieusement, et ceci pour une bonne raison. Si elle est prématurée et dictée par la tendance, l'adaptation de cet emblème individuel peut sonner l'hallali d'une personnalité d'entreprise.

Aussi est-il réjouissant de voir nombre de marques figurant dans ce second volume de *Logo Design* tenir compte, en matière de formation et de développement futur, de la tradition, du présent qui en résulte et de l'avenir éventuel, non comme d'une question annexe mais comme d'un point absolument central. Odo Marquard a intitulé l'un de ses essais « Bâtir l'avenir sur la tradition ». Je ne puis qu'être d'accord avec lui.

Biography
Uli Mayer-Johanssen (MetaDesign)

www.metadesign.de   Location: Berlin   Position: Managing Director/
                         Year founded: 1990   Chief Design Officer

In early 1990, Uli Mayer-Johanssen founded the corporate design agency MetaDesign plus GmbH together with two partners. Since then, MetaDesign has developed into Germany's leading agency for integrated brand management. As the executive board's managing director, Mayer-Johanssen is responsible for the agency's general focus and the methods and strategies of corporate identity and corporate-design processes. Mayer-Johanssen took a degree in graphic and set design in Stuttgart. In 1986 she was awarded a diploma at the Visual Communications Department of the Hochschule der Künste, Berlin (Berlin College of Art). Her first position was with the design agency FAB Kommunikation in Berlin. She served as FAB's managing partner before establishing MetaDesign.

Uli Mayer-Johanssen hat Anfang 1990 zusammen mit zwei Partnern in Berlin die Corporate-Design-Agentur MetaDesign plus GmbH gegründet. Seither hat sich das Unternehmen zu Deutschlands führender Agentur in Sachen integrierter Markenführung entwickelt. Mayer-Johanssen zeichnet als Managing Director im Vorstand für die Ausrichtung der Agentur sowie für Methode und Strategie von Corporate Identity- und Corporate-Design-Prozessen verantwortlich. Sie hat zunächst ein Studium in Grafikdesign und Bühnenbild in Stuttgart absolviert. 1986 erwarb sie zusätzlich ihr Diplom am Fachbereich der Visuellen Kommunikation an der Hochschule der

Künste in Berlin. Ihre erste berufliche Station vor der Gründung von MetaDesign war die Design-Agentur FAB Kommunikation in Berlin, deren geschäftsführende Gesellschafterin sie zuletzt war.

Au début de l'année 1990, Uli Mayer-Johanssen fonde l'agence de communication d'entreprise MetaDesign plus GmbH avec deux associés. Depuis, MetaDesign s'est imposée en Allemagne comme le chef de file des agences de gestion intégrée de marque. En qualité de présidente du directoire, Uli Mayer-Johanssen est responsable de la démarche générale de l'agence, ainsi que des méthodes et des stratégies appliquées à l'identité corporative et aux procédures de communication de l'entreprise. Elle est titulaire d'un diplôme d'art graphique et de scénographie (Université de Stuttgart). En 1986, elle a été diplômée par le Département de communications visuelles du Hochschule der Künste, Berlin (Académie des beaux-arts de Berlin). Son premier employeur a été l'agence de communication FAB Kommunikation de Berlin, dont elle est devenue directrice associée avant de créer MetaDesign.

WHAT BRANDING IS ALL ABOUT TODAY

Looked at from the outside, brands seem to consist of a few elements – some colours, some typefaces, a strapline or slogan, all topped off with a logo or symbol, sometimes of an apparently allegorical nature but frequently consisting of a simple typeface. Sometimes a brand also embraces sound or music, and even smells. All of these ingredients seem to be mixed up and then plastered apparently more or less at random over everything the product or organisation owns or influences.

In reality though it's a tad more complicated than that. Branding is the channel through which the product, or the company, or a variety of other organisations from a symphony orchestra to a city, presents itself to all its audiences. The brand is intended to create a reputation and invoke trust, admiration, and even a sense of belonging in the people at whom it is directed. The visual manifestations of the brand, the logos, colours and so on, are simply, sometimes perhaps not so simply, the symbols of what lies behind. Branding today is increasingly significant

Äußerlich bestehen Marken nur aus wenigen Elementen: ein paar Farben, einige Schriftarten, ein Werbeslogan oder Motto, ergänzt durch ein Logo oder Symbol von manchmal sinnbildlicher Natur, das oft jedoch nur aus einem einfachen Schriftbild besteht. Bisweilen werden auch Töne, Musik und sogar Gerüche einbezogen. All diese Zutaten scheinen miteinander vermischt und dann mehr oder weniger willkürlich über alles gestülpt zu werden, was zum Produkt bzw. zur Organisation gehört oder darauf Einfluss nimmt.

Tatsächlich jedoch ist es etwas komplizierter. Durch Markenbildung präsentiert sich das Produkt, das Unternehmen oder jede andere Organisation (vom Sinfonieorchester bis zur Stadt) seiner gesamten Zielgruppe. Die Marke soll Reputation schaffen und Vertrauen, Bewunderung, ja sogar ein Zugehörigkeitsgefühl bei all jenen erwecken, an die sie sich wendet. Die visuellen Erscheinungsformen der Marke wie Logos, Farben usw. sind einfach – manchmal auch nicht so einfach – Symbole dessen, was sich hinter der Marke verbirgt.

Vues de l'extérieur, les marques semblent se composer de rares éléments – quelques couleurs, quelques polices d'imprimerie, un grand titre ou slogan, le tout surmonté d'un logo ou d'un symbole, parfois d'ordre apparemment allégorique mais se résumant souvent à un simple caractère. Il arrive qu'une marque recouvre également des sons ou de la musique, voire même des odeurs. Tous ces ingrédients semblent avoir été mélangés, puis plaqués plus ou moins au hasard sur tout ce que le produit ou l'organisation possède ou influence.

En réalité, c'est un tantinet plus compliqué que ça. La stratégie de marque est le canal par lequel le produit, l'entreprise ou une série d'autres entités allant de l'orchestre symphonique à la municipalité, se présentent à tous leurs publics. La marque est conçue pour créer une notoriété et susciter confiance, admiration, voire même un sentiment d'appartenance chez le public auquel elle s'adresse. Les manifestations visuelles de la marque, les logos, les couleurs, etc. symbolisent simplement, encore que pas si simplement parfois, ce qu'il y a

BY WALLY OLINS

and influential because it is about identity: it embraces the identity of the brand itself and also, by a process of osmosis, the identity of the people who use it or are otherwise involved with it.

So it's all quite complex. But that isn't the way it started. Modern branding began in the 19th Century with a few household products. The idea was to create a consistent, coherent, trustworthy reputation across a range of mundane household goods which ordinary working people could buy. Up till then, food and drink had been subject to adulteration, read any Dickens or Balzac novel – plenty of dirty water and chalk in the milk and a lot of brick dust in the jam. Then, for the first time ever, people could trust what they bought. Sunlight soap, Kellogg's cornflakes, and Heinz soups are all brands with their roots deep in the over-the-counter household stores of the 19th Century. They set the tone for the massive branded household-product business that followed, using colours, standardised logos, and all the rest of it to underline

Markenbildung gewinnt heute zunehmend an Bedeutung und Einfluss, denn es geht um Identität: Diese umfasst sowohl die Identität der Marke selbst, als auch, durch einen Osmoseprozess, die Identität der Menschen, die diese Marke nutzen oder auf andere Weise mit ihr verbunden sind.

Das Thema ist also ziemlich komplex, doch das war es nicht immer. Die moderne Markenbildung begann im 19. Jahrhundert mit einigen Haushaltswaren. Die Grundidee bestand darin, eine einheitliche, eingängige und vertrauenswürdige Reputation für einige alltägliche Haushaltsgüter zu schaffen, die sich durchschnittliche Arbeitnehmer leisten konnten. Bis dahin waren Nahrungsmittel oder Getränke oft gepanscht, wie man in den Romanen von Dickens oder Balzac nachlesen kann: jede Menge verschmutztes Wasser, Kreide in der Milch und viel Ziegelstaub in der Marmelade. Jetzt konnte man zum ersten Mal den Produkten vertrauen, die man kaufte. Sunlight Soap, Kellogg's Cornflakes und Heinz-Suppen – alles Marken, die fest im 19. Jahrhundert verwurzelt sind.

derrière. Aujourd'hui, la stratégie de marque revêt une importance d'autant plus forte et grandissante qu'elle porte sur l'identité : celle de la marque elle-même, mais aussi, par extension, l'identité des gens qui l'utilisent ou entretiennent un quelconque rapport avec elle.

La chose est donc assez complexe. Mais il n'en a pas toujours été ainsi. La stratégie de marque moderne a débuté au 19e siècle avec quelques produits domestiques. L'idée consistait à créer une réputation solide, cohérente et crédible, autour d'une gamme de produits de première nécessité, banals et à la portée des bourses les plus modestes. Jusqu'alors, la nourriture et la boisson avaient été adultérées, lisez pour vous en convaincre n'importe quel roman de Dickens ou de Balzac – eau sale et craie à foison dans le lait, poussière de brique dans la confiture… Là, pour la toute première fois, les gens allaient enfin pouvoir croire en ce qu'ils achetaient. Le savon Sunlight, les flocons d'avoine Kellogg et les soupes Heinz sont autant de marques dont les racines remontent aux bazars

consistency and create trust, confidence, and respect.

This was the pattern that lasted till round about the last quarter of the 20th Century. Of course, brands moved into clothes, luxury goods, cars and other products, but the pattern was established and sustained by the household-products branding business. The people who created brands used heavy advertising aimed mainly at one audience group – housewives. And then it all began to change. Starting in the 1970s, a complex mix of interrelated, mutually reinforcing patterns emerged that completely overturned the rigidly defined advertising-dominated world of household products branding.

Brands quite suddenly burst out from the narrow, strictly codified world in which they had been bred and over a period of a very few years became a commercial and then a cultural phenomenon of unparalleled power and influence.

They migrated from representing household products to retail to corporations themselves and then beyond so that now brands have become – whether we like it or not – part of the very air we breathe.

These new companies had very unusual ideas about branding. Body Shop hardly advertised. Starbucks reinvented coffee (some might say for the worse) and encouraged customers to lounge around all day reading the papers, like they had in a nineteenth-century Viennese Konditorei – the entire environment of Starbucks is the brand. And so are the people who work in it. Starbucks is not just a product but is an environmental and a behavioural, or service brand. Nike refused to recognise, or at least ignored, the traditional differences between above- and below-the-line advertising, a shibboleth greatly respected by traditional branding people. What's more, when Nike went retail, it built exhibition centres and monuments to itself. Timberland is, like Body Shop, associating itself with green issues. These brands take over huge international events. In other words,

Sie bildeten die Grundlage des sich anschließenden gewaltigen Geschäfts mit Marken-Haushaltswaren und arbeiteten mit Farbe, einheitlichen Logos usw., um ihre Kontinuität zu unterstreichen und Vertrauen bzw. Respekt zu schaffen.

Dieses Schema hatte ungefähr bis ins letzte Viertel des 20. Jahrhunderts Gültigkeit. Natürlich entstanden Marken für Kleidung, Luxusgüter, Autos und andere Produkte, doch das Verfahren an sich war durch die Markenbildung für Haushaltswaren begründet und aufrechterhalten worden. Die Markenschöpfer führten erhebliche Werbemaßnahmen durch, die sich hauptsächlich an eine bestimmte Zielgruppe richteten: die Hausfrauen. Und dann änderte sich alles. Seit den 1970er Jahren entstanden komplexe, miteinander verwobene und sich gegenseitig unterstützende Verfahren. Sie brachten die starr definierte, werbebeherrschte Welt der Markenbildung für Haushaltsprodukte ins Wanken.

Ganz plötzlich brachen Marken aus der engen und genau festgeschriebenen Welt aus, die sie hervorgebracht hatte, und wurden innerhalb weniger Jahre zu einem kommerziellen und dann zu einem kulturellen Phänomen von beispielloser Macht und Einfluss.

Von bloßen Repräsentanten für Haushaltswaren entwickelten sich Marken zu eigenständigen Unternehmen und weit darüber hinaus, sodass sie nun allgegenwärtig sind.

Diese neuen Unternehmen hatten sehr ungewöhnliche Ideen bezüglich der Markenbildung. Body Shop warb kaum, Starbucks erfand den Kaffee neu (manche mögen behaupten zum Schlechteren) und ermunterte seine Kunden, den ganzen Tag zu faulenzen und Zeitung zu lesen wie in den Wiener Konditoreien des 19. Jahrhunderts. Das ganze Starbucks-Umfeld gehört zur Marke, das gilt auch für die Mitarbeiter. Starbucks ist nicht einfach nur ein Produkt, sondern eine Umfeld- und Verhaltens- bzw. eine Dienstleistungsmarke. Nike weigerte sich, die traditio-

grand public du 19ᵉ siècle. Elles ont ouvert la voie au grand business des marques domestiques de masse qui a suivi, en recourant aux couleurs, aux logos standardisés et à tout ce qui s'en suit, pour souligner leur solidité et inspirer confiance, stabilité et respect.

Tel est le modèle qui s'est perpétué à peu près jusqu'au dernier quart du 20ᵉ siècle. Bien entendu, les marques se sont étendues aux vêtements, aux produits de luxe, aux automobiles et à d'autres produits, mais le modèle était établi et soutenu par le secteur des produits ménagers. Les créateurs de marques usait abondamment de la publicité, avec pour principale cible un segment de la population : les ménagères. Et c'est alors que tout a commencé à changer, dans les années 70, avec l'émergence d'un faisceau complexe de modèles qui, se renforçant les uns les autres, bouleversèrent littéralement le monde rigide et basé sur la publicité des produits domestiques de marque.

Brusquement, des marques se mirent à éclore de ce petit monde aux codes stricts dont elles étaient issues et, en quelques années à peine, devinrent un phénomène commercial, puis culturel, au pouvoir et à l'ascendant sans pareils.

De représentants de produits domestiques, elles devinrent détaillants pour les entreprises, puis davantage encore, de sorte qu'aujourd'hui – que cela nous plaise ou non– les marques font partie de l'air que nous respirons.

Ces nouvelles sociétés avaient de bien curieuses idées en matière de stratégie de marque. Body Shop misait résolument sur la publicité. Starbucks réinventait le café (hélas, diront certains) et encourageait ses clients à faire salon toute la sainte journée devant un journal, comme dans les pâtisseries viennoises au 19ᵉ siècle – l'environnement de Starbucks tout entier est la marque. De même que le personnel qui y travaille. Starbucks n'est pas qu'un produit, c'est une prestation de marque, d'ordre environnemental et comportemental. Nike refusait d'admettre, ou tout au moins ignorait, les différences classiques entre

they have created their own media. Above all, new brands target individuals, not socio-economic groups.

These new brands blew holes in the traditional marketing/branding business. But it didn't stop there. Brands migrated once again – this time into services. In the 1990s the service industry, led by a combination of IT and deregulation, went into explosive growth. All the statistics in every advanced country show a relative decline in manufacturing and a growth in services from the mid '70s.

Service industries are now massive brand-builders. Some of the biggest companies in the world are now service companies of one kind or another. Telefonica, France Telecom, Vodafone, Ryanair, EasyJet are all massive brands built around service not products and these barely existed before the turn of the 21st century.

Nowadays most services are heavily branded and many of the people who are in charge of managing them have been trained in the traditional school of great consumer brands – product brands. But the attempt to manage service brands as though they are product brands has created vast problems.

Product brands are about products. Kit Kat, a classic product brand, doesn't answer back, doesn't get tired, isn't anxious, is always ready to perform and always tastes the same. Service brands aren't like that. Service brands are about people. People who represent the organisation lose their tempers, get tired and anxious, and sometimes have just had enough that day. Call centres are staffed with people, not chocolate bars. Every experience with a product brand is identical. Every experience with a service brand is different.

For the customer, the person who represents the brand is the brand. If he or she doesn't perform properly, the relationship between the brand and the customer may collapse. The skills required to teach staff to live the brand have much more in common with managing people than with conventional marketing management.

nellen Unterschiede zwischen Above- und Below-the-line-Werbung anzuerkennen oder ignorierte sie zumindest; diese Attribute wurden von traditionellen Markenschöpfern in hohem Maße beachtet. Doch damit nicht genug: Als Nike in den Einzelhandel einstieg, errichtete die Marke sogar eigene Ausstellungszentren und Monumente. Timberland setzt, genau wie Body Shop, auf das Umweltthema. Diese Marken führen gewaltige internationale Events durch. Sie haben also ihre eigenen Medien kreiert. Neue Marken zielen nicht auf sozioökonomische Gruppen, sondern vor allem auf Einzelpersonen ab.

Diese neuen Marken torpedierten die traditionellen Strukturen der Vermarktung/ Markenbildung. Und die Entwicklung war nicht aufzuhalten. Marken wandelten sich noch einmal – diesmal im Bereich der Dienstleistungen. Ausgelöst durch staatliche Deregulierung und Fortschritte im IT-Bereich entwickelte sich der Dienst- leistungssektor in den 1990er Jahren explosionsartig. Ab Mitte der 1970er Jahre zeigen die Statistiken in allen fortschritt- lichen Ländern einen relativen Rückgang der Fertigungsindustrien und ein Wachstum der Dienstleistungsbranchen.

Im Dienstleistungssektor werden heute massiv Marken entwickelt. Einige der größten Unternehmen der Welt sind Dienstleistungsunternehmen: Telefonica, France Telecom, Vodafone, Ryanair, EasyJet – alles große Marken, die nicht aus Produkten, sondern aus Dienstleistungen entstanden und wie es sie vor der Wende zum 21. Jahrhunderts kaum gab.

Heute sind die meisten Dienstleistungen stark mit Marken verknüpft. Viele der Markenschöpfer, die für die Marken- führung verantwortlich sind, haben die traditionelle Schule der großen Verbraucher- und Produktmarken durchlaufen. Doch der Versuch, Dienstleistungsmarken wie Produktmarken zu führen, hat zu gewaltigen Problemen geführt. Bei Produktmarken geht es um Produkte. Kit Kat, eine klassische Produktmarke, widerspricht nicht, wird nicht müde, ist nicht ängstlich, ist immer leistungsbereit und schmeckt immer gleich. Dienstleistungsmarken

publicité média et hors média, un mot d'ordre grandement respecté par les traditionalistes du secteur. Qui plus est, lorsque Nike se mit au détail, elle construisit des centres d'exposition et des monuments à sa propre grandeur. Comme Body Shop, Timberland s'associe à des manifestations environnementales. Ces marques relayent des événements internationaux de très grande envergure; elles ont créé leur propre média. Enfin, et surtout, les nouvelles marques visent des cibles individuelles, pas des groupes socio-économiques.

Ces nouvelles marques ont affaibli le secteur traditionnel du marketing et de la valorisation de marque. Mais la chose ne s'est pas arrêtée là. Les marques ont opéré un nouveau changement de cap – cette fois en direction des services. Dans les années 90, l'industrie des services, survolée par un cocktail de technologies de l'informa- tion et de déréglementation, a connu une croissance explosive. Toutes les statistiques dans les pays industrialisés montrent un relatif recul de la production et un essor des services à partir du milieu des années 70.

Les industries de service sont désormais de grands créateurs de marques. Quelques- unes des plus grosses sociétés au monde sont aujourd'hui des sociétés de services d'un type ou d'un autre. Telefonica, France Télécom, Vodafone, Ryanair, EasyJet sont toutes des marques de masse construites autour de services et non pas de produits, une chose qui n'existait pratiquement pas avant le tournant du 21e siècle.

De nos jours, la plupart des services sont associés à une marque et la plupart des personnes chargées de les gérer ont été formées à l'école traditionnelle des marques de produit. Mais vouloir gérer les marques de services comme s'il s'agissait de marques de produit a été la source de graves problèmes.

Les marques de produit concernent des produits. Kit Kat, marque de produit classique, ne se lasse pas, n'a pas d'angoisses, est toujours prête et a toujours le même goût. Les marques de services ne sont pas comme ça. Elles concernent les gens. Les gens qui représentent l'entreprise perdent

In a product brand the most important audience is the customer – customers come first. But in a service brand the most important audience is your own staff – your own people come first. And this is what the new breed of brand manager is just starting to learn.

While product brands are pretty much ok, service brands are mostly still pretty awful. Hanging on to call centres for hours, putting up with rude airline staff, all that petty harassment which comes from badly managed service brands, is now part of our daily life. It will get better of course, but slowly. Brand managers, like most managers, are fairly conservative, they hate change and they cling on to outdated mantras like the belief that the most important audience for the brand is the customer.

While all that is going on branding continues to make relentless and inexorable progress into every kind of activity and into all our lives. Branding is getting really big. Sport, charities, the arts, and places, cities, regions and even the nation, are all branded. Dubai is a brand. Manchester United is a brand. The Berlin Philharmonic is a brand. You may not care for it much, but there isn't much sign that any of it will stop.

Why? Because we all need to belong and to express our sense of belonging and that's what the brand enables us to do.

sind anders: Hier geht es um Menschen. Menschen, die die Organisation repräsentieren, verlieren ihre Geduld, werden müde und können ängstlich sein; manchmal haben sie auch einfach keine Lust. Callcenter beschäftigen Menschen, keine Schokoriegel. Jede Erfahrung mit einer Produktmarke ist identisch. Jede Erfahrung mit einer Dienstleistungsmarke ist anders. Für den Kunden ist die Person, die die Marke repräsentiert, die Marke selbst. Handelt sie unzureichend, kann die Beziehung Kunde – Marke scheitern. Mitarbeitern beizubringen, die Marke zu „leben", hat mehr mit Menschenführung zu tun als mit konventionellem Marketing-Management. Bei einer Produktmarke besteht die wichtigste Zielgruppe aus den Kunden – der Kunde ist König. Doch bei einer Dienstleistungsmarke besteht die wichtigste Zielgruppe aus den eigenen Mitarbeitern – das eigene Personal ist König. Dies beginnt die neue Generation von Markenmanagern gerade zu lernen.

Während es bei den Produktmarken kaum etwas zu beanstanden gibt, kann man das von den Dienstleistungsmarken leider nicht behaupten – die meisten sind immer noch recht verbesserungswürdig. Sich stundenlang mit Callcentern herumzuschlagen, unhöfliches Flugpersonal in Kauf zu nehmen – all diese kleinen Ärgernisse, die man von schlecht geführten Dienstleistungsmarken kennt, gehören mittlerweile zu unserem Alltag. Natürlich wird das besser werden, aber langsam. Markenmanager sind wie die meisten Manager ziemlich konservativ – sie halten oft an einem veralteten Credo fest, etwa daran, dass die wichtigste Zielgruppe der Marke die Kunden sind.

Währenddessen macht die Markenbildung unaufhaltsam Fortschritte und drängt in jegliche Aktivität und in unser Leben. Sie hat sich bereits beachtlich ausgedehnt. Sport, Wohltätigkeitsorganisationen, die Künste sowie Orte, Städte, Regionen und sogar Nationen tragen Markenzeichen: Dubai ist eine Marke. Manchester United ist eine Marke. Die Berliner Philharmonie ist eine Marke. Und es sieht nicht danach aus, als wäre dies aufzuhalten. Warum? Weil wir alle irgendwo dazugehören und unser Zugehörigkeitsgefühl ausdrücken möchten – genau das ermöglicht eine Marke.

leur calme, se fatiguent et se font du souci. Les centres d'appels ont pour personnel des personnes, pas des barres chocolatées. Avec une marque de produit, toutes les expériences sont identiques. Avec une marque de service, elles sont toutes différentes.

Pour le client, la personne qui représente la marque est la marque elle-même. Si cette personne ne se comporte pas comme il le faut, la relation entre la marque et le client peut rompre. Les aptitudes pour apprendre au personnel à vivre la marque ont davantage à voir avec la gestion des hommes qu'avec la gestion de marketing classique.

Pour la marque de produit, le public qui compte le plus est le client. Pour la marque de service, le public le plus important est sa propre équipe. Et cela, la nouvelle génération de gestionnaires de marque commence juste à l'apprendre.

Si les marques de produit sont relativement acceptables, celles de services laissent encore grandement à désirer pour la plupart. Mariner des heures durant au bout de la ligne d'un centre d'appels, endurer le manque d'éducation du personnel d'une compagnie d'aviation et toutes les menues rebuffades qui sont la conséquence des services mal gérés, tout cela fait désormais partie de notre quotidien. Cela s'arrangera bien sûr, mais il faudra du temps.

Et pendant ce temps-là la stratégie de marque fait son chemin, inexorablement, et elle progresse dans tous les secteurs d'activité, ainsi que dans nos propres vies. La stratégie de marque est réellement en pleine expansion. Le sport, les associations caritatives, les arts, ainsi que les sites, les villes, les régions, la nation elle-même, tout est marque. Dubaï est une marque. Manchester United est une marque. Le Philharmonique de Berlin est une marque. Peut-être n'y prêtez-vous guère attention, mais il ne semble pas que cela doive prendre fin.

Pourquoi ? Parce que nous avons tous besoin d'appartenir et d'exprimer notre sentiment d'appartenance, et c'est cela, justement, que la marque nous permet de faire.

Biography
Wally Olins (Saffron Brand Consultants)

http://saffron-consultants.com   Location: London   Position: CBE/Chairman
                                  Year founded: 2001

Born in London, Wally Olins is Chairman of Saffron Brand Consultants of London, New York, and Madrid. He is one of the world's leading practitioners in corporate identity and branding. After Oxford he went into advertising in London, and was sent to India where his first big job was as head of what became Ogilvy & Mather in Mumbai, where he lived for five years. He came back to London and co-founded Wolff Olins, being its Chairman until 1997. Olins has also taught at many business schools, including London Business School, Said Business School at Oxford, Lancaster University, Imperial College Business School, Copenhagen Business School, and Duxx University in Mexico, and he frequently holds seminars on branding and communication issues around the world.

Der in London geborene Wally Olins ist Präsident von Saffron Brand Consultants in London, New York und Madrid. Er ist einer der weltweit führenden Experten für Corporate Identity und Markenentwicklung. Nach Abschluss seines Studiums in Oxford arbeitete er in der Werbung in London und wurde nach Indien geschickt, wo er seine erste große Aufgabe als Leiter der Agentur übernahm, aus der Ogilvy & Mather in Mumbai (Bombay) entstand. Dort lebte er fünf Jahre, kehrte nach London zurück und war einer der Mitbegründer der Agentur Wolff Olins, deren Vorsitz er bis 1997 innehatte. Zudem hat Olins an vielen Business Schools unterrichtet, unter anderem an der London Business School, der Said Business School in Oxford, der Lancaster University, der Imperial College Business School, der Copenhagen Business School und der Duxx University in Mexiko. Er hält häufig Seminare zu den Themen Markenentwicklung und Kommunikation auf der ganzen Welt ab.

Né à Londres, Wally Olins est le président de Saffron Brand Consultants, implanté à Londres, New York et Madrid. Il est l'un des experts mondiaux en matière d'identité d'entreprise et de valorisation de marque. Après Oxford, il intègre le secteur de la publicité, à Londres, et il est envoyé en Inde ; il s'y voit confier pour première grande mission la direction de ce qui deviendra Ogilvy & Mather à Mumbai, où il vivra cinq ans. Il rentre alors à Londres et y co-fonde la société Wolff Olins, dont il sera le président jusqu'à 1997. Wally Olins a également enseigné dans diverses écoles de hautes études commerciales, dont la London Business School, la Said Business School d'Oxford, la Lancaster University, l'Imperial College Business School, la Copenhagen Business School et la Duxx University à Mexico, et il dirige fréquemment des séminaires sur la stratégie de marque et la communication, un peu partout dans le monde.

THE MOST BEAUTIFUL FRENCH COME FROM NEW YORK: EXHIBITION ID

Challenges in cultural marketing

In order to attract attention, cultural institutions have to operate in the same strategic manner as commercial enterprises. The content is different and, of course, the way it is employed is different. Anyone who wants to formulate a cultural message that will really capture people's attention needs to investigate its characteristics just as intensively as would be the case with product and company branding. An exhibition, a museum, theatre, opera or cultural institution, has to know what it is there for, what makes it special, and, above all, how it wants to position itself. The environment in which you operate and within which you have to assert yourself is also an important factor. The competition comes not only from within the same ranks as your own particular area but with the whole of the leisure and media sector, all of which canvasses for public attention with its diverse range of products. That ever-diminishing resource 'time' becomes the biggest hurdle. To stand out, you have to reach the public with

Herausforderungen für das Marketing im Kulturbereich

Um Aufmerksamkeit zu erreichen, müssen Kulturinstitutionen inzwischen ebenso strategisch agieren wie Wirtschaftsunternehmen. Die Inhalte sind andere, und man muss sie natürlich auch anders aufbereiten. Wer eine Botschaft formulieren will, die tatsächlich das Interesse der Menschen weckt, muss sich mit den eigenen Besonderheiten genauso intensiv auseinandersetzen, wie das bei Produkt- oder Unternehmensmarken der Fall ist. Eine Ausstellung, ein Museum, ein Theater, eine Oper oder Kulturinstitution müssen wissen, wofür sie stehen, was sie besonders macht und vor allem, wie sie sich positionieren wollen. Dazu zählt auch das Umfeld, in dem man agiert und gegen das es sich zu behaupten gilt. Denn Konkurrenz besteht nicht nur innerhalb der eigenen Reihen: Der gesamte Freizeit- und Medienbereich wirbt mit seinen vielfältigen Angeboten um die Aufmerksamkeit, und die immer knapper werdende Ressource Zeit wird zu einer immer größeren

Des défis en matière de marketing culturel

Pour attirer l'attention, les institutions culturelles doivent user des mêmes stratégies que les entreprises commerciales. Le contenu diffère bien entendu, de même que la manière de les employer. Quiconque souhaite formuler un message culturel capable de retenir vraiment l'attention du public doit en analyser les caractéristiques aussi exhaustivement qu'il le ferait dans le cas d'un produit ou de la valorisation d'une marque. Une exposition, un musée, un théâtre, un opéra ou une institution culturelle, doit connaître sa propre raison d'être, ce qui le rend spécial et, surtout, comment il souhaite se positionner. L'environnement dans lequel il œuvre et dans lequel il doit s'imposer est également un facteur important. La concurrence ne se résume pas aux rangs du domaine dans lequel opère l'institution, elle peut provenir des nombreuses ramifications du secteur des loisirs et des médias, qui toutes s'efforcent de capter l'attention du public avec diverses gammes de produits. Le temps, cette peau de chagrin, s'avère en

DIE SCHÖNSTEN FRANZOSEN KOMMEN AUS NEW YORK.

FRANZÖSISCHE MEISTERWERKE DES 19. JAHRHUNDERTS AUS DEM METROPOLITAN MUSEUM OF ART, NEW YORK. 1. JUNI BIS 7. OKTOBER 2007.
NEUE NATIONALGALERIE, BERLIN. KULTURFORUM POTSDAMER PLATZ. EINE AUSSTELLUNG DER STAATLICHEN MUSEEN ZU BERLIN. ERMÖGLICHT
DURCH DEN VEREIN DER FREUNDE DER NATIONALGALERIE UND DIE WESTLB AG. **WWW.METINBERLIN.ORG**

messages and content which communicates successfully and which is relevant, interesting and unique. How that can be achieved is illustrated in the development process of the cultural marketing campaign "The Most Beautiful French Come from New York".

Beginning the campaign "The Most Beautiful French Come from New York"

The initial situation we were faced with was this: an exhibition, organised by the Friends of the National Gallery (*Verein der Freunde der Nationalgalerie*, VFN), which aimed to be the cultural event of the summer of 2007 and to attract 400,000 to 500,000 visitors in the course of four months. Berliners were a particular target audience, even more so than in the 2004 exhibition "MoMA in Berlin". Although the interest in cultural exhibitions put on in conjunction with New York's Metropolitan Museum of Art (Met) has increased in Germany in general, it is still not easy to address. To achieve a comparable resonance, a similar, strong attention-attracting dynamic of communication was required. A close analysis of the preconditions and general framework of the exhibition revealed that the Met's 19th-Century French masterpieces constitute one of its most prized collections. The collection is also a jewel in the crown of the history of art, documenting the artistic pathway into modernity and covering the subject much more than Impressionism does with its prominent protagonists. It should be made clear that not all of the collection was to come to Berlin, only a certain selection. Important 19th-Century artists such as Manet, Degas, Pissarro, Monet, Cézanne, Gauguin, Matisse, and Rodin were to have their works exhibited. So much for the facts, but would it be enough just to talk about the individual artists and their work?

Another aspect of the exhibition emerged during the analysis and this was the journey made by the artworks, i.e. these were works of art that had made their way from France to America and which would now be returning to Europe, or more exactly to Berlin.

Hürde. Wer sich durchsetzen will, muss die Menschen mit Botschaften und Kommunikationsinhalten erreichen, die relevant, interessant und besonders sind. Wie das gelingen kann, soll der Entwicklungsprozess der Kulturmarketingkampagne „Die schönsten Franzosen kommen aus New York" exemplarisch aufzeigen.

Auf dem Weg zur Kampagne „Die schönsten Franzosen kommen aus New York"

Die kommunikative Ausgangssituation: Die Ausstellung, veranstaltet vom Verein der Freunde der Nationalgalerie (VFN), sollte das Kulturereignis des Sommers 2007 werden und binnen vier Monaten 400.000 bis 500.000 Besucher begrüßen. Stärker als noch bei der Ausstellung „Das MoMA in Berlin" im Jahre 2004 sollten insbesondere auch Berliner in die Schau gelockt werden. Zwar ist das Interesse an Kunstausstellungen im Zuge des Metropolitan Museum of Art (Met) in Deutschland generell gestiegen. Aber an dieses Interesse lässt sich nicht beliebig anknüpfen. Um eine vergleichbare Resonanz zu erzielen, bedurfte es eines ähnlich aufmerksamkeitsstarken Kommunikationsimpulses. Eine eingehende Analyse der Voraussetzungen und Rahmenbedingungen der Ausstellung zeigte: Die französischen Meisterwerke aus dem 19. Jahrhundert bilden eine der wertvollsten Sammlungen des Met. Diese Sammlung ist ein Juwel der Kunstgeschichte, sie dokumentiert den Weg der Kunst in die Moderne. Sie thematisiert somit weit mehr als den Impressionismus und seine herausragenden Protagonisten. Zudem musste deutlich werden, dass nicht das gesamte Metropolitan Museum of Art nach Berlin kommen sollte, sondern ein bestimmter Ausschnitt der gesamten Sammlung. Mit Manet, Degas, Pissarro, Monet, Cézanne, Gauguin, Matisse und Rodin werden herausragende Künstler des 19. Jahrhunderts und ihre Werke präsentiert. So weit zu den Fakten, aber genügte es, über einzelne Künstler und ihre Werke zu reden?

Ein weiterer Aspekt der Ausstellung drängte sich bei der Analyse immer mehr in den Vordergrund: Die Reise der Kunst – ging

l'occurrence l'obstacle le plus sévère. Pour attirer l'attention, il faut toucher le public avec des messages et des contenus communicateurs, mais aussi pointus, intéressants et uniques. La manière d'y parvenir est illustrée par le processus de création de la campagne de marketing culturel « Les plus beaux Français viennent de New York ».

Démarrage de la campagne « Les plus beaux Français viennent de New York »

La situation initiale que nous avons dû affronter était la suivante : une exposition, organisée par l'Amicale de la Nationalgalerie (*Verein der Freunde der Nationalgalerie*, VFN), qui aspirait à devenir l'événement culturel de l'été 2007 et à attirer entre 400 000 et 500 000 visiteurs dans un intervalle de quatre mois. Les Berlinois en étaient la cible particulière, plus encore qu'en 2004 lors de l'exposition « MoMA in Berlin ». Bien que l'intérêt pour les expositions culturelles montées en collaboration avec le Metropolitan Museum of Art de New York (Met) se soit accru en Allemagne de manière générale, il n'est toujours pas aisé de faire mouche. Pour obtenir un retentissement comparable, une dynamique de communication aussi accrocheuse était donc nécessaire. Une analyse attentive des conditions préliminaires et de l'ossature générale de l'exposition révéla que les chefs-d'œuvre du 19ᵉ siècle français étaient l'une des collections les plus précieuses du Met. La collection est également un des joyaux de la couronne de l'histoire de l'art, en ce qu'elle témoigne du passage à l'art moderne et couvre le sujet bien plus largement que ne le fait l'Impressionnisme avec ses principaux protagonistes. Il devait être explicite que seule une sélection, et non toute la collection, voyagerait à Berlin. Des œuvres d'artistes majeurs du 19ᵉ siècle tels Manet, Degas, Pissarro, Monet, Cézanne, Gauguin, Matisse et Rodin y seraient exposées. Voilà pour les faits, mais suffirait-il de parler des artistes individuels et de leur travail ?

Un autre aspect de l'exposition se fit jour au cours de l'analyse : le voyage des œuvres d'art ; en effet, elles avaient fait leur chemin de la France à l'Amérique, et voilà qu'elles

DIE
SCHÖNSTEN
FRANZOSEN
KOMMEN AUS
NEW YORK.

In the course of a workshop with the people responsible for the VFN and the Berlin State Museums, key questions were discussed to identify a consensus about the relevance and significance of a number of individual aspects of the exhibition. The initial aim was to gather together as broadly as possible everything that connected the people in charge with the idea of the exhibition. What expectations and aspects of the exhibition lay hidden? What was special or unique about it? What was the goal and which themes should be used?

From this conceptual base, the various content-oriented facets of the exhibition were singled out and stated more precisely, using pictorial aids. In this way, a collective perception could be gradually developed, which formed the binding framework for any further details. This process also contributed to clarifying the significance of individual themes and values. After all, you cannot communicate everything at the same time: essential matters must be brought into focus and an appropriate way found to achieve that. The differentiating

es doch um Kunstwerke, die ihren Weg aus Frankreich nach Amerika gefunden hatten und nun zeitweilig wieder nach Europa, genauer gesagt nach Berlin, kommen sollten.

Um gemeinsam eine Vorstellung von der Relevanz und der Bedeutung einzelner Aspekte der Ausstellung herauszuarbeiten, wurden in einem Workshop mit den Verantwortlichen des VFN und der Staatlichen Museen Berlin alle zentralen Fragen erörtert. Ziel war es, zunächst einmal umfassend zu sammeln, was die verant-wortlichen Köpfe alles mit der Idee der Metropolitan-Ausstellung verbanden. Was verbarg sich an Vorstellungen und Aspekten hinter dieser Ausstellung? Was war das Besondere, das Einzigartige an ihr? Welche Ziele gab es, welche Themen sollten zum Tragen kommen?

Auf der begrifflichen Ebene wurden zunächst die vielfältigen inhaltlichen Facetten der Ausstellung gesammelt und mittels der Übersetzung in eine bildliche Dimension weiter präzisiert. So konnte man sukzessive

allaient retourner en Europe, ou plus exactement à Berlin.

Au cours d'un atelier avec les responsables de VFN et des Musées nationaux de Berlin, diverses questions clé furent débattues pour trouver un consensus quant à l'importance et la signification d'un certain nombre d'aspects individuels de l'exposition. L'objectif initial était de rassembler aussi largement que possible tout ce qui pouvait relier les personnes responsables avec l'idée de l'exposition. Quelles attentes et quels aspects y avait-t-il derrière ? Qu'avait-elle de spécial et d'unique ? Quel était l'objectif et quels thèmes devait-on utiliser ?

Sur cette base conceptuelle, les différentes facettes de contenu de l'exposition furent isolées, puis établies plus précisément à l'aide d'illustrations. Une perception collective se dégagea ainsi, peu à peu, tel un cadre où placer tous les détails ultérieurs. Le processus permit également de clarifier la signification des questions et valeurs individuelles. Après tout, on ne peut pas tout communiquer en même temps : des

aspects of the exhibition could be expressed in terms of themes such as "eternal paradise", "beauty", "overcoming borders", and "the sensuality of the painter".

The mood that emerged from this analysis enabled the whole process to be carried forward and made into a real experience. What was missing was a concise overall motif that would tie the exhibition together, give the event a strong position, and excite the general public.

Outline and final layout

An outline was developed, based on the results of the analysis and from the workshop: the journey the works of art made from New York to Berlin. 150 French masterpieces from America. French from America? There was something wonderfully confusing about the history of this collection, which was also used to promote it. The campaign played with this confusion and condensed it into the slogan "The Most Beautiful French Come from New York". The presentation then used some incisive and recognisable elements, such as the striped border with colours that evoked the French tricolour and the Stars and Stripes and which at the same time reminded Berliners of the trusty air-mail postal service. In addition, the memorable sanserif font Avant Garde was used, a typeface often seen on placards in the America of the 1950s and '60s.

A new cultural brand with a catchy appearance was created. Once the first phase of the external promotion became familiar, initially using a concise typographic-placard motif, the communication ran forward, inserting direct references to the collection inside this visual frame. Motifs followed, comprising details from works of art that conveyed the mood of the exhibition: the informality, the colours, the light, the breaking of taboos in portrayal and content, the beauty in detail. Nevertheless, the familiar brand elements remained: the frame, slogan, colours and font. To give a communicative brand a sustainable anchoring, constants are needed to provide instant recognisability.

eine gemeinsame Vorstellung entwickeln, die den verbindlichen Rahmen für alles Weitere darstellte. Dieser Prozess trug auch dazu bei, sich über die Bedeutung einzelner Themen und Werte klar zu werden. Schließlich kann man nicht alles gleichzeitig kommunizieren: Das Wesentliche muss in den Fokus gerückt und ein adäquater Weg der Vermittlung gefunden werden. Als differenzierende Aspekte der Ausstellung fanden sich Begriffe wie „Ewiges Paradies", „Schönheit", „Grenzen überwinden" und „Sinnlichkeit der Malerei".

Die Stimmung, die sich hinter diesen Beschreibungen abzeichnet, galt es zu transportieren und erlebbar zu machen. Was noch fehlte, war eine prägnante Geschichte, die die Ausstellung bündelt, um das Ereignis nachhaltig zu positionieren und die Menschen dafür zu begeistern.

Leitidee und finale Gestaltung

Auf Basis aller Ergebnisse aus Analyse und Workshop wurde die Leitidee entwickelt: die Reise der Bilder von New York nach Berlin. 150 französische Meisterwerke kommen aus Amerika. Franzosen aus Amerika? In der Geschichte dieser Sammlung liegt eine wunderbare Irritation, die für die Kommunikation genutzt wurde. Die Kampagne spielte mit dieser Irritation und kondensierte sie im Slogan „Die schönsten Franzosen kommen aus New York". Und die Gestaltung fand dafür prägnante, wiedererkennbare Elemente: Der gestreifte Rahmen, der mit seinen Farben ebenso an die Trikolore wie an die Stars and Stripes erinnert, gleichzeitig aber auch insbesondere für die Berliner die vertrauten Luftpostbriefe zitiert. Dazu die einprägsame Schrift, die Grotesk-schrift „Avant Garde", eine im Amerika der fünfziger und sechziger Jahre weit verbreitete Plakatschrift.

Eine neue Kulturmarke mit einem einpräg-samen Auftritt war geschaffen. Nachdem sie in der ersten Phase der externen Kommu-nikation zunächst über ein prägnantes Typo-Plakatmotiv bekannt gemacht wurde, stellte das Kommunikationskonzept im weiteren Verlauf innerhalb dieser visuellen Klammer konkrete Bezüge zur Sammlung

points essentiels doivent être mis en lumière et une manière appropriée d'y parvenir doit être trouvée. Les traits distinctifs de l'exposition pouvaient dès lors être exprimés par des termes tels que « paradis éternel », « beauté », « s'affranchir des frontières » et « la sensualité du peintre ».

L'atmosphère qui se dégageait de cette analyse avait permis de mener à bien le processus et d'en faire une expérience réelle, mais il manquait cependant un motif d'ensemble suffisamment concis pour ficeler le tout, positionner fermement l'exposition et séduire le grand public.

Ebauche et maquette finale

Une ébauche fut mise au point à partir des résultats de l'analyse et du travail d'atelier : le voyage qu'avaient fait les œuvres d'art de New York à Berlin. 150 chefs d'œuvre d'Amérique. Français d'Amérique ? L'histoire de cette collection avait quelque chose de merveilleusement confus, que l'on décida également d'utiliser pour la promotion. La campagne a donc joué avec cette confusion et l'a condensée dans le slogan « Les plus beaux Français viennent de New York ». Des éléments frappants et reconnaissables ont été utilisés pour la présentation, notamment le liseré rayé aux couleurs du drapeau tricolore français et des *Stars and Stripes*, qui, pour les Berlinois, rappelait en même temps leur ponctuel service postal aérien. De plus, on a retenu la fameuse police sans sérif Avant-garde, un caractère très fréquent sur les affiches américaines entre les années 50 et 60.

Une nouvelle marque culturelle à l'allure séduisante venait de naître. Une fois la première phase de promotion externe devenue familière, en recourant tout d'abord à un motif typographique concis, la communication se poursuivit par l'insertion de références directes à la collection dans ce cadre visuel. Des motifs suivirent, avec notamment des détails d'œuvres d'art capables de transmettre l'atmosphère de l'exposition : non-conformisme, couleurs, lumière, tabous du portrait et du contenu brisés, beauté du détail. Néanmoins, les éléments leitmotiv de la marque demeu-

Page 17: *Exhibition poster. ///* **Seite 17**: *Ausstellungsplakat. ///* **Page 17** : *Affiche d'exposition.*

Previous spread: *Printed material used to promote the exhibition. ///* **Vorhergehende Seite:** *Werbemappe zur Ausstellung. ///* **Double page précédente** : *Supports promotionnels de l'exposition.*

Right: *Backlit posters in Berlin. ///* **Rechts:** *Rückseitig beleuchtete Plakate in Berlin. ///* **A droite** : *Affiches rétro éclairées à Berlin.*

Press and publicity work as a part of the branding strategy

The media reaction to the exhibition and its advertising campaign was remarkable. Analysis by the Friends of the National Gallery documented 1,828 articles in the German print media about "The Most Beautiful French Come from New York". The press was happy to carry the theme and slogan. The campaign press and publicity work made such a media reaction possible. MetaDesign and Friends of the National Gallery were able to profit from their joint experience on "MoMA in Berlin" during the theoretical preparatory work and its practical implementation, namely by forming early media partnerships and constantly generating new themes that attracted attention, in particular outside the features pages. In the end, the press coverage did most of the advertising work for the exhibition. A similarly effective media budget would have been prohibitive for Friends of the National Gallery.

her. Es folgten Motive, deren Ausschnitte aus Kunstwerken die Stimmung der Ausstellung vermittelten: das Leichte, die Farben, das Licht, die Tabubrüche in Darstellung und Inhalt, die Schönheit im Detail. Erhalten blieben aber stets die gelernten Elemente der Marke: der Rahmen, der Slogan, die Farben und die Schrift. Um eine Marke in der Kommunikation nachhaltig zu verankern, müssen Konstanten für eine schnelle Wiedererkennung sorgen.

Presse- und Öffentlichkeitsarbeit als Teil der Markenstrategie

Die Medienresonanz auf die Ausstellung und ihre Kampagne war beachtlich. Die Auswertung des Vereins der Freunde der Nationalgalerie verzeichnete 1.828 in deutschen Printmedien erschienene Artikel zu „Die schönsten Franzosen kommen aus New York". Die Presse nahm also das Thema und den Slogan dankbar auf. Mit der Presse- und Öffentlichkeitsarbeit zur Kampagne wurde die Basis für eine derartige Medienresonanz gelegt. Hier konnten

raient : le cadre, le slogan, les couleurs et la police de caractères. Pour ancrer solidement une marque qui communique, il faut lui associer des constantes instantanément identifiables.

Le travail de presse et de publicité comme partie intégrante de la stratégie de marque

Les médias réagirent remarquablement bien à l'exposition et à sa campagne de publicité. Une analyse effectuée par l'Amicale de la NationalGalerie recense pas moins de 1828 articles dans la presse allemande au sujet de « Les plus beaux Français viennent de New York ». La presse se montra ravie de relayer le thème et le slogan, une réaction qu'il faut porter au crédit de la campagne de presse et du travail publicitaire. Durant le travail théorique préparatoire et sa mise en pratique, MetaDesign et *Verein der Freunde der Nationalgalerie* surent mettre à profit leur expérience conjointe lors de « MoMA in Berlin », notamment en nouant très tôt des liens de partenariat avec la presse et en générant sans cesse de nouveaux thèmes

No clear profile without a clear strategy

Cultural institutions have the difficult task of trying to attract attention on a very low budget. The means they have available must be used to maximum effect. That can only happen when communication and presentation go hand in hand, and the results are strategic processes whose basis is the clarification of the fundamental content, ideas, and values to be conveyed.

This unusual process worked very well for "The Most Beautiful French…": the exhibition was attended by 680,000 visitors over 111 exhibition days, i. e. around 6,100 visitors a day. 40 per cent came from Berlin, a higher percentage than with the MoMA exhibition. Around 90 per cent of visitors said the exhibition had met their expectations and 60 per cent were "completely" happy. The campaign for "The Most Beautiful French Come from New York" made no false promises, but adequately communicated the special aspects of the exhibition and provided a perfect experience. That is what counts in the end.

MetaDesign und der Verein der Freunde der Nationalgalerie in der theoretischen Vorarbeit und praktischen Umsetzung sicher auch von den gemeinsamen Erfahrungen der Ausstellung des MoMA in Berlin profitieren: im Vorfeld Medienpartner gewinnen, immer wieder neue Themen generieren, die insbesondere jenseits des Feuilletons für Aufmerksamkeit sorgen etc. Letztlich hat die Berichterstattung in der Presse einen Großteil der Werbung für die Ausstellung erzeugt. Ein vergleichbar wirkungsvolles Medienbudget wäre für den Verein der Freunde der Nationalgalerie unbezahlbar gewesen.

Kein klares Profil ohne eine klare Strategie

Kulturinstitutionen haben die schwierige Aufgabe, mit einem äußerst geringen Budget auf sich aufmerksam zu machen. Mit den zur Verfügung stehenden Mitteln muss ein Maximum erreicht werden. Das kann gelingen, wenn Kommunikation und Gestaltung Hand in Hand gehen und sie Ergebnis eines strategischen Prozesses sind,

capteurs d'attention, en particulier en dehors de leurs propres pages. A terme, c'est la couverture de presse qui assura le plus gros du travail publicitaire de l'exposition. Un budget presse de cette envergure aurait été inabordable pour l'amicale de la *Nationalgalerie*.

Pas de profil clair sans stratégie claire

Les institutions culturelles n'ont pas la tâche facile : elles doivent attirer l'attention avec un très faible budget. Il leur faut dès lors tirer le meilleur parti des moyens dont elles disposent. Elles ne peuvent y parvenir que lorsque la communication et la présenta-tion avancent main dans la main, et que les résultats sont des processus stratégiques ayant pour base la clarification du contenu fondamental, des idées et des valeurs à transmettre.

Ce processus inhabituel a très bien fonctionné dans le cas de « Les plus beaux Français… » : l'exposition a été vue par 680 000 personnes sur 111 jours, autrement dit une moyenne de 6100 visiteurs par

From left to right: *Public advertising at subway station in Berlin; bus signage; exhibition shop.* /// **Von links nach rechts:** *Außenwerbung in einer U-Bahn-Station in Berlin; Reklame an einem Bus; Museums-Shop.* /// **De gauche à droite :** *Publicité dans une station de métro de Berlin ; signalisation de bus ; boutique de l'exposition.*

dessen Basis die Klärung der wesentlichen Inhalte, Ideen und Werte ist, die es zu vermitteln gilt.

Für „Die schönsten Franzosen" hat sich dieser für den Kulturbereich sicher ungewöhnliche Prozess gelohnt: Die Ausstellung begrüßte 680.000 Besucher an 111 Ausstellungstagen, also rund 6.100 Besucher pro Tag. Darunter waren 40 Prozent aus Berlin – und damit prozentual weit mehr Berliner als beim Besuch des MoMA. Rund 90 Prozent der Besucher gaben an, dass das Erlebte ihren Erwartungen entsprochen hat, und 60 Prozent waren „voll und ganz" zufrieden. Die Kampagne „Die schönsten Franzosen kommen aus New York" hat also keine falschen Erwartungen geweckt, sondern das Besondere der Ausstellung adäquat kommuniziert und für ein perfektes Erlebnis gesorgt. Das ist es, was zählt.

jour. 40 pour cent d'entre eux venaient de Berlin, soit un pourcentage supérieur à l'exposition montée avec le MoMA. Environ 90 pour cent des visiteurs ont assuré que l'exposition avait comblé leurs attentes et 60 pour cent se sont déclarés « absolument » enchantés. La campagne de « Les plus beaux Français viennent de New York » n'a rien promis d'irréalisable, elle a au contraire communiqué adéquatement sur les aspects particuliers de l'exposition et procuré à son public une expérience parfaite. Et c'est en définitive ce qui compte.

DIE SCHÖNSTEN FRANZOSEN KOMMEN AUS NEW YORK.

Left: *Exhibition poster.* /// **Links:** *Ausstellungs-plakat.* /// **A gauche** : *Affiche d'exposition.*

Profile
MetaDesign

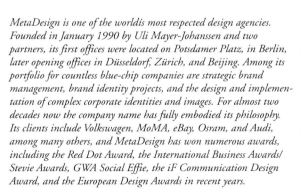

www.metadesign.de   Location: Berlin   Year founded: 1990

MetaDesign is one of the world's most respected design agencies. Founded in January 1990 by Uli Mayer-Johanssen and two partners, its first offices were located on Potsdamer Platz, in Berlin, later opening offices in Düsseldorf, Zürich, and Beijing. Among its portfolio for countless blue-chip companies are strategic brand management, brand identity projects, and the design and implementation of complex corporate identities and images. For almost two decades now the company name has fully embodied its philosophy. Its clients include Volkswagen, MoMA, eBay, Osram, and Audi, among many others, and MetaDesign has won numerous awards, including the Red Dot Award, the International Business Awards/ Stevie Awards, GWA Social Effie, the iF Communication Design Award, and the European Design Awards in recent years.

Bei MetaDesign handelt es sich um eine der angesehensten Designagenturen der Welt. Nach der Gründung durch Uli Mayer-Johanssen gemeinsam mit zwei Partnern im Januar 1990 lagen die ersten Büroräume am Potsdamer Platz in Berlin. Später kamen weitere Agenturbüros in Düsseldorf, Zürich und Peking hinzu. Zu dem Portfolio der Agentur für zahllose erstklassige Unternehmen gehören strategische Markenführung, Projekte über Markenidentität sowie das Design und die Realisierung komplexer Projekte im Bereich Corporate Identity und Imagebildung. Seit fast

zwei Jahrzehnten verkörpert das Unternehmen nun seine Philosophie. Zu seinen Kunden gehören, neben vielen anderen, Volkswagen, MoMA, eBay, Osram und Audi. MetaDesign hat zahlreiche Auszeichnungen erhalten, darunter den Red Dot Award, die International Business Awards/Stevie Awards, GWA Social Effie, den iF Communication Design Award und die European Design Awards in den letzten Jahren.

MetaDesign est l'une des agences de design les plus prestigieuses au monde. Fondée en janvier 1990 par Uli Mayer-Johanssen et deux associés, elle a ouvert ses premiers bureaux sur la Potsdamer Platz, à Berlin, puis d'autres à Düsseldorf, Zürich et Beijing. Pour les innombrables sociétés de premier plan figurant à son portefeuille, elle assure diverses fonctions : gestion stratégique de marque, projets d'identité de marque, conception et mise en œuvre d'images et d'identités corporatives complexes. Depuis maintenant une vingtaine d'années, le nom de la société incarne pleinement sa philosophie. Parmi ses clients, citons Volkswagen, MoMA, eBay, Osram et Audi, entre beaucoup d'autres ; MetaDesign a par ailleurs remporté de nombreux prix, notamment, dans les dernières années, le Red Dot Award, les International Business Awards/Stevie Awards, le GWA Social Effie, le iF Communication Design Award, et les European Design Awards.

BIG & SMALL, EAST & WEST: HOW DESIGN CAN IMPROVE BRANDS

Andrea Wulf on Sasha Vidakovic

Sasha Vidakovic's brand identity strategies bridge many worlds. This versatile approach gives him a different perspective towards brands, the markets, and aesthetic sensibilities in general. He came to branding steeped in the influence of poster art, where striking images and the use of a few words were capable of telling extraordinary stories. "In Yugoslavia it was never so sophisticated that we were trained as graphic designers. We were inspired by Malevich, Rodchenko or El Lissitzky," he explains.

With experience of working with a variety of agencies and clients he learned the tools of the trade that have transformed branding in the past two decades. Rather than just relying on intuition, talent, and artistic expression, as he had been taught to do in art school, Sasha embraced the analytical approach and intensive research that distinguished these big brand strategies. What gives his work its distinctive flavour is that he has fused his cultural and artistic background from Eastern Europe with his

Andrea Wulf über Sasha Vidakovic

Sasha Vidakovics Markenidentitätsstrategien überbrücken viele Welten. Durch seinen vielseitigen Ansatz bekommt er einen anderen Blickwinkel auf Marken, Märkte und allgemeine ästhetische Feinheiten. Er begann seine Arbeit im Bereich Markenbildung unter dem Einfluss der Posterkunst. In diesem Bereich konnten Künstler mit markanten Bildern und wenigen Worten außergewöhnliche Geschichten erzählen. „In Jugoslawien war dies nie so hoch entwickelt, dass wir zu Grafikdesignern ausgebildet wurden. Wir wurden von Malewitsch, Rodtschenko oder El Lissitzky inspiriert", erklärt er.

Durch seine Erfahrung in der Arbeit mit verschiedenen Agenturen und Kunden erlernte er das Handwerkszeug, das die Markenbildung in den letzten beiden Jahrzehnten umgewandelt hat. Statt sich nur auf Intuition, Talent und künstlerischen Ausdruck zu verlassen, wie es in der Kunsthochschule vermittelt wurde, bezog Sasha den analytischen Ansatz und die

Andrea Wulf à propos de Sasha Vidakovic

Les stratégies d'identité de marque de Sasha Vidakovic couvrent de nombreux domaines. Cette souplesse dans la démarche lui donne une perspective différente des marques, des marchés et des sensibilités esthétiques en général. Il est venu à la valorisation de marque, tout imprégné encore de l'influence de l'art de l'affiche, où les images frappantes et le recours à une poignée de mots sont capables de raconter d'extraordinaires histoires. « En Yougoslavie, ça n'a jamais été tellement sophistiqué d'étudier le design graphique. Nous étions inspirés par Malevich, Rodchenko ou El Lissitzky », explique-t-il.

Au contact d'une grande variété d'agences et de clients, il a appris les savoir-faire qui ont transformé la valorisation de marque dans les deux dernières décennies. Plutôt que de s'en remettre à l'intuition, au talent et à l'expression artistique, comme on le lui avait enseigné aux beaux-arts, Sasha s'est tourné vers l'approche analytique et

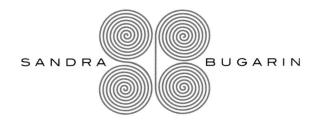

SANDRA BUGARIN

Clockwise from top left: *Logo, package design for flagship stores, and promotional printed material for Sandra Bugarin.* ///
Im Uhrzeigersinn von oben links: *Logo, Verpackungsdesign für Flagship-Stores und Werbemappe für Sandra Bugarin.* ///
Dans le sens des aiguilles d'une montre, depuis l'angle supérieur gauche : *Logo et conception d'ensemble pour flagship stores (boutiques vaisseaux amiral) et supports promotionnels pour Sandra Bugarin.*

Above: *Logo and package design for FINO VINO.* /// **Oben:** *Logo und Verpackungsdesign für FINO VINO.* /// **Ci-dessus** *: Logo et conception d'ensemble pour FINO VINO.*

commercial experience in the West. He returns often to Eastern Europe as a way of stimulating his mind and refreshing his approach, but as with all his work he doesn't regard this as a one-way street. It's an inspiring exchange in which all sides profit as he is also applying his success with big Western brands to the new emerging markets.

For Sasha, the beauty of working like this is that he can apply the lessons he has learned in the world of global companies to smaller brands. He uses the same rigour but at the same time he can develop a close relationship with the owners of these businesses, and can as a result witness the speedy execution of his work. "They often require big ideas, but they tend to need an intuitive leap. It's a process which keeps my brain alive, and is necessary preparation for the slower, bigger and corporate jobs."

In 2006, for example, a group of intellectuals and wine lovers in Belgrade started a business to import the best wines from

intensive Recherche mit ein, die diese Strategien für große Marken unterschieden. Seine Arbeit erhält ihre unverwechselbaren Merkmale durch die Verbindung seines kulturell und künstlerisch osteuropäisch geprägten Hintergrundes mit seinen kommerziellen Erfahrungen im Westen. Er kehrt häufig nach Osteuropa zurück, um sich neue Anregungen zu holen und seine Arbeitsweise aufzufrischen. Das ist für ihn und seine Arbeit keine Einbahnstraße, sondern er betrachtet dieses Pendeln als inspirierenden Austausch, von dem alle Seiten profitieren, da er seinen Erfolg bei großen westlichen Marken auf den neu entstehenden Märkten einsetzt.

Für Sasha liegt die Schönheit dieser Arbeit darin, dass er das, was er in der Welt der globalen Unternehmen gelernt hat, auf kleinere Marken anwenden kann. Er arbeitet mit der gleichen Strenge, kann aber gleichzeitig eine enge Verbindung zu den Eigentümern dieser Marken entwickeln und demzufolge die schnelle Realisierung seiner Arbeit miterleben. „Sie wollen oft eine große Idee haben, doch

la recherche intensive qui distinguent les stratégies de grandes marques. S'il émane de son travail ce parfum si particulier, c'est qu'il y a allié son propre background culturel et artistique d'Europe de l'Est avec l'expérience commerciale acquise à l'Ouest. Il retourne fréquemment à ses origines, pour se stimuler intellectuellement et rafraîchir son approche créative, mais comme avec tout ce qu'il fait, il n'y voit pas un processus unilatéral. Un échange s'instaure, fructueux pour les deux côtés puisqu'il fait profiter les nouveaux marchés émergents de sa réussite avec les marques du monde occidental.

Pour Sasha, la beauté de ce mode de travail tient au fait de pouvoir mettre au service de petites marques ce qu'il a appris auprès des grandes. Il s'y emploie avec la même rigueur mais peut en même temps nouer des relations étroites avec leurs propriétaires et, par conséquent, être témoin des prompts résultats de son travail. « Ils réclament souvent de grandes idées, mais ont en général besoin d'un ‹ saut intuitif ›. Cela maintient mon

Right: *Logo, bottle, and box for Olynthia. ///*
Rechts: *Logo, Flasche und Verpackung für Olynthia. /// A droite : Logo, bouteille et boîte pour Olynthia.*

France, Italy and Spain in a "personal quest for good taste." The name was FINO VINO, and Sasha was asked to brand the business. He began by questioning the owner. "Sometimes I think of myself as a branding shrink," he says. "They lie down on the sofa and I analyse their visions as well as business realities." One of his favourite processes is to persuade brand-owners to describe their brands as if they were an object, a piece of music, an animal, or a piece of furniture. FINO VINO's owner said it was like a horse, a cypress tree, a pair of handcrafted Italian shoes, and the music of Erik Satie. "Suddenly it was obvious what was needed," says Sasha. "They were classical but with a touch of modernity. They were like wine, which you sense in part with your mouth, but which you finish with your brain." The result was an elegant serifed logo in which some of the letter strokes are removed, leaving it to the viewer to complete the form. The colour is a gradation from red to burgundy as if printed with wine itself, and thus the whole image retains a direct, poetic simplicity.

benötigen eher einen intuitiven Sprung nach vorn. Dieser Prozess hält meinen Verstand am Leben und stellt die nötige Vorbereitung für die zeitaufwendigeren und größeren Aufgaben in großen Unternehmen dar."

2006 wurde beispielsweise in Belgrad von Intellektuellen und Weinliebhabern, denen sehr am guten Geschmack gelegen war, eine Firma zu dem Zweck gegründet, die besten Weine aus Frankreich, Italien und Spanien zu importieren. Sie gaben der Firma den Namen FINO VINO, und Sasha wurde gebeten, eine Marke für dieses Unternehmen zu entwerfen. Er begann damit, den Eigentümer zu befragen. „Manchmal sehe ich mich selbst als eine Art Marken-Psychotherapeut", sagt er. „Meine Kunden liegen sozusagen auf dem Sofa, und ich analysiere ihre Visionen und den unternehmerischen Rahmen." Eines seiner Lieblingsverfahren besteht darin, die Markenbesitzer dazu zu bringen, ihre eigene Marke so zu beschreiben, als wäre sie ein Gegenstand, ein Musikstück, ein Tier oder ein Möbelstück. Die Eigentümer von

esprit en alerte, et c'est une préparation nécessaire pour les projets d'entreprise de plus grande envergure, par nature plus lents. »

En 2006, par exemple, un groupe d'intellectuels et d'amateurs de vin belgradois crée une société pour importer des grands crus de France, d'Italie et d'Espagne ; il s'agit en quelque sorte de satisfaire une « quête du bon goût personnelle ». Ils la baptisent FINO VINO et demandent à Sasha de mettre au point leur stratégie de marque. Celui-ci commencera par interroger le propriétaire. « Parfois, je me fais l'effet d'un psy », plaisante-t-il. « Ils s'allongent sur le divan et j'analyse leurs visions, ainsi que les réalités du business. » L'un des moments qu'il préfère est celui où il persuade les propriétaires de marques de décrire ces dernières comme s'il s'agissait d'objets, de morceaux de musique, d'animaux ou de meubles. Le propriétaire de FINO VINO assimile la sienne à un cheval, un cyprès, une paire de chaussures italiennes et la musique d'Erik Satie. « Soudainement, ce dont ils avaient besoin

29

Maks is a Zagreb boutique and fashion brand which has been trading for more than thirty years. In 2004, the daughter of the original proprietor took over, and asked Sasha to create a new brand with the aim of broadening appeal beyond the existing customer-base. In this instance, rather than asking questions, he could look at and feel the clothes. "They were simple, usually in cotton and linen. Full of overlaps, very laid-back, very loose. They were made on a small scale. The brand had to mirror these qualities." The result was a hand-dotted composition that looks something like a cloud of dandelion heads, inspired by a few rustic, craftsman-like marks Sasha saw on a terracotta pot. He imagined this brand not as the repeated application of a logo on letterheads and bags, but as a playful and ever-changing experience: for instance, a model might be branded with this circular tattoo or a child might blow the circles as if they were bubbles, etc.

Sasha responded to the challenge of another fashion brand in a different way: Sandra Bugarin is a designer in Belgrade, who was aiming at the top-end of the Western market. Sasha's solution was to research motifs and costumes from the region. "Almost certainly the solution is within the problem," he says. The result was a stylised folk motif of spirals, which at the same time spells out the initial letters of the brand. It is both rooted in the regional experience, and honed and polished by Sasha so that it shines out in the new context of high streets in the West in the form of labels as well as on bags and boxes.

Sasha is clear that he is not trying to develop a personal visual style: "I want everything I do to be different. I try to crawl inside the skin of the companies that I work for. I want to express what is inside them, not impose something from the outside." As evidence of this, he points to Olynthia, a family-owned virgin olive-oil producer on a tiny island in the Adriatic. There he criss-crossed the island, took photographs of ancient olive trees, and picked up twigs. He even shared a glass (or two) of grappa with the locals.

FINO VINO meinten, die Marke sei wie ein Pferd, wie eine Zypresse, wie ein Paar handgearbeiteter italienischer Schuhe und wie die Musik von Erik Satie. „Plötzlich war es ganz offensichtlich, was zu tun war", sagt Sasha. „Sie waren klassisch, doch mit einer leichten Modernität. Sie waren wie ein Wein, den man teilweise im Mund schmeckt, doch eigentlich im Kopf zur Vollendung bringt." Das Ergebnis war ein elegantes, mit Serifen versehenes Logo, in dem einige Buchstabenstriche entfernt wurden und bei dem es dem Betrachter überlassen bleibt, die Form zu vervollständigen. Die Farbe besteht aus einer Abstufung von Rot zu Burgunderrot, als ob sie mit dem Wein selbst gedruckt worden wäre. Das verleiht dem gesamten Bild eine unmittelbare und poetische Schlichtheit.

Maks ist sowohl eine Boutique in Zagreb als auch eine Modemarke, die bereits seit mehr als 30 Jahren im Handel ist. 2004 übernahm die Tochter des Eigentümers das Unternehmen und bat Sasha, eine neue Marke zu kreieren. Diese sollte das Ziel verfolgen, die Produkte über den bisherigen Kundenbestand hinaus ansprechend zu machen und die Zielgruppe auszuweiten. In diesem Fall stellte Sasha keine Fragen, sondern beschäftigte sich mit der Kleidung und befühlte sie. „Sie war einfach und meist aus Baumwolle und Leinen. Voller Überlappungen, sehr locker und luftig. Die Kleidung wurde in kleiner Stückzahl hergestellt. Die Marke musste diese Eigenschaften widerspiegeln." Das Ergebnis war eine handgepunktete, wolkenartige Struktur, die ein wenig an Löwenzahnköpfe erinnerte, inspiriert durch einige rustikale handwerkliche Abdrücke, die Sasha auf einem Terrakotta-Topf gesehen hatte. Er stellte sich diese Marke nicht als eine sich wiederholende Applikation eines Logos auf Briefköpfen und Taschen vor, sondern als spielerische und sich ständig verändernde Erfahrung: Zum Beispiel kann ein Modell mit dieser kreisförmigen Tätowierung gekennzeichnet werden oder ein Kind kann die Kreise wegpusten, als wären sie Seifenblasen etc.

Sasha stellte sich der Herausforderung einer weiteren Modemarke auf noch andere Weise: Sandra Bugarin ist eine

m'est apparu clairement », affirme Sasha. « Ils étaient classiques, mais avec une touche de modernité. Ils étaient comme le vin, qu'on sent en partie avec la bouche, mais dont on achève l'analyse intellectuellement. » Le résultat sera un élégant logo à base de caractères avec empattement dont certains jambages ont été omis, laissant au lecteur le soin d'en compléter le dessin. La couleur, un dégradé allant du rouge au bourgogne, semble avoir été imprimée avec du vin, et l'image tout entière y gagne une simplicité directe et poétique.

Maks est une boutique et une griffe de mode de Zagreb existant depuis plus de trente ans. En 2004, ayant pris l'affaire en main, la fille du propriétaire d'origine demande à Sasha de créer une nouvelle marque, avec pour objectif de renforcer le pouvoir d'attraction du label parmi sa clientèle. Pour ce faire, et plutôt que de poser des questions, il a le loisir d'examiner et de toucher les vêtements. « Ils étaient simples, en coton et en lin pour la plupart. Avec des tas de superpositions, très décontractés, très amples. Ils étaient fabriqués à très petite échelle. La marque devait refléter ces qualités. » Le résultat, une composition en pointillé exécutée à la main et évoquant vaguement un nuage d'aigrettes de pissenlits, a été inspiré à Sasha par le motif rustique d'une poterie artisanale. Il voit dans cette marque, non pas un logo reproduit à l'envi sur en-têtes et sacs, mais une expérience, drôle et en perpétuelle évolution : un modèle, par exemple, peut être estampillé d'un tatouage circulaire, ou un enfant souffler les cercles comme s'il s'agissait de bulles de savon, etc.

Sasha a également relevé le défi d'une autre griffe de mode, différemment cette fois : Sandra Bugarin, une styliste belgradoise, visait le haut de gamme du marché occidental. Sasha lui a proposé la solution suivante : chercher parmi les motifs et les costumes de la région. « C'est presque à tous les coups dans le problème que réside la solution », selon lui. Le résultat est un motif folklorique en forme de spirale, qui a été stylisé pour former les initiales de la marque. Il traduit un enracinement dans la tradition locale et, épuré et poli

The result is a large, oily "O" embraced by olive leaves, intended for use on packaging. The label is stripped of all superfluities – it's image-led and draws attention to itself like a poster. "This is an honest olive oil brand, which uses the most essential elements in the simplest way," says Sasha.

It's all about the process, he explains, it's about finding out what the brand stands for and what the clients need. "I listen, that's the most important thing." Whether he works for big brands such as Harrods, the World Wildlife Fund for Nature, or AZIMUT Yachts, or for smaller companies in Belgrade, Sasha is obsessed with finding the most perfect solution for each particular brand. "I'm not interested in lacing my idiosyncratic signature over a brand", he says, "it's about them not me."

Designerin aus Belgrad, die auf die Spitze des westlichen Marktes abzielte. Für sie bestand Sashas Lösung darin, Motive und Trachten aus der Region zu recherchieren. „Fast immer liegt die Lösung innerhalb des Problems", sagt er. Das Ergebnis war ein stilisiertes volkstümliches Motiv aus Spiralen, das gleichzeitig die Anfangsbuchstaben der Marke darstellte. Dieses Motiv wurzelte zum einen in der Region und wurde zum anderen von Sasha fein geschliffen und poliert, sodass es im neuen Kontext der westlichen Haupteinkaufsstraßen in Form von Labeln sowie auf Taschen und Schachteln glänzen konnte.

Sasha macht deutlich, dass er nicht versucht, einen persönlichen visuellen Stil zu entwickeln: „Ich möchte, dass sich alles voneinander unterscheidet, was ich mache. Ich versuche, den Unternehmen, für die ich arbeite, sozusagen unter die Haut zu kriechen. Ich will ausdrücken, was in diesem Unternehmen steckt, und nicht etwas von außen aufzwingen." Als Beispiel dafür verweist er auf Olynthia: Dieses Familienunternehmen produziert auf einer winzigen Insel im Adriatischen Meer natives Olivenöl. Er erforschte die Insel kreuz und quer, fotografierte alte Olivenbäume und sammelte Zweige. Er trank mit den Einheimischen sogar ein (oder zwei) Gläser Grappa. Das Ergebnis ist ein großes, öliges und von Olivenblättern umrahmtes „O", das für Verpackungen bestimmt ist. Das Label hat nichts Überflüssiges an sich – es wird nur durch das Bild geprägt und zieht die Aufmerksamkeit auf sich wie ein Poster. „Dies ist eine ehrliche Olivenölmarke, die die wesentlichsten Elemente auf einfachste Art einsetzt", sagt Sasha.

Sasha erklärt, es gehe ihm dabei um den Prozess, und er wolle herausfinden, für was die Marke steht und was die Kunden brauchen. „Ich höre zu, das ist das Wichtigste." Ob er nun für große Marken arbeitet wie zum Beispiel Harrods, World Wildlife Fund for Nature, AZIMUT-Yachten oder für kleinere Firmen in Belgrad – Sasha ist stets davon besessen, für jede einzelne Marke die perfekte Lösung zu finden. „Ich bin nicht daran interessiert, einer Marke meine eigenwillige Signatur aufzudrücken", sagt er, „es geht um die Marke, nicht um mich."

par Sasha, brille de tous ses feux sur les grands boulevards de l'Occident sous forme de labels, ainsi que sur les sacs et les cartons d'emballage.

Pour Sasha, une chose est tout à fait claire, il n'envisage pas de créer de style visuel personnel : « Je veux que tout ce que je fais soit différent. Je veux me glisser dans la peau des entreprises pour lesquelles je travaille. Je veux exprimer ce qu'elles ont en elles, pas imposer quelque chose d'extérieur. » Et, pour preuve, il nous parle d'Olynthia, un petit producteur d'huile d'olive familial installé sur une minuscule île de l'Adriatique. Il a sillonné les lieux en tous sens, photographié les vieux oliviers et ramassé des rameaux. Il a même bu un (ou deux) verres de grappa avec les habitants. Le résultat est un « O », gros et gras, entouré de feuilles d'olivier, conçu pour figurer sur l'emballage. Le label est dépouillé de tout ornement superflu – il est expressif et attire l'attention à la manière d'une affiche. « Il s'agit d'une honnête marque d'huile d'olive, qui recourt et va à l'essentiel de la manière la plus simple », conclut Sasha.

Ce qui compte, c'est le processus, explique-t-il, c'est de découvrir ce que représente la marque et ce dont les clients ont besoin. « J'écoute, c'est le plus important. » Qu'il travaille pour des grandes marques comme Harrods, the World Wildlife Fund for Nature ou AZIMUT Yachts, ou pour de petites sociétés belgradoises, Sasha n'a de cesse de trouver la solution idéale pour chaque marque. « Je ne tiens pas à apposer ma propre signature sur une marque », précise-t-il, « c'est d'eux qu'il s'agit, pas de moi. »

Facing page: *Invitation for fashion show, promotional poster, and in-store decoration for Maks.* /// **Gegenüberliegende Seite:** *Einladung zu einer Modenschau, Werbeplakat und Gestaltung eines Maks-Geschäftsraumes.* /// **Page opposée :** *Invitation à un défilé de mode, affiche promotionnelle et décoration intérieure pour Maks.*

Biography
Sasha Vidakovic (SViDesign)

www.svidesign.com

Location: London
Year founded: 2006

Position: Creative Director/
Founder

Having been trained in Yugoslavia and having worked for almost two decades for some of the most influential branding companies in London and Milan, Sasha Vidakovic combines Eastern European and Western influences, the artistic and the corporate world, the small and the large-scale. He is a brand architect and a craftsman, a strategist and a designer. Vidakovic came to Britain in the early 1990s just before the war broke out across Yugoslavia and worked in London as design and creative director for Interbrand, Enterprise IG (now Brand Union) and Conran Design Group; after that he spent four years in Milan with Landor Associates before setting up SViDesign in 2006. His clients have included a broad range from car brands to charity organisations, from cosmetics to manufacturers, and luxury items to food.

Sasha Vidakovic wurde in Jugoslawien ausgebildet und arbeitete fast zwei Jahrzehnte für einige der einflussreichsten Unternehmen für Markenbildung in London und Mailand. Er verbindet erfolgreich osteuropäische und westliche Einflüsse, die künstlerische und unternehmerische Welt, den kleinen und den großen Maßstab. Er ist Markenarchitekt und Handwerker, Stratege und Designer. Vidakovic kam in den frühen 1990er Jahren nach Großbritannien, kurz bevor in Jugoslawien der Krieg ausbrach, und arbeitete in London als Design- und Kreativdirektor für Interbrand, Enterprise IG (heute Brand Union) und die Conran Design Group. Anschließend

verbrachte er vier Jahre in Mailand bei Landor Associates und gründete schließlich 2006 das Beratungsunternehmen SViDesign. Seine Kunden kommen aus vielen Bereichen: von Automarken zu Wohlfahrtsorganisationen, von Kosmetikfirmen zu Fabriken und von Luxusgütern zu Nahrungsmitteln.

Formé en Yougoslavie et ayant travaillé pendant près de vingt ans pour quelques-unes des plus grandes sociétés de valorisation de marque à Londres et Milan, Sasha Vidakovic mêle influences d'Europe orientale et d'Europe occidentale, monde de l'art et de l'entreprise, petite et grande échelle. Il est à la fois designer de marque et artisan, stratège et styliste. Vidakovic arrive en Grande-Bretagne au début des années 90, juste avant que la guerre ne déchire la Yougoslavie. Sasha collaborera à Londres en qualité de designer et directeur de la création pour Interbrand, Enterprise IG (actuellement Brand Union) et Conran Design Group ; il passera ensuite quatre années à Milan chez Landor Associates, avant de monter SViDesign en 2006. Son très large portefeuille de clients comprend depuis des marques automobiles à des associations caritatives, en passant par des fabricants de cosmétiques, des industriels, des produits de luxe et des produits alimentaires.

THE CORE ELEMENTS OF A DESIGN STUDIO CORPORATE IDENTITY

An often-heard excuse from agencies is: We're too busy and don't have the time to look after our own corporate identity (CI). The shoemaker's son always goes barefoot…

– I beg your pardon?

Shouldn't that be the first thing you do when you start an agency or brand? This situation often surprised me at various agencies in the past. Why wasn't the agency's brand handled in the same way as the client's? Why was the chance to rise above the competition and secure a place within the market not taken? An agency is also a brand and has to be treated like one. Presenting a strong public image is important – just as important as establishing an internal identity.

I think the acting out of a CI is an important point, and one which I often find missing at large agencies. It is a shame when agency employees are unable to identify with the CI.

Eine verbreitete Ausrede von Agenturen lautet: Wir haben zuviel zu tun und keine Zeit, uns um unsere eigene Corporate Identity (CI) zu kümmern. Der Schuster hat ja die schlechtesten Leisten …

– Wie bitte?

Sollte das nicht das Erste sein, das man in Angriff nimmt, wenn man eine Agentur oder eine Marke gründet? Das hat mich in der Vergangenheit bei verschiedenen Agenturen oft gewundert: Warum wird die eigene Marke nicht genauso behandelt wie ein Kundenauftrag – warum wird nicht die Chance genutzt, sich abzuheben und sich so seinen Platz am Markt zu sichern? Eine Agentur ist auch eine Marke und muss genauso behandelt werden. Ein starkes Image ist für die Außenwirkung wichtig, genauso wie es wichtig ist, intern eine Identifikation mit der Agentur zu schaffen.

Gerade das Ausleben einer CI halte ich für einen wichtigen Punkt, den ich oft bei großen Agenturen vermisst habe. Ich finde

Dans les agences, on entend fréquemment l'excuse suivante : Nous sommes trop occupés, nous n'avons pas le temps de soigner notre propre identité corporative (IC). Les cordonniers sont toujours les plus mal chaussés…

– Comment dites-vous ?

Est-ce que ça ne devrait pas être le premier souci quand on lance une agence ou une marque ? Une chose m'a souvent étonné, par le passé, au sein de différentes agences : pourquoi la marque de l'agence n'était-elle pas gérée de la même façon que celles de la clientèle ? Pourquoi ne saisissait-on pas la chance de la hisser au-dessus du lot et d'asseoir sa position sur le marché ? Une agence est également une marque, et il faut donc la traiter comme telle. Présenter une solide image publique est important – tout aussi important qu'établir une identité interne.

J'estime fondamentale l'image qu'une IC offre d'elle-même, et c'est là quelque chose qui manque souvent à mon avis dans les

DIGITAL COMMUNICATION & DESIGN STUDIO

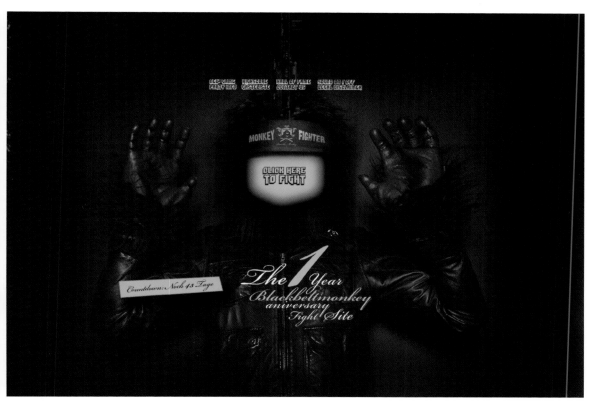

Previous spread: Main logo and 1ˢᵗ anniversary promotional website. /// **Vorhergehende Seite:** *Hauptlogo und Website zum einjährigen Bestehen. ///* **Double page précédente :** *Logo principal et site Web promotionnel du 1ᵉʳ anniversaire.*

A CI has to fit with the agency and the employees should live it and care for it with the required level of detail. It is particularly important in attracting new clients and winning over new employees – and not only by highlighting prized customers and awards won. A brand cannot survive on positioning and branding ideas alone. It is vital to have an image, a first impression of the stringent CI. A comparison can be made with a new, young band that is virtually unknown. As well as the sound, an attitude, an interesting background and a catchy name are important to help it get noticed. These factors are almost as important to success as the music (or the product) itself.

It is easy to talk when assessing others without having to be assessed yourself. This is probably true, but for me it was exactly these experiences and impressions that made me want to do things differently. I had my first chance to practise early on. In 2004, I started to work on my own portfolio, my own brand alongside my regular job, and to give the whole thing

es immer schade, wenn eine Agentur es nicht schafft, eine Identifikation der Mitarbeiter mit der CI zu schaffen.

Eine CI muss zu der Agentur passen, und die Mitarbeiter sollten sie leben und pflegen, und zwar mit allen Details, die dafür nötig sind. Das ist besonders wichtig, um nicht nur durch Prestigekunden und Awards neue Kunden anzulocken und neue Mitarbeiter zu gewinnen. Eine Marke lebt schließlich nicht allein von der Positionierung und der Markenidee, sondern auch ganz stark vom Look, vom ersten Eindruck, von der Stringenz der CI. Das ist vergleichbar mit einer neuen, jungen Band, die noch keiner kennt. Neben dem Sound ist eine Haltung, ein interessanter Background und ein griffiger Name wichtig, um wahrgenommen zu werden. Das ist fast genauso ein Erfolgsfaktor wie die Musik, sprich: wie das Produkt selbst.

Nun hat man leicht reden, wenn man nur wertet, selbst aber nicht bewertet wird. Ja, das ist sicherlich wahr, aber genau diese Erfahrungen und Eindrücke stärkten in

grandes agences. Il est fort regrettable que le personnel d'une agence n'ait pas d'IC à laquelle s'identifier.

L'IC doit s'ajuster à l'agence et le personnel doit l'assumer comme sienne et y veiller avec le soin requis. Ceci revêt une importance toute particulière à l'heure de s'attirer de nouveaux clients et de nouveaux collaborateurs – et pas uniquement en mettant en avant clients récompensés et prix empochés. Une marque ne saurait survivre seulement d'idées de positionnement et de stratégie. Il est vital d'avoir une image, une première empreinte d'IC rigoureuse. On pourrait comparer cela avec un groupe de musique, par exemple, un groupe nouveau, jeune et pratiquement inconnu. A part le son, il lui faut une attitude, un background et un nom accrocheur pour se faire remarquer. Ces facteurs sont presque aussi importants pour réussir que la musique (ou le produit) en soi.

Il est aisé de donner des conseils quand on n'a pas soi-même à se faire conseiller. Certes,

Left: *Variation of the logo and collateral applications of the corporate identity.* /// **Links:** *Abwandlung des Logos und verschiedene Umsetzungen der Corporate Identity.* /// **A gauche :** *Variante du logo et diverses présentations de l'identité visuelle de l'entreprise.*

Right: *Orientation signage for the building where the studio is located.* /// **Rechts:** *Hinweisschild für das Gebäude, in dem sich das Studio befindet.* /// **A droite :** *Signalisation de l'immeuble où est installé le studio.*

a stringent branding and an interesting name. The result was "stereoplastic", a platform that still helps me today and which has shown me that even a small creative professional from Germany can cause waves internationally by developing ideas based on common sense and persuasive visuals.

But that's enough about the past. Let's talk about the present – my present and hopefully my future and the future of the other monkeys. Let's talk about blackbeltmonkey.

Following salaried positions with agencies such as Razorfish, e7 and BBDO Interone, and some freelancing, I finally wanted to start my own business. The time was right and, as fate would have it, I knew or met the right people to make it happen. I made a start on June 1, 2007 and founded the blackbeltmonkey studio with Oliver Bentz and Marcellus Gau.

As well as choosing a name, which took over six weeks, it was clear that we urgently

mir den Wunsch, es anders zu machen. Die ersten Möglichkeiten zum Üben kamen früh, als ich im Jahr 2004 anfing, neben meinem festen Job an meinem eigenen Portfolio, meiner eigenen Marke zu basteln, um dem Ganzen ein stringentes Branding und einen interessanten Namen zu geben. Das Resultat war „stereoplastic", das mir als Plattform bis heute gute Dienste erwiesen und mir gezeigt hat, dass man als kleiner Kreativer aus Deutschland international für Aufmerksamkeit sorgen kann, wenn man es vernünftig und visuell überzeugend aufzieht.

Genug über die Vergangenheit geredet. Sprechen wir über die Gegenwart, meine Gegenwart und hoffentlich auch meine Zukunft und die der anderen monkeys – reden wir über blackbeltmonkey.

Nach den Festanstellungen bei Agenturen wie Razorfish, Elephant Seven und BBDO Interone und meiner Zeit als Freelancer wollte ich endlich meinen eigenen Laden gründen. Die Zeit war reif, und wie das Schicksal es wollte, kannte und traf ich die

mais dans mon cas ce sont justement des expériences et des impressions de ce genre qui m'ont conduit à vouloir faire les choses autrement. La première chance m'en a été donnée assez tôt. En 2004, j'ai commencé à élaborer mon propre portefeuille, ma propre marque, parallèlement à mon job régulier, en tâchant de trouver pour l'ensemble une stratégie de marque rigoureuse et un nom frappant. C'est ainsi qu'est née « stereoplastic », une plateforme qui me sert encore aujourd'hui et qui m'a montré que même un tout petit créateur indépendant venu d'Allemagne peut faire des vagues à l'échelle internationale en développant des idées basées sur des images convaincantes et de bon sens.

Mais assez parlé du passé. Parlons du présent – mon présent et espérons-le mon avenir et celui des autres « monkeys ». Parlons de blackbeltmonkey.

Après plusieurs emplois salariés dans des agences comme Razorfish, Elephant Seven et BBDO Interone, et quelques boulots freelance, j'ai fini par vouloir monter ma

needed a strong and stringent CI in order to be taken seriously. Being in charge of design development, it was my job to make an early start on implementing the first ideas. In the event, it was almost too early. We let our attention focus a little too much on a cool and innovative website instead of steadily developing the CI. The whole process left us wanting and we had three different opinions. A bit of back-pedalling, an annoyed Flash developer, and we started again from scratch. I first developed some rough mood-boards and tried things out to see what was possible. The three of us then talked things through and found some common ground: a colour, a typography, and, most importantly, a logo we all liked and could identify with.

Even though I am of the opinion that design should not be a democratic process, it is nevertheless important that the people who represent the image created also support it.

The blackbeltmonkey logo comprises a modified font and a handwritten and vectorised script that together form a word-branding that emphasises the polemic nature of the name. The black belt is the highest rank in karate and a good metaphor for the more than ten years of experience we have in this business. On the other side is the monkey, standing for crazy and creative lateral thinking. We wanted to make it clear that we see ourselves neither as a "normal" agency nor a total hotshop. As Bono from U2 once aptly said, "We don't want to be *in*, because being *in* means that you are on the way to being *out*". To this I would add the following sentence: "It is better to achieve lasting success than to be a one-hit wonder and spend the rest of your life sadly retelling the story even though no one wants to hear it."

Of course, a logo on its own is not a CI. As well as the logo there is also an emblem that gives the blackbeltmonkey a face and creates an icon. We chose the colours black, in reference to the black belt, white, for the blank sheet of paper on which ideas

richtigen Leute, um das in die Tat umzusetzen: Am 1. Juni 2007 habe ich zunächst mit Oliver Bentz und Marcellus Gau angefangen und das Studio blackbeltmonkey gegründet.

Neben der Namensfindung, die gut sechs Wochen gedauert hat, war klar, dass wir früh eine stringente und starke CI brauchten, um wahrgenommen zu werden. Da ich für die Designentwicklung verantwortlich war, fing ich schon bald mit der Umsetzung erster Ideen an – beinahe zu früh. Denn wir legten unser Augenmerk überstürzt auf eine coole und innovative Website, statt erst einmal langsam die CI zu entwickeln. Das Ganze führte dann auch nicht zum gewünschten Ergebnis. Wir hatten drei verschiedene Meinungen. Also wurde zurückgerudert, der freie Flasher verprellt und wieder ganz von vorne gestartet. Ich entwickelte zunächst grobe Moodboards und probierte so alles Mögliche aus. Wir besprachen die Dinge dann zu dritt und fanden die ersten Bausteine: eine Farbe, eine Typo und vor allem ein Logo, das wir alle mochten und in dem sich jeder wiederfand.

Auch wenn ich der Meinung bin, dass Design nicht basisdemokratisch sein sollte, ist es dennoch wichtig, dass die, die das Erscheinungsbild vertreten, auch dahinter stehen.

Das Logo von blackbeltmonkey besteht zum einem aus einem abgewandelten Font und einer handgeschriebenen und vektorisierten Schrift, die zusammen als Wortmarke die beiden Pole im Namen unterstreichen. Als höchster Rang im Karate ist der Blackbelt eine geeignete Metapher, um unsere über zehnjährige Erfahrung in der Branche zu unterstreichen. Auf der anderen Seite der Monkey, der für das andere, verrückte und kreative Querdenken steht. Wir wollten damit klar stellen, dass wir uns weder als eine weitere "normale" Agentur sehen noch als reiner Hotshop. Bono von U2 hat treffenderweise mal gesagt: „Wir möchten nicht in Mode sein, denn ‚in' sein heißt, dass man auf dem besten Wege ist, ‚out' zu sein". Ich würde das noch mit einem Satz ergänzen: „Es ist

propre affaire. C'était le bon moment et le hasard a voulu que je connaisse ou que je rencontre les gens qu'il fallait pour y parvenir. Je me suis jeté à l'eau le 1er juin 2007 et j'ai fondé le studio blackbeltmonkey avec Oliver Bentz et Marcellus Gau.

A part choisir un nom, ce qui nous a demandé six semaines, il était clair que nous avions urgemment besoin d'une IC solide et rigoureuse afin d'être pris au sérieux. Etant chargé de la conception du design, j'aurais dû me hâter de trouver les premières idées. A ce stade, il était encore trop tôt. Nous nous sommes un peu trop focalisés sur le site Web, que nous voulions brillant et novateur, au lieu de nous atteler à la création de l'IC. Ça nous a laissés tous les trois totalement insatisfaits, chacun campant sur ses propres opinions. Après un rien de rétropédalage, quelques contrariétés avec un développeur de Flash, nous avons fait table rase et tout recommencé de zéro. J'ai tout d'abord ébauché quelques prototypes et essayé des trucs pour voir. Puis, ensemble, nous avons tout posé sur la table et finalement trouvé un terrain d'entente : une couleur, une typographie et, plus important encore, un logo qui nous plaisait à tous les trois, et avec lequel nous pouvions nous identifier.

Même si je pense que le processus conceptuel n'a pas à être démocratique, il faut tout de même que les gens qui représentent une création aient foi en elle.

Le logo de blackbeltmonkey fait appel à une police modifiée et à une typo manuscrite et vectorisée qui, à elles deux, composent une griffe venant rehausser la nature polémique de la dénomination. La ceinture noire, le plus haut grade en karaté, est aussi une excellente métaphore pour l'expérience de plus de dix ans que nous avons du secteur. De l'autre côté, il y a le « monkey », le singe qui élucubre et crée des trucs fous et décalés. Nous voulions qu'il soit clair que nous ne nous prenons ni pour une agence « normale », ni totalement pour une hot shop. Comme l'a très judicieusement dit Bono, le chanteur de U2, « Nous ne voulons pas être ‹ in ›, car être ‹ in › signifie qu'on n'est pas très loin

form, and a light blue that we use for all digital visualisation. Furthermore, the CI includes our five agency rules, which we use as a handbook for our co-operative work and external image. The core elements of the blackbeltmonkey CI had been found.

We developed a provisional teaser-website based on the CI with a background video of our opening party. It contained introductory information about us, as well as links to our portfolios and our joint show-reel. The video used stop-motion footage of the party. We found that the stop-motion technique was ideally suited to show that our agency was in motion and was hungry to stay in motion.

The feedback from the teaser-website was overwhelmingly good – so good that it stayed online for almost six months.

We concentrated on tackling all types of media at once, so that anyone who came into contact with the blackbeltmonkey brand would come across a stringent and lived-out CI. Within a few months we had matching corporate nameplates outside the office, individual business cards with our photographs and the current agency rules that we had each selected on them. Furthermore, the office walls were decorated with the logo and the emblem so everyone knew where they were…first impressions make a big impression!

In addition to all these vital elements just as much time was used putting the CI on to everyday working tools such as presentations, invoices, email footers, letterheads and work tables. This is a step that takes a lot of time, but one that should be made at the beginning of a company start-up to establish a standardised system and documentation for everyone as early as possible.

Once we had collected together enough cases from our first clients and our work, we ventured further with our "real" agency website. It is based on the look of the blackbeltmonkey teaser-website and our show-reels, and the agency's

besser, konstante Leistung zu bringen, als einen einzigen Hit gelandet zu haben, von dem man noch nach Jahren melancholisch jedem erzählt, der es nicht hören will."

Nun, ein Logo macht noch keine CI aus. Neben dem Logo entstand noch ein Wappen, bei dem wir dem blackbeltmonkey ein Gesicht gaben und damit auch ein Icon kreierten. Als Farbe wählten wir Schwarz als Bezug zum schwarzen Gürtel, Weiß für das leere Blatt Papier, auf dem Ideen entstehen, und ein Hellblau, das wir als Visualisierung für alles Digitale wählten. Zur CI gehören außerdem unsere fünf Agenturregeln, die wir als Leitfaden für das gemeinsame Arbeiten und für den Außenauftritt nutzen. Die Kernelemente der CI für blackbeltmonkey waren nun gefunden.

Auf Basis der CI entwickelten wir eine provisorische Teaser-Seite, die mit einem Video unserer Einweihungsparty hinterlegt war. Darauf waren die ersten Infos über uns zu sehen, zusammen mit Links zu unseren Portfolios und unserem gemeinsamen Showreel. Das Video zeichneten wir im Stop-Motion-Verfahren auf der Party auf. Stop Motion fanden wir als Style treffend, um zu zeigen, dass die Agentur sich in Bewegung befindet und auch hungrig in Bewegung bleibt.

Das Feedback war für eine Teaser-Seite überwältigend gut – so gut, dass die Seite fast ein halbes Jahr online blieb.

Wir konzentrierten uns darauf, alle Medien gleichzeitig anzugehen, sodass jeder, der mit der Marke blackbeltmonkey in Berührung kommt, eine stringente und von uns gelebte CI vorfindet. Innerhalb des ersten Monats hatten wir passende Firmenschilder draußen am Büro, individuelle Visitenkarten mit Fotos von uns und der jeweiligen Agenturregel, die sich jeder von uns ausgesucht hatte. Außerdem wurden die Bürowände mit Logo und Wappen dekoriert, damit auch jeder weiß, wo er sich befindet … der erste Eindruck zählt ja bekanntlich!

Neben all diesen notwendigen Elementen verging ebensoviel Zeit, die CI konse-

d'être ‹ out ›. » A quoi j'ajouterais ceci : « Mieux vaut une réussite durable qu'un succès sans lendemain dont on racontera toute sa vie la triste histoire à des gens qui ne veulent pas l'entendre. »

Certes, à lui seul, un logo ne fait pas une IC. A l'instar du logo, nous avons aussi un emblème qui donne un visage à blackbeltmonkey et impose une icône. Nous avons retenu trois couleurs, le noir, en référence à la ceinture noire, le blanc, pour la feuille de papier où les idées prennent forme, et un bleu clair que nous utilisons pour la visualisation numérique. En outre, cette IC comprend les cinq grandes règles de l'agence, employées à la manière d'un raccourci de notre travail de groupe et de notre image externe. Les principaux éléments de l'IC de blackbeltmonkey avaient été trouvés.

Nous avons mis au point une amorce sous forme de site Web provisoire basé sur l'IC, avec en arrière-plan une vidéo de notre fête d'inauguration. On y trouvait des informations élémentaires sur nous, ainsi que des liens à nos portfolios et à notre show-reel commun. La vidéo utilisait un métrage image par image de la fête. A nos yeux, la technique image par image traduit idéalement l'idée que notre agence est en mouvement et qu'elle entend le rester.

Le feedback de ce site-amorce a été formidablement bon – si bon même qu'il est resté on-line près de six mois.

Nous nous sommes illico pourvus de toutes sortes de supports afin que toute personne prenant contact avec la marque blackbeltmonkey l'associe avec un IC à la fois rigoureux et expressif. Au bout de quelques mois, nous disposions de plaques sur la façade, de cartes de visite individuelles avec nos photos et les grandes règles de l'agence choisies par chacun. Ensuite, les murs du bureau ont été agrémentés du logo et de l'emblème, afin que tout le monde sache où il était… Premières impressions, grosses impressions !

Outre ces éléments primordiaux, autant de temps a été consacré à créer, conformé-

style is represented by an extensive case presentation, a humorous slant, and the stop-motion technique. The website aims to mirror exactly what we are about: digital, creative and emotional communication.

Our studio (we decided against the term "agency") is now one year old, and we are still working on the details of the CI. Like I said, it's a continuous process, but it remains enjoyable.

When a CI is running smoothly, any work done on it doesn't interfere with day-to-day activities, despite what many people say.

Furthermore, it's a great way to engage new employees and get them to participate in the development of the studio.

I often use comparisons with the music industry, which I again use here to finish: I believe a good CI, the appearance that a brand has, is similar to learning how to play an instrument. You decide on an instrument and then whenever you play it you have to keep on practising to get good, to get better, or to become a virtuoso.

quent allen alltäglichen Arbeitsmitteln wie Präsentationen, Rechnungen, E-Mail-Footern, Anschreiben und Arbeitstabellen aufzudrücken. Das ist ein Schritt, der zwar mit viel Arbeit verbunden ist, aber gerade am Anfang einer Firmengründung getan werden sollte, um früh ein einheitliches System und Arbeitsunterlagen für alle zu schaffen.

Als wir durch die ersten Kunden und Arbeiten genug Cases zusammenhatten, wagten wir uns erneut an unsere „richtige" Agenturseite. Die Seite von blackbeltmonkey basiert auf dem Look unserer Teaser-Seite und unseres Showreels, eine große Darstellung der Cases, eine humorvolle Tonalität und das Stop-Motion-Verfahren als Style für die Agenturdarstellung. Die Seite sollte das widerspiegeln, was wir tun: digitale, kreative und emotionale Kommunikation.

Unser Studio (wir haben uns bewusst gegen den Begriff „Agentur" entschieden) ist jetzt ein Jahr alt, und wir arbeiten immer noch an Details der CI. Wie ich schon sagte – das ist eine stetige Weiterentwicklung, die aber auch sehr viel Spaß macht.

Wenn die CI funktioniert, dann hält die Arbeit an ihr auch nicht die tägliche Arbeit auf, wie viele gerne argumentieren.

Außerdem ist es eine tolle Möglichkeit, neue Mitarbeiter einzubinden und sie an unserem Studio mitgestalten zu lassen.

Ich verwende oft Vergleiche mit der Musikbranche, daher auch hier in meinem Schlusswort: Ich glaube, dass eine gute CI, also das Erscheinungsbild einer Marke, ähnlich wie das Erlernen eines Instruments ist. Man entscheidet sich für eines, und dann muss man, so lange man es spielt, immer weiter üben, um gut, besser oder gar einzigartig zu werden.

ment à l'IC, les outils de travail quotidiens tels que présentations, factures, bas de page de courrier électronique, en-têtes de lettre et tables de travail. C'est une étape laborieuse mais par laquelle toute start-up doit passer afin d'établir un système et une documentation standard pour tout le monde, aussi tôt que possible.

Quand nous avons eu amassé suffisamment de dossiers sur nos premiers clients et notre travail, nous avons abordé la construction de notre « vrai » site web. Il repose sur le look du site-amorce de blackbeltmonkey et sur nos show-reels, et le style de l'agence s'y exprime par un long dossier de présentation, un point de vue humoristique et la technique image par image. Le site Web se veut le reflet fidèle de ce que nous représentons : une communication numérique créative et émotionnelle.

Notre studio (terme que nous avons préféré à « agence ») a maintenant un an, et nous travaillons encore à parfaire les détails de son IC. Comme je le dis souvent, c'est un « work in progress », mais qui reste agréable.

Quand une IC marche bien, le travail qu'on y apporte ne perturbe pas les activités quotidiennes, en dépit de ce que beaucoup pensent.

Et puis c'est un excellent moyen d'embaucher de nouveaux employés et de les amener à prendre part au développement du studio.

Je nous compare souvent avec l'industrie de la musique, et j'y recourrai encore ici pour conclure : à mon avis, construire une bonne IC, c'est-à-dire l'apparence qu'offre une marque, revient à apprendre à jouer d'un instrument. On choisit l'instrument et puis il faut travailler encore et encore pour devenir un bon instrumentiste, puis un meilleur instrumentiste, puis, un jour peut-être, un virtuose.

blackbeltmonkey™

hello@blackbeltmonkey.com

Biography
Mike John Otto (blackbeltmonkey)

www.blackbeltmonkey.com   Location: Hamburg   Position: Co-founder/
                                          Year founded: 2007   Creative Director

After studying visual communication Mike John Otto worked freelance in London until, in 2000, he became Senior Designer at the Razorfish agency. After almost two years at Razorfish he became Art Director with Elephant Seven in Hamburg, until at the beginning of 2003 he went to work for Interone (part of the BBDO group). His work for BMW and MINI has garnered many awards in Cannes and D&AD, as well as at the Art Directors Club Germany, and has also been recognised at ceremonies such as Clio, Cresta, New York Festivals and Effie. In mid-2007 he founded the blackbeltmonkey studio together with two former colleagues from Interone. Blackbeltmonkey is a digital communication agency and design studio and forms the interface between classic and digital communication, focusing on digital campaigns (online specials) and digital branding.

Nach dem Studium der visuellen Kommunikation arbeitete Mike John Otto zunächst frei in London, bis er 2000 als Senior Designer bei der Agentur Razorfish begann. Nach knapp zwei Jahren dort wechselte er als Art Director zu Elephant Seven in Hamburg, bis er Anfang 2003 zu Interone (BBDO Group) ging. Seine Arbeiten für BMW und MINI wurden mehrmals sowohl in Cannes als auch vom D&AD sowie vom Art Directors Club Deutschland ausgezeichnet und erhielten viele weitere Awards wie Clio, Cresta, New York Festivals und Effie. Mitte 2007 gründete Otto zusammen mit zwei

ehemaligen Interone-Kollegen das Studio blackbeltmonkey. Es versteht sich als digitale Werbeagentur und Design-Studio und bildet die Schnittstelle zwischen klassischer und digitaler Kommunikation mit einem Schwerpunkt auf digitalen Kampagnen (Online-Specials) und digitalem Branding.

Après des études de communication visuelle, Mike John Otto travaille comme freelance à Londres et devient en 2000 responsable du design de l'agence Razorfish, où il restera deux ans avant d'être nommé directeur artistique de Elephant Seven à Hambourg, puis, début 2003, d'intégrer l'agence Interone (appartenant au groupe BBDO). Son travail pour BMW et MINI lui a valu plusieurs récompenses à Cannes et au D&AD, ainsi qu'au Art Directors Club Germany, et il a également été récompensé lors de cérémonies telles que Clio, Cresta, New York Festivals et Effie. Mi-2007, il a fondé le studio blackbeltmonkey avec deux anciens confrères de Interone. Le studio de communication numérique et design Blackbeltmonkey assure l'interface entre la communication classique et le numérique ; elle est axée sur les campagnes numériques (en particulier on-line) et sur le branding numérique.

THE MAKING OF
BURTON
OUTWEAR
FALL/WINTER
2007

When we started the studio in 1997, our vision was to break through the barriers standing between certain audiences or subcultures (street, hip-hop, skateboarding, etc.) and the commercial brands trying to reach these groups. At the time, marketing attempts were generally off-base and actually alienating. There seemed to be a lack of understanding in regard to access/placement and also literal and visual language. Coming from those contemporary cultures ourselves, we basically started designing campaigns that appealed to us directly but with an instinct for what we'd need to reach a broader audience. We brought art back into advertising, which had mostly disappeared since the poster campaigns of the '60s, and laid the groundwork for boutique guerrilla marketing. Once we got a few corporate accounts it was evident that our strategies worked and it sort of exploded from there.

Our vision for identity starts with trying to be as real as possible about a brand and knowing that we are placing that brand in a market where the consumer is judge and

Als wir 1997 das Studio gründeten, bestand unsere Vision darin, die Barrieren zwischen bestimmten Zielgruppen oder Subkulturen (Street, Hip-Hop, Skateboarding etc.) und den kommerziellen Marken zu durchbrechen, die versuchen, diese Gruppen zu erreichen. Zu jener Zeit lagen Marketingversuche im Allgemeinen ziemlich daneben und wirkten sogar eher abschreckend. Scheinbar fehlte ein Verständnis für den Zugang und die Platzierung sowie die Sprache und visuelle Ausdrucksweise. Da wir selbst in diesen zeitgenössischen Kunstformen zu Hause waren, starteten wir im Wesentlichen mit der Entwicklung von Kampagnen, die uns selbst direkt ansprachen, und nutzten unseren Instinkt, um herauszufinden, wie wir eine größere Zielgruppe erreichen konnten. Wir brachten die Kunst in die Werbung zurück, die seit den Posterkampagnen der 60er Jahre meist verloren gegangen war, und legten das Fundament für das Guerilla-Marketing der Boutiquen. Als wir dann einige Unternehmen als Kunden gewinnen konnten, war es offensichtlich, dass unsere Strategie funktionierte.

Lorsque nous avons lancé le studio en 1997, notre objectif était de briser les barrières entre certains publics ou sub-cultures (rue, hip-hop, skateboard, etc.) et les marques commerciales, en essayant d'atteindre ces groupes. A l'époque, les tentatives de marketing étaient généralement marginales et, en fait, excluantes. Il semblait y avoir un manque de compréhension en matière d'accès/positionnement, mais aussi de langage textuel et visuel. Etant nous-mêmes issus de ces cultures contemporaines, nous avons commencé à concevoir des campagnes qui nous plaisaient, à nous, mais avec un feeling pour l'audience plus large que nous cherchions à toucher. Nous avons ramené l'art à la publicité, d'où il avait quasiment disparu depuis les campagnes d'affichage des années 60, et préparé le terrain pour le marketing alternatif en boutique. Au bout de quelques comptes sociaux obtenus, nous avons compris que nos stratégies fonctionnaient, et c'est à partir de là que ça a commencé à s'emballer.

jury. On the positive side, this keeps us from having to do work we'd feel crappy about, and in reality, receptive audiences are there just waiting to be entertained by advertising in one way or another. People keeping up with cultural trends and alt lifestyles, in particular, will always respond to something new.

We initially define the primary goals of a project by asking the client a lot of questions so as to get as close to their true vision of their brand as possible; their goals and expectations; why are they seeking this market in particular; the brand's real or perceived competition, and so on.

We also take care to spend the time needed to help the client communicate his or her personal likes and dislikes regarding existing marketing, from strategies to colours. In addition to building an element of trust with the client and helping to open communication channels, this helps ensure that we don't waste time taking the client in a direction they will not approve of. After that initial stage, we move to research mode and begin to engage in a sort of immersion with the brand, essentially wearing the shoes of the consumer, so to speak, which leads to planning and brainstorming. The design phase comes soon after.

We recently designed the thread packages for Burton's youth and men and women's Fall/Winter 2007 snowboard apparel line. The project consisted of taking blank Burton garments and embellishing each one based on a unique theme. We'd be given a loose directive based on a word or location, like "Cheyenne" or "Tangiers". They were more like exotic clues. We designed top-to-bottom with each theme – everything from logos to patterns, labels, stitching, buttons, and whatever else came to mind. The placement had to be done as well. It was an intense project with a short deadline.

The project was expansive and seemed almost esoteric at first. We had little time to waste and a lot of concept-work to do

Unsere Vision für die Markenidentität beginnt mit dem Versuch, bei einer Marke so echt wie möglich zu sein und im Hinterkopf zu behalten, dass wir diese Marke auf einem Markt platzieren, in dem der Konsument urteilt und entscheidet. Das Positive daran ist, dass wir keine Arbeit machen müssen, bei der wir uns schlecht fühlen. Tatsächlich warten empfängliche Zielgruppen nur darauf, durch Werbung auf die eine oder andere Art unterhalten zu werden. Besonders Personen, die mit kulturellen Trends und alternativen Lifestyles Schritt halten, werden gegenüber etwas Neuem immer empfänglich sein.

Zunächst definieren wir die grundlegenden Ziele eines Projektes, indem wir dem Kunden eine Menge Fragen stellen, sodass wir der wahren Vision des Kunden über seine Marke so nahe wie möglich kommen: die Ziele und Erwartungen des Kunden, warum der Kunde ausgerechnet auf diesen Markt abzielt, die tatsächliche oder wahrgenommene Konkurrenz usw.

Wir achten auch darauf, uns genügend Zeit zu nehmen, dem Kunden bei der Kommunikation seiner persönlichen Vorlieben oder Abneigungen hinsichtlich des bereits vorhandenen Marketings zu helfen, von den Strategien bis hin zu den Farben. Dies schafft eine Vertrauensbasis bei den Kunden und öffnet Kommunikationswege. So verlieren wir keine Zeit damit, die Kunden in eine falsche Richtung zu lenken. Nach dieser Anfangsphase gehen wir zur Recherche über und beginnen, uns auf die Marke einzulassen, indem wir sozusagen in sie eintauchen. Dabei versetzen wir uns im Wesentlichen in die Lage des Kunden und starten mit Planung und Brainstorming. Die Designphase folgt kurz darauf.

Wir entwarfen neulich das Zuschnittdesign für die Bekleidungsreihe Burton's Snowboard Herbst/Winter 2007 für Jugendliche, Frauen und Männer. Das Projekt bestand darin, unbearbeitete Kleidungsstücke von Burton nach einem besonderen Thema zu gestalten. Wir bekamen dazu vage Anweisungen, die auf einem Wort oder

Pour nous, l'identité consiste à jouer autant que possible la carte de l'authenticité de la marque, sachant que nous la plaçons sur un marché où le consommateur est le seul juge. Le côté positif, c'est que ça nous évite d'avoir à faire un boulot qui nous semble nul ; d'ailleurs, en fait, la seule chose que veulent les publics destinataires c'est que la publicité les divertisse d'une façon ou d'une autre. Les gens qui suivent les tendances culturelles et, en particulier, les styles de vie alternatifs, répondront toujours aux nouveautés.

Nous définissons tout d'abord les objectifs fondamentaux d'un projet en posant des tas de questions aux clients, de manière à coller aussi près que possible à la manière dont ils perçoivent leur propre marque ; à leurs objectifs et leurs attentes ; à la raison pour laquelle ils visent ce marché plutôt qu'un autre, aux concurrents réels ou perçus comme tels de la marque, etc.

Nous nous efforçons également de consacrer le temps nécessaire à aider le client à communiquer ses goûts ou ses aversions pour le marketing existant, depuis les stratégies jusqu'aux couleurs. Outre la confiance qu'elle contribue à cimenter entre nous et le client, cette manière de procéder facilite l'ouverture de canaux de communication et nous donne l'assurance de ne pas risquer de perdre de temps en menant le client dans une direction qu'il n'approuve pas. Après cette phase initiale, nous passons à la recherche et entamons avec la marque une espèce d'immersion, en nous mettant pour ainsi dire dans les chaussures du consommateur, immersion qui débouche sur une planification et des séances de remue-méninges. La phase conceptuelle vient ensuite.

Nous avons récemment conçu la passementerie des vêtements de snow-board Burton pour les lignes ado, homme et femme de la collection automne/hiver 2007. Le projet a consisté à prendre des spécimens de modèles Burton et à les agrémenter en déclinant un thème unique. Nous avions pour vague fil conducteur un mot et une

Previous spread: *Concept design for the youth collection. ///* **Vorhergehende Seite:** *Konzeptdesign für die Jugendkollektion. ///* **Double page précédente :** *Design conceptuel pour la collection Jeunesse.*

Bottom and right: *Research and logo studies on the theme "Highlander" for the men's collection. ///* **Unten und rechts:** *Recherchen und Studien für das Logo zum Thema „Highlander" für die Herrenkollektion. ///* **En bas et à droite :** *Recherches et études de logo sur le thème « Highlander » pour la collection Homme.*

BLK/MRKT

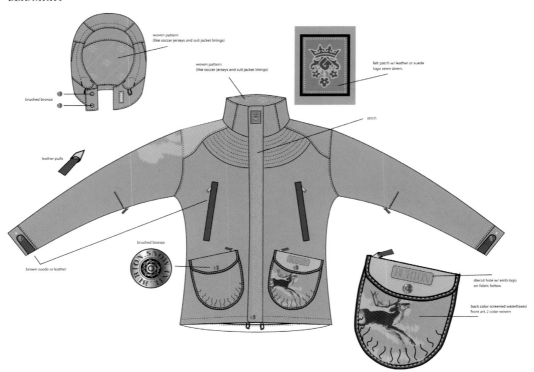

before we could realise the full project. The most difficult and challenging aspect was the amount of research needed to execute each theme properly in a unique, yet un-naive way. It was important that we fully understood each theme so we could put our heads into that place. Another challenge was managing everything – as a team, you don't have down-time with a complex project like this so we had to keep organised and in creative motion for the duration.

The high point of the project for our team was probably all the exercises in application (design vs. material, etc.) of the artwork we were developing while exploring multiple and diverse cultures. We all felt like we had travelled the world for a year when it was completed. Working with Burton was also great because they gave us complete creative control and were open to just about anything we could dream up. That made the project a lot of fun as well. The best solution we created for Burton was to give them more options than they asked for –

einem Ort basierten, wie zum Beispiel „Cheyenne" oder „Tanger". Sie dienten mehr als exotische Anhaltspunkte. Wir entwarfen bei jedem Thema komplett alles vom Logo bis zum Design, von den Labeln über die Nähte bis zu den Knöpfen und was uns sonst noch einfiel. Auch die Platzierung musste durchgeführt werden – ein intensives Projekt mit einem engen Zeitrahmen.

Das Projekt war sehr umfangreich und erschien zunächst fast esoterisch. Wir hatten nur wenig Zeit und mussten eine Menge Konzeptarbeit erledigen, bevor wir das gesamte Projekt realisieren konnten. Der schwierigste und anspruchvollste Aspekt dabei war die nötige Recherchearbeit, damit jedes Thema richtig und auf einmalige, nicht naive Art ausgeführt werden konnte. Dabei war es wichtig, dass wir jedes Thema umfassend durchdrungen hatten und es so in unserem Gedächtnis fixieren konnten. Eine weitere Herausforderung bestand im Management des Gesamtprojektes – als Team hat man bei einem solch komplexen Projekt keinen Stillstand, deshalb mussten

destination, « Cheyenne » et « Tanger », à titre d'indices exotiques plutôt qu'autre chose. Nous avons tout conçu de A à Z pour chaque thème – tout, du logo aux motifs, en passant par les labels, les coutures, les boutons et tout ce qui peut venir à l'esprit. Nous avons également assuré la mise en place. Un projet intense, on le voit, et avec une échéance très courte.

Le projet se dilatait sans cesse et, au départ, semblait quelque peu hermétique. Nous avions peu de temps à perdre et beaucoup de travail conceptuel à faire avant d'y mettre un point final. La grosse difficulté, mais aussi le plus grand défi, tenait à la quantité de recherches nécessaires pour exécuter chaque thème adéquatement, d'une manière unique mais sans excès de simplicité. Il nous fallait nous pénétrer entièrement de chaque thème pour être en phase avec les lieux d'inspiration. Autre défi, il fallait tout gérer – pour une équipe, il n'y a pas d'heures improductives avec un projet de cette complexité, et nous avons donc dû nous organiser, pour tenir la distance en restant créatifs.

Left: *"Manchester" snowboard jacket and detailing close-ups for the women's collection. ///* **Links**: *Snowboard-Jacke „Manchester" und Detailabbildungen für die Damenkollektion. ///* **A gauche** : *Veste de snowboard « Manchester » et gros plans détaillés pour la collection Femme.*

Right: *Pattern and logo on the theme "Cheyenne" for the women's collection. ///* **Rechts**: *Muster und Logo zu dem Thema „Cheyenne" für die Damenkollektion. ///* **A droite** : *Motif et logo sur le thème « Cheyenne » pour la collection Femme.*

Next spread: *Sketches and studies for the youth collection. ///* **Nächste Seite**: *Zeichnungen und Studien für die Jugendkollektion. ///* **Double page suivante** : *Croquis et études pour la collection Jeunesse.*

this goes against our normal convention, but in this case we knew Burton had an excellent creative team and they were able to pick and choose from a wide range of potential solutions and apply them across the whole line. Each designer on the team did about 10 pages of thumbnails or loose reference compositions for each theme initially. As the project progressed, the best designs were chosen.

The project was presented on digital "boards" – everything was presented digitally from start to finish. Once sent to the client, the boards went through an internal review and the final designs were chosen for build-out. In regard to the final result, Burton seemed very pleased and it was cool to see the designs applied to actual garments and hit the market. Nothing seemed to go wrong – we have great management and a team of people with cross-over capabilities, and as we have also worked with Burton for years, there were no surprises on either side. After that, Burton handled the production side of the pieces we created. We call

wir für die gesamte Projektdauer organisiert und in kreativer Bewegung bleiben.

Für unser Team bestand der Höhepunkt des Projektes wahrscheinlich darin, all die künstlerische Arbeit in Anwendungsmöglichkeiten umzusetzen (z.B. das Design mit dem Material abzugleichen etc.), die wir entwickelten, während wir viele verschiedene Kulturen erforschten. Am Ende des Projektes fühlten wir uns, als wären wir ein Jahr lang auf Weltreise gewesen. Die Zusammenarbeit mit Burton war auch deshalb so großartig, weil wir die vollständige kreative Verantwortung bekamen und Burton offen gegenüber allem war, was wir uns einfallen ließen. Dadurch hat uns das Projekt sehr viel Spaß gemacht. Unsere beste, für Burton entwickelte Lösung bestand darin, dem Unternehmen mehr Optionen als angefragt anzubieten. Dies steht zwar im Gegensatz zu unserem normalen Verfahren, doch in diesem Fall wussten wir, dass Burton über ein hervorragendes Kreativteam verfügte, das unter mehreren möglichen Lösungen eine Auswahl treffen und diese auf die gesamte Serie

Le point culminant, dans notre cas, a probablement été les opérations de mise en œuvre (design/matériel, etc.) du travail artistique issu de notre périple à travers toutes sortes de cultures. Quand il a été terminé, nous avions l'impression d'avoir sillonné le monde une année entière. Nous avons également aimé travailler avec Burton parce qu'ils nous ont laissé carte blanche pour la création et se sont montrés réceptifs à tout ; impossible de rêver mieux. Du coup, nous nous sommes éclatés avec ce projet. Et nous avons proposé à Burton davantage de solutions qu'ils n'en demandaient – chose contraire à nos habitudes, mais en l'occurrence nous savions que Burton avait une excellente équipe créative, parfaitement en mesure de trier et de choisir parmi une large gamme de solutions potentielles, puis de les appliquer à toute la ligne. Chaque designer de l'équipe a initialement pondu environ 10 pages de croquis ou de crayonnages pour chaque thème. A mesure que le projet avançait, les meilleurs d'entre eux ont été retenus.

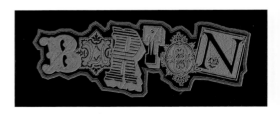

Above: *Patterns for the youth collection. ///*
Oben: *Muster für die Jugendkollektion. ///*
Ci-dessus : *Motifs pour la collection Jeunesse.*

Right: *Snowboard jacket and detailing for the youth collection. ///* **Rechts:** *Snowboard-Jacke und Details für die Jugendkollektion. ///* **A droite :** *Veste de snowboard et détails pour la collection Jeunesse.*

everything out to spec (material, position, etc.) and they have it produced through their vendors. We have a lot of experience with apparel design so we have acquired a pretty good understanding of how the end-product will look based on our directives.

Projects like this are very important to our team, as we love being here, we really do take pride in everything we do and the important thing is to have fun as well. It's one of the biggest advantages about having a small but experienced staff. We all have to rely on each other very much and there's virtually no room for holes within the relationship of the group. This project necessitated each and every one of our team members working diligently and responsibly, alone and together, and I think it served to reinforce our knowledge that we have a special thing going on here at BLK/MRKT. A smart and dedicated team is a must – organisation is essential and In & Out Burger is a lifesaver.

anwenden konnte. Zu Anfang entwickelte jeder Designer und jede Designerin im Team für jedes einzelne Thema ungefähr zehn Seiten Miniaturbilder oder schnelle Ideenskizzen. Im Verlauf des Projekts wurden die besten Vorschläge ausgewählt.

Das Projekt wurde auf digitalen „Boards" präsentiert – wie alles von Anfang bis Ende digital präsentiert wurde. Nachdem die digitalen Boards zum Kunden gesendet worden waren, durchliefen sie eine interne Prüfung, und die endgültigen Designs zur Weiterbearbeitung wurden ausgewählt. Burton war offenbar sehr zufrieden mit dem Ergebnis, und es war fantastisch zu sehen, wie die Designs auf der Bekleidung umgesetzt wurden und schließlich den Markt eroberten. Es gab keinerlei Probleme – wir haben ein hervorragendes Management und ein vielseitiges Mitarbeiterteam. Zudem arbeiten wir auch schon seit Jahren mit Burton, und nie kam es zu irgendwelchen bösen Überraschungen. Burton brachte nun die von uns entwickelten Stücke in die Produktion. Wir gaben alles frei (Material, Position etc.), und Burton

Le projet a été présenté sur « planches » numériques – tout a d'ailleurs été présenté numériquement du début à la fin. Après envoi au client, les planches ont été soumises à un examen interne, puis les dessins retenus mis en fabrication. Chez Burton, on a été apparemment très satisfait du résultat et nous avons eu le plaisir de voir nos créations et les vêtements de la collection faire un malheur sur le marché. Tout a marché comme sur des roulettes – nous avons une bonne gestion, une excellence synergie d'équipe, et puis cela fait tant d'années que nous collaborons avec Burton qu'il n'y a eu de surprises ni d'un côté ni de l'autre. A partir de là, Burton s'est occupé de produire les pièces que nous avions créées. Nous avons tout préparé au millimètre près (matériel, position, etc.) et ils ont fait fabriquer par leurs fournisseurs. Nous avons beaucoup d'expérience en matière de design vestimentaire, aussi avons-nous une idée assez précise de l'apparence qu'aura le produit fabriqué selon nos directives.

De tels projets sont très importants pour notre équipe, et comme nous aimons ce

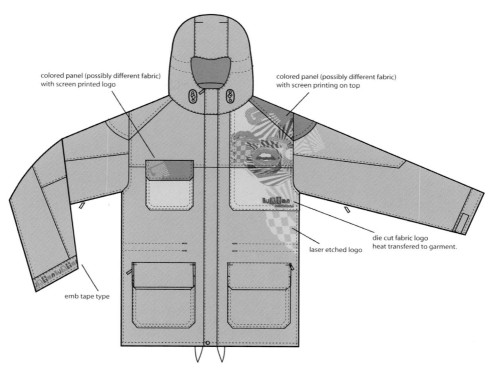

colored panel (possibly different fabric) with screen printed logo

colored panel (possibly different fabric) with screen printing on top

die cut fabric logo heat transfered to garment.

laser etched logo

emb tape type

ließ die Kleidung durch seine Lieferanten produzieren. Wir haben viel Erfahrung im Bereich Bekleidungsdesign und deshalb ein recht gutes Verständnis dafür entwickelt, wie das Endprodukt auf Grundlage unserer Anweisungen aussieht.

Projekte wie dieses sind für unser Team sehr wichtig. Wir lieben es, hier zu arbeiten, und sind wirklich stolz auf alles, was wir tun. Zudem ist es wichtig, dass wir auch Spaß an unseren Projekten haben. Es ist ein großer Vorteil, ein kleines, aber erfahrenes Mitarbeiterteam zu haben. Wir müssen uns alle sehr aufeinander verlassen, und es gibt praktisch keinen Platz für Lücken in den Beziehungen innerhalb der Gruppe. Dieses Projekt erforderte, dass jedes Teammitglied sorgfältig und verantwortungsvoll arbeitete, allein oder zusammen mit anderen Teammit- gliedern. Ich denke, das Projekt stärkte uns in unserem Bewusstsein, dass unsere Arbeit hier bei BLK/MRKT etwas Besonderes ist.

que nous faisons, nous en tirons une réelle fierté, l'important étant aussi de se faire plaisir. C'est l'un des plus gros avantages de travailler avec une équipe peu nombreuse mais expérimentée. Nous dépendons tous beaucoup les uns des autres et il n'y a virtuellement pas de place pour les désaccords au sein du groupe. Ce projet demandait que tous les membres de l'équipe sans exception y collaborent avec efficacité et responsabilité, seuls et ensemble, et je pense qu'il aura contribué à renforcer en nous le sentiment qu'il se passe quelque chose de tout à fait particulier au sein de BLK/MRKT. Une équipe intelligente et disponible est un must – l'organisation est essentielle… et In & Out Burger nous sauve la vie.

STITCHING

RUBBER/FELT PATCH

SCREENPRINT

SHREDDED PATCH

STITCHING

SCREENPRINT

EMBROIDERY

HIGH_DENSITY (gloss) SCREENPRINT (ALL BLACK)

Left top: *Illustration and detailing for the youth collection.* /// **Links oben:** *Illustrationen und Details für die Jugendkollektion.* /// **En haut à gauche :** *Illustrations et détails pour la collection Jeunesse.*

Left bottom: *Sketches for the youth collection.* /// **Links unten:** *Zeichnungen für die Jugendkollektion.* /// **En bas à gauche :** *Croquis pour la collection Jeunesse.*

Biography
Dave Kinsey (BLK/MRKT)

www.blkmrkt.com.com   Location: Los Angeles   Position: Creative Director
                                 Year founded: 1997

Born in Pittsburgh in 1971, Kinsey is part of a growing dimension of urban contemporary artists changing the scene of traditional and non-traditional art and visual media. After attending the Art Institute of Pittsburgh, with an emphasis on fine-art illustration, he honed his design skills at the Art Institute of Atlanta, graduating in 1993. He moved to the West coast a year later to pursue a job offer and founded the creative design agency BLK/MRKT. He has also been featured in such publications as The New York Times, Black Book *and BLK/MRKT One* and Two, *and has been invited to speak at numerous institutions such as The Art Center College of Design, UCLA, Montserrat College of Art, and most recently at the Semi-Permanent conference in Sydney.*

Dave Kinsey wurde 1971 in Pittsburgh (USA) geboren. Er gehört zur wachsenden Zahl urbaner, zeitgenössischer Künstler, die die Szenen der traditionellen und nicht-traditionellen Kunst sowie der visuellen Medien verändern. Nach dem Besuch des Art Institute of Pittsburgh, wo er mit dem Schwerpunkt Kunst-Illustration studiert hatte, verfeinerte er seine Designfertigkeiten am Art Institute of Atlanta, wo er 1993 seinen Abschluss machte. Ein Jahr später zog Kinsey an die Westküste, um einem Jobangebot zu folgen, und gründete die Agentur für kreatives Design BLK/MRKT. Über Kinsey wird in Publikationen wie The New York Times, Black Book *und* BLK/MRKT One *und* Two *berichtet. Er wird von zahlreichen Institutionen zu Vorträgen eingeladen, unter anderem vom Art Center College of Design, vom UCLA, vom Montserrat College of Art und kürzlich zur Semi-Permanent Konferenz in Sidney.*

Né à Pittsburgh en 1971, Kinsey est l'un de ces artistes contemporains urbains qui, en toujours plus grand nombre, bouleversent la scène des arts traditionnels et non traditionnels et de l'audio-visuel. Après des études à l'Art Institute de Pittsburgh, spécialisées dans l'illustration d'art, il perfectionne ses talents de dessinateur à l'Art Institute d'Atlanta, dont il obtient le diplôme en 1993. Répondant à une offre d'emploi, il s'établit sur la côte ouest un an plus tard et fonde l'agence de communication BLK/MRKT. Il a également collaboré à des publications telles que The New York Times, Black Book *et* BLK/MRKT One *et* Two, *et il a été invité à s'exprimer dans de nombreuses institutions comme* The Art Center College of Design, UCLA, Montserrat College of Art *et, plus récemment, à l'occasion de la conférence semi-permanente de Sydney.*

LOGO GENERATOR FOR A MUSIC CENTRE: INTERVIEW WITH STEFAN SAGMEISTER

T: Can you describe the work you do, and what is your vision for identity?
S: *I am an Austrian graphic designer running a design office in NYC. In general, I think branding is overrated, most international branding agencies are visual polluters and many identity designers take sameness too seriously.*

T: How do you think that your work can build a strong identity?
S: *Through smart thinking, good designing and relentless applying.*

T: What are the key things you look at when you start a project?
S: *Does the client need a new logo/identity? If yes, should this identity be static or dynamic? Who is the audience? How can it stand out and maximise impact with fewer applications?*

T: Can you describe one project you have done recently?
S: *We were asked to develop a new visual identity for the music centre Casa da Música in Porto, Portugal, built by Dutch architect Rem Koolhaas.*

T: Können Sie Ihre Arbeit und Ihre Vision zur Markenidentität beschreiben?
S: *Ich bin ein österreichischer Grafik-designer und leite eine Designagentur in New York. Generell denke ich, dass die Markenbildung überbewertet wird, dass die meisten internationalen Agenturen für Markenbildung visuelle Umweltverschmutzer sind und dass viele Identity-Designer Markenbildung zu ernst nehmen.*

T: Wie können Sie durch Ihre Arbeit eine starke Markenidentität schaffen?
S: *Durch kluges Denken, gutes Design und unerbittliche Umsetzung.*

T: Welche Dinge sind für Sie zu Beginn eines Projektes entscheidend?
S: *Braucht der Kunde ein neues Logo oder eine neue Identität? Falls ja, soll diese Identität statisch oder dynamisch sein? Wer ist die Zielgruppe? Wie kann ich die Identität hervorheben und ihre Wirkung mit weniger Anwendungen maximieren?*

T: Pouvez-vous nous parler de votre travail et de votre perception de l'identité ?
S: *Je suis un créateur de graphisme autrichien qui dirige une agence de communication à New York. En général, j'estime que la valorisation de marque est surestimée, la plupart des agences de branding sont des pollueurs visuels et beaucoup de concepteurs d'identité se prennent trop au sérieux.*

T: Comment, à votre avis, votre travail contribue-t-il à construire une solide identité ?
S: *Par la justesse du raisonnement, l'adéquation de la conception et la rigueur de la mise en œuvre.*

T: Quels sont les aspects auxquels vous veillez particulièrement quand vous abordez un projet ?
S: *Je me demande si le client a besoin d'un nouveau logo, d'une nouvelle identité ? Si oui, cette identité doit-elle être statique ou dynamique ? Quel est le public ? Comment faire différent et maximiser l'impact avec moins d'applications ?*

2º ANIVERSÁRIO
CASA DA MÚSICA

13,14 e 15 Abril 2007

13 Abril|Sex

ONP À SEXTA
Orquestra Nacional do Porto

Concerto de Gala
2º Aniversário

21:30 | Sala Suggia

Stefan Asbury *direcção musical*

Ludwig van Beethoven
Abertura nº 3 de Leonora
Leonard Bernstein
Suite de On the Waterfront
Dmitri Shostakovich/
James Conlon
*Suite para Orquestra de Lady
Macbeth de Mtsensk*

14 Abril|Sáb

AO MEIO DIA
Otto Michael Pereira *violino*
Prémio Jovens Músicos 2005

12:00 | Sala 2 | Entrada livre

Otto Michael Pereira *violino*
João Crisóstomo *piano*

Ludwig van Beethoven | Giuseppe
Tartini | Henri Wieniawski
Tomaso Antonio | Pablo Sarasate

Stefan Sagmeister
Conferência
16:00 | Sala 2 | Entrada livre

PIANO
Grigori Sokolov *piano*
18:00 | Sala Suggia

Franz Schubert | Alexander
Scriabin

URBAN VIBE
Dizzee Rascal | Deize
Tigrona | Tetine | Buraka Som
Sistema
23:00 | Parque

15 Abril|Dom

AO MEIO DIA
Orquestra Nacional do Porto
12:00 | Sala Suggia
Entrada livre

Stefan Asbury *direcção musical*

Concerto para famílias
comentado por Gabriela
Canavilhas

Programa
Ludwig van Beethoven
Leonard Bernstein

casa da música

T: What was the challenge of this project, the most difficult things to address?
S: *Our initial desire was to design an identity without featuring the building. Most architecturally interesting music-centre identities I had studied worldwide turned their architecture into a cold, static logo, forgoing the musical content at the centre of the building's DNA. This desire proved impossible because as we studied the structure more we realised that the building itself is a logo. Koolhaas calls this "the organisation of various layers of meaning", which translates into "logo-making".*

T: What were the high points of this project, the best solutions you generated?
S: *We did try to avoid another rendering of a building by developing a system where this recognisable, unique, modern form transforms itself like a chameleon from application to application, changes from media to media, where the physical building itself is the ultimate (in very high resolution, so to speak) rendering in a long line of logos. We achieved this by designing a "Casa da Música Logo Generator", a custom-designed piece of*

T: Können Sie ein Projekt beschreiben, das Sie vor Kurzem durchgeführt haben?
S: *Wir wurden gebeten, für das Musik-zentrum Casa da Música im portugiesischen Porto eine neue visuelle Identität zu schaffen. Das Gebäude wurde von dem holländischen Architekten Rem Koolhaas erbaut.*

T: Was waren die Herausforderungen und die größten Schwierigkeiten bei diesem Projekt?
S: *Unser anfänglicher Wunsch bestand darin, eine Identität zu schaffen, ohne das Gebäude herauszustellen. Die meisten architektonisch interessanten Musikhäuser, die ich weltweit studiert habe, wandelten ihre Architektur in ein kaltes und statisches Logo um, ohne dabei den zentralen musika-lischen Inhalt des Gebäudes und ihre eigene Identität zu berücksichtigen. Dieser Wunsch war nicht umzusetzen, da wir bei näherer Betrachtung der Baustruktur feststellten, dass das Gebäude selbst ein Logo ist. Koolhaas nennt dies die „Organisation von verschiedenen Bedeutungsschichten", was sich mit „Entwicklung eines Logos" übersetzen lässt.*

T: Pouvez-vous nous décrire un projet dont vous vous êtes occupé récemment ?
S: *On nous demandé de créer la nouvelle identité visuelle de la Casa da Música de Porto, Portugal, une œuvre de l'architecte hollandais Rem Koolhaas.*

T: Quel était le défi de ce projet, les choses les plus difficiles à maîtriser ?
S: *Notre souhait initial était de créer une identité sans faire allusion au bâtiment. Parmi les identités des salles de spectacle ayant une architecture particulière que j'ai pu étudier dans le monde, un grand nombre faisait de cette architecture un logo statique et froid, renonçant au contenu musical niché au cœur de l'ADN de l'édifice. Ce souhait s'est révélé irréalisable ; en effet, plus nous étudions la structure, plus nous nous rendions compte que le bâtiment est un logo en lui-même. Koolhaas appelle ça « organisation de plusieurs couches de sens », ce qui peut se traduire par « logo-making ».*

T: Quels ont été les points culminants de ce projet, les meilleures solutions que vous ayez trouvées ?

Previous spread: *Poster for 2ⁿᵈ anniversary of Casa da Música music centre, April 2007. ///* **Vorhergehende Seite:** *Plakat zur Feier des zweijährigen Bestehens des Musikzentrums Casa da Música, April 2007. ///* **Double page précédente :** *Affiche pour le second anniversaire du centre musical Casa da Música, avril 2007.*

Left: *Casa da Música building designed by Rem Koolhaas. ///* **Links:** *Die Casa da Música, entworfen von Rem Koolhaas. ///* **A gauche :** *La Casa da Música, une œuvre de Rem Koolhaas.*

Right: *Vectorised shapes of the views of the building to be used as the basis for the logo. ///* **Rechts:** *Vektorisierte Formen der Gebäude-ansichten, die als Basis für das Logo dienen. ///* **A droite :** *Profils vectorisés des vues du bâtiment ayant servi de base pour le logo.*

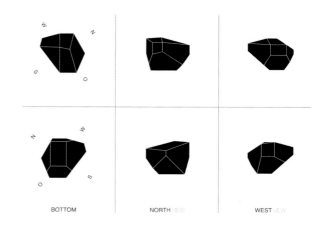

BOTTOM   NORTH VIEW   WEST VIEW

software connected to a scanner which transforms any image in a matter of seconds into a matching Casa da Música logo.

T: What were the implications of the creation of the new identity in the company/brand?
S: *Our goal was to show the many different kinds of music performed in one house. Depending on the music filling it, the house changes its character and works like dice cubes by displaying the different views and facets of the music.*

T: Could you please talk about the work-flow, the time you spent on the projects, the different phases of the projects?
S: *We started by meeting with everybody in Porto, from the president to the musical director and the house manager, to get a good idea about the house itself, and attended numerous performances. We worked about 12 weeks on the initial presentation, and another 12 on the final overall identity. Since then, various aspects of the identity have still needed updating.*

T: Was waren die Höhepunkte dieses Projekts und die besten Lösungen, die Sie entwickelt haben?
S: *Wir wollten vermeiden, schon wieder das Gebäude darzustellen, und entwickelten ein System, mit dem diese bemerkenswerte, einzigartige und moderne Form sich selbst wie ein Chamäleon von einer Anwendung zur anderen und von Medium zu Medium verändert. Dabei stellt das physische Gebäude selbst die ultimative Wiedergabe einer langen Serie von Logos (sozusagen „hochaufgelöst") dar. Wir erreichten dies, indem wir einen „Casa da Música Logo-Generator" entwickelten. Das ist eine selbst entwickelte Software, die mit einem Scanner verbunden ist. Diese Software verwandelt jedes Bild innerhalb von Sekunden in ein passendes Casa-da-Música-Logo.*

T: Welche Auswirkungen hatte die Schaffung der neuen Identität des Unternehmens bzw. der Marke?
S: *Unser Ziel bestand darin, die vielen verschiedenen Arten von Musik zu zeigen, die in diesem Haus gespielt werden können. Je nach der Art der Musik, die das Haus*

S: *Nous nous sommes efforcés d'éviter un rendu d'architecture de plus, en créant un système grâce auquel cette silhouette reconnaissable, unique et moderne se transforme d'application en application, comme un caméléon, se modifie de support en support, l'édifice physique lui-même étant le dernier rendu (en très haute définition, pour ainsi dire) d'une longue série de logos. Nous y sommes parvenus en mettant au point le « Casa da Música Logo Generator », un progiciel personnalisé connecté à un scanner qui transforme en quelques secondes n'importe quelle image en un logo assorti à celui de la Casa da Música.*

T: Quelles étaient les implications de la création de cette nouvelle identité pour la société ou la marque ?
S: *Notre objectif était de montrer les nombreux types de musique qui trouvent place dans cet établissement. En fonction de la musique qui y est interprétée, l'édifice change de caractère et fonctionne à la manière d'un dé dont on découvre ainsi les différentes faces et apparences musicales.*

Casa da Musica - logo generator

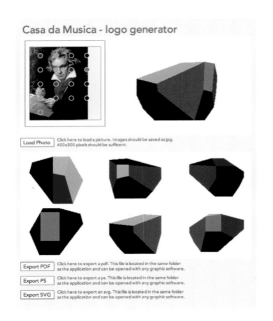

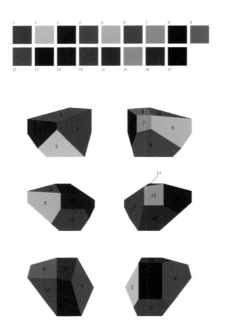

casa da música

Left: *Logo Generator software; picture with points applied, from where the colour palette will be taken; final poster; colour palette to be used to produce the logo.* /// **Links:** *Die Logo-Generator-Software; an einem Bild sind Punkte aufgebracht, aus denen sich die entsprechende Farbpalette zusammensetzt; das fertige Poster; Farbpalette, die zur Erstellung des Logos verwendet wurde.* /// **A gauche :** *Logiciel générateur de logos ; image avec le marquage de points d'où sera tirée la palette de couleurs ; affiche finale ; palette de couleurs à employer pour créer le logo.*

Right and bottom: *Series of studies of images for the Logo Generator.* /// **Rechts und unten:** *Serie von Bildstudien für den Logo-Generator.* /// **En bas à droite :** *Séries d'études d'images pour le générateur de logos.*

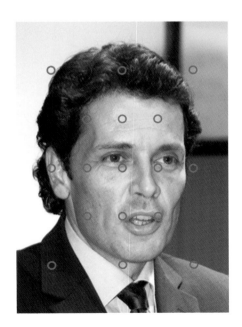
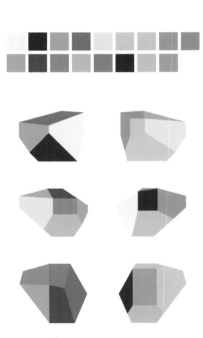

T: Can you describe the number of applications you created, and why the necessity to have them?

S: *We generated many versions of the logo, always fitting EXACTLY to the applications, because they both (logo and application itself) use the same digital data. Not only was an entire logo system and sub-logo system developed, the identity is also used as the PRIMARY visual element on the entire advertising effort.*

T: What were the things that went wrong, and how did you correct them?

S: *We presented our work first to the client and once, in front of 600 people, to the citizens of Porto. Both presentations went very well. There were some minor questions about the sub-identities but they were quickly resolved. We lost the marketing director Guta Moura Guedes to another cultural institution, and as she was the one who championed the project, also lost a friend within the institution.*

T: Can you describe the particularities involved in the production of the final product, or in the implementation of it?

erfüllt, ändert das Haus seinen Charakter und ähnelt Würfeln, die die verschiedenen Blickwinkel und Aspekte der Musik darstellen.

T: Können Sie bitte den Arbeitsablauf, den Zeitaufwand und die verschiedenen Phasen des Projekts beschreiben?

S: *Zuerst setzten wir uns mit den relevanten Personen in Porto zusammen, vom Präsidenten über den Musikdirektor bis zum Hausverwalter, um einen genauen Eindruck vom Haus selbst zu bekommen. Zudem nahmen wir an zahlreichen Veranstaltungen teil. Wir arbeiteten ungefähr 12 Wochen an der Erstpräsentation, und weitere 12 Wochen an der endgültigen Gesamtidentität. Seitdem mussten verschiedene Aspekte der Identität weiter aktualisiert werden.*

T: Können Sie die Anwendungen beschreiben, die Sie geschaffen haben, und erläutern, warum sie notwendig waren?

S: *Wir entwickelten viele Versionen des Logos, die immer exakt zu den Anwendungen passten, denn beide (das Logo und die Anwendung selbst) verwenden die gleichen digitalen Daten. Es wurde nicht nur ein*

T: Pourriez-vous nous parler du déroulement du travail, du temps que vous avez passé sur les projets, de leurs différentes phases ?

S: *Nous avons commencé par rencontrer tout le monde à Porto, du président au directeur musical et au gérant de la maison, afin de prendre la véritable mesure de l'établissement, et puis nous avons assisté à de nombreux spectacles. Nous avons travaillé environ 12 semaines à la présentation initiale, puis encore 12 semaines pour peaufiner l'identité. Depuis, plusieurs aspects de cette identité ont dû être actualisés.*

T: Pouvez-vous décrire le nombre d'applications que vous avez créées, et nous dire en quoi elles étaient nécessaires ?

S: *Nous avons mis au point plusieurs versions du logo, en veillant à ce qu'elles collent EXACTEMENT aux applications, car tous deux (logo et application) utilisent les mêmes données numériques. Non seulement nous avons créé un système intégral de logo et de sub-logo, mais nous avons utilisé l'identité comme élément visuel PRINCIPAL de l'ensemble du processus publicitaire.*

orquestra nacional
do porto

Left: *Series of posters for Casa da Música. ///*
Links: *Plakatserie für die Casa da Música. ///*
A gauche : *Série d'affiches pour la Casa da Música.*

Right: *Logo options using typography and patterns. ///* **Rechts:** *Logo-Optionen unter Verwendung von Typografie und Strukturen. /// A droite : Possibilités de logo utilisant diverses typographies et divers motifs.*

remix ensemble

S: *Casa da Música employed two new Portuguese designers in-house, Sara Westermann and André Cruz, whose task is to take care of the incredible amount of day-to-day design needs for the venue as well as being the guardians of the new identity internally. If you don't implement every aspect of a new identity yourself, you have to learn to let certain things go and be as they are.*

gesamtes Logo-System und Sub-Logo-System entwickelt, sondern auch die Identität als hauptsächliches visuelles Element in der gesamten Werbemaßnahme verwendet.

T: Welche Dinge haben nicht funktioniert und wie konnten Sie diese korrigieren?
S: *Wir stellten unsere Arbeit zunächst dem Kunden vor und dann 600 Menschen in Porto. Beide Präsentationen verliefen sehr gut. Es gab einige kleinere Probleme mit den Sub-Identitäten, doch die waren schnell gelöst.*

T: Können Sie die Besonderheiten beschreiben, die in der Erstellung oder Durchführung des Endprodukts lagen?
S: *Casa da Música beschäftigt zwei neue portugiesische Designer im Haus: Sara Westermann und André Cruz. Ihre Aufgaben bestehen darin, die unglaubliche Nachfrage an Design zu decken, das tagtäglich für den Veranstaltungsort nötig ist, und die neue Identität intern zu verwalten. Falls man nicht jeden Aspekt einer neuen Markenidentität selbst durchführt, muss man lernen, bestimmte Dinge so zu lassen, wie sie sind.*

T: Qu'est-ce qui a posé problème et comment avez-vous rectifié le tir ?
S: *Nous avons présenté notre première mouture au client, puis tout de suite, devant 600 personnes, aux habitants de Porto. Les deux présentations se sont très bien passées, hormis quelques broutilles concernant les sub-identités, qui ont d'ailleurs été rapidement résolues. En cours de route, la directrice du marketing, Guta Moura Guedes, nous a quittés pour une autre institution culturelle, et comme c'était elle qui avait défendu le projet au départ, nous avons également perdu une excellente amie au sein de l'institution.*

T: Pouvez-vous nous décrire les particularités intrinsèques à la mise au point ou à l'implantation du produit final ?
S: *La Casa da Música a embauché en interne deux nouveaux designers portugais, Sara Westermann et André Cruz, dont la mission est de satisfaire l'incroyable quantité de besoins que la salle peut avoir au quotidien, et de veiller à la nouvelle identité au sein de l'institution. Si vous ne mettez pas en œuvre vous même tous les aspect d'une nouvelle identité, il faut apprendre à laisser aller certaines choses telles qu'elles sont.*

SERVIÇO EDUCATIVO

Patrocínio **Superbock**

01 Junho|Sex

António Victorino d'Almeida
Concerto para tuba e orquestra
Richard Strauss:
Till Eulenspiegels lustige Streiche

Filme/Concerto|Space Ensemble
As Aventuras Do Príncipe Achmed

02 Junho|Sáb

Ritmos Urbanos Jorge Queijo

Narrativas Sonoras Rui Penha
Sonoridades Líquidas João Ricardo
de Barros Oliveira

Ritmos Do Mundo Jorge Queijo

Digital Jam|Rui Penha

Filme/Concerto|Space Ensemble As
Aventuras Do Príncipe Achmed

Compor Com Hyperscore Rui Penha

De Festivais Dos Anos 60
Álvaro Costa

03 Junho|Dom

Orquestra Nacional Do Porto

GUDGIGUOGI DADA Ana Paula Almeida,
Katarzyna Peceira

SONORIDADES LÍQUIDAS João Ricardo
Barros de Oliveira

DJ Classic: audição musical com
crianças e jovens Jorge Ribeiro

casa da música

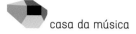

Left: *Poster for educational service in the institution. ///* **Links:** *Plakat für den pädagogischen Dienst der Institution. ///* **A gauche :** *Affiche pour services éducatifs dans l'institution.*

Right: *Casa da Música logo variations. ///* **Rechts:** *Logo-Variationen für die Casa da Música. ///* **A droite :** *Variantes de logo pour la Casa da Música.*

Biography
Stefan Sagmeister (Sagmeister Inc.)

www.sagmeister.com

Location: New York
Year founded: 1993

Position: Founder/
Creative Director

A native of Austria, Stefan Sagmeister received his MFA from the University of Applied Arts in Vienna and, as a Fulbright Scholar, a master's degree from the Pratt Institute in New York. He formed the New York-based Sagmeister Inc. in 1993 and has since designed for clients as diverse as the Rolling Stones, HBO, and the Guggenheim Museum. Having been nominated five times for the Grammies he finally won one for the Talking Heads boxed set. He has also won practically every important international design award. In 2008, a comprehensive book entitled Things I have Learned in my Life so Far *was published by Abrams. Stefan also teaches in the graduate department of the School of Visual Arts in New York and lectures extensively on all continents.*

Der gebürtige Österreicher Stefan Sagmeister schloss sein Studium an der Universität für angewandte Kunst in Wien ab und erhielt als Fulbright-Stipendiat ein Master-Diplom am Pratt Institute in New York. Er gründete 1993 Sagmeister Inc. mit Sitz in New York und hat seitdem für so unterschiedliche Kunden wie die Rolling Stones, HBO und das Guggenheim Museum gearbeitet. Nachdem Stefan Sagmeister bereits fünfmal für die Grammy-Verleihung nominiert wurde, gewann er schließlich einen Grammy für das Talking Heads Boxed Set. Zudem hat er praktisch jeden wichtigen internationalen Preis für Design erhalten. 2008 erschien sein umfassendes Buch mit

dem Titel Things I have Learned in my Life so Far *bei Abrams. Stefan Sagmeister unterrichtet im Graduiertenstudiengang der School of Visual Arts in New York und hält zahlreiche Vorträge und Vorlesungen auf allen Kontinenten.*

Né en Autriche, Stefan Sagmeister a étudié à l'Université des arts appliqués de Vienne et, en tant qu'étudiant du programme Fulbright, il a été diplômé par le Pratt Institute de New York. A New York, il a fondé en 1993 la société Sagmeister Inc. et, depuis, il a créé pour des clients aussi divers que les Rolling Stones, HBO et le Musée Guggenheim. Nominé cinq fois aux Grammies, il a finalement remporté ce prix pour un coffret des Talking Heads. Au demeurant, il a pratiquement obtenu toutes les récompenses internationales de quelque importance. En 2008, un livre exhaustif intitulé Things I have Learned in my Life so Far *(Ce que j'ai appris jusqu'ici) a été publié par Abrams. Stefan enseigne également au graduate department de l'Ecole des arts visuels de New York et donne des conférences sur tous les continents.*

THE NATIONAL CHINESE TV COMPETITION IDENTITY

Moving into its new headquarters in Beijing was considered by CCTV, the Chinese television giant (which provides almost 90 per cent of the 1.3 billion inhabitants of the People's Republic with 16 thematic channels), to be the right time to deal with its outdated corporate identity as part of an ambitious project which also involved the signage system within and around the new building. The new CCTV headquarters are a revolutionary design by Rem Koolhaas and Ole Scheeren of OMA of Rotterdam. A cultural centre (TVCC), a service building, and a media park are also part of the site totalling 20 hectares in the Beijing Central Business District. The entire complex offers 550,000 square metres of office and studio floors.

Ever since it was first revealed, the architectural design has been recognised as groundbreaking because of its striking form: an open rectangle with two slightly sloping glass and steel towers which embrace each other high up in the sky. The building reaches a height of 230 metres, thus redefining the Beijing skyline, a true

Der Umzug in die neue Hauptniederlassung in Peking schien CCTV, dem chinesischen Fernsehgiganten (der fast 90 Prozent der 1,3 Milliarden Chinesen mit 16 Spartenkanälen versorgt) der geeignete Zeitpunkt zu sein, seine unzeitgemäße Firmenidentität im Zuge eines ambitionierten Projekts zu überarbeiten, das auch das Leit- und Orientierungssystem innerhalb und außerhalb des neuen Gebäudes mit einschloss. Die neue Hauptniederlassung der CCTV-Gruppe wird vom revolutionären Design von Rem Koolhaas und Ole Scheeren von OMA (Rotterdam) geprägt. Zu der insgesamt 20 Hektar großen Anlage im zentralen Geschäftsbezirk von Peking gehören auch ein Kulturzentrum (TVCC), ein Dienstleistungsgebäude und ein Mediapark. In dem gesamten Komplex steht eine Fläche von 550.000 Quadratmetern für Büro- und Studioetagen zur Verfügung.

Schon bei der ersten Präsentation des architektonischen Entwurfs wurde er wegen seiner markanten Form als bahnbrechend betrachtet: ein offenes Rechteck mit zwei

CCTV, le géant de la télévision chinoise (avec seize chaînes thématiques, il fournit près de 90 % des 1,3 milliards d'habitants de la République Populaire) a jugé que son emménagement dans un nouveau siège social, à Pékin, était une excellente occasion de revoir son image de marque désuète, dans le cadre d'un ambitieux projet comprenant également la signalétique intérieure et extérieure du nouvel édifice. Le nouveau quartier général de CCTV est une création révolutionnaire de Rem Koolhaas et Ole Scheeren, du cabinet d'architectes OMA de Rotterdam. Un centre culturel (TVCC), un bâtiment de service et un mediaparc font également partie du site, qui occupe au total 20 hectares dans le quartier d'affaires central de Pékin. Dans son ensemble, le complexe offre quelque 550 000 mètres carrés de bureaux et de studios.

Dès sa présentation, la création architecturale a été qualifiée de révolutionnaire en raison de sa forme surprenante : un rectangle ouvert formé par deux tours d'acier et de verre légèrement inclinées, qui s'assemblent très

Previous spread: *New logo applied to an outdoor sign (top) and a vehicle (bottom). ///* **Vorhergehende Seite:** *Das neue Logo auf einem Außenschild (oben) und auf einem Fahrzeug (unten). ///* **Double page précédente** *: Nouveau logo appliqué à une signalisation extérieure (en haut) et sur un véhicule (en bas).*

landmark. The cultural centre that rises next to the main building resembles an opened-out boot.

The architecture has a strong iconic quality. The existing corporate visual identity of CCTV sticks out bleakly against the futuristic construction. The current logo consists of two one-dimensional atom rings that have served as its symbol from the day CCTV was established, back in 1958. Later, a second logotype was introduced including the letters CCTV in a typeface that was strongly modelled on the CNN logo. This is the logo that was mainly used in the top corner of the television screen. Both the original symbolic rings as well as the CCTV type done in the nineties were realised internally and are still in use.

Now with the new headquarters being constructed, a tender for the new identity of CCTV was held. Because of its great reputation in the fields of visual identity, branding, and signage, our Rotterdam-based Studio Dumbar was invited to participate. Eventually a total of nine agencies

leicht geneigten Türmen aus Glas und Stahl, die weit oben durch einen winkelförmigen Querriegel miteinander verbunden sind. Das Gebäude erreicht eine Höhe von 230 Metern und definiert somit die Skyline von Peking neu – ein echtes Wahrzeichen. Das Kulturzentrum erhebt sich neben dem Hauptgebäude und gleicht einem Stiefel.

Die Architektur weist eine starke ikonische Qualität auf. Die bestehende visuelle Unternehmensidentität der CCTV-Gruppe verblasst neben der futuristischen Konstruktion. Das derzeitige Logo besteht aus zwei eindimensionalen Atomringen und dient der Gruppe bereits seit der Gründung von CCTV im Jahre 1958 als Symbol. Später wurde ein zweites Logo eingesetzt, das die Buchstaben CCTV in einer stark an das Logo von CNN anlehnten Typo darstellt. Dieses Logo erschien hauptsächlich in der oberen Ecke des Fernsehbildschirms. Sowohl die originalen symbolischen Ringe als auch die CCTV-Typo, die in den 1990er Jahren entstand, wurden intern entwickelt und sind nach wie vor in Gebrauch.

haut dans le firmament. L'édifice culmine à 230 mètres, redéfinissant ainsi la ligne d'horizon de Pékin, dont il devient un point de référence. Le centre culturel qui se dresse près du bâtiment principal ressemble à une botte ouverte.

L'architecture possède une forte qualité iconique. Or, l'image de marque visuelle de CCTV jure cruellement avec la construction futuriste. Le logo se compose en effet de deux anneaux d'atome unidimensionnels, symboles de la chaîne depuis son lancement en 1958. Plus tard, CCTV en a eu un second, qui, lui, joue de caractères fortement inspirés du logo de CNN. C'est celui-ci qui s'affiche dans l'angle supérieur de l'écran de télévision. Les anneaux symboliques, tout comme le sigle CCTV datant des années quatre-vingt-dix, ont été créés en interne et sont encore en usage.

Avec la construction du nouveau siège, un appel d'offres a été lancé pour la création de la nouvelle image de CCTV. En raison de son excellente réputation dans les domaines de l'identité visuelle, de la

Left: *New logo on black background and with Chinese wording.* /// **Links:** *Das neue Logo auf schwarzem Hintergrund und mit chinesischem Namenszug.* /// **A gauche :** *Nouveau logo sur fond noir avec légende en chinois.*

Right: *Old logos used previously and given as reference to the competitors.* /// **Rechts:** *Die bisher genutzten alten Logos, die den Mitbewerbern als Referenz dienten.* /// **A droite :** *Anciens logos fournis aux candidats à titre de référence.*

were admitted to the bidding, including two international studios. From the beginning, one important restriction was made: the current logos were not to be totally redone, but to be revitalised. A complete plan was to be presented within two months, without any financial compensation, as is often the case in China. Some 30 experts from all over the world worked together to present a comprehensive plan that provided a new visual identity concept including a new, or rather revitalised logo, a complete way-finding throughout the building and a visiting loop through the public areas. However, this well thought-out conceptual design was not chosen. CCTV granted the assignment to a Chinese agency instead (even though not mentioned in the original tender), with the argument that their plan was four times cheaper than ours.

Studio Dumbar proposal for the new CCTV visual identity

In the case of a building that speaks with the power of an icon, the obvious thing to do is to use the strong image language in

Nach dem Bau der neuen Hauptniederlassung wurde eine Ausschreibung für die neue Identität von CCTV durchgeführt. Aufgrund unserer guten Reputation in den Bereichen visuelle Identität, Markenbildung, Leit- und Orientierungssysteme wurde Studio Dumbar (Rotterdam) eingeladen, an der Ausschreibung teilzunehmen. Insgesamt wurden neun Agenturen für die Abgabe eines Angebotes zugelassen, darunter zwei internationale Studios. Von Anfang an gab es eine wichtige Einschränkung: Die bestehenden Logos sollten nicht völlig neu entwickelt, sondern wiederbelebt werden. Innerhalb von zwei Monaten sollte ein vollständiger Entwurf präsentiert werden – ohne Vergütung, wie es in China oft der Fall ist. Weltweit arbeiteten etwa 30 Experten zusammen, um einen umfassenden Entwurf zu präsentieren, der ein neues Konzept für die visuelle Identität einschließlich eines neuen (oder besser: wiederbelebten) Logos vorsah, außerdem einen vollständigen Wegeplan des Gebäudes und einen Besucherrundweg durch die öffentlichen Bereiche. Dieses gut durchdachte konzeptionelle Design wurde jedoch

stratégie de marque et de la signalisation, notre agence de Rotterdam, le Studio Dumbar, a été invitée à y participer. Au total, neuf agences, dont deux études internationales, ont été retenues parmi les soumissionnaires. D'emblée, une restriction de taille a été imposée : les logos actuels ne devaient pas être totalement modifiés, sinon rajeunis. Un plan complet devait être présenté dans les deux mois, sans la moindre compensation financière, comme c'est souvent le cas en Chine. Une trentaine d'experts du monde entier se sont réunis pour mettre au point un plan exhaustif fournissant une nouvelle image de marque, avec en particulier un logo tout neuf, ou plutôt rajeuni, une signalisation complète pour tout l'édifice et un circuit de visite dans les zones publiques. Mais ce n'est pas ce design parfaitement conçu qui a été retenu. CCTV a attribué le contrat à une agence chinoise (qui pourtant ne figurait pas parmi les soumissionnaires originaux), sous prétexte que son plan était quatre moins onéreux que le nôtre.

the logo design. The CCTV building has the potential to become the single icon by which Beijing is recognised throughout the world, comparable to what the Eiffel Tower is for Paris. Nevertheless CCTV chose to hold on to the red, green and blue atom rings together with the abbreviation CCTV. Firstly, a new typeface had to be designed. Everything that called the CNN logo to mind was eliminated. A new robust, monumental, and dominant typeface was developed to emphasise the nature of the new building. One striking aspect is that the letters T and V remain chained, whereas both Cs are flattened at the upper and lower edge, thus accentuating the curve on the left side and creating a strong abstract-like image; as if they were set free from what they stand for (China Central).

In the client's view, the atom rings give a strong association with the phenomenon of television. We tried to find a solution for the static, even droll image, by detaching the rings. The colour range was made more dynamic and in the logo, the abbreviation and the symbol changed places. Now the

nicht ausgewählt. Mit der Begründung, ihr Entwurf sei viermal günstiger als der unsrige, vergab CCTV den Auftrag stattdessen an eine chinesische Agentur (obwohl diese in der ursprünglichen Ausschreibung nicht genannt war).

Der Vorschlag von Studio Dumbar für die neue visuelle Identität von CCTV

Bei einem Gebäude, das eine solche Symbolkraft ausstrahlt, ist es naheliegend, dieses in das Logo einzubinden. Das Gebäude der CCTV-Gruppe hat das Potenzial, zu dem Wahrzeichen zu werden, für das Peking in der ganzen Welt bekannt sein wird, ähnlich wie der Eiffelturm in Paris. Trotzdem entschied CCTV, an den roten, grünen und blauen Atomringen mit dem Unternehmenskürzel CCTV festzuhalten. Zunächst musste eine neue Typo entworfen werden. Alles, was an das CNN-Logo erinnerte, wurde beseitigt. Um den Charakter des neuen Gebäudes zu betonen, wurde ein neuer, robuster, imposanter und dominanter Schriftzug entwickelt. Auffällig ist, dass die Buchstaben T und V

La proposition du Studio Dumbar pour la nouvelle image de marque de CCTV

Dans le cas d'un immeuble doué d'un tel pouvoir iconique, user de la force de l'image pour le logo semblait être la solution la plus évidente. Le bâtiment de la CCTV a tout en effet pour devenir le symbole qui fera reconnaître Pékin dans le monde entier, à l'instar de la Tour Eiffel dans le cas de Paris. CCTV a néanmoins préféré conserver les anneaux d'atome rouge, vert et bleu, ainsi que l'abréviation CCTV. Tout d'abord, un nouveau caractère devait être choisi. Tout ce qui rappelait de près ou de loin le logo de CNN a été supprimé. Un nouveau caractère, robuste, massif et puissant a été mis au point pour souligner la nature du nouvel édifice. Un des aspects marquants en l'occurrence tient à l'entrelacement des lettres T et V, tandis que le bord supérieur et inférieur des C a été aplati, accentuant la courbe du côté gauche et créant une image fortement abstraite ; un peu comme si les lettres prenaient leurs distances de ce qu'elles signifient (Chine Centrale).

Left: *Frames of an animation of the logo projected on the headquarters building designed by Rem Koolhaas. ///* **Links:** *Bilder einer Animation des Logos, die auf das Hauptgebäude projiziert werden. Das Gebäude wurde von Rem Koolhaas entworfen. ///* **A gauche :** *Images d'une animation du logo projetées au siège central conçu par Rem Koolhaas.*

Right: *Simulation of the entrance of the building with animated projections on the walls. ///* **Rechts:** *Simulation des Eingangsbereiches des Gebäudes mit animierten Projektionen auf den Wänden. ///* **A droite :** *Simulation de l'entrée du bâtiment, avec des films d'animation projetés sur les murs.*

still image of the rings gives the impression of something that is always in motion. This impression is even stronger in other applications. Fragments of the atom rings, always in different constellations, different positions, and different colours, are employed in all imaginable identity carriers. It looks as though each image of the rings in motion was made at a different moment. There are endless possibilities. The most spectacular employment of this visual branding is on the outside of the CCTV building itself. Using the characteristic diagonal steel grid, LED lights form animated portions of the original atom rings in all possible colours. Fifty years after it was first created, the logo is truly revitalised, as was commissioned by CCTV. Moreover, even without the letters CCTV the symbol will now be recognised as belonging to a modern and dynamic media company.

The new signage system proposed to CCTV

A transparent and logical signage system is of essential importance in a complex of

verkettet bleiben, während beide Cs am oberen und unteren Ende abgeflacht sind und deshalb die Kurve auf der linken Seite hervorheben und ein starkes, abstrahiertes Bild schaffen, als seien sie von dem losgelöst, wofür sie stehen (China Central).

Aus Sicht des Kunden sind die Atomringe sehr stark mit dem Phänomen Fernsehen verknüpft. Wir versuchten, für das statische, sogar lustige Bild eine Lösung zu finden, indem wir die Ringe voneinander lösten. Die Farbpalette wurde dynamischer gestaltet, im Logo tauschten Kürzel und Symbol die Plätze. Nun erweckt das starre Bild der Ringe den Eindruck, fortwährend in Bewegung zu sein. Dieser Eindruck verstärkt sich noch je nach Verwendung. Fragmente der Atomringe (immer in unterschiedlichen Konstellationen, Positionen und Farben) werden auf allen Identitätsträgern eingesetzt. Es scheint, als sei jedes Bild der sich bewegenden Ringe zu einem anderen Zeitpunkt erstellt worden. Die Möglichkeiten sind endlos. Die eindrucksvollste Verwendung dieses visuellen Markendesigns ist außerhalb des

Aux yeux du client, les anneaux d'atome suggèrent puissamment le phénomène télévisuel. Nous avons donc tenté de trouver une solution pour animer cette image statique, voire étrange, en dissociant les anneaux. La gamme de couleurs a été dynamisée et, sur le logo, l'abréviation et le symbole ont changé de place. Ainsi l'image inanimée des anneaux donnait-t-elle désormais l'impression d'être en perpétuel mouvement, impression encore plus forte avec certaines autres applications. On retrouvait des fragments d'anneaux d'atome, toujours dans différentes constellations, positions et couleurs, sur tous les supports possibles et imaginables. Un peu comme si chaque image d'anneaux en mouvement avait été créée à un moment différent. Les possibilités étaient innombrables. Mais c'est à l'extérieur de l'édifice lui-même que prenait place la manifestation la plus spectaculaire de cette stratégie visuelle de marque. Utilisant la caractéristique armature d'acier en diagonale, des lampes à électroluminescence composaient sur la façade des fragments d'anneaux mobiles et multicolores. Cinquante ans après sa

Top: *Catalogue cover and vehicle signage.* ///
Oben: *Katalogdeckblatt und Fahrzeug-*
beschriftung. /// **En haut** : *Couverture du*
catalogue et signalisation sur véhicule.

Right: *Sign design on a headquarters'*
corridor. /// **Rechts:** *Hinweisschild in einem*
Flur im Hauptgebäude. /// **A droite** : *Design*
signalétique dans un couloir du siège social.

buildings of this magnitude with its great variety of functions. Employees as well as visitors should be able to find out where in the building they are in an easy way at any time. Elements of the morphological language of the architecture were used for the signage on the outside in the same way that it would have been obvious to play with the shape of the building in the logo. Within the building hexagonal panels refer to the basic plate form. Distinct typography and use of colour make it clear to anyone what part of the building they are in. The materials used differ from area to area. The office areas have signs made of wood and marble, in the hotel section glass fibre is used, and in the broadcast area the material used is granite and travertine. Materials will always match the surrounding interior design of the particular area.

Without light, television cannot exist. The reference to this condition became an important element in the proposed signage. Particularly in the live-broadcasting area, the branded light concept and multimedia applications will come back in

CCTV-Gebäudes zu finden. Das charakteristische diagonale Stahlnetz des Gebäudes nutzend, werden die Atomringe mittels Leuchtdioden in ständig wechselnden Ausschnitten und Farben als bewegte Lichtfolgen sichtbar. Fünfzig Jahre nach seiner Erstellung ist das Logo wahrhaft wiederbelebt, wie die CCTV-Gruppe es in Auftrag gegeben hatte. Zudem kann man nun sogar ohne die Buchstaben CCTV erkennen, dass das Symbol zu einer modernen und dynamischen Mediengesellschaft gehört.

Der Vorschlag für ein neues Leit- und Orientierungssystem

In einem Gebäudekomplex dieser Größe mit seinen vielfältigen Funktionen ist ein transparentes und logisches Leit- und Orientierungssystem von grundlegender Bedeutung. Sowohl Angestellte als auch Besucher sollten jederzeit problemlos erkennen können, wo im Gebäude sie sich befinden. So wie wir im Logo mit der Architektur hätten spielen wollen, wurden auch morphologische Elemente der architektonischen Formensprache für

création, le logo avait été vraiment rajeuni, conformément aux exigences de CCTV. De plus, même sans les lettres CCTV, le symbole est maintenant reconnu comme celui d'une chaîne de télévision moderne et dynamique.

Le nouveau système de signalisation proposé à CCTV

Dans un immeuble de cette envergure où coexistent toutes sortes de fonctions, un système de signalisation logique et transparent est d'une importance primordiale. Employés et visiteurs doivent pouvoir y trouver facilement leur chemin, à tout moment. Nous avons donc employé, pour la signalisation extérieure, certains éléments du langage morphologique de l'architecture, de la même façon qu'il nous avait semblé évident de jouer avec la forme du building pour le logo. Dedans, les panonceaux hexagonaux renvoient à la forme de base. Une typographie distincte et le recours à la couleur permettent à quiconque de savoir dans quelle partie de l'immeuble il se trouve. Les matériaux,

different ways to emphasise the dynamics of television-making. Illuminated panels provide a more dynamic signage, making it possible to adapt to events taking place at different times. The same concept of way-finding was created for the TVCC building with multimedia displays providing any added real-time information.

The visitors' loop

The aforementioned dynamics of television-making as well as the exceptional architecture of the CCTV building will attract visitors in great numbers, from both mainland China and abroad. A visitors' loop is a way to make the building accessible for everyone, enabling the passage of crowds of people through the public areas in a controlled way and at the same time adding an extra attraction to the building. We proposed the visitors' loop as a total experience, which begins right at the entrance. There, people would walk through a 4-D tunnel packed with the latest information technology and multimedia tools. The walls, as well as the floor and

das Orientierungssystem außerhalb des Gebäudes eingesetzt. Innerhalb des Gebäudes weisen hexagonale Tafeln den Weg. Die klare Typographie und der Einsatz von Farben machen jedem klar, in welchem Teil des Gebäudes er sich befindet. Die verwendeten Materialien unterscheiden sich je nach Bereich und sind jeweils auf das Design der umgebenden Inneneinrichtung abgestimmt: In den Bürobereichen ist die Beschilderung aus Holz und Marmor gefertigt, im Hotelbereich wird Fiberglas verwendet, und im Sendebereich sind die Schilder aus Granit und Travertin.

Ohne Licht kann Fernsehen nicht existieren. Diese Abhängigkeit spielte bei unserem Vorschlag für das Leit- und Orientierungssystem eine wichtige Rolle. Besonders im Live-Sendebereich werden das Lichtkonzept und die Multimedia-Anwendungen der Marke unterschiedlich aufgegriffen, um die Dynamik bei der Produktion von Fernsehsendungen zu unterstreichen. Mit Leuchttafeln lässt sich die Beschilderung dynamischer gestalten und kann an Veranstaltungen angepasst werden, die zu

eux aussi, sont différents selon les espaces : bois et marbre pour les panneaux de signalisation des bureaux, fibre de verre pour ceux de l'hôtel, granit et travertin pour la partie consacrée aux émissions. L'harmonie est toujours assurée entre les matériaux et le design environnemental d'un espace donné.

Sans lumière, pas de télévision possible. Aussi la référence à cette condition était-elle un élément majeur de la signalisation proposée. Dans la partie occupée par les plateaux des émissions en live, en particulier, l'image conceptuelle de luminosité et les applications multimédias reviennent à différents égards souligner les dynamiques de la pratique télévisuelle. Des panneaux lumineux y assurent une signalisation plus dynamique, permettant en outre de les adapter à des événements programmés à différentes heures. Le même concept de pilotage a été créé à l'intention de l'édifice de TVCC, à l'aide d'écrans multimédias affichant toutes sortes d'informations complémentaires en temps réel.

Below: *Schematics of the coding and routing of the sign system of CCTV's headquarters ///* **Unten:** *Schemata für die Programmierung des Leit- und Orientierungssystems im CCTV-Hauptgebäude. ///* **Ci-dessous :** *Schémas de codage et de routage du système de signalisation du siège social de CCTV.*

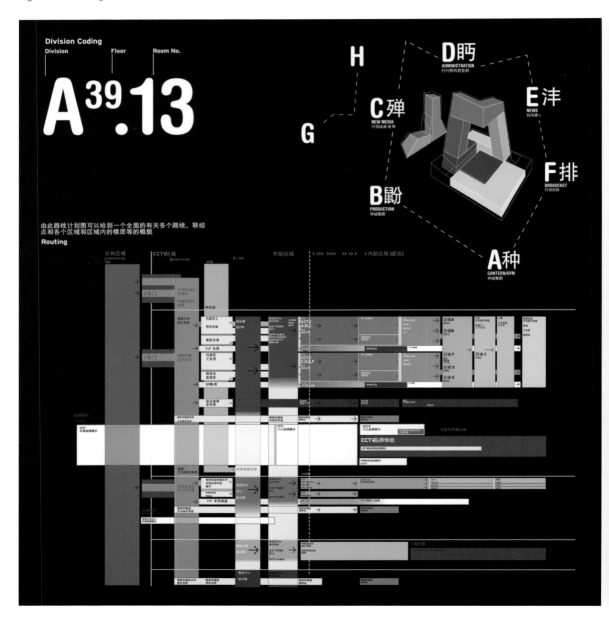

Below: *Totems and sign design for both interior and exterior of the building ///* **Unten:** *Pylone und Beschriftungsdesign für den Innen- und den Außenbereich des Gebäudes. ///* **Ci-dessous :** *Totems et design signalétique à l'intérieur et à l'extérieur du bâtiment.*

Exterior sign program

Interior sign program

Area Identification

Material Palette

ceiling of this tunnel, serve as large screens showing dynamic animations. Instead of just entering a building, visitors undergo the most fascinating experience in which they are literally surrounded by sound and images. Later in the studio tour, they would be confronted with displays showing stage reconstructions, studio equipment, production material, behind-the-scenes information, and the stars of television, stretching from CCTV's past to its future. All the exhibits, the graphics on the wall, and the videos and animations, are presented according to the context of the Visual Branding as developed by Studio Dumbar.

unterschiedlichen Zeiten stattfinden. Das gleiche Konzept der Orientierung wurde für das TVCC-Gebäude entwickelt, wobei Multimedia-Anzeigen in Echtzeit alle möglichen zusätzlichen Information bieten können.

Der Besucherrundweg

Die oben erwähnte Dynamik bei der Produktion von Fernsehsendungen sowie die außergewöhnliche Architektur des CCTV-Gebäudes wird eine große nationale und internationale Besucherschar anziehen. Über einen Besucherrundweg sollte das Gebäude jedermann zugänglich gemacht werden, indem Besuchergruppen durch die öffentlichen Bereiche gelenkt werden und das Gebäude somit eine weitere Attraktion bietet. Wir schlugen den Besucherrundweg als Gesamterlebnis vor, das bereits am Eingang beginnt. Dort sollten die Besucher durch einen 4-D-Tunnel geführt werden, der mit der neuesten Informationstechnologie und mit Multimedia-Tools ausgerüstet ist. Die Wände, der Boden und die Decke dieses Tunnels dienen als riesige Projektions-

Le circuit des visiteurs

Intérêt pour la pratique télévisuelle évoquée plus haut, attrait de l'exceptionnelle architecture de l'édifice, il est probable que les lieux attireront un très grand nombre de visiteurs, de Chine et d'ailleurs. Un circuit à l'intention des visiteurs est une façon de les rendre accessibles à tous, en maîtrisant la circulation des groupes à travers les espaces publics et en donnant au bâtiment un charme supplémentaire. Nous avons proposé un circuit visiteurs conçu comme une véritable expérience : il débutait dès l'entrée dans le building ; on y traversait tout d'abord un tunnel en 4-D, bourré d'outils multimédias et d'informations technologiques de la dernière génération. Faisant fonction d'écrans, les murs, ainsi que le sol et le plafond de ce tunnel, montraient des films d'animation. Au lieu de pénétrer simplement dans l'édifice, les visiteurs vivaient ainsi la plus captivante des expériences, littéralement baignés de sons et d'images. Un peu plus loin, ils seraient confrontés avec des écrans diffusant des images du montage des plateaux, de

Left: *Simulation of the sign system reflecting the architecture of the building.* /// **Links**: *Simulation des Beschilderungssystems, das die Architektur des Gebäudes widerspiegelt.* /// **A gauche** : *Simulation du système signalétique reproduisant l'architecture du bâtiment.*

Right: *Sign design applied to an internal corridor in the building.* /// **Rechts**: *Entwurf für die Beschilderung eines Flures innerhalb des Gebäudes.* /// **A droite** : *Signalisation dans un couloir à l'intérieur du bâtiment.*

flächen und zeigen Animationen. Statt einfach nur ein Gebäude zu betreten, sollten die Besucher faszinierende Erfahrungen machen, indem sie buchstäblich von Klängen und Bildern umhüllt würden. Später auf der Studio-Tour sollten sie auf Bildschirme treffen, auf denen Bühnenrekonstruktionen, Studioausstattungen, Produktionsmaterial, Hintergrundinformationen sowie Fernsehstars gezeigt würden – von der Vergangenheit der CCTV-Gruppe bis hin zu zukünftigen Projekten. Alle Ausstellungsgegenstände, die Grafiken an den Wänden, Videos und Animationen sollten in Übereinstimmung mit der visuellen Markenbildung präsentiert werden, das von Studio Dumbar entwickelt wurde.

l'aménagement des studios, de la production du matériel, ainsi que des infos sur les coulisses et les vedettes de la télé, bref tout un panorama de l'histoire de la CCTV. Tous ces éléments, graphiques muraux, films vidéo et d'animation se présentaient bien entendu conformément à la stratégie de marque mise au point par le Studio Dumbar.

FLOOR
11 - 38

NEW MEDIA

C

B 09 LOBBY
行行照构简览畴

CANTEEN
行行照构简览畴

B 07 STUDIO CONTROLROOMS
行行照构简览畴

B 04 STUDIO TWOTHOUSAND
行行照构简览畴

B 04 STUDIOS EIGHTHUNDRED
行行照构简览畴

STUDIOS FOURHUNDRED
行行照构简览畴

STUDIOS TWOHUNDRED
行行照构简览畴

Left: *Detail of signage applied on a textured wall. /// **Links:** Detail des Leitsystems auf einer Wandstruktur. /// **A gauche** : Détail de signalisation sur un mur texturé.*

Biography
M. de Boer & T. Dorresteijn (Studio Dumbar)

www.studiodumbar.com   Location: Rotterdam   Position: Partners
         Year founded: 1977

Michel de Boer was educated at the Academy of Fine Arts and Higher Technologies in Rotterdam. In 1989 he became creative managing partner at Studio Dumbar where he is responsible for the creative output. His portfolio includes projects for Apple, Allianz, Shell, KPN, the Dutch Police, and Nike. He has won several awards, including the D&AD Golden and Silver Awards. In 2005 he became professor at the Instituto Universitario Architettura in Venice. Tom Dorresteijn is a partner in Studio Dumbar and a strategist in the field of branding, design, and communication. He has been closely involved with setting up Studio Dumbar's joint venture in China. He was Chairman of "Platform Creating Brands" 2002–2004 of the BNO (the Board of Dutch Designers), and was elected President of the BNO in 2006.

Michel de Boer wurde an der Akademie für Bildende Kunst und Höhere Technologie in Rotterdam ausgebildet. 1989 wurde er zum kreativen geschäftsführenden Partner bei Studio Dumbar, wo er für die kreative Produktion verantwortlich ist. Sein Portfolio umfasst Projekte für Apple, Allianz, Shell, KPN, die niederländische Polizei und Nike. Er gewann mehrere Auszeichnungen, darunter die D&AD Golden and Silver Awards. 2005 wurde er Professor am Instituto Universitario Architettura in Venedig. Tom Dorresteijn ist nicht nur Partner im Studio Dumbar, sondern auch ein Stratege in den Bereichen Markenbildung, Design und Kommunikation. Tom

war maßgeblich am Aufbau des Joint Ventures von Studio Dumbar in China beteiligt. Er war 2002 bis 2004 Vorsitzender der „Platform Creating Brands" des BNO (dem Interessensverband niederländischer Designer) und wurde 2006 zum Präsidenten des BNO gewählt.

Michel de Boer a fait ses études à l'Académie des beaux-arts et des hautes technologies de Rotterdam. En 1989, il est devenu directeur associé du Studio Dumbar où il a la responsabilité de la création. Son portefeuille comprend des projets pour Apple, Allianz, Shell, KPN, la police hollandaise et Nike. Il a remporté plusieurs prix, dont les D&AD Golden and Silver Awards. Depuis 2005, il enseigne à l'Institut universitaire d'architecture de Venise. Tom Dorresteijn, autre associé de Studio Dumbar, est un grand spécialiste de la valorisation de marque, du design et de la communication. Il a pris étroitement part à la création de la société en participation du Studio Dumbar en Chine. Président de la « Platform Creating Brands » 2002–2004 du BNO (Board of Dutch Designers), il a été élu président du BNO en 2006.

ELECTRO FOLK: MTV'S NEW VISUAL LANGUAGE FOR EMERGING MARKETS

As far as brands are concerned, MTV can consider itself one of the biggest brands in the world. When MTV Emerging Markets (MTV in Central Eastern Europe, Africa, and the Middle East) needed to re-launch its identity across Poland, Romania, Slovenia, Croatia, Serbia, Montenegro, Macedonia, Bosnia and Herzegovina, Turkey, Lithuania, Latvia, Estonia, and Ukraine, it needed a branding that could live up to the expectations of the MTV brand and would speak to its very new audiences.

The task was to create a brand identity that could both appeal to these diverse regions and be made to work in a variety of ways and across different platforms; because each region has a different set-up, it needed to be modular and flexible with elements that could be adopted, adapted, expanded on, and localised by all channels so that we could all share a common theme while being able to build the MTV brand around our local audience and culture. The toughest challenge was to come up with a strong concept that could appeal to all regions, with their diverse cultures, tastes, humour, and sensibilities.

Geht es um Marken, kann sich MTV als eine der größten Marken der Welt betrachten. Als MTV Emerging Markets (MTV in Mittel- und Osteuropa, Afrika und im Nahen Osten) seinen Neustart in Polen, Rumänien, Slowenien, Kroatien, Serbien, Montenegro, Mazedonien, Bosnien-Herzegowina, in der Türkei, in Litauen, Lettland, Estland und in der Ukraine plante, erforderte dies eine Identität, die den Erwartungen an die Marke MTV gerecht werden und die neuen Zielgruppen ansprechen würde.

Es galt, eine Markenidentität zu entwickeln, die sowohl in diesen unterschiedlichen Regionen Anklang findet, als auch auf verschiedene Arten und über diverse Plattformen wirken kann. Aufgrund der spezifischen Eigenarten jeder Region musste sie modular und flexibel sein und Elemente enthalten, die übernommen, angepasst und erweitert sowie auf allen Kanälen lokalisiert werden konnten, um ein gemeinsames Thema übergreifend verwenden und gleichzeitig die Marke MTV um unsere regionale Zielgruppe und

En matière de marques, MTV peut se considérer comme l'une des plus grandes au monde. Lorsqu'il a fallu relooker les marchés émergents de MTV (Europe centrale et orientale, Afrique et Moyen Orient) à travers la Pologne, la Roumanie, la Slovénie, la Croatie, la Serbie, le Monténégro, la Macédoine, la Bosnie-Herzégovine, la Turquie, la Lituanie, la Lettonie, l'Estonie et l'Ukraine, une stratégie de marques capable de satisfaire les attentes de MTV et de parler à ses nouveaux publics s'est avérée nécessaire.

La mission consistait à créer une identité de marque à la fois séduisante pour ces diverses régions et susceptible de fonctionner de très différentes façons et sur différents supports et plateformes ; chaque région ayant sa propre implantation, il fallait qu'elle soit modulaire et souple, avec des éléments pouvant être adoptés, adaptés, étendus et localisés par tous les canaux, de manière à ce que nous puissions tous partager un thème commun en construisant la marque MTV au sein de notre public et de notre culture locale. Le plus ardu aura

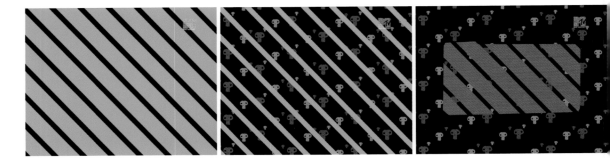

Previous spread: *Promotional stickers featuring the new characters and logos.* ///
Vorhergehende Seite: *Werbe-Sticker mit den neuen Figuren und Logos.* /// **Double page précédente** : *Autocollants promotionnels montrant les nouveaux caractères et les logos.*

I thought of storytelling as the unifying trend: it is a universal language that speaks to everyone in every part of the world. Stories told using simple and universal body language and characterised by surreal, somewhat dark humour. I also started to be influenced by the new electro wave that had begun crowding the arts and underground scene in Eastern Europe. With these criteria in mind, I immersed myself in these regions. After travelling through each country and meeting the individual creative teams as well as local artists and musicians in town and bars, I struck upon the idea of electro and folk. I realised that folk as a tradition and a source for culture is still very much alive in Eastern Europe, and at the same time, these regions are looking at the same sources as we are for inspiration; they are digitally savvy, and even more technologically curious and experimental.

So you get a strange co-existence of the old and the new. That was the beginning of Electro Folk. The Electro/Folk ethos is based on the tension between the past and

Kultur herum aufbauen zu können. Die größte Herausforderung bestand in der Entwicklung eines tragfähigen Konzepts, das trotz großer Unterschiede in Kultur, Geschmack, Humor und Empfindsamkeiten alle Regionen gleichermaßen ansprechen sollte.

Als gemeinsamen Nenner dachte ich an das Geschichtenerzählen als universelle Sprache, die jeden Menschen überall auf der Welt anspricht – surreale Geschichten mit einer Prise schwarzen Humors, die in einfacher, allgemein verständlicher Körpersprache dargestellt werden sollten. Außerdem wurde ich zunehmend von der neuen Elektro-Welle beeinflusst, die gerade die Kunst- und Untergrundszenen in Osteuropa eroberte. Mit diesen Kriterien im Hinterkopf bereiste ich intensiv alle Regionen. Nachdem ich jedes Land besucht und die jeweiligen kreativen Teams sowie lokale Künstler und Musiker in Städten und Bars getroffen hatte, entstand die Idee von „Electro" und „Folk". Ich erkannte, dass „Folk" (Volkstum) als Tradition und kulturelle Quelle in Osteuropa immer

été de produire un concept fort, capable de plaire dans toutes les régions, chacune avec sa culture, ses goûts, son humour et sa propre sensibilité.

Le conte, langage planétaire parlant à tous et dans le monde entier, m'a semblé un filon unificateur. Des histoires qu'on raconte dans un langage simple et universel, caractérisé par un humour légèrement noir, presque surréaliste. J'ai également subi l'influence de la nouvelle vague Electro qui commençait à envahir les arts et la scène underground de l'Europe de l'Est. Avec ceci en tête, je me suis plongée dans l'étude de ces régions. Après avoir voyagé un peu partout, rencontré les équipes individuelles de création et bu des coups avec les artistes et les musiciens locaux, je me suis attelée à l'idée de l'Electro Folk, ayant compris que le folklore, en tant que tradition et source de culture, reste très vivant en Europe orientale, et qu'en même temps, ces régions ont le regard tourné vers les mêmes sources d'inspiration que nous ; ils sont parfaitement au courant de tout

From left to right: Frames of the animated bumpers (which announce the next coming programme). /// Von links nach rechts: Einzelbilder aus den animierten Trennern (die das nächste Programm ankündigen). /// De gauche à droite : Images de spots d'animation (annonçant la prochaine émission).

he future: the interplay between the slick, he fast, and the electronically aware digital culture and the traditional spirit of folk storytelling. The Electro component needed o be fast and minimal to assure the look sits well on air as well as online and within digital environments. The Folk component s the soul of the look, the story behind he graphics, drawn from the commonly shared tradition of storytelling. Each region has old stories rooted in folk tales populated by dark humour and strange characters, whose stories are told in the break bumpers (mini spots that fill in between programmes).

Once the concept of Electro Folk was created, I needed to assemble a team. I didn't go for an agency, as rebranding your channels is a personal and intimate project: it determines both look and feel, so I kept the whole project in-house right from the start and pulled together a small team of very creative, enthusiastic and talented freelancers. I knew that each one of them would have been perfect for this project because they also travelled around

noch sehr lebendig ist. Gleichzeitig lassen sich die osteuropäischen Regionen von den gleichen Quellen inspirieren wie wir auch; sie haben Erfahrung mit digitalen Medien und sind technologisch sogar noch interessierter und experimentierfreudiger.

Folglich besteht ein eigenwilliges Nebeneinander von Alt und Neu. Dies war der Anfang von Electro Folk. Das Ethos von Electro/Folk basiert auf der Spannung zwischen Vergangenheit und Zukunft: dem Zusammenspiel zwischen der cleveren, schnellen und elektronisch versierten digitalen Kultur und dem traditionellen Geist des volkstümlichen Geschichtenerzählens. Die Electro-Komponente musste schnell und minimal gestaltet sein, damit sie als Fernsehsendung und online sowie in digitalen Umgebungen auch gut aussieht. Die Folk-Komponente ist die Seele und die Geschichte hinter den Grafiken, die von der gemeinsamen Tradition des Geschichtenerzählens geprägt sind. Jede Region kennt alte Geschichten, die in volkstümlichen Sagen wurzeln, mit schwarzem Humor gespickt und merkwürdigen Figuren

ce qui touche le numérique, et plus curieux encore en matière de technologie et d'expérimental.

Ancien et nouveauté y coexistent donc assez étrangement. C'est ainsi qu'a démarré l'identité Electro Folk, dont le système de valeurs repose sur la tension entre le passé et l'avenir : le jeu entre la virtuosité, la vitesse, la conscience électronique de la culture numérique et l'esprit de la tradition orale. La composante Electro devait être rapide et minimale afin que le look passe aussi bien à l'antenne que on-line ou sur environnement numérique. La composante Folk, elle, est l'âme de l'image, l'histoire qui se cache derrière l'infographie, tirée de la tradition orale commune. Chaque région a sa mémoire, enracinée dans des récits folkloriques peuplés d'humour noir et de personnages étranges, dont les histoires sont racontées lors de reprises d'écran de coupure publicitaire (bref spots de remplissage entre des programmes).

Une fois que j'ai eu créé le concept d'Electro Folk, il a fallu que je forme une

the regions a lot and shared a passion and a sensibility for Eastern European culture, from art-house cinema and animation, to gipsy music and humour. The team was made up of Anrick, Art Director, Serge, Illustrator, Alex, Animator, and a couple of AFX Designers.

I deliberately started with a very undefined brief. I gathered quite a lot of research material from old books of fairy-tales borrowed from friends (some beautiful ones from Tbilisi, Georgia) and had a general direction, with a lot of visual reference, but no specifics.

I wanted to work it out by taking inspiration from all the people involved and so it became a collaborative process with one person working on the interpretations of another. We started by having Serge, our illustrator, spending three weeks crafting a clan of folk-tale-inspired characters and then from this set we started brainstorming about them and their stories. We then moved to animating the stories. I wanted the animation to have a real tangible and hand-made feel to it, so I decided to go back to the old craft of traditional animation, where every frame is painstakingly drawn on a real piece of paper. This was a very laborious process and is quite rare nowadays when everyone opts for fast-and-cheap like Flash Animation, whose result is definitely quicker but lacks the warm satisfaction of a hand's touch to it.

I wanted the look to be heavily textured, as well as hand-drawn. But it also needed to be digital, minimal, and fast, in order to reflect the digital platforms we live on. MTV is taking creative challenges into the mobile and online worlds and I wanted our look to be as comfortable there as it is on air. For the Navigation Menus and End-boards, we got inspired by old animation gifs, which are the most traditional art forms of early computer aesthetics. I wanted to use storytelling for the break bumpers only and have a clean minimal look for the info menus. We combined this with a really bold and large font for the Headlines with a hand-drawn quality

bevölkert sind. Diese Geschichten werden als Trenner eingesetzt (als Mini-Spots zwischen einzelnen Programmen).

Nachdem das Konzept von Electro Folk entworfen war, musste ich ein Team zusammenstellen. Ich wollte mich nicht an eine Agentur wenden, da die Marken-neubildung für einen Fernsehkanal ein vertrauliches, eng gebundenes Projekt ist: Das Look and Feel wird festgelegt. Ich hielt daher das gesamte Projekt von Anfang an intern und bildete ein kleines Team aus sehr kreativen, begeisterten und talentierten Freiberuflern. Ich wusste, dass jeder von ihnen für dieses Projekt perfekt geeignet sein würde, denn auch sie waren viel durch die Regionen gereist und teilten die Leiden-schaft und das Verständnis für die osteuro-päische Kultur, vom Arthouse-Kino und Zeichentrickfilm bis hin zur Zigeunermusik und dem Humor. Zum Team gehörten Art Director Anrick, Illustrator Serge, Animator Alex und einige AFX-Designer.

Ich begann mit einem bewusst offen gehaltenen Vorgehen. Ich hatte viel Material aus alten Märchenbüchern gesammelt, die ich mir von Freunden geliehen hatte (einige wunderschöne Ge-schichten aus Tiflis, Georgien), und hatte bereits eine grobe Vorstellung mit zahlreichen visuellen Ver-weisen, aber nichts Konkretes.

Dieses Material wollte ich auswerten, indem ich die Einfälle aller beteiligten Personen mit einfließen ließ. So entstand ein gemeinschaftlicher Prozess, bei dem jeder mit den Ideen des anderen arbeitete. Wir begannen mit unserem Illustrator Serge, der drei Wochen damit zubrachte, eine Figurenfamilie zu schaffen, die durch Volksmärchen inspiriert war. Nachdem wir anschließend Ideen zu diesen Figuren und ihren Geschichten gesammelt hatten, machten wir uns daran, die Geschichten zu animieren. Da ich der Meinung war, dass die Animationen ein Gefühl von Materialität und Handarbeit vermitteln sollten, entschied ich mich, auf das alte Handwerk des traditionellen Trickfilms zurückzugreifen, bei dem jedes einzelne Bild sorgfältig auf einen Bogen Papier

équipe. Je ne me suis pas adressée à une agence car la revalorisation de nos chaînes est un projet intime et personnel qui suppose à la fois une image et un feeling ; j'ai donc décidé de mener le projet en interne de A à Z et j'ai constitué pour cela une petite équipe de graphistes indépen-dants très créatifs, enthousiastes et talentueux. Je savais qu'ils étaient parfaits pour ce projet car ils avaient tous pas mal voyagé dans les régions concernées et partageaient une même passion et une même sensibilité pour la culture de l'Europe orientale, du cinéma d'auteur et d'anima-tion à la musique et à l'humour gitans. Cette équipe se composait d'Anrick, directeur artistique, de Serge, illustrateur, d'Alex, animateur, et de deux graphistes AFX.

J'ai délibérément commencé par un programme plutôt vague, et rassemblé pas mal de matériel de recherche en piochant dans de vieux bouquins de contes de fées empruntés à des amis (dont quelques-uns absolument magnifi-ques venant de Tbilissi, Géorgie) ; j'avais certes une direction générale et de très nombreuses références visuelles, mais rien de vraiment spécifique.

Je voulais y parvenir en m'inspirant de tous les gens impliqués et ça s'est donc transformé en une collaboration, avec une personne travaillant à partir des interpré-tations d'une autre. Pour commencer, Serge, notre illustrateur, a passé trois semaines à croquer un groupe de personnages inspirés du folklore et, à partir de cela, nous avons commencé à élucubrer et à leur échafauder une histoire. Puis nous sommes passés à l'animation des histoires. Cette animation, nous voulions qu'elle ait un caractère artisanal marqué, aussi avons-nous décidé de revenir au bon vieux procédé d'autre-fois, où chaque image est méticuleusement dessinée sur une vraie feuille de papier. Cette technique, il est vrai très laborieuse, est plutôt rare de nos jours où tout le monde préfère les procédés rapides et bon marché comme Flash Animation, dont le résultat est effectivement plus vite obtenu, mais n'a pas la chaleur inhérente au dessin fait à la main.

to it – Fatso – and kept Helvetica for clear body-text (time of shows, etc).

There were a few funny stories during this re-brand period. Serge, our illustrator, was stung by a bee whilst cycling in to the office one morning on one of the most important days for our deliveries and his hand swelled to such an unimaginable size we had to send him to a hospital. In the last week of the animation deadlines a fire broke out in the room next to us, and since all the animation was created on real pieces of paper we were trying to re-enter the building every other minute to save the art-work from the fire. All went well.

The nicest surprises were the way the regions naturally identified with some of the characters we had created. People believed that some of the characters were specifically inspired by local stories, even though all we did was brainstorm over a few examples inspired by our imagination and from memories of childhood fairy-tales. And the funniest surprise was when MTV Adria identified one of the characters in

gezeichnet wird. Dieses sehr arbeitsintensive Vorgehen wird heute ziemlich selten angewendet, wo jeder sich für schnelle und günstige Methoden entscheidet, etwa die Animation mit Flash. Damit gelangt man zweifellos zügig zu Resultaten, doch fehlt ihnen die wohlige Zufriedenheit einer von Hand erstellten Arbeit.

Die Animation sollte deutlich texturiert und handgezeichnet wirken. Gleichzeitig musste sie aber auch einen digitalen, reduzierten und schnellen Charakter haben, um den digitalen Plattformen zu entsprechen, mit denen wir leben. MTV stellt sich den kreativen Herausforderungen der Mobiltelefon- und Online-Welten, und unser Design sollte dort genauso gut aussehen wie auf dem Fernsehschirm. Bei den Navigationsmenüs und Endboards wurden wir von alten Gif-Animationen inspiriert, der klassischen Kunstform früher Computer-Ästhetik. Ich wollte das Geschichtenerzählen ausschließlich als Trenner einsetzen und den Infomenüs ein klar reduziertes Aussehen verleihen. Wir kombinierten dies mit einem handgeschrie-

Je voulais une image fortement texturée, et dessinée à la main. Mais il fallait aussi qu'elle soit numérique, minimale et rapide, de manière à refléter les plateformes digitales où nous évoluons. MTV relève des défis créatifs dans les secteurs du portable et de la connectique, et je voulais donc que notre image soit aussi agréable qu'elle l'est à l'antenne. Pour les menus Navigation et les Endboards, nous nous sommes inspirés des vieux formats GIF, autrement dit les plus anciennes formes artistiques de l'esthétique informatique initiale. Je ne voulais utiliser le conte que pour les reprises d'écran de coupure publicitaire et avoir une image minimale bien nette pour les menus Info. Nous avons combiné cela avec un caractère d'imprimerie très large et gras pour la titraille, rappelant un peu l'écriture à la main – le Fatso – et nous avons réservé l'Helvetica pour la clarté des corps de texte (horaires de programmes, etc.).

Il nous est arrivé quelques anecdotes assez drôles pendant cette période de refonte de l'image. Serge, notre illustrateur, a été piqué par une abeille, un matin, tandis

one of the bumpers (the guy with the hair growing) with a local legend about Kralj Matjaž, a legendary hero in Slovenia, possibly based on a real-life king of Hungary: the legend says that he is asleep under Mount Peca in the Alps. When his beard grows and reaches seven times around the stone table, he will awake and bring a golden era to the Slovenes.

Electro Folk proved a successful and long-lasting branding thanks to the research and the passion that comes from collaborative work and a rich and diverse network of creatives from all over the regions; it is also a brand identity which offered all our channels a flexible package whilst directly making reference to the local culture of many of our viewers.

ben anmutenden, wirklich fetten, großen Schriftfont (Fatso) für die Headline und wählten die Helvetica für den reinen Bodytext (Zeitangaben u. Ä.).

Während wir an der Markenneubildung arbeiteten, kam es zu seltsamen Ereignissen: Unser Zeichner Serge wurde von einer Biene gestochen, als er eines Morgens ins Büro radelte – und das an einem für die Abgabe unserer Animationen wichtigen Tag. Seine Hand schwoll so stark an, dass wir ihn ins Krankenhaus bringen mussten. In der letzten Woche vor dem Fertigstellungstermin brannte es im Nachbarraum, und wir versuchten unermüdlich, in das Gebäude zu gelangen, um die Originalzeichenvorlagen vor den Flammen zu retten. Beides ging gut aus.

Die schönste Überraschung für uns war die Art, wie sich die Regionen mit einigen der von uns geschaffenen Figuren wie selbstverständlich identifizierten. Einige Zuschauer glaubten, dass manche unserer Figuren konkret von lokalen Erzählungen inspiriert worden seien, obwohl wir uns

qu'il pédalait en direction du bureau ; l'ennui c'est que nous avions ce jour-là une livraison hyper importante à faire, et que sa main a tellement enflé qu'il a fallu l'envoyer à l'hôpital. La dernière semaine, juste au moment de rendre l'animation, un incendie s'est déclaré dans la pièce d'à côté, et comme le travail avait pour support de vraies planches de papier, nous avons tout tenté pour pénétrer dans l'immeuble afin de les sauver des flammes. Tout c'est heureusement bien passé.

Les plus belles surprises, ce sont les régions qui nous les ont réservées en s'identifiant naturellement avec les personnages que nous avions créés. Les gens ont vraiment cru que certains d'entre eux s'inspiraient d'histoires locales, alors qu'en fait nous nous étions bornés à cogiter à partir de quelques exemples issus de notre imagination et de souvenirs des contes de notre enfance. La surprise la plus drôle, nous l'avons eue lorsque MTV Adria a identifié un personnage de l'un des spots (celui dont les cheveux poussent) avec la légende de Kralj Matjaž, héros mythique de Slovénie,

Previous spread: *Sketches of the main characters. ///* **Vorhergehende Seite:** *Entwurfszeichnungen der Hauptfiguren. ///* **Double page précédente :** *Croquis des personnages principaux.*

From left to right: *Characters applied to the bumpers in different animations. ///* **Von links nach rechts:** *Verschiedene Animationen der Figuren aus unterschiedlichen Trenner-Animationen. ///* **De gauche à droite :** *Personnages employés pour les spots, avec différentes animations.*

doch nur anhand einiger Entwürfe und aufgrund unserer Erinnerungen an die Märchen aus Kindertagen zu unseren Ideen haben inspirieren lassen. Lustig fanden wir, als MTV Adria eine unserer Figuren aus den Trennern (den Kerl mit dem wachsenden Haar) mit einer lokalen Legende über Kralj Matjaž in Verbindung brachte, einen sagenumwobenen slowenischen Helden, der möglicherweise auf einen wahrhaftigen König von Ungarn zurückgeht: Der Legende nach schläft er unter dem Berg Petzen. Wenn sein Bart so lang gewachsen ist, dass er siebenmal um den Steintisch herum-passt, wird er erwachen und die Slowenen zu einem goldenen Zeitalter führen.

Dank der Recherche, der Leidenschaft, die durch gemeinschaftliche Arbeit entstand, und des wertvollen, vielfältigen Netzwerkes kreativer Menschen aus allen Regionen erwies sich Electro Folk als erfolgreiche und langlebige Marke. Es ist zudem eine Markenidentität, die auf allen MTV-Kanä-len flexibel eingesetzt werden konnte und gleichzeitig direkt auf die regionale Kultur vieler unserer Zuschauer Bezug nahm.

probablement inspiré par un véritable roi de Hongrie : selon cette légende, le monarque en question dormirait sous le Mont Peca, dans les Alpes. Lorsque sa barbe aura poussé et fait sept fois le tour de la table de pierre où il repose, il s'éveillera et restaurera l'âge d'or en Slovénie.

La valorisation de la marque Electro Folk a été une réussite durable grâce à la recherche et à la passion découlant d'un travail en collaboration et d'un réseau riche et diversifié de créatifs de toutes les régions ; il s'agit également d'une identité de marque qui offre à toutes nos chaînes un paquet flexible tout en faisant directement référence à la culture locale de nombre de nos audiences.

 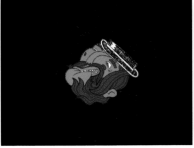 

Top: *Frames of an animated character.* /// Oben: *Einzelbilder einer animierten Figur.* /// En haut : *Images d'un personnage d'animation.*

Bottom: *Sketches of visual language for the project.* /// Unten: *Skizzen zu der visuellen Sprache des Projektes.* /// En bas : *Croquis de langage visuel pour le projet.*

Right: *Final frame of a bumper. ///* **Rechts:**
Das letzte Bild eines Trenners. /// **A droite :**
Image finale d'un spot.

Biography
Marta Di Francesco (MTV Europe)

www.mtv.com/
mtvinternational

Position: Creative Director

Marta Di Francesco currently works as a creative director for MTV Networks International. Her experience covers branding, animation, and developing concepts and new content. She is a creative gipsy and is constantly seeking fresh talent and ideas, working with creatives from all backgrounds and disciplines. She developed the MTV Emerging Markets Rebrand, creating a strong conceptual brand for MTV's Eastern European channels. One of her current projects is a pan-European campaign scouting for new talents, embracing the Internet as the new way to reach out to MTV audiences everywhere. Before MTV, she was a director for Turner Broadcasting where she worked on a whole range of branding and short-form content projects.

Marta Di Francesco ist zurzeit als Creative Director für MTV Networks International tätig. Ihre Sachkenntnisse umfassen Markenbildung, Animation sowie die Entwicklung von Konzepten und neuen Inhalten. Sie ist eine Art kreative Zigeunerin, immer auf der Suche nach unverbrauchten Talenten und Ideen, und arbeitet mit kreativen Menschen unterschiedlichster Hintergründe und Disziplinen zusammen. Sie entwickelte die Markenneubildung für MTV Emerging Markets und schuf dabei eine starke konzeptionelle Marke für die MTV-Kanäle in Osteuropa. Aktuell sucht sie u. a. nach neuen Talenten für eine gesamteuropäische Kampagne, die das Internet als weitere Möglichkeit nutzt, die MTV-Zuschauer überall auf der Welt zu erreichen. Bevor Marta Di Francesco zu MTV kam, war sie als Direktorin bei Turner Broadcasting tätig, wo sie an einer Reihe von Projekten zu Markenbildung und Kurzinhalten mitwirkte.

Marta Di Francesco est actuellement directrice de la création pour MTV Networks International. Son expérience va de la stratégie de marque à l'animation, en passant par la création de nouveaux concepts et contenus. Créative et bohème, elle est constamment en quête d'idées et de nouveaux talents et travaille avec des concepteurs de tous horizons et de toutes disciplines. Elle s'est occupée de la stratégie de MTV sur ses marchés émergents, créant une solide identité conceptuelle de marque pour les chaînes MTV d'Europe orientale. Parmi plusieurs projets, elle planche actuellement sur une campagne paneuropéenne de recherche de nouveaux talents, qui met à profit Internet comme nouveau moyen d'atteindre les audiences de MTV partout dans le monde. Avant MTV, elle a exercé un poste de direction chez Turner Broadcasting, où elle a travaillé à toutes sortes de projets de valorisation et de publicité.

IDENTITY IN THE DIGITAL ERA: PICTOMATO FOR MOBILE

Pictomato is an Internet-based platform for creating personalised avatars. An avatar is the appearance an Internet user takes on in a virtual world, and here it should be viewed as a graphic affirmation of a person's identity, character, or even sense of humour on the Internet, on blogs, game platforms, and social networks. An avatar on the Internet is to a person what a logo is to a company.

Whereas a logo aims to represent the activity, history, values, and strengths of a company, an avatar is supposed to characterise a person and that person's personality in a virtual world. One person can use entirely different avatars depending on the network, forum or medium frequented. This is why people often have many avatars that they use playfully or instinctively, depending on the moment. How do I express my emotions or feelings when I am in front of my computer screen? How do I represent, describe or sell myself in a virtual world? These are the questions that, in various forms, the avatar creator or user must answer at some point.

Pictomato ist eine internetbasierte Plattform zum Erzeugen personalisierter Avatare. Ein Avatar ist das Erscheinungsbild, das ein Internetbenutzer in einer virtuellen Welt annehmen kann, und wird hier als grafische Ausformung der Identität, des Charakters oder sogar des Humors einer Person im Internet, in Blogs, auf Spieleplattformen und in Social Networks betrachtet. Ein Avatar im Internet entspricht in Bezug auf eine Person dem, was ein Logo für ein Unternehmen ist.

Während ein Logo zum Ziel hat, Aktivitäten, Geschichte, Werte und Stärken eines Unternehmens darzustellen, soll ein Avatar eine Person und deren Persönlichkeit in einer virtuellen Welt charakterisieren. Je nach Netzwerk, Forum oder Medium kann eine Person völlig unterschiedliche Avatare benutzen. Aus diesem Grund haben Internetbenutzer häufig viele Avatare, die sie je nach Situation spielerisch oder instinktiv einsetzen. Wie drücke ich meine Emotionen oder Gefühle aus, wenn ich vor dem Computerbildschirm sitze? Wie präsentiere, beschreibe

Pictomato est un site permettant de créer des avatars personnalisés. Un avatar est l'apparence qu'adopte un internaute dans un monde virtuel ; il faut y voir l'affirmation graphique de l'identité d'une personne, d'un caractère, voire d'un sens de l'humour, sur Internet ou sur des blogs, des plateformes de jeux et des réseaux sociaux. L'avatar sur Internet est à l'individu ce que le logo est à la société.

De même que le logo vise à représenter l'activité, l'histoire, les valeurs et les points forts d'une société, l'avatar, lui, est censé caractériser la personnalité d'un individu dans le monde virtuel. Une personne peut utiliser des avatars radicalement différents selon le réseau, le forum ou le support qu'elle fréquente. C'est pourquoi les gens en ont souvent plusieurs, dont ils usent selon l'humeur ou l'intuition, et en fonction du moment. Comment faire pour exprimer mes émotions ou mes sentiments quand je suis face à l'écran de l'ordinateur ? Comment me représenter, me décrire ou me vendre dans un monde virtuel ? Telles sont les questions

FIRST CREATION'S WEBSITE FOR MOBILE

Previous spread: *Poster for the project launch.*
/// **Vorhergehende Seite:** *Plakat zur Einführung des Projektes.* /// **Double page précédente :** *Affiche de lancement du projet.*

True design and graphic work come into play when choosing one or more avatars. This is so not only because the avatars are supposed to represent you and present your image on the Net, but also because they must be eye-catching (each must make an impact and display individual graphic styles, types and colours among so many other avatars). They must also be reasonably readable and understandable by other Internet users (i. e. they must be composed of simple forms because they most often appear in much reduced size). Finally, they must be appreciated by other Internet users – seduction therefore also comes into play in avatar creation. An avatar can take different forms, such as photos or drawings of individuals, animals, or even objects. Developments in technology make avatars seem increasingly lifelike. They will undoubtedly soon be linked with sounds or melodies in the near future. Today, these virtual elements are widely recognised and used on a daily basis by many avid Internet users. They are therefore universal and rise above many common barriers (social status, age, language).

oder verkaufe ich mich in einer virtuellen Welt? Dies sind die Fragen, die der Schöpfer oder Benutzer eines Avatars irgendwann auf die eine oder andere Art beantworten muss.

Bei der Wahl eines oder mehrerer Avatare kommt die wahre Design- und Grafikarbeit ins Spiel – nicht nur, weil Avatare eine Person und deren Erscheinungsbild im Internet repräsentieren, sondern auch, weil sie einen Blickfang darstellen müssen (ein Avatar muss neben den vielen anderen Avataren eigenständig wirken können, einen individuellen grafischen Stil und Typ aufweisen sowie eine individuelle Farbgebung zeigen). Sie müssen zudem für andere Internetbenutzer einigermaßen lesbar und verständlich sein (sie sollten beispielsweise aus einfachen Formen bestehen, da sie meistens stark verkleinert dargestellt werden). Und letztendlich müssen sie von anderen Internetbenutzern anerkannt werden – daher spielt bei der Schaffung von Avataren auch Verführung eine Rolle. Avatare können verschiedene Formen annehmen, zum Beispiel Fotos

auxquelles, sous diverses formes, tout créateur d'un avatar ou tout internaute est forcément amené à répondre à un moment donné.

Un vrai travail d'infographie s'impose à l'heure de choisir un ou plusieurs avatars. Non seulement parce que les avatars sont supposés vous représenter et présenter votre image sur la Toile, mais encore parce qu'il faut qu'ils soient accrocheurs (chacun d'eux doit avoir un impact et afficher des couleurs, un style et un caractère personnels au milieu de tant d'autres avatars). Ils doivent être raisonnablement lisibles et compréhensibles par d'autres internautes (c'est-à-dire qu'ils doivent se composer de formes simples car ils apparaîtront souvent en dimensions réduites). Enfin, ils doivent être appréciés par les autres internautes – la séduction joue donc également un rôle dans la création de l'avatar. Un avatar peut adopter différentes formes, telles que photos ou dessins de personnages, d'animaux, voire d'objets. Les progrès technologiques permettent désormais de

Left: *Promotional material featuring samples of characters to be created using the website.* /// **Links:** *Werbematerial mit Beispielen für Figuren, die über die Website erstellt werden können.* /// **A gauche** : *Supports promotionnels, avec notamment des échantillons de personnages à créer en utilisant le site Web.*

Right: *Poster for the project launch.* /// **Rechts:** *Plakat zur Einführung des Projektes.* /// **A droite** : *Affiche de lancement du projet.*

Pictomato Project

The notion of a unique and original creation seemed important to us. The Pictomato concept was born after we realised that there did not yet exist an artistic platform which allowed people to design their own avatars with simple, creative tools. This would enable Internet users to express their creativity by giving them access to tools that stimulate their imagination. The Pictomato platform offers Internet users the opportunity to create avatars with their own image online, and a virtual gallery of a thousand faces helps make each avatar truly individual. Moreover, several style libraries with varying complexity have also been created. There are currently a dozen different thematic style libraries, such as coats of arms, portraits and stylised characters. The graphic themes used can be also different. Finally, new style libraries will be created on a regular basis according to new trends or desires/requests made by users.

In addition to these creative aspects, Pictomato allows its avatar designers to

oder Zeichnungen einzelner Personen, Tiere oder sogar Objekte. Durch technologische Weiterentwicklungen erscheinen Avatare zunehmend realistisch. Sie werden in naher Zukunft zweifellos mit Tönen oder Melodien verbunden sein. Heute sind diese virtuellen Elemente weitgehend anerkannt und werden von vielen begeisterten Internetbenutzern täglich benutzt. Sie sind daher allgemeingültig und überwinden viele alltägliche Barrieren (sozialer Status, Alter, Sprache).

Pictomato Project

Die Vorstellung eines einzigartigen und originären Designs erschien uns wichtig. Das Pictomato-Konzept wurde ins Leben gerufen, nachdem wir erkannt hatten, dass es noch keine künstlerische Plattform gab, mit deren Hilfe Benutzer ihre eigenen Avatare mit einfachen kreativen Tools gestalten können. Wir wollten den Internetnutzern die Möglichkeit bieten, ihrer Kreativität Ausdruck zu verleihen, indem wir ihnen Zugang zu Tools erleichtern, die ihre Vorstellungskraft

créer des avatars de plus en plus ressemblants. Dans un futur proche, il est probable qu'ils seront associés à des sons ou à des mélodies. Pour l'heure, ces éléments virtuels sont largement reconnus et utilisés au quotidien par beaucoup d'avides internautes. Ils sont par conséquent universels et surmontent presque toutes les barrières courantes (statut social, âge, langue).

Le projet Pictomato

La notion de création unique et originale nous semblait importante. Le concept de Pictomato est né lorsque nous nous sommes avisés qu'il n'existait pas de plateforme artistique permettant au gens de concevoir leurs propres avatars à l'aide d'outils simples et créatifs. Autrement dit nous avons voulu donner aux internautes la possibilité d'exprimer leur créativité en leur facilitant l'accès à des outils stimulant leur imagination. La plateforme Pictomato offre aux internautes l'opportunité de créer des avatars à leur image on-line ; ils y trouvent une galerie virtuelle avec des

 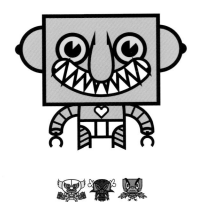 

Above: *Characters for use on mobile phones and variations that can be configured for download. ///* **Oben:** *Figuren zur Verwendung auf Mobiltelefonen und Varianten, die für den Download konfiguriert werden können. ///* **Ci-dessus :** *Personnages pour téléphones portables et variantes à configurer pour téléchargement.*

interact with each other through its Community. Each design registered generates a mini-blog that allows users to rank, annotate or comment on the design. Often, there are series of designs created based on a particular style or theme, and a graphic dialogue that rises above language barriers then begins.

There are several different applications the Pictomato platform may be used for. It can be used to personalise your mobile phone or your profile on forums, blogs, and social networks. It can also be used as a free graphic-design tool to exhibit designs simply in the gallery. Users can decide whether or not to exhibit their work, and if they do decide to do so, their creations will be shown in the gallery and can be downloaded by all site-users. Each time a user downloads a creation, credits are awarded to the designer. Our main idea is to unite as many users as possible on this project, even if the target audience is still teens and young adults (ages 12 to 35), as well as reaching innovative product-users and opinion

anregen. Die Pictomato-Plattform bietet Internetbenutzern die Möglichkeit, Avatare nach ihren eigenen Vorstellungen online zu kreieren. Sie finden dort eine virtuelle Galerie aus tausenden von Gesichtern, die sie dabei unterstützt, einen ganz individuellen Avatar zu gestalten. Außerdem wurden auch mehrere unterschiedlich umfangreiche Vorlagensammlungen erstellt. Zur Zeit sind ein Dutzend verschiedener thematischer Vorlagensammlungen verfügbar, zum Beispiel Wappen, Portraits und stilisierte Figuren. Auch die verwendeten grafischen Themen können sich unterscheiden. Aufgrund neuer Trends oder der Wünsche bzw. Anfragen der Benutzer werden letztlich regelmäßig neue Vorlagensammlungen geschaffen.

Neben diesen kreativen Aspekten ermöglicht Pictomato seinen Avatar-Designern, innerhalb ihrer Community miteinander zu interagieren. Jedes registrierte Design erstellt einen Mini-Blog, über den die Benutzer das Design anordnen, erläutern und kommentieren können. Häufig wird

milliers de visages qui les aide à créer un avatar vraiment unique. De plus, plusieurs bibliothèques de style d'une grande richesse ont également été créées. Il y a actuellement une douzaine de bibliothèques de styles sur différentes thématiques telles que armoiries, portraits et personnages stylisés. Les thèmes graphiques utilisés peuvent également être différents. Finalement, des bibliothèques de nouveaux styles seront régulièrement créées en fonction des nouvelles tendances ou des désirs et des demandes exprimés par les utilisateurs.

À part ces aspects relatifs à la création, Pictomato permet aux créateurs d'avatars de communiquer entre eux par le biais de sa Communauté. Chaque dessin enregistré génère un mini-blog sur lequel les internautes peuvent le classer, le noter ou laisser des commentaires à son sujet. On trouve souvent des séries de dessins reposant sur une thématique ou un style particulier, et un dialogue graphique s'instaure alors, surmontant les barrières linguistiques.

leaders who have access to both high-speed Internet connections and mobile telephones. To date, the site exists in French and English, and is currently being translated into Korean, and all users can download their creations or offer them on international mobile phone networks. The Pictomato site was officially launched in June 2008. After one month, there were already 140 users and 1,200 avatars available for downloading.

eine Serie von Designs kreiert, die auf einem bestimmten Modell oder Thema basieren, und dann kann ein grafischer Dialog jenseits der sprachlichen Barrieren beginnen.

Die Pictomato-Plattform kann für verschiedene Anwendungen genutzt werden. Die Benutzer können ihr Mobiltelefon oder ihr Profil in Foren, Blogs und in Social Networks individuell anpassen. Sie kann auch als kostenloses Grafikdesign-Tool verwendet werden, nur um die Avatar-Entwürfe in der Galerie zu zeigen. Die Benutzer können selbst entscheiden, ob sie ihre Arbeit zeigen möchten oder nicht. Falls sie die Präsentation wählen, werden ihre Kreationen in der Galerie gezeigt und können von allen Benutzern der Website heruntergeladen werden. Jedes Mal, wenn ein Benutzer ein Design herunterlädt, erhält der Designer eine Anerkennung. Unser Leitgedanke besteht darin, bei diesem Projekt so viele Benutzer wie möglich zusammenzuschließen, selbst wenn die Zielgruppe noch immer aus Teenagern und jungen Erwachsenen im Alter von 12 bis 35 Jahren besteht, sowie innovative Produktbenutzer und Meinungsführer zu erreichen, die Zugang sowohl zu Hochgeschwindigkeits-Internetverbindungen als auch zu Mobiltelefonen haben. Bis jetzt existiert die Website auf Französisch und Englisch und wird zurzeit ins Koreanische übersetzt. Alle Benutzer können ihre Entwürfe herunterladen oder sie über internationale Mobiltelefon-Netzwerke anbieten. Die Pictomato-Website wurde offiziell im Juni 2008 gestartet. Nach einem Monat gab es bereits 140 Benutzer, und 1.200 Avatare standen zum Download bereit.

La plateforme sert à plusieurs différentes applications. On peut l'employer pour personnaliser son téléphone portable ou son profil sur un forum, un blog ou un réseau social. On peut également y recourir comme à un instrument de design graphique gratuit, simplement pour exposer des dessins dans la galerie. Les utilisateurs décident d'exposer ou de ne pas exposer leur travail et, s'ils le font, leurs créations sont accrochées dans la galerie et peuvent être téléchargées par les utilisateurs du site. Chaque fois qu'un internaute en télécharge une, des crédits sont accordés à son auteur. Notre idée principale est de réunir le plus grand nombre possible d'utilisateurs sur ce projet, même si le public cible est encore très jeune (de 12 à 35 ans), ainsi que de toucher des utilisateurs novateurs et des prescripteurs ayant accès aussi bien à l'ADSL qu'au téléphone portable. A ce jour, le site existe en français et en anglais, et il est en cours de traduction en coréen ; tous les utilisateurs peuvent télécharger leurs créations ou les proposer sur les réseaux internationaux de téléphones portables. Le site Pictomato a été officiellement lancé en juin 2008. Au bout d'un mois, il comptait déjà 140 utilisateurs et 1200 avatars disponibles en téléchargement.

Left: *Samples of characters on the Pictomato website.* /// **Links:** *Beispiele von Figuren auf der Pictomato-Website.* /// **A gauche :** *Echantillons de personnages sur le site Web de Pictomato.*

Profile
Atelier Télescopique

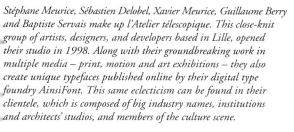

www.ateliertelescopique.com   Location: Lille, France   Year founded: 1998

Stéphane Meurice, Sébastien Delobel, Xavier Meurice, Guillaume Berry and Baptiste Servais make up l'Atelier télescopique. This close-knit group of artists, designers, and developers based in Lille, opened their studio in 1998. Along with their groundbreaking work in multiple media – print, motion and art exhibitions – they also create unique typefaces published online by their digital type foundry AinsiFont. This same eclecticism can be found in their clientele, which is composed of big industry names, institutions and architects' studios, and members of the culture scene.

Stéphane Meurice, Sébastien Delobel, Xavier Meurice, Guillaume Berry und Baptiste Servais bilden gemeinsam das Atelier Télescopique. Die eng verbundene Gruppe aus Künstlern, Designern und Entwicklern eröffnete 1998 ihr Studio mit Sitz in Lille (Frankreich). Neben ihrer innovativen Arbeit in verschiedenen Medien (Print, Film und Kunstausstellungen) kreieren sie außerdem einzigartige Typografien, die sie online über ihre digitale Fontfabrik AinsiFont veröffentlichen. Dieser gleiche Eklektizismus spiegelt sich auch in ihrer Klientel, die die großen Namen der Industrie, von Institutionen und Architektenstudios ebenso einschließt wie namhafte Mitglieder des Kulturbetriebs.

Stéphane Meurice, Sébastien Delobel, Xavier Meurice, Guillaume Berry et Baptiste Servais sont les fondateurs de l'Atelier télescopique. Ce groupe très homogène d'artistes, d'infographistes et de créatifs basé à Lille (France) a ouvert son studio en 1998. Outre un travail révolutionnaire dans divers medias – édition, cinéma et expositions d'art – ils ont également créé des caractères originaux, que leur fonderie digitale Ainsifont publie on-line. Le même éclectisme se retrouve parmi leur clientèle, qui se compose de grands noms de l'industrie, d'institutions et d'études d'architectes, ainsi que de membres de la scène culturelle.

EXPLORING THE SUNDANCE CHANNEL IDENTITY ONLINE

In the spring of 2007, Sundance Channel approached Tender to completely redesign and re-envision sundancechannel.com. Faced with the challenge of taking an already compelling and highly unique brand and finding ways for it to succeed and grow in the digital domain, Tender created a new website that not only translated an on-air property into an online destination, but also provided a platform for new content and a destination for true user-participation.

Our mission was to design a site experience that completely reflected and enhanced the sundancechannel.com brand ideals of independence in thought, action, and lifestyle while still serving the functional needs of a television website. The successful finished product would attract, organise, and empower diverse communities of independent thinkers, while also providing Sundance Channel with the means to share a more curatorial perspective on relevant issues.

At Tender we imagined a site that could be everything that Sundance Channel wanted to be for its audience: a vibrant source of

Im Frühling 2007 kam Sundance Channel auf Tender zu und gab die vollständige Neugestaltung und Neuausrichtung von sundancechannel.com in Auftrag. Damit konfrontiert, eine bereits sehr überzeugende und einzigartige Marke zu übernehmen und Wege zu finden, diese im digitalen Bereich zu Wachstum und Erfolg zu führen, kreierte Tender eine neue Website, die nicht nur Sendeinhalte ins Netz stellte, sondern auch eine Plattform für weiterführende Inhalte und unmittelbare Benutzerbeteiligung bot.

Unsere Aufgabe war es, eine Website zu schaffen, die die Markenideale von sundancechannel.com, unabhängig zu denken, zu handeln und zu leben, 1:1 widerspiegelt und fördert und gleichzeitig den funktionalen Anforderungen einer Website für einen Fernsehsender gerecht wird. Das erfolgreiche Endprodukt sollte unterschiedlichste Communities unabhängig Denkender anziehen, organisieren und zur Teilnahme bewegen. Gleichzeitig sollte Sundance Channel die Möglichkeit erhalten, sich bei relevanten Themen entsprechend einzubringen.

Au printemps 2007, Sundance Channel a contacté Tender en vue du relookage et de la refonte totale de sundancechannel.com. Confronté au défi de trouver pour cette marque, d'ores et déjà attractive et unique en son genre, des moyens de réussir et de grandir dans le domaine du numérique, Tender a créé un nouveau site Web qui a le mérite, non seulement de traduire on-line le caractère télévisuel de son propriétaire, mais encore de constituer à la fois une plateforme pour de nouveaux contenus et une destination pour une vraie participation de l'audience.

Notre mission consistait à créer un site qui reflèterait pleinement et mettrait en évidence les valeurs d'indépendance que véhicule la marque sundancechannel.com en matière d'opinion, d'initiatives et de mode de vie, tout en continuant de répondre aux besoins fonctionnels propres au site d'une chaîne TV. Le résultat attendu devait être capable d'attirer, d'organiser et de laisser s'exprimer divers courants d'opinion indépendants, tout en donnant à Sundance Channel le moyen de partager

sundance
CHANNEL.

for a change."

MY PROFILE | LOGOUT | SEARCH

FILMS   SERIES   EXCLUSIVES   SCHEDULE   VIDEOS   PHOTOS   FESTIVAL

VISION VOICE

FILM:
2046

SERIES:
HOUSE OF BOATENG

BLOCK:
ASIA EXTREME: THE
EYE 2

SPOTLIGHT:
MICHEL GONDRY

DISCUSSION:
JOHN212

"It's one thing to swap clothes with a
friend, but it's quite another swap-
ping clothes stores..."

BLOGS:
TREEHUGGER

"Artists Project Earth, a British
non-profit that raises money to fight
climate change and prvide disaster
relief..."

| Tonight | The Talent Given Us | Dirty Filthy Love | Ellie Parker |
| Full Schedule | 6:15pm | 8pm | 10pm |

---

sundance
CHANNEL.

MAILING LISTS | LOGIN | SEARCH

VISION VOICE

FILMS   SERIES   EXCLUSIVES   SCHEDULE   VIDEOS   PHOTOS   FESTIVAL   BLOGS   DISCUSSIONS   SPOTLIGHT   SELECTS

SCHEDULE:
THURSDAY DECEMBER 23

Current Time Zone: **EST**

▼ Time	▶ Title	▶ Genre	▶ Director	▶ Rating
1:30PM	ICONOCLASTS SEASON 2: EPISODE 6: DAVE CHAPELLE + MAYA ANGELOU	Series		14
3:00PM	THE BEST MAN	Drama	Malcolm D. Lee	14
4:00PM	ICONOCLASTS SEASON 2: EPISODE 6: DAVE CHAPELLE + MAYA ANGELOU	Series		14
NOW PLAYING 5:00PM	▶ BREATHLESS	Drama	Malcolm D. Lee	14
7:00PM	ICONOCLASTS SEASON 2: EPISODE 6: DAVE CHAPELLE + MAYA ANGELOU	Series		14
7:30PM	THE BEST MAN	Drama	Malcolm D. Lee	14
PRIMETIME				
8:00PM	HOUSE OF BOATENG: EPISODE 5	Series		14
9:30PM	DARK WATER	Drama	Bruce Weber	14
10:00PM	HARVEY KRUMPET	Documentary	Marcos Bernstein	14
11:00PM	KATH & KIM SEASON 3: SITTING ON A PILE	Comedy		14
12:00PM	HARVEY KRUMPET	Documentary	Brian Percival	14

‹ DECEMBER 2006 ›

			1	2	3	4
5	6	7	8	9	10	11
12	13	14	15	16	17	18
19	20	21	22	23	24	25
26	27	28	29	30	31	

VIEW E-GUIDE »
PRINTABLE SCHEDULE »
PRINTABLE FILM DESCRIPTIONS »

Search current listings   »

NOW PLAYING:
BREATHLESS

PLAYING NEXT:
ICONOCLASTS:
CHAPELLE + ANGELOU

| What's On Tonight | The Talent Given Us | Dirty Filthy Love | Ellie Parker | Asia Extreme |

Site Map   About   Feedback   Policies   Shop   © 2006 Sundance Channel L.L.C. All rights reserved

community, a curator of interesting and challenging cultural perspectives, and a springboard for thought and action. We proposed that Sundance Channel transform its website into a destination by leveraging their on-air content and brand as a kernel for a larger site designed around audience interests, values, and goals. What we envisioned for the project went beyond the traditional conception of a website. It was more in-line with the definition of application. *Sites* are one-way conduits for pushing information at *viewers*. *Applications* are dynamic, innovative, and responsive landscapes meant to be explored by *users*. While a website is often little more than an outlet for delivering and replicating the same homogeneous content from a single perspective to countless users, a web application can truly interact with and bring users together, can encourage and enable users to discover, create, and share content.

We began by organising the site into two complementary halves. One side housed all on-air content, and the other served as the expressive outlet for Sundance Channel and its loyal viewers. These main sections of the site we named Vision and Voice, respectively. While Vision acts as an informational resource for visitors interested in the channel's programming and films, Voice provides a home for blogs, discussions, channel-curated content, and other non-programming related activities and content. The two sides of the site do not exist independently; they feed off each other in ways designed to bring a user from one side of this related content to the other via contextual links.

With the Voice & Vision organisational paradigm in place, we moved on to the first of three main challenges: using the site to instigate the creation of communities. We envisioned ways of fostering community by incorporating interactive features that engage users in expressing and exploring ideas, thoughts, and actions related to the values they shared with the brand. A prime example, and one that demonstrates the philosophy of approaching sundancechannel.com as an application, is the Eco-mmunity Map.

Bei Tender stellten wir uns eine Website vor, die alles enthalten sollte, was Sundance Channel für seine Zielgruppe sein wollte: eine sprudelnde Quelle für die Community, ein Kurator für interessante, anspruchsvolle kulturelle Blickwinkel sowie ein Sprungbrett für Ideen und Aktionen. Wir schlugen vor, die Sundance-Channel-Website zu einem Treffpunkt umzuformen, indem die Sendeinhalte und die Marke als Kern für eine größere Site genutzt werden, die rund um Interessen, Werte und Ziele der Zielgruppe erstellt wird. Was wir für das Projekt vorsahen, ging über die traditionelle Konzeption einer Website hinaus. Es entsprach eher der Definition einer Anwendung. *Websites* sind Einwegkanäle zur Übertragung von Informationen an den *Betrachter*. *Anwendungen* sind dynamische, innovative und engagierte Landschaften, die vom *Benutzer* erforscht werden sollen. Während eine Website häufig lediglich ein Ausgangskanal für die Übermittlung und Wiederholung der gleichen homogenen Inhalte aus einer einzigen Perspektive an zahllose Benutzer ist, bietet eine Webanwendung die Möglichkeit, mit den Benutzern zu interagieren, sie zusammenzuführen und sie darüber hinaus dazu zu ermutigen und ihnen dabei behilflich zu sein, neue Inhalte zu entdecken, zu gestalten und weiterzugeben.

Zunächst gliederten wir die Website in zwei sich gegenseitig ergänzende Hälften. Die eine sollte den gesamten Sendeinhalt aufnehmen, die andere als Sprachrohr für Sundance Channel und seine treuen Zuschauer dienen. Wir nannten diese Hauptbereiche der Website „Vision" beziehungsweise „Voice". Während Vision als Informationsquelle für Besucher dient, die am Programm und den Filmen des Kanals interessiert sind, bietet Voice eine Heimat für Blogs, Diskussionen, redaktionell betreute Inhalte und andere programmunabhängige Aktivitäten und Themen. Die beiden Seiten der Website bestehen nicht unabhängig voneinander; sie nähren sich gegenseitig, indem ein Benutzer durch kontextabhängige Links von einer inhaltsbezogenen Seite auf die andere gelangt.

une perspective plus médiatrice sur les questions d'importance.

Tender a donc imaginé un site qui pouvait être tout ce que Sundance Channel souhaitait qu'il soit pour ses audiences : une source de convivialité, un médiateur de perspectives culturelles intéressantes et stimulantes, et un tremplin pour l'esprit et l'action. Nous avons proposé à Sundance Channel de transformer son site Web en une destination, en prenant le contenu télévisuel et la marque pour assise d'un site plus large conçu autour des intérêts, des valeurs et des aspirations de l'audience. Ce que nous envisagions pour ce projet allait bien au-delà de la conception traditionnelle du site Web. Nous étions plus près de la définition d'application. Les *sites* sont des canaux à sens unique que l'on bourre d'informations à l'intention de *spectateurs*. Les *applications* sont des environnements dynamiques, novateurs et réactifs conçus pour être explorés par des *utilisateurs*. Alors que le site Web n'est souvent guère qu'un distributeur fournissant sempiternellement le même contenu homogène et univoque à d'innombrables usagers, l'application, elle, peut vraiment rassembler les utilisateurs, les faire communiquer et les encourager à découvrir, créer et partager des contenus, en leur en donnant les moyens.

Nous avons commencé par organiser le site en deux moitiés complémentaires. L'une accueillait le contenu télévisuel proprement dit, l'autre faisait fonction de plateforme de communication entre Sundance Channel et ses fidèles auditeurs. Ces grandes sections du site, nous les avons respectivement baptisées Vision et Voice. Tandis que Vision renseigne les visiteurs désireux de connaître la programmation et les films que diffuse la chaîne, Voice accueille des blogs, des forums, les contenus médiés par la chaîne et toutes sortes de rubriques et d'activités sans rapport avec les programmes. Les deux côtés du site n'existent pas l'un sans l'autre ; ils s'alimentent réciproquement de manière à amener l'utilisateur à passer d'un côté à l'autre par le biais de liens contextuels.

Une fois le paradigme Voice & Vision mis en place, nous nous sommes attaqués au premier de trois principaux défis : utiliser

Previous spread: *Main page for the portal (top); page showing a selection of movies (bottom).* /// **Vorhergehende Seite:** *Hauptseite für das Portal (oben); Seite mit einer Auswahl an Filmen (unten).* /// **Double page précédente** : *Page principale du portail (en haut) ; page montrant une sélection de films (en bas).*

Right: *Page with film preview and discussion room.* /// **Rechts:** *Seite mit Filmvorschau und Diskussionsforum.* /// **A droite** : *Page avec avant-première et forum de discussion.*

Created as a companion to the content found in Sundance Channel's Green programming, the Eco-mmunity Map was developed in conjunction with Google as a global map to which individuals, groups, organisations, and companies could post their services and events by location. While the Eco-mmunity Map is not directly tied to Sundance Channel programming, it is tied to the values of the Sundance Channel brand by attracting and empowering an active community. While so many television channels have worked to capitalise on the "green" frenzy by merely green-washing their on-air line-up with token programming, the Eco-mmunity Map has become the biggest destination online for people looking for green businesses and activities in their neighbourhood – and has as a consequence established Sundance Channel as an authority on all things green.

Our second challenge was presenting the site as a rich destination for on-brand content. While most television websites show content only related to what is currently on-air or coming up, the goal

Die Struktur von Voice & Vision in Händen, wandten wir uns der ersten von drei großen Herausforderungen zu: die Site zu nutzen, um die Bildung von Communities zu initiieren. Wir malten uns Wege zu deren Aufbau aus, indem wir interaktive Funktionen einbauten, über die die Benutzer ihre Ideen, Gedanken und Aktivitäten hinsichtlich der Werte ausdrücken, untersuchen und weitergeben, die sie mit der Marke teilen. Ein Paradebeispiel dafür und wie man die Philosophie von sundancechannel.com als Anwendung darstellen kann, ist die Eco-mmunity Map. Sie begleitet die Inhalte der »grünen« Programme bei Sundance Channel und wurde in Verbindung mit Google als globale Karte entwickelt, in die Privatpersonen, Gruppen, Organisationen und Unternehmen ihre Dienste und Veranstaltungen ortsgebunden einstellen konnten. Die Eco-mmunity Map ist zwar nicht direkt in die Programmgestaltung von Sundance Channel eingebunden, aber mit den Werten der Marke Sundance Channel verbunden, indem sie eine aktive Gemeinschaft anzieht und teilnehmen lässt. So

le site pour stimuler la création de communautés. Nous avons envisagé des moyens d'encourager la convivialité en incorporant des dispositifs interactifs qui invitent les utilisateurs à exprimer et mettre en œuvre des idées, des points de vue et des actions en accord avec les valeurs qu'ils partagent avec la marque. Un premier exemple, représentatif de la philosophie qui sous-tend notre choix d'approcher sundancechannel.com à la manière d'une application, pourrait être ce que ce que nous avons appelé Eco-mmunity Map. Sorte de manuel sur les programmes de Sundance Channel ayant trait à l'écologie, Eco-mmunity Map a été mis au point en collaboration avec Google : il s'agit d'une carte globale où quiconque, personnes, groupes, organismes et sociétés, peut afficher localement ses services et événements. Bien qu'elle ne soit pas directement liée aux programmes de Sundance Channel, Eco-mmunity Map l'est en revanche aux valeurs de la marque Sundance Channel, en attirant et en donnant une visibilité à une active communauté. Tandis que tant de chaînes de télévision s'emploient à

for sundancechannel.com was defined to be more curatorial. We sought ways to present on-brand and on-value content from a variety of sources that could attract new users to the Sundance Channel brand and eventually pay back to the on-air programming through increased interest and viewership. The presentation of diverse content from diverse sources also allows the site to target and serve the needs of specific groups. To this end, we created features like the Independent Film Database, Artists Spotlights, the Select Programming Series, Blogs, and more. Each feature offers a dynamic way to discover content that resonates with the values of the Sundance Brand and also cultivates community interaction, facilitated by discussion forums, a user ratings engine, and content sharing tools – ways of fostering reflection, sharing ideas, and ultimately dialogues within the digital property.

The third challenge in our three-part strategy for bringing the Sundance Channel brand into the digital domain was to seek non-linear, but completely intuitive ways for the site to reveal itself to a user. We wanted a content-rich site that was neither overwhelming in its options nor limiting in its lack of choice – and we wanted to enable users to discover content according to their interests and tastes instead of being pushed down a linear selection of unappealing choices. The process of discovery was made enjoyable when the choices were clarified – proving that deep hierarchical structures are not always the best vehicle for discovery. The website as application allowed users quickly to uncover new content by offering them informed choices and intuitive navigation.

What we ended up articulating through our efforts with Sundance Channel was a new framework for evaluating how a brand performs in the digital arena. We discovered that a website *as application* can and should focus a community of dedicated users on powerful and engaging narratives that share their values with the brand. It is a symbiotic relationship that develops between the translation of a

viele Sendeanstalten haben versucht, aus der Begeisterung für »grüne« Themen Nutzen zu ziehen, indem sie lediglich ihrem TV-Programm mit ein paar grünen Sendereihen einen ökologischen Anstrich geben, die Eco-mmunity Map hingegen wurde zur wichtigsten Internetadresse für Menschen, die nach grünen Unternehmen und Aktivitäten in ihrer Nachbarschaft suchen – als Folge davon hat sich Sundance Channel als Autorität für alle grünen Themen etabliert.

Unsere zweite Herausforderung bestand darin, die Website als lohnende Anlaufstelle für markenkonforme Inhalte darzustellen. Während die meisten Fernsehsender nur Inhalte zeigen, die aktuell auf Sendung oder angekündigt sind, definierten wir das Ziel für sundancechannel.com eher in Richtung Beratung. Wir suchten nach Wegen, die Inhalte der Marke und ihre Werte mittels verschiedener Quellen darzustellen, die neue Benutzer auf die Marke Sundance Channel aufmerksam machen sollten, was sich schließlich für das TV-Programm durch erhöhtes Interesse und mehr Zuschauer auszahlen würde. Die Präsentation diverser Inhalte unterschiedlicher Herkunft ermöglicht der Website auch, auf die Bedürfnisse bestimmter Gruppen abzuzielen und einzugehen. Zu diesem Zweck entwickelten wir Funktionen wie die Independent Film Database, Artists Spotlights, die Select-Programming-Serie, Blogs und anderes. Bei jeder Funktion kann man auf lebendige Weise Inhalte entdecken, bei denen die Werte der Sundance-Marke mitschwingen und die die Interaktionen der Community fördern. Das wird durch Diskussionsforen, ein Beurteilungssystem für Benutzer und Content Sharing Tools möglich – alles Wege, die inhaltliche Auseinandersetzung zu fördern, Ideen weiterzugeben und letztendlich zum Dialog auf der digitalen Plattform.

Die dritte Herausforderung unserer dreiteiligen Strategie zur Markeneinführung von Sundance Channel in den digitalen Bereich war es, nach nichtlinearen, rein intuitiven Wegen für die Website zu suchen, mittels derer sie vom Benutzer erschlossen werden könnte. Wir wollten

capitaliser la « fièvre verte » en se contentant de repeindre leur antenne en vert, avec en prime quelques programmes, Eco-mmunity Map est devenue la plus importante destination on-line pour tous ceux qui cherchent autour d'eux des établissements et des activités écologiques – imposant par conséquent Sundance Channel comme une autorité en la matière.

Notre second défi consistait à présenter le site comme une destination riche de contenus relatifs à la marque. Alors que la plupart des sites Web affichent des contenus exclusivement consacrés aux programmes à l'antenne ou à venir, l'objectif marqué par sundancechannel.com était beaucoup plus médiateur. Nous avons donc cherché des moyens de présenter la marque et ses valeurs, à partir d'une variété de sources capables d'attirer de nouveaux utilisateurs vers la marque Sundance Channel, un public dont, l'intérêt et l'audience grandissant, l'antenne finirait par bénéficier. La présentation de contenus divers provenant de sources diverses permet également au site de cibler des groupes spécifiques et de répondre à leurs besoins. A cette fin, nous avons créé plusieurs dispositifs, notamment une base de données cinématographiques indépendante, des rubriques telles que Artists Spotlights (Pleins feux sur…), Select Programming Series, ainsi que des blogs, entre autres. Chaque rubrique offre une manière dynamique de découvrir un contenu en harmonie avec les valeurs de la marque Sundance, qui cultive en outre l'interaction conviviale, facilitée par des forums de discussion, un comparateur de prix et des outils sociaux – moyens d'encourager la réflexion, le partage des points de vue et, à terme, le dialogue au sein du domaine numérique.

Le troisième défi de notre stratégie en trois parties pour positionner la marque Sundance Channel dans le domaine numérique consistait à chercher des voies détournées, mais totalement intuitives, pour permettre au site de se révéler à l'utilisateur. Nous voulions un site riche en contenus, avec ni trop, ni trop peu de possibilités – et nous voulions que les utilisateurs puissent découvrir les

brand – like Sundance Channel – from a living, dynamic embodiment of brand values into a living, dynamic community of users. The statistics back up this finding: the number of visits to the Sundance Channel site has more than doubled since site launch. The number of unique visitors has gone up more than three-and-a-half times. Perhaps most importantly, the number of returning visitors has also gone up – meaning the amount of loyal members of the Sundance Channel community has risen dramatically. What this means is that the Sundance Channel has extended and increased its presence on the web in a very real and effective way – and has done so without watering down or changing its core brand values – it has done so, rather, in the opposite manner, by leveraging the strength and integrity of its brand values and by encouraging users to share them.

eine inhaltsreiche Website, die weder durch vielfältige Optionen überwältigt noch durch fehlende Auswahlmöglichkeit eingrenzt – und wir wollten, dass die Besucher nach eigenem Gutdünken und Vorlieben Inhalte entdecken können, anstatt wenig ansprechenden linearen Vorgaben folgen zu müssen. Entdecken macht Spaß, wenn die Auswahlmöglichkeiten klar sind – hier wird deutlich, dass stark verzweigte hierarchische Strukturen für Entdeckungen nicht immer am besten geeignet sind. Wird eine Website als Anwendung gestaltet, können Benutzer neue Inhalte schnell erschließen, weil sachbezogene Auswahlmöglichkeiten und eine intuitive Navigation zur Verfügung stehen.

Das Ergebnis unserer Arbeit mit Sundance Channel war ein neuer Bezugsrahmen zur Beurteilung dessen, wie sich eine Marke auf der digitalen Bühne behauptet. Wir entdeckten, dass eine Website als *Anwendung* eine engagierte Usercommunity, die ihre Werte mit der Marke teilt, auf eindringliche, fesselnde Berichte und Schilderungen fokussieren kann und sollte. Es handelt sich um eine symbiotische Beziehung, die sich aus der Umsetzung einer Marke wie Sundance Channel von einer lebendigen, dynamischen Verkörperung der Markenwerte zu einer lebendigen, dynamischen Gemeinschaft von Nutzern entwickelt. Die Statistiken belegen diese Erkenntnis: Die Zahl der Besuche auf der Sundance-Channel-Website hat sich seit der Einführung der Site mehr als verdoppelt, die der Einmal-Besucher ist um das 3,5-fache gestiegen. Vielleicht am wichtigsten ist jedoch, dass sich die Zahl der Besucher, die wiederholt auf die Website zugreifen, ebenfalls erhöht hat – das heißt, dass die Zahl der treuen Mitglieder der Sundance-Channel-Community drastisch gestiegen ist. Somit hat Sundance Channel seine Internetpräsenz auf sehr reale, effektive Weise ausgeweitet und erhöht – ohne seine wichtigsten Markenwerte abzuschwächen oder zu verändern. Stattdessen wurde genau das Gegenteil erreicht, indem die Stärken und die Integrität der Markenwerte wirksam eingesetzt und die Benutzer ermutigt wurden, sie mit dem Sender zu teilen.

contenus au gré de leurs intérêts et de leurs goûts, non pas à l'issue d'une sélection linéaire de choix sans attrait. Le processus de découverte devenait agréable grâce à la clarté des choix – ce qui prouve que les structures très hiérarchisées ne sont pas toujours le meilleur vecteur pour la découverte. Vu comme une application, le site Web permettait aux utilisateurs de découvrir rapidement un nouveau contenu en leur donnant la possibilité de choisir en connaissance de cause et de naviguer intuitivement.

En définitive, nous avons élaboré pour Sundance Channel un nouveau cadre permettant d'évaluer le fonctionnement d'une marque sur la scène numérique. Nous avons découvert que, vu comme une application, le site Web peut et doit focaliser une communauté dédiée d'utilisateurs sur des contenus attrayants et forts qui partagent avec la marque des valeurs communes. Il s'agit d'une relation symbiotique qui évolue au fil de la traduction d'une marque – comme Sundance Channel – de l'incarnation vivante et dynamique des valeurs de cette marque à la constitution d'une communauté d'utilisateurs vivante et dynamique. Les statistiques en font foi : sur le site de Sundance Channel, le nombre de visites a plus que doublé depuis le lancement. Le nombre de visiteurs individuels s'y est multiplié par trois et demi. Plus important encore, peut-être, le nombre de visiteurs qui récidivent a également augmenté – d'où une hausse spectaculaire du nombre de membres assidus au sein de la communauté de Sundance Channel. Cela signifie que Sundance Channel a vraiment élargi et renforcé sa présence sur la toile – et elle l'a fait sans s'édulcorer ni modifier les valeurs-clés de son image de marque. Elle y est parvenue, tout au contraire, en s'appuyant sur la force et la cohérence de ses valeurs de marque et en encourageant ses utilisateurs à les partager.

Bottom: *Opening page for a movie. ///*
Unten: *Startseite eines Films. ///* En bas :
Page de démarrage pour un film.

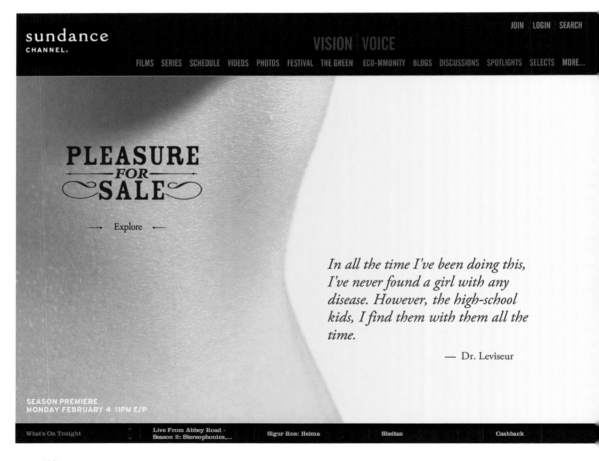

sundance
CHANNEL.

for a change.

Left: *Community pages at the Sundance Movie Channel.* /// Links: *Community-Seiten des Sundance Movie Channels.* /// A gauche : *Pages d'accueil de la chaîne Sundance Movie Channel.*

Biography
Dean Di Simone (Tender)

www.tendercreative.com   Location: New York   Position: Founder/
Year founded: 2005   Creative Director

Tender is focused on helping clients communicate through graphic design, branding, environmental design, and interactivity. Tender specialises in the conception, design, and development of experience-driven projects in various media. Recent awards and publications include the Communication Arts Design Annual, the AIGA Design Annual, Metropolis Magazine, *and SPA-de Magazine. Dean Di Simone has been the creative director and designer on a series of award-winning branding, print, broadcast, and interactive projects. He continues to engage academia through teaching and has taught at Yale University, Columbia University, and at the University of Pennsylvania where he is currently an Adjunct Assistant Professor in Architecture.*

Der Schwerpunkt der Arbeit von Tender besteht darin, Kunden dabei zu unterstützen, mittels Grafik-, Marken- und Umweltdesign sowie interaktiv zu kommunizieren. Tender spezialiert sich auf die Konzeption, das Design und die Entwicklung von Projekten, die auf Benutzererfahrung basieren und in verschiedenen Medien einsetzbar sind. Zu den neuesten Auszeichnungen und Veröffentlichungen gehören der Communication Arts Design Annual, der AIGA Design Annual, das Metropolis Magazine *und das* SPA-de Magazine. *Dean Di Simone ist Creative Director und Designer einer Reihe preisgekrönter Projekte im Bereich Markenidentität, Print, Rundfunk, Fernsehen*

und Online. Er ist nach wie vor als Dozent an Universitäten tätig und lehrte an der Yale University, an der Columbia University sowie an der University of Pennsylvania, wo er zurzeit als Lehrbeauftragter für die Fachrichtung Architektur arbeitet.

Le cabinet Tender aspire à aider ses clients à communiquer, par le biais de l'infographie, de la stratégie de marque, du design environnemental et de l'interactivité. Il est spécialisé dans la conception, le design et le développement de projets empiriques sur divers supports. Parmi les prix et publications les plus récentes, nous citerons les suivants : Communication Arts Design Annual, AIGA Design Annual, Metropolis Magazine, SPA-de Magazine. *Dean Di Simone a été le directeur de la création et le designer de plusieurs projets interactifs, audiovisuels, éditoriaux et de valorisation de marque qui ont été primés. Il continue de faire école en enseignant, en particulier aux universités de Yale, de Columbia et de Pennsylvanie, où il est actuellement professeur assistant en architecture.*

VUELING: LOW COST, HIGH STYLE IN THE SKIES ABOVE BARCELONA

At 7:15 a.m. on July 1, 2004, a plane bound for Paris took off from Barcelona. This was the first flight of Vueling Airlines, a brand-new Spanish carrier whose entire identity – from nose to tail, from staff-customer interactions to online interfaces – was designed by Saffron Brand Consultants. Within a year of this maiden flight, Vueling had become the third largest online retailer in Spain and had broken nearly every category norm in the low-cost airline sector, successfully distinguishing itself through service and style – the two paramount parameters of a service brand.

The first New Generation airline in Europe

Barcelona entrepreneurs Carlos Muñoz and Lázaro Ros had a plan for an airline. In their words: "We wanted to create an airline where paying less wouldn't equate to lowered standards for service, comfort, and style, and when it makes promises of everyday low prices for tickets, these prices actually exist." Pitted against the likes of

Am 1. Juli 2004 hob um 7:15 Uhr in Barcelona ein Flugzeug mit dem Ziel Paris ab. Es handelte sich um den ersten Flug der Vueling Airlines, einer brandneuen spanischen Fluglinie, deren gesamte Identität – von der Nase bis zum Heck, von den Gesprächen zwischen Mitarbeitern und Kunden bis hin zum Online-Interface – von Saffron Brand Consultants geschaffen wurde. Innerhalb eines Jahres nach diesem Jungfernflug entwickelte sich Vueling zur drittgrößten Online-Fluglinie in Spanien und brach nahezu alle Kategoriestandards in der Billigflugbranche, indem sie sich von anderen Anbietern durch Service und Stil abgrenzte – die beiden wichtigsten Parameter einer Dienstleistungsmarke.

Die erste Fluglinie der neuen Generation in Europa

Die in Barcelona ansässigen Unternehmer Carlos Muñoz und Lázaro Ros hatten die Idee für eine neue Fluglinie: „Wir wollten eine Fluglinie ins Leben rufen, bei der niedrige Preise nicht zu niedrigen Standards bei Service, Komfort und Stil führen und

7 h15, 1er juillet 2004, un avion à destination de Paris décolle de Barcelone. Il s'agit du premier vol de Vueling Airlines, une toute nouvelle compagnie espagnole dont l'image de marque – de A à Z, de la communication équipe/clientèle aux interfaces on-line – est l'œuvre de Saffron Brand Consultants. Dans l'année suivant ce vol inaugural, Vueling deviendra le troisième détaillant on-line d'Espagne et transgressera pratiquement toutes les règles catégorielles du secteur des compagnies aériennes low-cost, réussissant à se hisser aux premières places grâce à son service et son style – les deux paramètres suprêmes d'une marque de services.

La première compagnie aérienne de la nouvelle génération en Europe

Les entrepreneurs barcelonais Carlos Muñoz et Lázaro Ros avaient un plan pour une compagnie aérienne. Pour reprendre leurs propres paroles : « Nous voulions créer une compagnie aérienne où payer moins ne signifierait pas d'avoir à rabaisser les niveaux de service, de confort et de style ;

Previous spread: *Boarding card featuring the corporate identity. ///* **Vorhergehende Seite:** *Bordkarte mit der Corporate Identity. ///* **Double page précédente** *: Carte d'embarquement utilisant l'identité visuelle de l'entreprise.*

Iberia, British Airways, and Lufthansa as well as low-cost carriers Ryanair and easyJet, it was a grand ambition – to be "the first new generation airline in Europe" as well as the first Spanish airline based in fashionable and booming Barcelona – and it needed an identity, a name, a shape. And it needed as well to be noticeable, and bold.

Spanglish for "wow"

In Spain, Spanglish is hip; people say "footing", for instance, to mean running, or "siesting" to mean napping. In Spanish, *vuela* means to fly. Ergo, "Vueling". The novel name was further leveraged in its tone of voice by having Vueling break the deeply rooted and longstanding convention of companies using the formal Spanish *usted* form of address. All brand communications talk informally to you, right down to the on-board signage, which Airbus was asked to rewrite especially for Vueling's planes. Subsequent research has confirmed that one of the principal communications assets of Vueling is this distinctive language and vocal

bei der das Versprechen für täglich günstige Flugtickets tatsächlich auch eingehalten wird." Im Kampf gegen Fluggesellschaften wie Iberia, British Airways und Lufthansa sowie gegen Billigfluglinien wie Ryanair und easyJet war es das große Ziel, „die erste Fluglinie der neuen Generation in Europa" sowie die erste spanische Fluglinie mit Sitz im angesagten und boomenden Barcelona zu sein – und dazu brauchte man eine Identität, einen Namen und eine Gestalt. Darüber hinaus sollte die Marke auffällig und frech sein.

Spanglish für „Wow"

In Spanien ist *Spanglish* schick. Die Leute sagen zum Beispiel „footing", wenn sie Laufen meinen, oder „siesting" für ein Nickerchen am Mittag. *Vuela* bedeutet im Spanischen *fliegen*. Deshalb „Vueling". Der neue Name bricht weitere tief verwurzelte Konventionen der spanischen Unternehmenskommunikation und verzichtet auf die formelle Sie-Form einer Anrede. Die Marke kommuniziert per Du bis hin zur Beschilderung an Bord, die Airbus speziell

une compagnie, aussi, qui tiendrait ses promesses en mettant réellement à disposition, tous les jours, les tickets bon marché qu'elle se serait engagée à fournir. » Avec des concurrents tels qu'Iberia, British Airways et Lufthansa, mais aussi les transporteurs aériens low-cost Ryanair et easyJet, le projet était très ambitieux – devenir « la première compagnie aérienne de la nouvelle génération en Europe » et la première compagnie low-cost espagnole basée à Barcelone, ville en vogue et en pleine expansion – ; il lui fallait donc une image, un nom, une allure. Et il lui fallait aussi une visibilité et du caractère.

Le spanglish comme « effet surprise »

En Espagne, le spanglish est la mode ; on fait du « footing », par exemple, quand on court, ou du « siesting » quand on s'accorde une petite sieste. En espagnol, *vuela* signifie voler. D'où « Vueling ». Outre ce nom novateur, le ton employé par la compagnie pour s'adresser à son public a lui aussi eu un effet tremplin : Vueling a été la première à abandonner le

Left: *Application of the identity on airport personnel clothing, access stairs to the aircraft, and aircraft signage.* /// **Links:** *Umsetzung der Corporate Identity auf der Dienstkleidung des Flughafenpersonals, an der Einstiegstreppe zum Flugzeug und bei der Flugzeugbeschriftung.* /// **A gauche :** *Application de l'identité visuelle sur les vêtements du personnel de l'aéroport, les passerelles d'accès aux avions, et la signalisation des appareils.*

Right: *Aircraft signage design.* /// **Rechts:** *Entwurf der Flugzeugbeschriftung.* /// **A droite :** *Design signalétique des appareils.*

register. Some people like it, some don't, but everyone agrees it has a significant "wow" factor. It has been mimicked too, by other Spanish companies, similarly seeking a relaxed and unconventional image.

Design and instillation

"We looked at the colour spectrum of the industry at the time," recalls Saffron designer Virginia Sardón. "We found a niche in these colours, which also felt very Mediterranean, helping us convey the flavour of an airline from Barcelona." As Gabor Schreier, Saffron design director, puts it: "The visual elements of course gave Vueling a distinctive and appropriate look. But above everything, Vueling is about a different approach to air travel, so our creative input into every aspect of the business mattered enormously. We designed – in the biggest sense of the word design – as many brand 'touchpoints' as we could get our hands on."

Saffron's fingerprints are on everything, from the business cards to the in-flight

für die Flugzeuge von Vueling umgeschrieben hat. Nachfolgende Untersuchungen haben bestätigt, dass eine der hauptsächlichen Kommunikationswerte von Vueling in dieser charakteristischen Sprache und Tonlage liegt. Einige Leute mögen sie, andere nicht, doch alle sind sich darüber einig, dass sie einen erheblichen „Wow-Faktor" aufweist. Die Sprache wurde zudem von anderen spanischen Unternehmen imitiert, die ebenfalls nach einem ähnlichen zwanglosen und unkonventionellen Image suchten.

Design und Umsetzung

„Wir schauten uns das derzeitige Farbspektrum der Branche an", erinnert sich die Saffron-Designerin Virginia Sardón. „Wir fanden in diesen Farben eine Nische, die zudem ein sehr mediterranes Gefühl vermittelte und uns half, Lust auf eine Fluglinie aus Barcelona zu machen." Gabor Schreier, leitender Designer bei Saffron, drückt es so aus: „Natürlich bekam die Marke Vueling über die visuellen Elemente ihr unverkennbares und passendes Aussehen.

vouvoiement, convention enracinée de très longue date dans le secteur des compagnies aériennes. Elle s'adresse à ses passagers de manière informelle, y compris par le biais de la signalisation de bord, qu'Airbus a d'ailleurs été prié de modifier spécialement pour les appareils de Vueling. Des études sont venues confirmer que l'un de ses premiers atouts de communication est effectivement ce registre verbal et discursif différent. Certains apprécient, d'autres non, mais tout le monde s'accorde sur un point : ça surprend. D'autres compagnies aériennes espagnoles, en quête elles aussi d'une image décontractée et originale, l'ont d'ailleurs imitée depuis.

Design et formation

« Examinant la palette de couleurs en vigueur dans le secteur à l'époque », rappelle Virginia Sardón, designer chez Saffron, « nous avons constaté qu'il y avait une niche dans ces tons-là, que nous avons trouvé très méditerranéens et propres à transmettre le parfum d'une compagnie aérienne basée à Barcelone. » Comme le dit

Above: *Application of the identity on the aircraft seats and detail of personnel clothing with badge holder band.* /// **Oben:** *Umsetzung der Corporate Identity auf den Flugzeugsitzen und Detail der Dienstkleidung mit Ausweisband.* /// **Ci-dessus** : *Application de l'identité visuelle sur les sièges des appareils et détail des vêtements du personnel avec bande porte-badge.*

music. All brand expressions reflect *el espíritu Vueling* – the Vueling way – of being contemporary, cosmopolitan, straightforward and stylish. If you've ever flown on Iberia or Spanair, you'll grasp the "stand-out" this gives a Spanish airline.

From the beginning, Saffron advised Vueling's management, who understood and agreed that as a service brand the "human factor" was vital to the brand's cohesion and success. Therefore the identity work informed the airline's HR policies, and was also instilled through training sessions. "We taught them how to live and breathe and speak and write 'Vueling,'" explains consultant Juan Pablo Ramírez. "We trained the trainers: the head of the call centre, the head of PR, head of operations, and other brand guardians."

The brand's essence has been absorbed with gusto by Vueling's staff, even the pilots. Wrote one passenger in a review on airlinequality.com: "Crews were extremely professional and friendly, not your usual

Doch vor allem geht es bei Vueling um einen anderen Ansatz für Flugreisen. Daher war unser kreativer Input für jeden Aspekt des Unternehmens von enormer Bedeutung. Wir erstellten das Design – im umfassendsten Sinn des Wortes Design – für alle Marken-Berührungspunkte, die wir uns vorstellen konnten."

Die Handschrift von Saffron ist überall zu erkennen: von den Visitenkarten bis hin zur Musik. Alle Erscheinungsformen der Marke spiegeln *el espíritu Vueling* („den Vuelinggedanken"), und das bedeutet, zeitgemäß, kosmopolitisch, schnörkellos und stilvoll zu sein. Wer jemals mit Iberia oder Spanair geflogen ist, erkennt das „Herausragende", das diese Aspekte einer spanischen Fluglinie verleihen.

Von Anfang an beriet Saffron die Management-Ebene von Vueling. Dort hatte man verstanden und den Ansatz verinnerlicht, dass der „menschliche Faktor" für die Bindung und den Erfolg einer Dienstleistungsmarke entscheidend ist. Deshalb wurden die Arbeiten zur Markenidentität

Gabor Schreier, directeur de la création de Saffron : « Bien sûr, les éléments visuels donnent à Vueling une image différente et ad hoc ; mais, avant toute chose, Vueling est une manière différente de voler, aussi les idées créatives concernant tous les aspects de l'entreprise ont-elles énormément compté. En terme d'image, nous avons conçu – au sens propre du mot – autant de ‹ points de communication › que nous pouvions en manipuler. »

Saffron a laissé ses empreintes digitales un peu partout, des cartes de visite à la musique d'ambiance à bord des avions. Toutes les expressions de la marque reflètent *el espíritu Vueling* – l'esprit Vueling –, sa volonté d'être une compagnie contemporaine, cosmopolite, sans façon et élégante. Si vous avez jamais volé sur Iberia ou Spanair, vous apprécierez sans doute le « contraste ».

Saffron a tout de suite annoncé la couleur à la direction de Vueling, qui a compris et admis que, pour une entreprise de services, le « facteur humain » était vital à la cohésion

experience flying between Spain and France."

Notably, the in-flight magazine, just called 'Ling', is on-brand in terms of values, style and attitude, but these are manifested through the editorial content rather than the graphic design. Indeed, the publication's look and feel are completely different from the airline's. This reflects Saffron's view that consistency isn't the same thing as uniformity. It also adds to the appeal of the magazine by taking it beyond the realm of the usual self-published seatback rag.

Brand review

Four years after originating the identity, Saffron was called back for an extensive brand review, flying Vueling's domestic and international routes, taking notes and photographs of the journeys. Basic findings were that the farther from Barcelona one went, the weaker the brand's potency in expression, particularly when it came to personnel. Altogether, the review gave managers fresh insights they couldn't get any other way. Says Ramírez, who led the review: "This was the beauty of this exercise. It provided a snapshot of the complete business, not as industry statistics, like utilisation rates, but from the all-important view of the customer experience."

Results

As a brand identity, Vueling has been up for a number of awards, including the UK Design Effectiveness Awards (nominated) and Spanish Laus (won). As an airline, Vueling has earned countless accolades, from even as far away as America where in 2007 Forbes magazine's Forbestraveler.com pegged it as one of the 10 up-and-coming airlines, and Harvard Business School published a case study about Muñoz and the challenges he overcame in getting Vueling off the ground.

Significantly, whereas traditional low-cost airlines have a strong negative aspect to their image (having to do with cancellations without reimbursements, etc.), Vueling has managed to become seen as being higher quality and having more empathy.

der Personalabteilung der Fluglinie vorgestellt und auch während der Schulungseinheiten intensiv vermittelt. „Wir lehrten sie, ‚Vueling' zu leben, zu atmen, zu sprechen und zu schreiben", erklärt der Berater Juan Pablo Ramírez. „Das war echtes ‚Train the trainer': Wir bildeten die Vorgesetzten des Callcenters, der PR-Abteilung, der Arbeitsorganisation und andere Multiplikatoren der Marke aus."

Das Wesen der Marke wurde von den Vueling-Mitarbeitern mit viel Enthusiasmus aufgenommen, sogar von den Piloten. Ein Passagier schrieb in einer Bewertung bei airlinequality.com: „Die Besatzung war äußerst professionell und freundlich, was auf Flügen zwischen Spanien und Frankreich nicht zu unseren üblichen Erfahrungen gehört."

Besonders das Flugmagazin, das einfach ‚Ling' heißt, vertritt die Marke hinsichtlich der Werte, Stil und Gesinnung. Jedoch äußern sich diese eher durch den redaktionellen Inhalt als durch das Grafikdesign. In der Tat unterscheidet sich die Publikation in puncto Aussehen und Gefühl völlig von der Fluglinie. Dies spiegelt die Anschauung von Saffron wider, dass Kontinuität nicht mit Eintönigkeit gleichzusetzen ist, und erhöht die Anziehungskraft des Magazins über den üblichen Bereich der Sitzrückenlehnen hinaus.

Die Bewertung der Marke

Vier Jahre nach Entwicklung der Markenidentität wurde Saffron erneut beauftragt, eine umfangreiche Überprüfung der Marke durchzuführen. Dafür sollten Mitarbeiter von Saffron auf nationalen und internationalen Flügen mitfliegen und auf diesen Reisen Notizen und Fotos erstellen. Eines der grundlegenden Ergebnisse dabei war, dass die Ausdruckskraft der Marke umso schwächer wurde, je weiter man sich von Barcelona entfernte – insbesonders in Hinblick auf das Personal. Im Ganzen brachten die Bewertungen den Managern der Fluglinie neue Erkenntnisse, die sie sonst nicht erhalten hätten. Ramírez, der die Überprüfung leitete, sagt: „Das war das Schöne an dieser Aufgabe. Sie lieferte eine Momentaufnahme des gesamten

et à la réussite de l'image de marque. Aussi le travail sur l'image transparaît-il dans les politiques de ressources humaines de la compagnie, et a-t-il été inculqué au personnel par le biais de sessions de formation. « Nous leur avons appris à vivre et respirer ‹ Vueling ›, à parler et écrire ‹Vueling › », explique le consultant Juan Pablo Ramírez. « Nous avons formé les formateurs : la direction du centre d'appel, celle des relations publiques, la direction des opérations et autres garants de l'image de marque. »

Le personnel de Vueling, pilotes compris, a volontiers intégré l'essence de la marque. Sur airlinequality.com, on trouve cette évaluation d'un passager : « Les équipages sont extrêmement professionnels et aimables, chose peu commune sur les vols Espagne/ France si j'en crois mon expérience. »

A remarquer que la revue de bord, sobrement intitulée « Ling », est conforme à l'image de marque en termes de critères, de style et de posture, mais qu'elle le manifeste davantage au travers de sa ligne éditoriale que de sa conception graphique. La physionomie de la publication, ainsi que la sensation qu'il en émane, diffèrent complètement de celles de la compagnie. Cette apparence, qui traduit une conviction de Saffron, pour qui cohérence n'équivaut pas à uniformité, confère un attrait supplémentaire à la revue en la situant au-dessus du lot des feuilles de chou autopubliées qu'on trouve glissées dans les dossiers de fauteuil d'avion.

Révision de l'image de marque

Quatre ans après avoir créé cette image, Saffron a été invité à en faire une évaluation exhaustive, en volant sur les lignes nationales et internationales de Vueling, et en prenant des notes et des photos des voyages effectués. Il en est ressorti principalement ceci : plus on s'éloigne de Barcelone, plus la puissance d'expression de la marque s'amoindrit, en particulier en ce qui à trait au personnel. Dans son ensemble, l'évaluation a permis aux dirigeants de porter sur la situation un regard neuf qu'ils n'auraient pu avoir sans cela. Selon M. Ramírez, qui a dirigé cette évaluation : « L'intérêt de cet exercice tient

Above: *Catering package design and ticketing applications of the identity.* ///
Oben: *Entwurf der Verpackung für die Bordverpflegung und Umsetzung der Corporate Identity auf dem Flugticket.* ///
Ci-dessus : *Sacs repas et billets conformes à l'identité visuelle.*

Audiences who know and like Vueling regard it as the most *simpática* of all airlines. They describe it in words like fresh, enjoyable, young, simple, modern, clear, adventurous, cool and cosmopolitan.

This just in:

As of July 2008, Vueling, and an even newer low-cost Spanish airline called Clickair, are on the verge of a merger. All accounts indicate that the Clickair brand will yield abjectly to the Vueling identity. What stronger demonstration could there be of the success of the Vueling brand and the value of intangible assets in the airline sector? As Saffron's Ramírez puts it, "Clickair's brand is functional, utilitarian, colourless. And with brands, personality wins the day. Because personality affects people."

Unternehmens – nicht wie Branchen-statistiken oder Nutzungsstudien, sondern aus dem relevantesten Blickwinkel: dem der Kundenerfahrung."

Ergebnisse

Als Markenidentität wurde Vueling bei einer Reihe von Auszeichnungen nominiert, darunter die UK Design Effectiveness Awards (Nominierung) und der Spanish Laus (Preisträger). Als Fluglinie hat Vueling zahllose Auszeichnungen erhalten, sogar im weit entfernten Amerika, wo 2007 das Forum Forbestraveler.com des Forbes Magazine Vueling als eine der 10 vielver-sprechendsten Fluglinien auszeichnete. Dort veröffentlichte die Harvard Business School auch eine Fallstudie über Muñoz und über die Herausforderungen, denen er sich stellen musste, um Vueling abheben zu lassen.

Während das Image traditioneller Billig-flieger einen stark negativen Aspekt aufweist (was mit Stornierungen ohne Kostener-stattungen etc. zu tun hat), ist es Vueling

à ceci qu'il offre un instantané de l'entreprise tout entière, non pas des statistiques sectorielles, comme par exemple le taux d'utilisation, mais une vision essentielle de l'expérience de la clientèle. »

Résultats

Par son image de marque, Vueling a brigué un certain nombre de prix, dont les UK Design Effectiveness Awards (nominée) et les prix Laus (lauréate). En qualité de compagnie aérienne, elle a mérité d'innom-brables gages d'estime, parfois venus d'aussi loin que l'Amérique, où, en 2007, le magazine du groupe Forbes, Forbestraveler.com, l'a classée parmi les 10 compagnies aériennes les plus promet-teuses, et la Harvard Business School a publié une étude de cas sur Carlos Muñoz et les défis qu'il a dû relever pour faire décoller Vueling.

A noter qu'alors que les compagnies low-cost classiques ont une image franchement négative (à mettre au compte des annula-tions sans remboursement, etc.), Vueling

Right: *Identity applied to onboard safety instructions.* /// **Rechts:** *Die Umsetzung der Corporate Identity auf den Sicherheitsan-weisungen an Bord.* /// **A droite** : *Identité visuelle appliquée aux instructions de sécurité à bord de l'appareil.*

bezeichnenderweise gelungen, sein Image über höhere Qualität und mehr Einfühlungsvermögen aufzubauen. Zielgruppen, die Vueling kennen und mögen, betrachten diese Fluglinie als diejenige, die am meisten *simpática* ist. Sie beschreiben Vueling mit Worten wie frisch, angenehm, jung, einfach, modern, klar, abenteuerlich, cool und kosmopolitisch.

Gerade hereingekommen

Ab Juli 2008 stehen Vueling und eine sogar noch neuere spanische Billigfluglinie namens Clickair kurz vor einer Firmenfusion. Alle Berichte deuten darauf hin, dass sich die Marke Clickair der Identität von Vueling unterwirft. Welch größeren Beweis könnte es für den Erfolg der Marke Vueling und ihrer immateriellen Werte in der Flugbranche geben? Oder, um es mit den Worten von Juan Pablo Ramírez auszudrücken: „Die Marke Clickair ist funktional, utilitaristisch und farblos. Und bei Marken kann man nur mit Persönlichkeit gewinnen. Denn es ist die Persönlichkeit, die auf Menschen wirkt."

a trouvé le moyen d'être perçue comme plus aimable et de meilleure qualité. Les publics qui connaissent et aiment Vueling la tiennent pour la plus *simpática* de toutes les compagnies aériennes. Ils emploient pour la décrire des adjectifs tels que : nouvelle, agréable, jeune, simple, moderne, claire, audacieuse, décontractée et cosmopolite.

Dernière heure :

Depuis juillet 2008, Vueling et Clickair, une compagnie espagnole encore plus récente, sont en pourparlers de fusion. Tout indique que la marque Clickair va se couler sans résistance dans le moule de l'image Vueling. Quelle démonstration plus éclatante pourrait-il y avoir de la réussite de la marque Vueling et de la valeur des actifs incorporels dans le secteur des transports aériens ? Comme le conclut M. Ramírez de chez Saffron : « La marque Clickair est fonctionnelle, utilitaire et banale. Et en matière de marques, la personnalité a le vent en poupe. Parce que la personnalité touche les gens. »

Bottom: *The "Ling" in-flight magazine designed and produced by le cool Publishing from a brief by Saffron. ///* **Unten:** *Das Bordmagazin „Ling", entworfen und produziert von Le Cool Publishing im Auftrag von Saffron. ///* **En bas :** *« Ling », le magazine de bord conçu et produit par Le Cool Publishing sur un brief de Saffron.*

Left: *Signage at Madrid's Barajas Terminal 4, and the airline's homepage (brand identity by Saffron, cloud motif by ad agency S.C.P.F.) ///*
Links: *Beschilderung in Terminal 4 am Madrider Flughafen Barajas und die Homepage der Airline (Markenidentität von Saffron, das Wolkenmotiv von der Werbeagentur S.C.P.F.) /// A gauche : Signalisation dans l'aérogare 4 de l'aéroport de Madrid Barajas, et page d'accueil de la compagnie aérienne (identité visuelle par Saffron, motif en forme de nuages par l'agence de publicité S.C.P.F.).*

vueling

Biography
Jacob Benbunan (Saffron Brand Consultants)

http://saffron-consultants.com   Location: Madrid
Year founded: 2001

Position: Principal/CEO

Jacob Benbunan is the co-founder and CEO of Saffron. He has been advising companies on branding issues for 20 years. Saffron operates on a global basis out of four locations, London, Madrid, Mumbai, and New York. Its clients include AkzoNobel, Baker & McKenzie, Bajaj Auto, Lloyd's of London, Nationwide, Swiss Re, and Tata, among many others. Jacob was previously managing director of Wolff Olins, Madrid, in charge of Spain, Latin America, and France. He left Wolff Olins in 2000 to become CEO of OnoLab, the Internet and broadband arm of cable operator Ono. In 2001 he left OnoLab to start Saffron. Jacob holds a Masters in Industrial Management and a BSc in Industrial Engineering, cum laude, both from Boston University.

Jacob Benbunan ist Mitbegründer und CEO von Saffron. Seit 20 Jahren berät er Unternehmen in allen Fragen zur Markenidentität. Saffron ist von vier Niederlassungen in London, Madrid, Mumbai und New York aus weltweit tätig. Zu den Kunden des Beratungsunternehmens zählen u.a. AkzoNobel, Baker & McKenzie, Bajaj Auto, Lloyd's of London, Nationwide, Swiss Re und Tata. Jacobo arbeitete zunächst als Geschäftsführer für Wolff Olins (Madrid) und war dort für Spanien, Lateinamerika und Frankreich zuständig. Im Jahr 2000 verließ er Wolff Olins, um die Geschäftsführung von OnoLab zu übernehmen, dem Internet- und Breitbandzweig des Kabel-

betreibers Ono. 2001 stieg er bei OnoLab aus, um das Beratungsunternehmen Saffron zu gründen. Jacob Benbunan erwarb einen Mastertitel in Betriebswirtschaftslehre und einen Bachelor of Science cum laude in Wirtschaftsingenieurwesen, beide an der Boston University.

Jacob Benbunan est co-fondateur et PDG de Saffron. Il conseille les sociétés en matière d'image de marque depuis une vingtaine d'années. Saffron intervient dans le monde entier à partir de quatre sièges : Londres, Madrid, Mumbai (anciennement Bombay) et New York. Parmi ses nombreux clients, on trouve AkzoNobel, Baker & McKenzie, Bajaj Auto, Lloyd's of London, Nationwide, Swiss Re, et Tata. Jacob Benbunan a été auparavant directeur de Wolff Olins, à Madrid, où il était chargé de l'Espagne, de l'Amérique Latine et de la France. Il a quitté Wolff Olins en 2000 pour devenir PDG de OnoLab, la branche Internet et haut débit du câblo-opérateur Ono. En 2001, il a quitté OnoLab pour monter Saffron. Il est titulaire d'un master en gestion industrielle et d'un BSc (Bachelor of Science) en ingénierie industrielle, cum laude, tout deux délivrés par l'Université de Boston.

REJUVENATING WRANGLER WITH COMMUNICATIVE DESIGN AND DESIGNED COMMUNICATIONS

For a documentary entitled "Brand Iconics" about our philosophy of merging design with communications, we interviewed Larry Light, the Chief Marketing Officer of McDonald's, responsible for the global turnaround of the brand. He angrily recalled a television campaign McDonald's spent tens of millions on, trying to re-connect with young adults looking for a late night snack. The McMarketers and their famous agency had been running award-winning spots trying to convince the nightflies. Nothing happened. When Larry made his first store checks he realised why. To enter the McDonald's, the twenty-somethings had first to pass the McKindergarten in the front yard, and when they then came in the first thing they saw was a life-size Ronald McDonald, whilst family-friendly muzak was playing in the background. Larry simply replaced the Kindergartens with mobile toys that could disappear at night and changed the music tapes after dinner. The night people came back. How come the marketing and advertising professionals completely overlooked what was turning the customer

Für einen Dokumentarfilm mit dem Titel „Brand Iconics" über unsere Philosophie, Design und Kommunikation miteinander zu vereinigen, führten wir ein Interview mit Larry Light, dem Marketingleiter von McDonald's, der für die globale Neustrukturierung der Marke verantwortlich ist. Ungehalten erinnerte er sich an eine Fernsehkampagne, für die McDonald's eine Summe in zweistelliger Millionenhöhe ausgegeben hatte und die darauf abzielte, junge Erwachsene wieder für einen nächtlichen Imbiss bei McDonald's zu begeistern. Die Marketingexperten von McDonald's und ihre berühmte Agentur schalteten preisgekrönte Werbespots, um die Nachtschwärmer zu begeistern – es tat sich nichts. Als Larry die ersten Restaurants überprüfte, erkannte er den Grund: Um ein McDonald's-Restaurant zu betreten, mussten die Twens zunächst am McKindergarten vorbei, der häufig im vorderen Bereich der Restaurants eingerichtet ist. Wenn sie hereinkamen, sahen sie als Allererstes eine lebensgroße Ronald-McDonald-Figur, während aus den Lautsprechern familienfreundliche

Pour un documentaire intitulé « Images de marque », à propos de notre philosophie de fusion entre design et communication, nous avons interviewé Larry Light, responsable du marketing de McDonald's et chargé du redressement général de la marque. Il bouillait encore au souvenir d'une campagne télévisuelle où McDonald avait dépensé des dizaines de millions de dollars pour tenter de regagner les faveurs des jeunes noctambules en quête d'un en-cas tardif. Les « McMarketers » et leur célèbre agence avaient concocté des spots dignes de grands prix pour essayer de convaincre les couche-tard. Sans succès aucun. En faisant ses premières enquêtes sur les points de vente, Larry comprit pourquoi. Pour pénétrer dans un McDonald les plus de vingt ans devaient tout d'abord traverser le McKindergarten (espace garderie qui se trouve en façade, puis, une fois à l'intérieur, ils se retrouvaient nez à nez avec un Ronald McDonald grandeur nature, sur fond de musique d'ambiance familiale sympa-sympa. Larry se limita à remplacer les Kindergartens par des jouets mobiles qu'on pouvait escamoter en soirée, ainsi

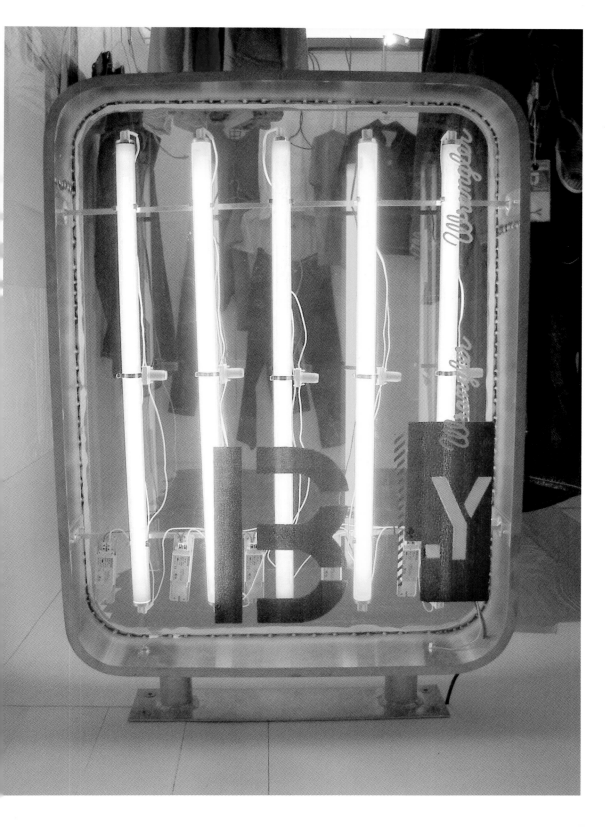

off about their core offer? "If the only tool you have is a hammer, you tend to see every problem as a nail."

Enter Wrangler

Wrangler was much in the same situation when we first met. The number two blue-jean brand in the world was downsizing for a while and searching for a new European advertising partner. Although it had been spending millions on cinema and television campaigns annually for the last two decades, it didn't get any return. From a design point of view, the advertising lacked its own look and feel, the only brand cue being a tiny logo in the corner. Young adults acknowledged the brand's authentic western spirit, but having only seen one classic jean and jacket outfit in the main film, from a product perspective they deemed it "nothing new" and "for cowboys not for us." Recent research shows that 55 % of brand preference among young adults is influenced by the design language of the brand instead of its advertising. In the

Hintergrundmusik dudelte. Larry ersetzte die Kindergarteneinrichtung einfach durch mobiles Spielzeug, das am Abend weggeräumt werden konnte, und änderte die Musik nach dem Abendessen. Die Nachtschwärmer kamen zurück. Warum übersahen die Marketing- und Werbeprofis völlig, was die Kunden am Kernangebot abschreckte? „Falls Ihr einziges Werkzeug ein Hammer ist, neigen Sie dazu, jedes Problem als einen Nagel anzusehen."

Der Fall Wrangler

Bei unserem ersten Treffen war Wrangler in einer ganz ähnlichen Situation. Die weltweit zweitgrößte Jeansmarke litt bereits seit einiger Zeit unter Umsatzrückgängen und war auf der Suche nach einem neuen europäischen Werbepartner. Obwohl Wrangler in den letzten zwei Jahrzehnten jährlich Millionen in Kino- und Fernsehkampagnen investiert hatte, blieben die Erträge aus. Hinsichtlich des Designs fehlte der Werbung ein individuelles Look & Feel – der einzige Hinweis auf die Marke war ein winziges Logo in der Ecke. Junge

qu'à changer les cassettes de musique après l'heure du dîner. Et les noctambules réapparurent. Comment est-il possible que les professionnels du marketing et de la publicité soient passés complètement à côté de ce qui détournait la clientèle de leur offre principale ? « Quand on a un marteau pour seul outil, on finit par voir n'importe quel problème comme un clou. »

Le cas Wrangler

Wrangler se trouvait à peu près dans la même situation quand nous avons fait connaissance. En nette perte de vitesse depuis quelques temps, la deuxième marque de blue-jeans du monde cherchait un nouveau partenaire publicitaire européen. Depuis une vingtaine d'année, elle dépensait pourtant des millions, chaque année, pour ses campagnes à la télé et au cinéma, mais le retour sur investissement restait quasiment nul. Du point de vue conceptuel, sa pub manquait de personnalité et d'atmosphère, le seul signe représentatif de la marque étant en effet un tout petit logo dans un coin de l'écran. Le jeune public reconnais-

Previous spread: *In-store display with the identity for the campaign.* /// **Vorhergehende Seite:** *Display in einem Geschäft mit der visuellen Identität der Kampagne.* /// **Double page précédente :** *Présentoir de magasin utilisant l'identité visuelle de la campagne.*

Left: *Series of applications of the logo and campaign identity on guerrilla advertising and photography.* /// **Links:** *Beispiele für die Umsetzung des Logos und der Kampagnenidentität im Bereich Guerilla-Marketing und -Fotografie.* /// **A gauche :** *Série d'applications du logo et identité visuelle pour la campagne sur le Guerrilla marketing (publicité et photographie).*

Right: *Logo designed for the campaign.* /// **Rechts:** *Logoentwurf für die Kampagne.* /// **A droite :** *Logo conçu pour la campagne.*

lifestyle business especially, advertising is in fact one of the weakest brand cues. Think of Apple. How much of the brand popularity is design-driven, how much is advertising? With a good brand, you don't notice where design stops and advertising starts. We learned that Wild West imagery wasn't relevant to today's urban youth, yet the simple cardboard cards on the jean pocket and the store materials were still oozing "saloon", putting the customer off at the point of purchase. Which, by the way, did not include the credible denim stores at that point. We decided to fix those key consumer touch-points first, and forget about cinema spots for a while. To align the people behind the brand, the first things produced were a brand book and video, visualising our strategy, and carving out our territory in product, design, communications and behaviour. This would express Wrangler's cowboy mindset in a modern and media-neutral way. Thinking about a matching language, we concluded that if a cowboy speaks at all, he says it short and bold. Like the joke: "Chuck Norris doesn't read books. He

Erwachsene erkannten zwar in der Marke die authentische Seele des Westerns, doch weil im Hauptfilm nur eine klassische Montur, bestehend aus Jeans und Jacke, zu sehen war, betrachteten sie das Produkt als „nicht neu" und „für Cowboys, nicht für uns". Neue Untersuchungen zeigen, dass 55 % der Markenpräferenz unter jungen Erwachsenen durch das Markendesign anstatt durch die Werbung beeinflusst wird. Besonders in den Lifestyle-Branchen ist die Werbung tatsächlich einer der schwächsten Markenhinweise. Denken Sie an Apple: Wie viel von der Popularität der Marke wird von Design und wie viel von der Werbung gesteuert? Bei einer guten Marke bemerken Sie nicht, wo das Design endet und wo die Werbung beginnt. Wir fanden heraus, dass das Image des Wilden Westens für die heutige urbane Jugend nicht von Bedeutung ist, und da die einfachen Pappkärtchen auf den Jeanstaschen und Dekomaterialien in den Geschäften immer noch die Aura von „Saloon" verströmten, schreckten die Kunden vom Kauf zurück. Das betraf übrigens nicht die glaubwürdigen Jeansgeschäfte. Wir beschlossen, uns

sait l'esprit authentiquement western de la marque, mais n'ayant vu dans le spot qu'un modèle classique de jean et de veste, il en concluait qu'il n'y avait là « rien de neuf » et que le produit n'était pas pour lui mais « pour cow-boys uniquement ». De récentes recherches ont montré que, chez les jeunes, 55 % des préférences en matière de marque sont influencées par le langage conceptuel de l'enseigne, et non par la publicité. Dans le secteur de l'art de vivre, la publicité est en fait l'un des plus faibles repères de marque. Voyez Apple par exemple. Dans sa popularité, quelle part faut-il attribuer au design et quelle part à la publicité ? Quand une image de marque est bonne, difficile de dire où finit le design et où commence la pub. Nous le savions, l'imagerie du Far Ouest n'est plus populaire aujourd'hui parmi la jeune clientèle urbaine ; du reste, l'étiquette cartonnée cousue sur la poche et la déco du magasin suintent une atmosphère tellement « saloon » qu'elles suffisent à éloigner l'acheteur du point de vente. Chose qui, notons-le au passage, ne concerne pas les toujours crédibles magasins Denim. Nous avons donc décidé de nous

Above: *Ice block with frozen jeans inside for a guerrilla advertising initiative; sticky tape used on most guerrilla advertising initiatives. ///* **Oben:** *Eisblock mit gefrorener Jeans für eine Guerilla-Marketing-Aktion; dieses Klebeband wurde bei den meisten Guerilla-Marketing-Aktionen verwendet. ///* **Ci-dessus** *: Bloc de glace contenant un jean pour la campagne de guérilla publicitaire ; bande autocollante utilisée pour la plupart des initiatives de guérilla publicitaire.*

stares them down until he gets the information he wants."

Hence the one-word campaign theme: WANTED. For copy, an American beat poetry style was applied. Launched in 22 countries throughout Europe and in Asia soon after, WANTED instantly connected with the brand name. Since the world already refers to Wrangler's home turf in the Wild West, the images were free to explore the more contemporary fashion side of the brand. Set in Northern American landscapes it showed new and unexpected combinations, adding tops and women's clothes to the wide set of images. Not only shooting for advertising, but also shooting all products for sales guides, brochures, and websites on the spot simultaneously. This continuous delivery of new product evidence in an authentic territory elevated the fashion relevance of the brand. Simultaneously, we created a new identity design. The brand's flag colours were re-instated. Blue and yellow. In bold graphics. Everything based on the new creative brand template

zunächst diesen Bedürfnissen der Hauptkunden zuzuwenden und die Werbespots im Kino eine Zeit lang außenvor zu lassen. Um die Menschen hinter der Marke auf eine Linie zu bringen, produzierten wir als Erstes ein Handbuch und ein Video zu der Marke, in denen wir unsere Strategie veranschaulichten und in puncto Produkt, Design, Kommunikation und Verhalten den Rahmen absteckten. Dies sollte die Cowboymentalität von Wrangler auf eine moderne und medienneutrale Art ausdrücken. Bei unseren Überlegungen zu einer passenden Sprache kamen wir zu dem Schluss, dass Cowboys, falls sie überhaupt etwas sagen, dieses kurz und verwegen äußern. Das ist wie dieser Witz: „Chuck Norris liest keine Bücher. Er zwingt sie mit seinem Blick nieder, bis er die gewünschten Informationen erhält."

Daraus entstand das Leitmotiv der Ein-Wort-Kampagne: WANTED. Der Werbetext wurde im Stil der amerikanischen Beat Poetry gehalten. Nach Einführung in 22 Ländern in ganz Europa und kurz darauf in Asien wurde WAN-

occuper en premier de ces points de communication avec la clientèle, et de laisser de côté les spots publicitaires pour un temps. Pour resserrer les rangs du public derrière l'enseigne, nous avons tout d'abord réalisé un manuel d'image de marque et un film vidéo, médité notre stratégie et délimité le territoire en termes de produit, de design, de messages et de comportement. L'idée consistait à exprimer l'esprit cow-boy de Wrangler d'une manière médiatique moderne et neutre. Recherchant le langage qui ferait mouche, nous sommes arrivés à la conclusion qu'un cow-boy, s'il a quelque chose à dire, le dit en deux mots et abruptement. Un peu à la manière de cette blague : « Chuck Norris ne lit pas de livres. Il les fixe du regard jusqu'à en tirer ce qu'il veut savoir. »

D'où le thème de la campagne, en un seul mot : WANTED. Avec un style très « beat generation » américaine. Lancé peu après dans 22 pays d'Europe et d'Asie, WANTED a instantanément été en phase avec le label. Puisque le monde entier associait déjà Wrangler aux territoires du Far Ouest, rien

of WANTED, a compass for all things executed. Key values: Bold, Inventive, Under-engineered, Low-tech, Rugged. These became the design values for all things two- and three-dimensional: trade fairs, point of sale, flagship-store interiors, websites, but also special product lines and licensed products.

Product design implanted the creative values

Being a leather patch on the behind, the brand was invisible in busy nightlife places, so T-shirts expressing the brand values were designed, the WANTED collector's items. The women's collection got a clear, more masculine-inspired direction. Models got the piercing eyes of a cowboy ready to draw. And to gain access to denim boutiques uninterested in the mainstream collection, an exclusive sub-label was created, proudly magnifying the brand's newfound iconics: B.Y. Blue and Yellow by Wrangler, with its own urbanised shades of blue and yellow, and under-engineered bus-shelter posters, just showing the tubes in blue and yellow inside. The mailing to shop owners and the press was a low-tech but irresistible viewmaster. Not only did B.Y. get the right stores, it made those boutiques rediscover items from the classic collections too, and the lines blurred. The highly branded collection created for Europe was even embraced and imported by hip New York City denim stores.

Brand behaviour followed the bravery displayed by the product. In an outdoor setting, bold was translated into the following buying strategy: "buildings, not billboards", emphasising the attitude of the brand. This applied mostly during fashion trade fairs, so consumers, professional "denimals" and the press were reached with one firm blow. In several European capitals we launched a winter collection frozen into ice blocks, roughly thrown on the streets and cars in shopping areas, to be chipped out by whoever passed by. It connected to successful store-promos and got loads of free publicity on- and offline.

TED sofort mit dem Markennamen in Verbindung gebracht. Nachdem die Welt bereits den Wilden Westen als Heimat von Wrangler betrachtete, konnte sich die Marke auf ein eher zeitgemäßes Erscheinungsbild der Kleidung konzentrieren. Die Werbefotos wurden in nordamerikanischen Landschaften geschossen und zeigten neue und unerwartete Kombinationen, zu denen nun auch Tops und Damenbekleidung gehörten. Die Aufnahmen wurden nicht nur für Werbezwecke erstellt, sondern an Ort und Stelle wurden gleichzeitig auch alle Produkte für Kataloge, Broschüren und Websites aufgenommen. Diese konstante Präsenz neuer Produkte in einer authentischen Landschaft verstärkte die Moderelevanz der Marke. Gleichzeitig schufen wir ein neues Design für die Markenidentität. Die Farben des Markensymbols wurden neu eingesetzt: Blau und Gelb in Fettdruck. Alles basierte auf dem neuen kreativen Markenmotiv WANTED, das als Richtschnur für alle Maßnahmen diente, die durchgeführt wurden. Folgende Schlüsselwerte entstanden: verwegen, innovativ, original, Low-Tech, rau. Das Design aller zwei- und dreidimensionalen Werbemaßnahmen wie Messen, Verkaufsorte, Flagship-Store-Ausstattung, Websites, aber auch besondere Produktlinien und lizenzierte Produkte orientierten sich an diesen Werten.

Produktdesign setzt kreative Werte um

Als Lederflicken auf dem Hinterteil war die Marke an den belebten Orten des Nachtlebens unsichtbar. Aus diesem Grund wurden T-Shirts entworfen, welche die Markenwerte ausdrückten und zu WANTED-Sammlerobjekten werden sollten. Die Damenkollektion erhielt eine klare und eher maskulin orientierte Richtung. Models setzten den durchdringenden Blick eines Cowboys auf, der bereit war, seine Waffe zu ziehen. Und um bei Jeans-Boutiquen Zugang zu finden, die an der Hauptkollektion nicht interessiert waren, wurde ein exklusives Sub-Label geschaffen, das stolz die neu entdeckten Kultsymbole der Marke herausstellte: B.Y. Blue and Yellow von Wrangler, mit ihren ganz eigenen urbanen Farbtönen von Blau und Gelb. Poster für Wartehäuschen an

n'interdisait d'y explorer en images le côté davantage contemporain et fashion de la marque. C'est donc dans des paysages d'Amérique du Nord que nous avons choisi de montrer des combinaisons nouvelles et inattendues, en ajoutant des modèles et des vêtements féminins au large éventail d'images. Et nous y avons tourné pour la publicité, certes, mais aussi pour tous les autres produits, simultanément : guides de vente, brochures et sites Web. Cette avalanche de témoignages de nouveaux produits, dans un décor authentique, a eu pour effet de rétablir la crédibilité de la marque en termes de mode. Simultanément, nous avons relooké le design. Les couleurs étendard de la marque, le bleu et le jaune, ont été restaurées. Avec un graphisme sobre. Tout repose sur le patron de la nouvelle image créative de WANTED, le gabarit utilisé pour toutes nos créations. Valeurs-clés : sobriété, inventivité, déstructuration, tradition, robustesse. Ce sont ces valeurs que nous avons employées partout, en deux – voire trois – dimensions : salons, points de vente, intérieurs des boutiques de l'enseigne, sites Web, mais aussi lignes spéciales et produits brevetés.

Le design de produit au service de l'implantation des valeurs créatives

Cousue sur la poche arrière, la pièce de cuir où figure la marque était invisible, surtout au milieu d'une foule dans les bars et les boîtes de nuit ; nous avons donc conçu des T-shirts exprimant les valeurs de la marque, les collectors WANTED. La collection femme a pris une direction nettement plus masculine. Nos modèles affichaient le regard acéré du cow-boy prêt à dégainer. Et pour faciliter l'accès aux boutiques Denim que n'intéressait pas la collection principale, une sous-marque exclusive vantant fièrement les toutes nouvelles valeurs iconiques a été créée : B.Y. Blue and Yellow by Wrangler, avec ses propres nuances urbaines de bleu et de jaune, et des affiches d'abribus déstructurées ne montrant que des tubes en bleu et jaune à l'intérieur. Le publipostage adressé aux propriétaires de boutiques et à la presse adoptait la forme d'une irrésistible visionneuse ancienne. Non seulement B.Y. a touché les bons points de vente, mais elle les a aidé à redécouvrir des modèles de la

WANTED

Previous spread: *Imagery used to identify the brand in the campaign.* /// **Vorhergehende Seite:** *Darstellungen zur Bestimmung der Marke in der Werbekampagne.* /// **Double page précédente :** *Imagerie utilisée pour identifier la marque pendant la campagne.*

Above: *Urban application of the visual language of the campaign.* /// **Oben:** *Umsetzung der visuellen Sprache der Kampagne im urbanen Umfeld.* /// **Ci-dessus :** *Application urbaine du langage visuel de la campagne.*

And after a teasing on- and offline promotional five Wrangler trucks rode into town the cowboy way. Out came "This Is Wanted", a 1000 square-metre event staging an all-senses brand experience. A three-level, free-standing monument designed to entertain consumers, business and press contacts with live rock music, Wrangler inspired art (in conjunction with *Dazed & Confused*), food and beverages, motorcycle stunts, DJs/VJs, a heritage hall, and product displays. The brand values were implemented into every section right down to the materials used for the structure and the food served. The event took place in Barcelona, Stockholm and Milan and received free publicity throughout Europe.

By delivering hundreds of design and communication messages a year, each visualising its unique point of view, Wrangler's structural downsizing turned into a substantial growth. Today, the "constantly moving brand" is on course with its double-digit growth strategy. To pull it off, you need focused creative

Bushaltestellen, die mit von innen angebrachten blauen und gelben Leuchtröhren angestrahlt wurden. Die Werbepost an Ladenbesitzer und Presse wurde mit wenig technischem Aufwand erstellt, hinterließ aber einen nachhaltigen Eindruck. B.Y. konnte nicht nur die richtigen Läden gewinnen, sondern diese Boutiquen entdeckten auch Artikel aus der klassischen Kollektion wieder, und die Produktlinien begannen, sich zu verwischen. Die starke, für Europa entworfene Markenkollektion wurde sogar von den schicken Jeansläden in New York angenommen und eingeführt.

Das Markenverhalten verkörperte den Mut, der durch das Produkt symbolisiert wird. In einer Außenkulisse wurde die Kaufstrategie „Keine Plakatwände, sondern Hauswände" entwickelt, welche die Gesinnung der Marke hervorheben sollte. Diese Strategie wurde überwiegend auf Modemessen angewendet, sodass Konsumenten, professionelle „Denimals" und die Presse auf einen Schlag erreicht werden konnten. In mehreren europäischen Hauptstädten führten wir eine Winterkollektion ein, die in Eisblöcken

collection classique, et les frontières se sont estompées. La collection très « marquée » créée pour l'Europe a même été élue et importée par les magasins Denim les plus branchés de New York.

La ligne de communication a été calquée sur la résolution affichée par le produit. Sur le terrain, la sobriété s'est traduite par la stratégie de vente suivante : « buildings, not billboards », soulignant ainsi l'attitude de la marque. Nous l'avons appliquée essentiellement pendant les salons du secteur, de façon à atteindre en bloc consommateurs, professionnels du jeans et organes de presse. Dans plusieurs capitales européennes, nous avons lancé une collection d'hiver figée dans des blocs de glace, qui tombaient du ciel au hasard sur les voitures et les trottoirs des quartiers commerçants, attendant que le premier passant venu en libère le contenu. Associée à une campagne de promotion en magasins très réussie, « Ice invasion » a bénéficié de tonnes de publicité on et off line.

Après cela, un teaser promotionnel on et off line mettant en scène cinq jeeps Wrangler a

leadership with a zero-tolerance attitude for wrong details, as a simple coffee cup can strengthen or weaken the brand image in the eyes of the marketing-savvy consumer. To avoid analysis paralysis, simply start with fixing the most important brand cues first. It may very well not be your ad.

eingefroren war, einfach auf Straßen und Autos in Einkaufsvierteln verteilt wurde und von Passanten aus dem Eis geschlagen werden konnte. Dies führte zu einer erfolgreichen Ladenwerbung, die on- und offline eine Menge kostenlose Publicity bekam.

Nach einer sehr ansprechenden on- und offline-Werbung rollten fünf Wrangler-Lastwagen auf Cowboy-Art in die Stadt. Daraus entwickelte sich die Veranstaltung „This Is Wanted", ein Bühnenereignis über 1.000 m², bei der die Marke mit allen Sinnen erlebt werden konnte. In einer freistehenden Konstruktion auf drei Ebenen wurden Kunden, die Geschäfts-welt und die Presse mit Live-Rockmusik sowie von Wrangler inspirierter Kunst (in Verbindung mit *Dazed & Confused*), Speisen und Getränken, Motorrad-Stunts, DJs/VJs, einer Kulturhalle und Produkt-ausstellungen unterhalten. Die Marken-werte wurden in jedem Bereich bis hin zu den Materialien der Konstruktion und den servierten Gerichten umgesetzt. Die Veranstaltung wurde in Barcelona, Stockholm und Mailand durchgeführt und erhielt in ganz Europa kostenlose Publicity.

Durch Hunderte von Design- und Kommunikationsbotschaften im Jahr, die jeweils ihre eigene Perspektive veranschau-lichten, konnte Wrangler seinen strukturellen Abbau in erhebliches Wachstum umwan-deln. Heute ist die „sich ständig bewegende Marke" mit seiner zweistelligen Wachs-tumsstrategie auf Erfolgskurs. Um dies zu erreichen, benötigt man eine gezielte kreative Leitung, die falsche Details absolut nicht durchgehen lässt, denn eine einfache Kaffeetasse kann in den Augen des marketingerfahrenen Kunden das Marken-image stärken oder schwächen. Um sich nicht von Umsatzanalysen lähmen zu lassen, fangen Sie einfach an, die wichtigsten Markensymbole zu verbessern. Es liegt sehr wahrscheinlich nicht an Ihrer Werbung.

imposé en ville le style cow-boy. Puis est venu « This Is Wanted », un événement artistique pluridisciplinaire sur une scène de 1000 mètres carrés. Un édifice modulaire sur trois étages conçu pour le plaisir du public, du secteur et de la presse, avec du rock live, de l'art inspiré par Wrangler (en collaboration avec *Dazed & Confused*), à boire et à manger, des cascades en motos, des DJ/VJ, une salle « Tradition » et des présentoirs de produit. Les valeurs de la marque étaient omniprésentes, jusqu'aux aliments servis et aux matériaux employés pour la structure. L'événement s'est déroulé à Barcelone, Stockholm et Milan, et il a bénéficié de publicité gratuite dans toute l'Europe.

En adressant des centaines de messages stratégiques et communicationnels par an, tous tendus vers une même direction, Wrangler a pu renverser la vapeur, se restructurer et recommencer à croître. Aujourd'hui, la « marque en perpétuel mouvement » est en passe d'atteindre le taux de croissance à deux chiffres qu'elle s'est fixée. Pour y parvenir, il faut une direction créative spécialisée, et ne pas tolérer la moindre erreur de détail, une simple tasse à café pouvant renforcer ou amoindrir l'image de marque aux yeux du consommateur publiphile. Pour éviter l'analyse paralysante, commencez tout d'abord par établir les repères fondamen-taux de la marque. Vous ne devriez pas le regretter.

Top and bottom: *Imagery of urban initiatives during the campaign.* /// **Oben und unten:** *Bilder von Aktionen im urbanen Umfeld während der Kampagne.* /// **En haut et en bas** : *Imagerie des initiatives urbaines pendant la campagne.*

Biography
Joost Perik (BSUR Amsterdam)

www.bsur.com

Location: Amsterdam
Year founded: 1994

Position: Co-founder/
Creative Director

Dutch copywriter Joost Perik was born in 1966 and is creative partner and co-founder of BSUR ("Be as you are") in Amsterdam. BSUR, born in 1994, is an award-winning Dutch international creative consultancy that delivers total branding solutions. It unites brand creation, brand re-engineering, new product development, identity design, integrated communications and brand activation. It has worked for brands such O'Neill Europe, Wrangler Europe and Asia, Davidoff Worldwide, Wyborowa Worldwide, Sara Lee International, Arrow Europe, Glamour, WE Fashion Europe, Corporate Express Worldwide and Bacardi Global Brands.

Der niederländische Werbetexter Joost Perik wurde 1966 geboren und ist ein kreativer Partner und Mitbegründer der Agentur BSUR („Be as you are") in Amsterdam. Bei BSUR handelt es ich um eine 1994 gegründete, international tätige, preisgekrönte Kreativ-Beratungsagentur mit Sitz in den Niederlanden, die Gesamtlösungen zur Markenidentität anbietet. Das Unternehmen verbindet Markenbildung, Marken-Umstrukturierung, Neuntwicklung von Produkten, Identitätsdesign, integrierte Komnunikation und Markenaktivierung. Zu den Kunden von BSUR zählen Marken wie O'Neill Europe, Wrangler Europe und Asia, Davidoff Worldwide, Wyborowa Worldwide, Sara Lee

International, Arrow Europe, Glamour, WE Fashion Europe, Corporate Express Worldwide und Bacardi Global Brands.

Joost Perik, copywriter hollandais né en 1966, est l'associé créatif et le co-fondateur de BSUR (« Be as you are ») à Amsterdam. BSUR, qui a vu le jour en 1994, est un cabinet de conseil en communication internationale hollandais, lauréat de plusieurs prix, qui fournit des solutions intégrales de stratégie de marque : création et relookage de marque, création de nouveaux produits, création d'image, communication intégrée et mise en œuvre de marque. Il a travaillé pour des marques telles que O'Neill Europe, Wrangler Europe et Asie, Davidoff Worldwide, Wyborowa Worldwide, Sara Lee International, Arrow Europe, Glamour, WE Fashion Europe, Corporate Express Worldwide et Bacardi Global Brands.

XINDAO: THE REDESIGN OF A SPORTS BRAND FROM CHINA

Xindao, a Dutch company, is a supplier of promotional gifts with over 22 years' experience and strong relations in China. Working with Xindao means working with a partner that knows all the ins and outs of the business, both on the Chinese and the European side. The name Xindao has many meanings in Chinese, one being "New Direction", which best expresses our philosophy: We build our business based on new ideas and through long-term relations with our customer.

About three years ago, Xindao were assessing how they could give themselves a unique selling point. They decided design was one of the avenues they could look into; they already had a large operation in Shanghai, dealing directly with the manufacturers, and it seemed a logical step to create a product design studio in Shanghai, so that way the designers would have direct contact with the factories producing the goods. The product design studio started with two product designers and has now grown to 17 people, of whom seven are highly educated international designers.

Das niederländische Unternehmen Xindao ist ein Anbieter von verkaufsfördernden Werbegeschenken mit über 22 Jahren Erfahrung und sehr engen Verbindungen nach China. Mit Xindao zu arbeiten bedeutet mit einem Partner zu arbeiten, der all die Tricks und Kniffe des Geschäfts kennt, sowohl auf der chinesischen als auch auf der europäischen Seite. Der Name Xindao hat im Chinesischen viele Bedeutungen – eine davon ist »Neue Richtung«, und diese drückt unsere Philosophie am besten aus: Wir bauen unser Unternehmen auf der Grundlage neuer Ideen und langjähriger Beziehungen zu unseren Kunden auf.

Vor ungefähr drei Jahren fragte man sich bei Xindao, wie man dem Unternehmen ein Alleinstellungsmerkmal geben könnte. Xindao entschied sich dafür, dass das Design einen möglichen Weg darstellen könnte. In Schanghai existierte bereits eine große Geschäftsstelle, die direkt mit den Herstellern in Verbindung stand. Daher erschien der Schritt logisch, ein Studio für Produktdesign in Schanghai zu gründen,

Xindao, une société hollandaise, fournit des cadeaux promotionnels depuis plus de 22 ans, en étroite relation avec la Chine. Travailler avec Xindao signifie travailler avec un partenaire qui connaît parfaitement les arcanes de la profession, du côté chinois comme du côté européen. Le nom Xindao a en Chine diverses significations, dont celle de « Nouvelle direction », qui exprime au mieux notre philosophie : Bâtir notre entreprise sur de nouvelles idées et au travers de relations à long terme avec la clientèle.

Il y a environ trois ans, s'interrogeant sur la manière de se donner un point de vente unique, les dirigeants de Xindao ont vu dans le design une voie à explorer ; ils avaient déjà un champ d'opération à Shanghai, traitant directement avec les fabricants, aussi la création sur place d'une agence de design produit semblait-elle une suite logique ; les concepteurs auraient ainsi des contacts directs avec les usines de fabrication. Cette agence, qui employait au départ deux créatifs, affiche aujourd'hui un effectif de 17 personnes, dont sept

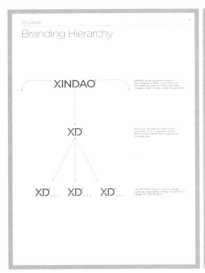

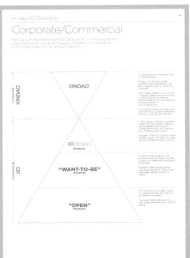

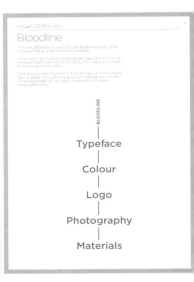

Each product category (Lifestyle, Bags, Tools, and Outdoors) has been assigned one product design art director. All designers have been educated at the Central Saint Martins Design School in London, considered Europe's leading design academy.

Research Studios' relationship with Xindao started off the back of this conscious shift in utilising design. With the product design studio being established, they turned their attention to the company's communication tools. Each year Xindao produce two catalogues, one 250-page/600+ product main catalogue, and one winter 80-page/100-product catalogue, and these are their key sales and communications tools. They decided to bring us in to work on the winter catalogue, this being a test run to see if design would benefit this area of their business. The result was obvious, that design would definitely benefit Xindao as a company.

The design of Xindao's branding and communication collateral was very much

sodass die Designer in direktem Kontakt mit den Fabriken stehen würden, die die Produkte herstellen. Das Designstudio begann zunächst mit zwei Produktdesignern und beschäftigt nun 17 Personen, von denen sieben hochqualifizierte internationale Designer sind. Jedes Produktsegment (Lifestyle, Taschen, Werkzeuge und Outdoor-Produkte) wurde einem Art Direktor für Produktdesign unterstellt. Alle Designer hatten ihre Ausbildung an der Central Saint Martins Design School in London erhalten, der führenden Design-Akademie Europas.

Die Beziehung zwischen Research Studios und Xindao begann vor dem Hintergrund dieser bewussten Veränderung für den Einsatz des Designs. Nach Gründung des Studios für Produktdesign kümmerte sich dieses um die Kommunikationsmittel des Unternehmens. Jedes Jahr produziert Xindao zwei Kataloge: einen 250-seitigen Hauptkatalog mit 600 Produkten und einen 80-seitigen Winterkatalog mit 100 Produkten, welche die wichtigsten Verkaufs- und Kommunikationsmittel

designers hautement qualifiés de diverses nationalités. Chaque catégorie de produits (Art de vivre, Maroquinerie, Outils et Extérieurs) a été assignée à un directeur artistique. Tous les designers ont fait leurs études à la Central Saint Martins Design School de Londres, qui est considérée comme la meilleure école d'art d'Europe.

C'est à la faveur de ce changement de cap délibéré vers le design qu'a débuté la relation de Research Studios avec Xindao. Une fois l'agence mise en œuvre, on s'est intéressé aux outils de communication de la société. Chaque année, Xindao publie deux catalogues, un catalogue général (250 pages / plus de 600 produits) et un catalogue Hiver (80 pages / une centaine de produits) ; ce sont là ses principaux outils de vente et de communication. Il a été décidé que nous nous attèlerions au catalogue Hiver ; c'était en quelque sorte un coup d'essai pour voir en quoi le design profiterait à cette branche de l'activité. Le résultat a été éclatant : oui, le design allait sans aucun doute être bénéfique pour la société Xindao.

Previous spread: *Stand design for a trade show, and wall lettering application.* /// **Vorher- gehende Seite**: *Gestaltung eines Messe- standes bei einer Fachausstellung und die Umsetzung des Schriftzuges auf einer Wand.* /// **Double page précédente** : *Design d'un stand sur un salon-exposition et lettrage mural.*

Left: *Key identity directions of the corporate identity manual.* /// **Links**: *Vorgaben für die Hauptidentität aus dem Corporate-Identity- Handbuch.* /// **A gauche** : *Directives clés du manuel d'identité visuelle de l'entreprise.*

Right: *The old logo.* /// **Rechts**: *Das alte Logo.* /// **A droite** : *Ancien logo.*

of the promotional gift industry and market's general visual language, so in essence there was nothing wrong with the design Xindao already had, it did its job safely and efficiently. The concept Xindao had behind designs was to push their positioning in China, something they did by using the colour red and the styling of their branding and tradeshow stand, which had the theme of a Chinese pagoda.

Again Xindao's current look and feel was doing its job, but it was restrictive in terms of creating a unique visual foothold in the marketplace. The Chinese angle to the brand had also run its course: with China becoming a strong capitalist global player, it was no longer viable to use this as an angle to make Xindao a unique company, the design was looking dated and tired.

What was needed was to embrace Xindao's new ethos of using design and being a specialist in their field. In an industry where product design and design awareness is light, and where the common industry trend is to carpet-bomb the marketplace

darstellen. Das Unternehmen entschied sich, uns bei dem Winterkatalog hinzuzu- ziehen, sozusagen als Testlauf, ob sich Design auf diesen Geschäftsbereich positiv auswirken würde. Das Ergebnis machte deutlich, dass Design für Xindao als Unternehmen definitiv einen Gewinn darstellen würde.

Das Design der Marken- und Kommuni- kationsmittel von Xindao entsprach sehr der allgemein gültigen visuellen Sprache des Marktes und der Branche für Werbege- schenke. Daher war im Wesentlichen nichts an dem Design auszusetzen, das Xindao bereits verwendete, da es seine Aufgabe sicher und effektiv erfüllte. Das Konzept hinter dem Design von Xindao bestand darin, die Positionierung in China auszubauen. Dazu verwendete das Unter- nehmen die Farbe Rot und das Motiv einer chinesischen Pagode für die Formgebung seiner Marken und des Messestandes.

Obwohl das damalige Look & Feel der Marke Xindao seine Aufgabe erfüllte, war es zu restriktiv, um visuell eindeutig am

L'image de marque et les supports de communication de Xindao étant tout à fait dans la ligne visuelle classique du marché et de l'industrie du cadeau promotionnel, il n'y avait pour l'essentiel rien à redire au design de l'entreprise, qui remplissait parfaitement son office. Xindao tentait à travers lui de renforcer son positionnement en Chine, exploitant à cet effet la couleur rouge et le thème de la pagode, aussi bien pour son image de marque que ses stands d'exposition sur les salons commerciaux.

Encore une fois, l'image actuelle de Xindao remplissait son office, mais, s'agissant de créer un point d'ancrage visuel unique sur le marché, elle manquait un peu d'ampleur. Et puis le symbolisme chinois lui aussi avait fait son temps : la Chine s'imposant comme un solide acteur de la scène capitaliste mondiale, il était contrepro- ductif de garder cet angle de vue pour positionner Xindao : son design était daté et fatigué.

Il fallait mettre en avant la volonté de Xindao de recourir au design et de s'imposer

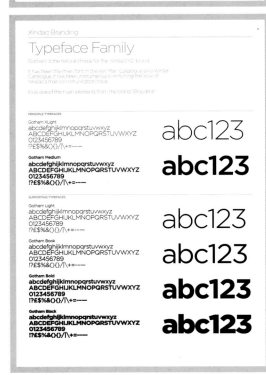

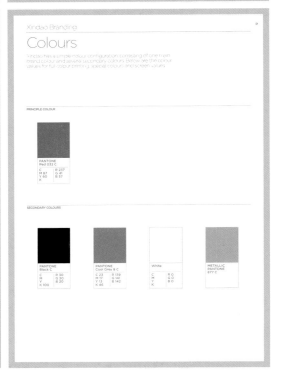

XD Design Branding
Logotype Anatomy

The XD Design logo comes from two weights of the font Gotham, which helps to tie everything together. The X and the D are taken directly from the Xindao logo, design is set in Gotham light.

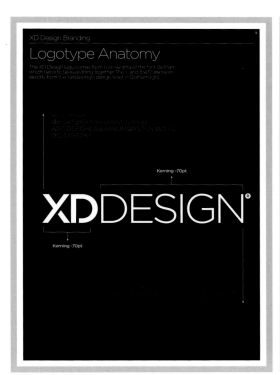

Kerning -70pt

Kerning -70pt

XD Design Branding
Photography – Product

Product photography should be functional but stylish, the photography has to show the devising elements of the product is including details, textures and materials. Cropped parts which are sometimes used with the main images to focus specific features. All products are shot on a black reflective surface, which emulate the look of the product and differentiates XD Design Products from standard Xindao products.

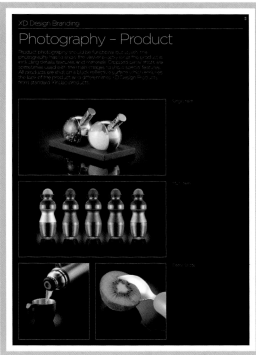

XD Design Branding
Photography – Mood

The idea of XD Design is pure product, so unlike the Xindao mood photography, this features nothing else but the XD Design products. The concept is to create stylish interesting imagery using the products as subject matter this draws attention to the design of the products and ultimately makes them more desirable.

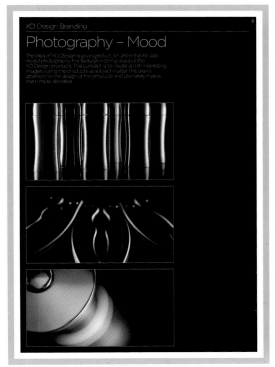

XD Design Branding
Materials

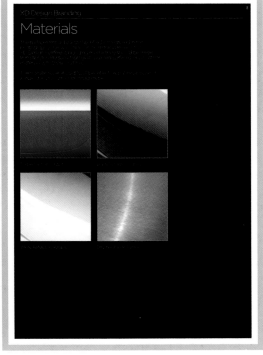

XDDESIGN®

Previous spread: *Technical guidelines and branding application pages of the corporate identity manual. ///* **Vorhergehende Seite:** *Styleguide und Richtlinien für die Umsetzung der Markenmerkmale – Seiten aus dem CI-Handbuch. ///* **Double page précédente :** *Pages consacrées aux normes techniques et à l'utilisation de l'image dans le manuel d'identité visuelle.*

Above: *Logo developed for the design division of the company. ///* **Oben:** *Das für den Designbereich des Unternehmens entwickelte Logo. ///* **Ci-dessus :** *Logo mis au point pour la division Design de l'entreprise.*

Right: *Catalogue cover design. ///* **Rechts:** *Entwurf des Katalog-Deckblatts. ///* **A droite :** *Couverture du catalogue.*

with as many products as possible, Xindao could create their own platform where they would be design-led and product-focused. So, in tandem with continuing to work on their Main and Winter catalogues we realised one of the key things that was needed was at the top end, the branding, and this could then create a strong platform for everything else that followed, creating a unique positioning in the market and all the elements that would support this.

During the process we accessed the design languages that are familiar to the industry, the market and to competitors. What we didn't want to do was design according to this formula, so we accessed the design trends to see how we could break that mould and create pioneering design solutions that would elevate Xindao from their competitors and in turn make them a pioneer of their own market. We wanted to achieve this while still being relevant and valid to their brand ethos and needs – it was about creating an innovative design solution that would grow with Xindao's needs far into the future. As product design

Markt Fuß zu fassen. Die chinesische Perspektive der Marke war ebenfalls überholt: Da sich China zu einer starken kapitalistischen Wirtschaftsmacht entwickelte, konnte man diesen Blickwinkel nicht länger dazu nutzen, Xindao als einzigartiges Unternehmen zu betrachten – das Design wirkte veraltet und müde.

Aus diesem Grund war es notwendig, dem neuen Ethos von Xindao bei der Verwendung von Design und als Spezialist in der Branche gerecht zu werden. In einem Industriezweig, in dem Produktdesign unterrepräsentiert und das Designbewusstsein gering ist, der allgemeine Geschäftstrend außerdem darin besteht, den Markt mit so vielen Produkten wie möglich zu bombardieren, konnte Xindao seine eigene Plattform schaffen, auf der sich das Unternehmen designorientiert und produktbezogen zeigte. Während wir also weiterhin an den Haupt- und Winterkatalogen arbeiteten, stellten wir fest, dass eine der notwendigsten Veränderungen am oberen Ende stattfinden musste: bei der Markenbildung. Diese könnte dann eine

comme un spécialiste de son secteur. Dans une industrie où le design de produit et la sensibilité pour le design restent faibles, et où la tendance générale consiste à bombarder littéralement le marché avec le plus grand nombre possible de produits, Xindao pourrait créer sa propre plateforme et se distinguer par une démarche conduite par la communication et axée sur le produit. Aussi, sans cesser de travailler aux catalogues (général et hiver), nous avons vite compris que nous avions besoin, avant toute chose, d'une image de marque, bref de dresser une plateforme solide pour tout ce qui allait suivre, en créant un positionnement unique sur le marché et tous les éléments susceptibles de le soutenir.

Pendant le processus, nous avons passé en revue les modes discursifs en vigueur dans l'industrie, sur le marché et parmi la concurrence. Nous voulions éviter de suivre les mêmes formules, d'où cet examen pour voir comment briser le moule et créer des solutions capables de hisser Xindao au-dessus de ses rivaux et d'en faire un précurseur sur leur propre marché. Nous

was the driving force of Xindao, a product hierarchy was created which in turn formed a strong brand hierarchy. At the top is Xindao the corporate brand, second to that is XD Design, the commercial brand, a select group of 20 flagships that are created by the in-house design team and which of course would be completely exclusive to Xindao, thus putting design right at the heart of the products and the brand. Below XD Design are another two tiers, where the brand becomes less strong as you drop down through the product hierarchies.

One of the design problems with Xindao is that the corporate brand has to be silent owing to the fact that companies buy their products to put their own branding on them, and therefore we had to find other ways to have a strong brand presence without interfering or polluting the distributors' and end customers' own brand. So to create the brand strategy we took the angle that a brand is more than just a logo: a brand is all the visual elements working individually, and working

starke Plattform für alles Folgende darstellen und somit eine eindeutige Positionierung am Markt schaffen sowie die Entwicklung aller dazu erforderlichen Elemente unterstützen.

Während dieses Prozesses beschäftigten wir uns mit der in der Branche, am Markt und im Wettbewerb geläufigen Designsprache. Wir wollten unser Design nicht nach dieser Formel entwickeln. Daher griffen wir die Designtrends auf, um zu sehen, wie wir diese Form verändern und bahnbrechende Designlösungen kreieren konnten, mit deren Hilfe sich Xindao von der Konkurrenz abheben und sich selbst zum Pionier auf dem eigenen Markt machen würde. Wir wollten dieses Ziel erreichen, indem das Markenethos und die Bedürfnisse von Xindao ihre Relevanz und Gültigkeit behielten – es ging darum, eine innovative Designlösung zu schaffen, die mit den Bedürfnissen von Xindao weit in die Zukunft wachsen könnte. Da das Produktdesign die treibende Kraft von Xindao war, wurde eine Produkthierarchie geschaffen, die wiederum eine starke

voulions y parvenir du moment qu'il y allait de l'éthique et des besoins de la marque – il s'agissait de créer une solution novatrice qui grandirait sur le long terme au gré des besoins de Xindao. Le design de produit étant l'énergie motrice de Xindao, une hiérachie entre produits a été établie qui à son tour s'est traduite par une solide hiérachie de marque. Au sommet, la marque Xindao, en dessous XD Design, la marque commerciale, un groupe sélectionné de 20 produits phare qui ont été mis au point en interne et, bien entendu, restent l'exclusivité de Xindao, situant le design au cœur de la production et de la marque. Puis, encore en dessous de XD Design, deux autres niveaux, l'empreinte de la marque s'estompant peu à peu à mesure qu'on descend dans la hiérachie des produits.

Un des problèmes, en l'occurrence, était que la marque Xindao doit rester blanche puisque les sociétés qui achètent ses produits y apposent leur propre label ; il nous fallait donc trouver d'autres moyens de renforcer sa présence sans faire d'ombre à celles des

harmoniously as a whole. By creating a distinctive style that is individual to Xindao in their marketplace, every element could be recognisable as "Xindao" and "XD Design". To do this we created a distinctive style for each of the facets that would be used throughout the visual tools, and this meant creating quite strict styling rules for typeface, colour, logo, photography, layout, and materials. This also meant that at the top of the branding hierarchy all these elements could be used together to create the strongest instance of the brand, and as you dropped down through the product hierarchies elements of the brand would begin to drop away, but there would still be a strong brand presence, creating a visual bloodline that could be traced back to the core branding – the logo. Also taken into consideration were the element relationships, i.e. all product photography is taken on a reflective surface, creating a reflection of the product, and thus the display stands and surfaces of the trade-show stands are also made out of reflective surfaces to achieve the same visual effect.

The outcome

Xindao now has a brand that has design at its heart, and this has extended through to all the applications of Xindao, to internal signage and stationery, catalogues, promotional tools, advertising, website design, and tradeshow booths all underpinned by a clear branding hierarchy and bloodline. Rather than being campaign-driven the brand is about timeless innovation and is flexible and modular enough to run alongside Xindao's growth and expansion into other markets.

Markenhierarchie formte. Ganz oben steht Xindao, die unternehmenseigene Marke. Als zweites kommt XD Design, die kommerzielle Marke – eine ausgewählte Gruppe von 20 Kernprodukten, die vom hauseigenen Designerteam entwickelt wurden und die natürlich vollständig zu Xindao gehören. Folglich ist das Design dieser Produkte und Marken sehr wichtig. Unterhalb von XD Design liegen zwei weitere Stufen, bei denen sich die Marke auf dem Weg durch die Produkthierarchien nach unten in der Wirkung abschwächt.

Eines der Probleme des Designs bei Xindao besteht darin, dass die unternehmenseigene Marke versteckt bleiben muss, da andere Unternehmen die Produkte kaufen und sie mit ihrer eigenen Marke kennzeichnen wollen. Aus diesem Grund mussten wir andere Möglichkeiten finden, um eine starke Markenpräsenz zu erhalten, ohne dabei die eigenen Marken der Zwischen-händler und der Endkunden zu beeinträch-tigen oder zu verderben. Für die Entwick-lung der Markenstrategie nahmen wir also den Standpunkt ein, dass eine Marke mehr ist als nur ein Logo: Bei einer Marke arbeiten alle visuellen Elemente indivi-duell und bilden zudem eine harmonische Gesamtheit. Durch die Schaffung eines charakteristischen Stils, der am Markt individuell zu Xindao gehört, könnte jedes Element als „Xindao" und „XD Design" erkennbar sein. Dafür entwickelten wir für jede Facette einen unverwechselbaren Stil, der bei allen visuellen Hilfsmitteln verwendet wurde. Dies bedeutete, ziemlich genaue Regeln für das Design von Schriftbild, Farbe, Logo, Fotografie, Layout und Materialien zu schaffen. Es bedeutete auch, dass an der Spitze der Markenhier-archie all diese Elemente zusammen verwendet werden könnten, um das stärkste Beispiel der Marke zu kreieren. Auf dem Weg nach unten durch die Produkthier-archien würden die Elemente der Marke nach und nach wegbrechen, doch es bliebe immer noch eine starke Markenpräsenz erhalten, die einen visuellen Stammbaum schafft, der bis zum Kern der Marke zurückverfolgt werden könnte: dem Logo. Auch die Beziehungen der Elemente wurden berücksichtigt: Alle Aufnahmen der Produkte wurden auf einer reflektie-

distributeurs et des consommateurs finals. Aussi, en dressant la stratégie, avons-nous pris pour angle de vue qu'une marque est davantage qu'un logo : elle est la somme de ses éléments visuels, lesquels fonctionnent à la fois isolément, et harmonieusement tous ensemble. Grâce au style différent, individuel, que nous allions créer pour Xindao sur le marché, chacun de ces éléments serait identifiable et identifié comme appartenant à « Xindao » et « XD Design ». Pour ce faire, nous avons créé un style différent pour chacune des facettes à utiliser au travers des outils visuels, ce qui signifiait de fixer des lignes assez strictes en termes de polices de caractères, de couleur, de logo, de photographie, de mise en pages et de matériaux. Cela signifiait également qu'au sommet de la hiérarchie de marque, tous ces éléments pourraient être associés au service de l'exemplarité du label, et que plus on descendrait dans les étages plus ils seraient mis en retrait, la présence de la marque restant néanmoins forte, telle une lignée dont on peut suivre la trace pour remonter jusqu'à l'image principale : le logo. L'élément relationnel a également été considéré : tous les clichés sont pris sur des surfaces réfléchissantes, où le produit se reflète, et les présentoirs ainsi que les surfaces des stands d'exposition ont eux aussi des surfaces réfléchissante pour obtenir le même effet visuel.

Le résultat

Aujourd'hui, le design est au cœur même de Xindao, au cœur de toutes les applica-tions de Xindao, de la signalisation interne aux fournitures de bureau, des catalogues aux supports promotionnels, de la publicité au site Web, en passant par les stands d'exposition, qui affichent clairement leur origine et leur « branding hierarchy ». Plus que sur la publicité, la marque est axée sur l'innovation intemporelle, elle est souple et suffisamment modulaire pour grandir à l'unisson de la croissance et de l'expansion de Xindao sur d'autres marchés.

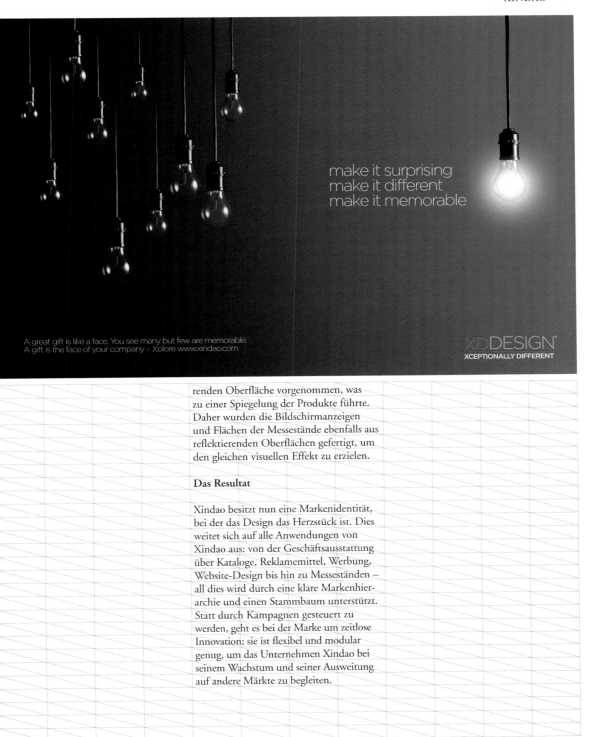

make it surprising
make it different
make it memorable

A great gift is like a face. You see many but few are memorable.
A gift is the face of your company – Xplore www.xindao.com

XD DESIGN®
XCEPTIONALLY DIFFERENT

renden Oberfläche vorgenommen, was
zu einer Spiegelung der Produkte führte.
Daher wurden die Bildschirmanzeigen
und Flächen der Messestände ebenfalls aus
reflektierenden Oberflächen gefertigt, um
den gleichen visuellen Effekt zu erzielen.

Das Resultat

Xindao besitzt nun eine Markenidentität,
bei der das Design das Herzstück ist. Dies
weitet sich auf alle Anwendungen von
Xindao aus: von der Geschäftsausstattung
über Kataloge, Reklamemittel, Werbung,
Website-Design bis hin zu Messeständen –
all dies wird durch eine klare Markenhier-
archie und einen Stammbaum unterstützt.
Statt durch Kampagnen gesteuert zu
werden, geht es bei der Marke um zeitlose
Innovation; sie ist flexibel und modular
genug, um das Unternehmen Xindao bei
seinem Wachstum und seiner Ausweitung
auf andere Märkte zu begleiten.

Contents

Welcome

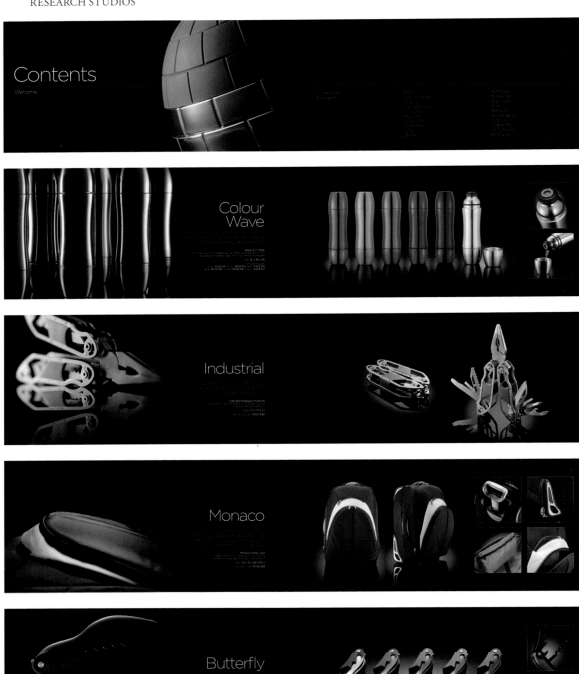

Colour Wave

Industrial

Monaco

Butterfly

Previous spread: *Advertising page. ///*
Vorhergehende Seite: *Werbeseite. /// Double*
page précédente : *Page publicitaire.*

Left: *Catalogue spreads. ///* **Links:**
Katalogseiten. /// **A gauche** : *Doubles pages*
de catalogue.

Biography
Jeff Knowles (Research Studios)

www.researchstudios.com   Location: London   Position: Art Director
                           Year founded: 1994

Jeff Knowles was born in 1976 in Rugby and graduated with a B.A. (Hons) in graphic design from The University of Salford, and directly from there he joined Research Studios London in the autumn of 1998. During his 10 years there Jeff has become one of the studio's longest-standing members of staff, and in turn one of the key art directors, and has become an integral part of the studio's evolution and growth. He has handled a large variety of projects, from large branding projects, publication design, packaging design, motion graphics and web design. Research Studios successfully operated as Neville Brody Studios for many years until he decided to expand, opening the first Research Studios in London in 1994. Since then Research has built up an extensive client list and has worked in all areas of design on projects of varying size and depth.

Jeff Knowles wurde 1976 in Rugby geboren. Er schloss sein Studium mit einem B.A. (Hons) in Grafikdesign an der University of Salford ab und begann sofort im Herbst 1998 seine Tätigkeit bei Research Studios, London. Nach zehn Jahren gehört Jeff zu den dienstältesten Mitarbeitern, ist einer der wichtigsten Art Direktoren und zudem unabdingbar für Wachstum und Entwicklung des Studios. Er führte viele verschiedene Projekte durch, von großen Projekten zur Markenidentität, über Publikationsdesign, Verpackungsdesign, bis hin zu Motion-Grafiken und Webdesign. Research Studios war

über viele Jahre erfolgreich als Neville Brody Studios tätig, bis man sich schließlich entschied, zu expandieren und 1994 die ersten Research Studios in London eröffnete. Seitdem hat Research einen umfangreichen Kundenstamm aufgebaut und arbeitet in allen Bereichen des Designs an Projekten von verschiedener Größe und mit unterschiedlichem Tiefgang.

Jeff Knowles est né en 1976 à Rugby et il est titulaire d'un baccalauréat ès art (avec mention) en design graphique (Université de Salford), après lequel il a directement intégré les Research Studios de Londre, à l'automne 1998. Au bout de dix ans de présence, Jeff en est l'un des plus anciens membres, ainsi que l'un des directeurs artistiques et artisans majeurs de l'évolution et de la croissance de l'agence. Il a traité une grande variété de projets (image de marque, publications, packaging, cinéma et sites Web). Research Studios a opéré avec succès sous le nom Neville Brody Studios pendant plusieurs années, avant de décider de s'étendre et d'ouvrir le premier Research Studios à Londres en 1994. Depuis, Research s'est constitué un solide portefeuille de clients et prête ses services dans tous les domaines de la communication, pour des projets de taille et d'envergure diverses.

THE HERITAGE OF THE MAYA: REDESIGNING AN ANCIENT IDENTITY

The native Maya lived in the Mesoamerican region (Central America) from about 1500 BC to 1519 AD. The Maya are one of the world's six cradles of early civilisation and their intelligent and beautiful written language is quite unknown to the western world, even to Central Americans, because it remained undeciphered for centuries. The Mayan scribes held a very privileged position in the socio-political system and were multi-talented – they were artists, sculptors, and calligraphers, and were also believed to be astronomers, mathematicians, historians and royal book-keepers. Original Mayan hieroglyphs were both ideographic and syllabographic.

As a Central American who lived in London for six years, living away from home inspired me to research (during my Masters studies at Central Saint Martins) and to attempt to resuscitate the unique Mayan scriptures, which had been undervalued by local graphic designers and could be reformed for application in contemporary visual communications.

Das Volk der Maya lebte etwa 1500 v. Chr. bis 1519 n. Chr. in der Region von Mesoamerika (Zentralamerika). Die Maya gehören zu den sechs Frühkulturen der Welt. Ihre intelligente und schöne Schriftsprache ist in der westlichen Welt und selbst den Zentralamerikanern wenig bekannt, da sie über Jahrhunderte nicht entziffert wurde. Die Schriftgelehrten der Maya nahmen in dem sozialpolitischen System eine sehr privilegierte Position ein und waren mehrfach talentiert: Sie waren Künstler, Bildhauer und Kalligrafen; zudem wird angenommen, dass sie als Astronomen, Mathematiker, Historiker und königliche Buchhalter tätig waren. Die ursprünglichen Hieroglyphen der Maya waren sowohl ideografisch als auch syllabografisch.

Als Zentralamerikanerin, die seit sechs Jahren in London lebt, hat mich das Leben fern der Heimat dazu angeregt, während meines Master-Studienganges am Central Saint Martins die einzigartigen Schriften der Maya zu erforschen und zu versuchen, sie wiederzubeleben. Diese Schriften

Les Mayas ont peuplé la Méso-Amérique (Amérique centrale) de 1500 avant J.-C. à 1519 après J.-C. La civilisation maya est l'un des six berceaux de l'humanité, mais son langage écrit, beau et intelligent, reste méconnu du monde occidental, et même de l'Amérique Centrale, car il a fallu des siècles pour le déchiffrer. Les scribes mayas occupaient une place privilégiée au sein du système politique et social et ils avaient de multiples talents. Artistes, sculpteurs et calligraphes, ils étaient aussi supposés être astronomes, mathématiciens, historiens et comptables royaux. Les hiéroglyphes mayas originales étaient à la fois idéographiques et syllabiques.

Originaire d'Amérique centrale, j'ai vécu six années à Londres et l'éloignement m'a amenée à étudier (pendant mes études de mastère au Collège Central Saint Martins) et à tenter de ressusciter les codes uniques de l'écriture maya, qui ont été sous-estimés par les designers graphiques locaux en dépit de ce qu'on pourrait en faire en les passant au crible de la communication visuelle contemporaine.

Previous spread: *The redesign of the iconography of a variety of Maya symbols.* ///
Vorhergehende Seite: *Die Neugestaltung der Ikonografie verschiedener Maya-Symbole.* ///
Double page précédente : *Réinterprétation iconographique de divers symboles mayas.*

Since 2004, I have been devising a graphic system called New Maya Language. It is a redesign of certain Mayan ideographs that express concepts and even whole sentences. My work parallels the principle of the Chinese-concept script where primary-root or Lego-like pictographs can be combined to generate compound pictographs that signify a more complex idea. For example, "Stone" + "Fire" has the combined meaning of "Lava stone" as a New Maya Language ideograph. Because the original Mayan written language was not democratic i.e. it was only known by a privileged class, my New Maya Language can help surpass language barriers and literacy disadvantages while at the same time enhancing users' experience and providing opportunities for learning in public locations, or simply being appreciated as an artform.

The project started using the "Joya de Cerén" UNESCO World Heritage Archaeological Site in El Salvador, as a case study for the creation of 23 New Maya Language pictograms set in the

wurden von den heimischen Grafikdesignern unterbewertet und konnten für die Anwendung in der zeitgenössischen visuellen Kommunikation neu gestaltet werden.

Seit 2004 entwickle ich ein grafisches System, das New Maya Language genannt wird. Es handelt sich um eine Neugestaltung bestimmter Maya-Ideogramme, die Konzepte und sogar ganze Sätze ausdrücken. Meine Arbeit gleicht dem Prinzip der chinesischen Schriftzeichen, bei denen Basis-Piktogramme wie Legosteine miteinander verbunden werden können, um einen komplexen Gedanken zu versinnbildlichen. Zum Beispiel haben die Begriffe „Stein" + „Feuer" als Ideogramm der New Maya Language die kombinierte Bedeutung von „Lavastein". Da die originale Schriftsprache der Maya nicht demokratisch bzw. nur einer privilegierten Klasse bekannt war, kann meine New Maya Language dabei helfen, Sprachbarrieren und Leseschwächen zu überwinden, während sie gleichzeitig die Erfahrungen der Anwender verbessert, Lernmöglich-

Depuis 2004, je mets au point un système graphique que j'ai baptisé Nouveau Langage Maya. Il s'agit d'une recréation de certains idéogrammes mayas exprimant des concepts, voire des phrases entières. Mon travail suit le principe de l'écriture conceptuelle chinoise où, à la manière d'un jeu de Lego, des racines principales pictographiques peuvent être combinées pour former des idéogrammes composés désignant une idée plus complexe. Par exemple, « Pierre » + « Feu » prennent une fois assemblés le sens de « Lave » dans le Nouveau Langage Maya. Sachant que l'écriture maya originale n'était pas démocratique, autrement dit qu'elle était réservée à une élite, mon Nouveau Langage Maya peut aider à surmonter les barrières linguistiques et les problèmes d'alphabétisation, tout en offrant par ailleurs au public des possibilités de l'expérimenter ou de l'apprendre, ou tout simplement de le contempler comme une forme d'art.

Le projet a débuté par l'étude de « Joya de Cerén », site archéologique salvadorien classé par l'UNESCO, en vue de créer

*Left: Book guide of the Maya symbols system
and signage application. /// **Links:** Handbuch
zum Symbolsystem der Maya und die Umsetzung auf Hinweisschildern. /// **A gauche :**
Guide pratique du système de symboles
mayas et de l'application signalétique.*

*Right: Sign system that originated the design
of the Maya symbols. /// **Rechts:** Leitsystem
auf der Grundlage der Maya-Symbole. ///
A droite : Système signalétique issu des
symboles mayas.*

orm of a guidebook and wood-carved
ootpath and a wayfinding system. The
pictograms' narrative tells the story of
the site, which was buried under ash by
a volcanic eruption around 590 AD, just
like Pompeii. It was preserved for centuries
until it was re-discovered in the 1970s.
The site documents the lifestyle and way
of living of the ordinary Mayan citizens,
their eating habits, social relations,
architecture, and agriculture – very unlike
the majestic religious temples more
commonly found in the region. The type
of remains found at the site became a
perfect representation of my objective:
democratising a dead written language that
in ancient times was unknown to common
citizens but had the possibility of being
understood by a general audience in our
times.

The challenge after generating the New
Maya Language proposal was to dissemi-
nate it. It is in the last five years that this
has been slowly achieved – the New Maya
Language has been taken forward to many
forms of visual communication, such as

keiten an öffentlichen Orten bietet oder
einfach als Kunstform betrachtet werden
kann.

Das Projekt begann damit, in einer
Fallstudie für die archäologische Stätte
„Joya de Cerén", einem UNESCO-Welt-
kulturerbe in El Salvador, 23 New Maya
Language-Piktogramme zu entwickeln.
Diese sollten in Form eines Führers, eines
hölzernen Fußpfades und eines Wegeplan-
Systems eingesetzt werden. Die Piktogram-
me erzählen die Geschichte des Ortes, der
ca. 590 n. Chr. während eines Vulkanaus-
bruchs unter Asche begraben wurde,
genau wie Pompeji. Die Stätte blieb über
Jahrhunderte bedeckt, bis sie schließlich in
den 1970er Jahren wiederentdeckt wurde.
Sie dokumentiert den Lebensstil und die
Lebensweise der gewöhnlichen Maya-
Bewohner, ihre Essgewohnheiten, sozialen
Bindungen, die Architektur und Land-
wirtschaft – sehr im Gegensatz zu den
majestätischen religiösen Tempeln, die
im Allgemeinen in der dortigen Region
gefunden wurden. Die Art der Überreste,
die in „Joya de Cerén" gefunden wurden,

23 pictogrammes en Nouveau Langage
Maya sous forme de topoguide et de
panneaux de signalisation sculptés sur bois.
Ces pictogrammes racontent l'histoire
du site, qui a été enseveli sous les cendres
à la suite d'une éruption volcanique en
590 avant J.-C., tout comme Pompéi.
Il a ainsi été préservé pendant des siècles,
jusqu'à sa redécouverte en 1970. Le site
rend compte du style et du mode de vie
des citoyens mayas ordinaires, de leurs
habitudes culinaires, de leurs relations
sociales, de leur architecture et de leur
agriculture – contrairement aux grandioses
temples religieux qui abondent dans la
région. Le type de vestiges qu'a livrés le
site s'est révélé une représentation parfaite
de mon objectif : démocratiser une écriture
morte, autrefois inconnue des gens
ordinaires, mais susceptible de nos jours
d'être appréhendée par le grand public.

Après la création de ce Nouveau Langage
Maya, la difficulté consistait à le diffuser.
Nous y sommes parvenus, lentement, dans
les cinq dernières années – il a été exploité
avec plusieurs formes de communication

new maya language

Frida Larios

brand identities, for example. I am citing four examples to illustrate how an ancient graphic mode of expression is being re-introduced to a Mesoamerican society that, since the Spanish conquest in the 15th Century, and from that point onwards, has been bombarded by western visual influences. Designers have played a detrimental role in looking for inspiration in the foreign rather than the local.

Hacienda San Lucas

The Hacienda San Lucas, located in the hill-tops of the Copán valley in Honduras, provides a spiritual, ecological, gastronomical, and cultural experience for the guests that stay at this family-run resort.

Inspired by the frog, water, wind, and human being hieroglyphs, the logotype had to reflect all these qualities and at the same time represent the Mayan archaeological site located within the property's precincts and where fertility rituals were practised in the midst of gigantic sculptures in the form of toads.

stellten die perfekte Repräsentation meines Zieles dar: die Demokratisierung einer toten Schriftsprache, die in antiken Zeiten den gewöhnlichen Bewohnern nicht bekannt war, aber die Möglichkeit bietet, in der heutigen Zeit von einem breiten Publikum verstanden zu werden.

Die Herausforderung bei der Umsetzung der New Maya Language bestand darin, die Bildsprache zu verbreiten. In den letzten fünf Jahren konnte dies langsam verwirklicht werden – die New Maya Language wurde in vielen Formen der visuellen Kommunikation eingesetzt, zum Beispiel für Markenidentitäten. Ich führe nachfolgend vier Beispiele an, um zu zeigen, wie eine grafische Ausdrucksform in eine mesoamerikanische Gesellschaft wiedereingeführt wurde, die seit der spanischen Eroberung im 15. Jahrhundert fortwährend durch westliche visuelle Einflüsse bombardiert wurde. Designer haben in diesem Prozess eine wenig schmeichelhafte Rolle gespielt, da sie eher im Ausland als in ihrer Heimatregion nach Inspirationen suchten.

visuelle, la création d'identités de marque par exemple. Je citerai ici cinq exemples pour illustrer la manière dont cet ancien mode d'expression graphique est réintroduit peu à peu dans une société méso-américaine qui, depuis la conquête espagnole au 15ᵉ siècle, a été bombardée de tous côtés par des influences visuelles occidentales. Les designers, en l'occurrence, ont joué un rôle funeste en allant chercher l'inspiration ailleurs plutôt que sur place.

La Hacienda San Lucas

Située dans les collines de la vallée de Copán au Honduras, la Hacienda San Lucas est un gîte rural exploité par une famille, dont les hôtes peuvent vivre une expérience à la fois spirituelle, écologique, gastronomique et culturelle.

Inspiré des idéogrammes représentant la grenouille, l'eau, le vent et l'homme, son logotype devait refléter toutes ces qualités et, en même temps, représenter le site archéologique maya qui se trouve dans l'enceinte de la propriété et où des rituels

Left: *Cover of the book with the complete redesign project.* /// **Links:** *Cover des Buches über das gesamte Projekt der Neugestaltung.* /// **A gauche :** *Couverture du livre contenant la totalité du projet de réinterprétation.*

Right: *Three contemporary logos using the Maya visual language.* /// **Rechts:** *Drei aktuelle Logos, die die visuelle Sprache der Maya verwenden.* /// **A droite :** *Trois logos actuels utilisant le langage visuel maya.*

Macaw Mountain

Macaw Mountain Bird Park & Nature Reserve is an innovative tropical-bird reserve in western Honduras that cares for rescued and endangered birds native to the Central American tropics.

For the ancient people of Mesoamerica, birds were an integral part of daily life and played fundamental roles in religion, art, and politics. Based on a Mayan sculpture, the logo promotes ecological conservation by reflecting human immersion into the richness of bird and plant diversity.

La Reina Maya

Mayan culture respected bees. As in a bee colony, the Mayan people believed harmony and justice could be reflected within their own society.

Bees and honey were used in rituals and were represented through deities like The Lord of the Bees, Bee Jaguar or Queen Bee, and the Bee Keeper.

Hacienda San Lucas

Die Hacienda San Lucas liegt auf den Hügelkuppen des Copán-Tals in Honduras. Das Familienunternehmen bietet seinen Gästen spirituelle, ökologische, gastronomische und kulturelle Erlebnismöglichkeiten. Inspiriert durch Hieroglyphen, die Frosch, Wasser, Wind und Mensch zeigen, sollte der Logotyp all diese Merkmale reflektieren und gleichzeitig die archäologische Mayastätte repräsentieren, die im Umfeld der Hacienda liegt. Dort wurde inmitten eines von riesigen Krötenskulpturen gebildeten Kreises ein Fruchtbarkeitsritual abgehalten.

Macaw Mountain

Beim Vogelpark und Naturschutzgebiet Macaw Mountain handelt es sich um einen innovativen Park für tropische Vögel im westlichen Honduras, der sich für gerettete und gefährdete Vögel einsetzt, die in den Tropen Zentralamerikas heimisch sind.

de fertilité étaient pratiqués au milieu de gigantesques sculptures à l'effigie du crapaud.

Le massif de Macaw

Le parc naturel et la réserve d'oiseaux du massif de Macaw, dans l'ouest du Honduras, se charge de secourir et de protéger les populations en danger d'oiseaux originaires des tropiques de l'Amérique centrale.

Pour les anciens peuples de Méso-Amérique, les oiseaux faisaient partie intégrante de la vie quotidienne et jouaient un rôle fondamental dans la vie religieuse, artistique politique. Basé sur une sculpture maya, le logo plaide pour la protection de la nature, en reflétant l'immersion de l'homme dans une faune et une flore extrêmement diverses et riches.

La Reina Maya

La culture maya était respecteuse des abeilles. Les Mayas pensaient qu'à l'instar d'une ruche leur propre société devait refléter l'harmonie et la justice.

La Reina Maya is a premium honey naturally produced in accordance with ancient practices. A reinterpretation of different polychrome vase depictions was used to design this brand packaging, illustrating a fusion of bee, honey, queen, and vessel.

No Smoking

I made the "No Smoking" New Maya Language sign available as a royalty-free, historically relevant pictogram. It is currently being used in dozens of public spaces across Mesoamerica, and even in Europe. It combines the smoke and upright human hand hieroglyphs as well as the red diagonal bar across, which readers have come to know as meaning "banned" in our times.

The New Maya Language is a true celebration of the Maya cultural and visual identity; it is an inspiration for present and future generations and brings new life to the sacred stones.

Für das alte mesoamerikanische Volk stellten Vögel einen unabdingbaren Teil ihres alltäglichen Lebens dar und spielten eine wichtige Rolle in Religion, Kunst und Politik. Das Logo basiert auf einer Maya-Skulptur und wirbt für den Schutz der Natur, indem es den menschlichen Einfluss auf den Artenreichtum der Vögel und Pflanzen reflektiert.

La Reina Maya

In der Maya-Kultur wurden Bienen respektiert. Die Mayas glaubten, dass sich in ihrer Gesellschaft Harmonie und Gerechtigkeit widerspiegelten, genau wie bei einem Bienenvolk.

Bienen und Honig wurden bei Ritualen eingesetzt. Dabei wurden die Bienen durch Gottheiten wie dem Herrn der Bienen, dem Bienen-Jaguar oder der Bienenkönigin und dem Bienenwächter repräsentiert.

La Reina Maya ist ein hochwertiger Honig, der natürlich und in Anlehnung an uralte Verfahren hergestellt wird. Die Verpackung für diese Marke wurde anhand einer Neuinterpretation verschiedener mehrfarbiger Vasen entwickelt und zeigt als Logo Elemente von Biene, Honig, Königin und Gefäß.

No Smoking

Ich habe das Symbol für „No Smoking" in der New Maya Language als lizenzfreies und historisch relevantes Piktogramm zur Verfügung gestellt. Es wird zur Zeit an Dutzenden von öffentlichen Orten in ganz Zentralamerika und sogar in Europa verwendet. Das Piktogramm kombiniert die Hieroglyphen für Rauch und eine erhobene menschliche Hand mit dem roten diagonalen Balken, den heutzutage jeder der Bedeutung „verboten" zuordnet.

Die New Maya Language feiert die kulturelle und visuelle Identität der Mayas. Sie ist eine Inspiration für gegenwärtige und zukünftige Generationen und verleiht den heiligen Steinen neues Leben.

Les abeilles et le miel étaient utilisés lors de rituels, et représentés par des dieux tels que le Seigneur des Abeilles, l'Abeille Jaguar ou la Reine des Abeilles, et l'Apiculteur.

La Reina Maya est une marque de miel de grande qualité, fabriqué dans le respect des procédés d'antan. C'est par réinterprétation de différents motifs de vases polychromes qu'a été conçu ce packaging d'image, illustrant une fusion entre abeille, miel, reine et vaisseau.

No Smoking

J'ai conçu ce pictogramme d'interdiction de fumer en Nouveau Langage Maya à titre gracieux. Il est actuellement utilisé dans des dizaines de lieux publics d'Amérique centrale et d'Europe. Il assemble les glyphes signifiant fumée et main levée avec la barre diagonale rouge que tout le monde associe aujourd'hui avec l'interdiction.

Le Nouveau Langage Maya est un véritable hommage à la culture et à l'identité visuelle de la culture maya ; il se veut une inspiration pour les générations actuelles et à venir, et tente de redonner vie aux pierres sacrées.

Right: *The royalty-free non-smoking pictogram. /// **Rechts:** Das lizenzfreie No-Smoking-Piktogramm. /// **A droite :** le pictogramme libre de droits « Défense de fumer ».*

Biography
Frida Larios (Ideas Frescas)

www.ideas-frescas.com
www.saposerpiente.com

Location: San Salvador
Year founded: 1999

Position: Founder/
Creative Director

Frida Larios has an MA in Communication Design from Central Saint Martins College of Art & Design. She has been a lecturer since 2000, at such places as the Escuela de Comunicación Mónica Herrera and the University of the Arts in London. She is founder and director of two design studios: Ideas Frescas in San Salvador, and Sapo Serpiente in Honduras. In 2005, she was the only Latin American to have ever won the Sign Design Award (Sign Design Society in London), for her MA project "New Maya Language Archaeological Site". In 1999, she was nominated for the Beatrice L. Warde Award by the ISTD (International Society of Typographic Designers) for excellence in typographic research in the UK. Frida has exhibited at Central Saint Martins' Lethaby Gallery, The Mall Galleries, St. Bride Printing Library, and the Embassy of El Salvador in London.

Frida Larios erhielt einen MA in Kommunikationsdesign am Central Saint Martins College of Art & Design. Sie arbeitet bereits seit 2000 als Dozentin und lehrt beispielsweise an der Escuela de Comunicación Mónica Herrera und der University of the Arts in London. Sie ist Gründerin und Direktorin von zwei Design-Studios: Ideas Frescas in San Salvador und Sapo Serpiente in Honduras. In 2005 war sie die einzige lateinamerikanische Künstlerin, die jemals den Sign Design Award (verliehen von der Sign Design Society in London) gewonnen hat – für ihr MA-Projekt „New Maya Language

Archaeological Site". In 1999 wurde sie für ihre hervorragende Leistung im Bereich typographische Forschung in Großbritannien und Nordirland für den Beatrice L. Warde Award durch die ISTD (International Society of Typographic Designers) nominiert. Frida stellte in Central Saint Martins' Lethaby Gallery, The Mall Galleries, St. Bride Printing Library und in der Embassy of El Salvador in London aus.

Frida Larios est titulaire d'un master of arts en design de la communication (Central Saint Martins College of Art & Design). Elle est maître de conférences depuis 2000, notamment pour la Escuela de Comunicación Mónica Herrera et l'University of the Arts de Londres. Elle a fondé et dirige deux studios de design : Ideas Frescas à San Salvador, et Sapo Serpiente au Honduras. En 2005, elle a été la seule latino-américaine à avoir jamais remporté le Sign Design Award (Sign Design Society de Londres), pour son projet de MA « New Maya Language Archaeological Site ». En 1999, elle a été nommée au Beatrice L. Warde Award par le ISTD (Société internationale de designers typographiques) pour l'excellence de ses recherches typographiques au Royaume Uni. Frida a exposé aux endroits suivants : Central Saint Martins' Lethaby Gallery, The Mall Galleries, St. Bride Printing Library, et à l'ambassade du Salvador à Londres.

CREATIVE INDUSTRY

ADVERTISING AGENCIES, ARCHITECTS & ARCHITECTURE OFFICES, ARTISTS, BRANDING COMPANIES, DESIGNERS & DESIGN OFFICES, FILM PRODUCTION STUDIOS, ILLUSTRATORS, INDUSTRIAL & PRODUCT DESIGNERS, PHOTOGRAPHERS

0001

001. Animal Days / Ego Grafik

0002. Intermedia Creative Group / Fritz Torres   0003. Circular 15, The Typographic Circle / Pentagram   0004. Two Worlds, Orange, France Telecom / KITA   0005. Drei Groschen Studio / HelloMe   0006. Christian Otto Studio / Christian Otto Studio   0007. Eramos Tantos Eramos Tantos Studio   0008. Hello Vanilla / Hello Vanilla   0009. Idea Espacios / Helou Design   0010. Ronda, Patricia Lascano / Estudio Garcia Balza   0011. g800 / Apfel Zet   0012. AV Produções / Interface Designers   0013. Torres Fotografía / Tholön Kunst   0014. LVL / LVL

0015. MatrizB / RacoSchneider   **0016.** GRACOM / Felix Beltran   **0017.** Diana Cabeza / ImagenHB   **0018.** Nippon Boy / KITA
0019.–0020. Landia / Rock Instrument Bureau   **0021.** Fatuus / Fatuus   **0022.** Pablo Vintimilla / Helou Design   **0023.** Non / Justin
Harder   **0024.** Reaktor / Fatuus   **0025.** Estudio Rosellini / ImagenHB   **0026.** JMW Architecture / Pixelerate   **0027.** Arquimia Architecture / Martino

0028. La Negrita / Damián Di Patrizio **0029.** KMDG Crew / DHM Graphic Design **0030.** Büro Ink / Büro Ink **0031.** Ronin Recruitment / Hawaii Design **0032.** Escobas / Escobas **0033.** Craftsmen / Attak **0034.** Jeremy Levine / SectionSeven **0035.** Molekül / Ego Grafik **0036.** Studio Jefrë / Push

0037

0038

0039

0040

0041

0042

0043

0044

0037. Hello Monday, *main logo* / Hello Monday   **0038.–0044.** Hello Monday, *characters* / Hello Monday

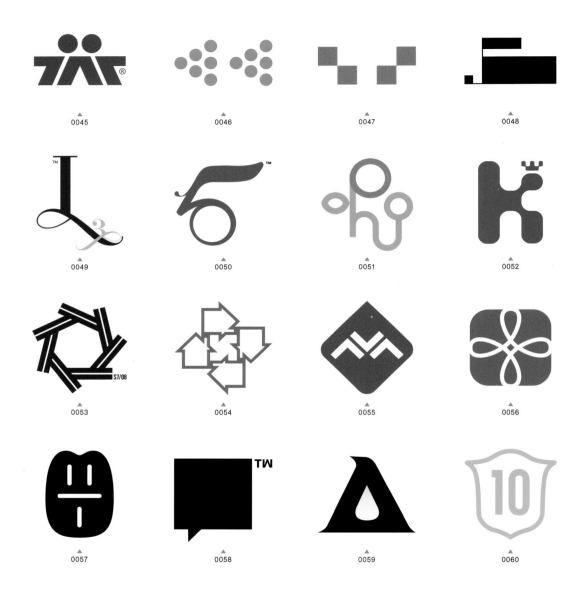

0045. Futatsu, Bleed / TNOP Design   **0046.** Projectgraphics / Projectgraphics   **0047.** Tipos / Felix Beltran   **0048.** Casper Balslev /
Hello Monday   **0049.** Triple L / Damián Di Patrizio   **0050.** Five Point O / il2d   **0051.** Phi / Apfel Zet   **0052.** King Emperor / King Emperor
0053. SectionSeven / SectionSeven   **0054.** Pon a Punto tu Casa, Quito Vivienda / Anima   **0055.** Marland Consultoria & Design /
Fabrika de Typos   **0056.** Caus Bambu / Comparsas   **0057.** ImagenHB / ImagenHB   **0058.** SpeachSquare / HelloMe   **0059.** A Penguin / Attak
0060. Camisa 10 Propaganda / Camisa 10 Propaganda

East

0061

DEMO

0062

aha!

0063

pluto

0064

formlos

0065

MALTHA

0066

HALF ™

0067

OWAK

0068

TNOP ®

0069

union

0070

Fold

0071

Dpt.

0072

0061. East Photographic / No Days Off **0062.** Proyecto Demo / Estudio González **0063.** Aha! / Pure Communication **0064.** Pluto Project Spaces / Eva Lindeman **0065.** Formlos / Forma **0066.** Maltha / Studio41 Designers **0067.** Half, Milos Milosevic / Branislav Design **0068.** Owar / Estudio González **0069.** TNOP / TNOP Design **0070.** Union / Uselo **0071.** Fold / FEED **0072.** Departement Interactive Services / Philippe Archontakis

 chokolat

0073

0074

0075

0076

0077

0078

ESPACE N

0079

matriz B

0080

expositivo

0081

0082

TOMMY CHANDLER PHOTOGRAPHY

0083

taylordesign studio

0084

0073. Chokolat / TAXI Toronto   **0074.** Greensky Films / Falko Ohlmer   **0075.** Antje Klein / Hafenbraut   **0076.** td designs, Tony Davis / entz creative   **0077.** Grundfaktor / Ocular Ink   **0078.** Primegate / Anders Kavcic   **0079.** Espace N / FEED   **0080.** MatrizB / RacoSchneider   **0081.** Colectivo Xpositivo / Escobas   **0082.** Photographic Interiors / Studio Output   **0083.** Tommy Chandler Photography / Listen Design   **0084.** Taylor Design Studio S.L. / Christian Otto Studio

0085

0086

0087

0088

0089

0090

0091

0092

0093

0094

0095

0096

0085. Wood Productions / Estudio González   **0086.** Project Album / il2d   **0087.** Illunatic / Illunatic   **0088.** Propaga / Uselo
0089. Oblicua / Oblicua   **0090.** Debriefing / Cabina   **0091.** Keenpixel / Ocular Ink   **0092.** VaryWell / VaryWell   **0093.** Firsteight /
Falko Ohlmer   **0094.** A2 Studio / Projectgraphics   **0095.** Green Volcano Software / Ocular Ink   **0096.** Modani / Vladimir Sijerkovic

0097

0098

0099

0100

0101

0102

0103

0104

0105

0106

0107

0108

0097. Ars Thanea / Ars Thanea **0098.** Loosefilms / Studio Output **0099.** Swirl / LVL **0100.** Rana / Uselo **0101.** Loading, Cristian Vargas / Typozon Studio **0102.** Jaydee / Negro **0103.** Normal / Negro **0104.** Kontra / Kontra **0105.** Jaydee / Negro **0106.** area3 / area3 **0107.** Design Deluxe / Caótica **0108.** Claudia Mahecha Design / Clusta Ltd.

0109

0110

TRE UKER

0111

0112

0113

0114

arquitectos

0115

0116

0117

0118

0109.–0110. Beautiful Decay / Ohyeah Studio   **0111.** Tre Uker / Ohyeah Studio   **0112.** Viva Architecture / Zappness   **0113.** CIC (Contemporary Image Collective) / eps51   **0114.** Cinimod Studio / Studio Makgill   **0115.** Furograma Architects / Martino   **0116.** Ambigram / Pentagram   **0117** Automatica / Tecnopop   **0118.** Voodoo / BBH

0119

0120

0121

0122

0123

0124

0125

0126

0127

0128

0129

0130

0131

0132

0133

0134

0119. Ecopartner, Original Impressions / Maria Loor   **0120.** Pink Elephants Inc. / Helou Design   **0121.** Permanent Unit / Permanent Unit   **0122.** Bluelounge Design / Bluelounge Design   **0123.** Metro Ferreiro / ImagenHB   **0124.** Estúdios Mega / Vinte Zero Um Design   **0125.** Artist House Holding / A.C.O.   **0126.** Miguel Ángel Aragonés Studio / Frontespizio   **0127.** I love xhoch4 / xhoch4   **0128.** Kiu Enviromental Design / GuaZa Studio   **0129.** Lategan Media Group / TAXI Toronto   **0130.** Ein Anna Dans / Ohyeah Studio   **0131.** Studio-A / WeEatDesign   **0132.** USOTA 2007 / USOTA   **0133.** Nalindesign / Nalindesign   **0134.** ReStart Associates / ReStart Associates

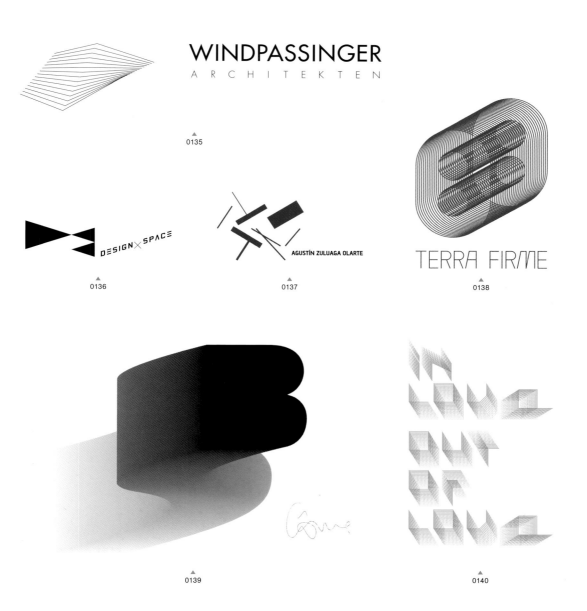

0135

0136

0137

0138

0139

0140

0135. Windpassinger Architekten / xhoch4   0136. Design x Space, Tunnel Studio / ReStart Associates   0137. Agustín Zuluaga Olarte / Cuartopiso   0138. Terra Firme Produtora / Tempo Design   0139. Bunch / Côme de Bouchony   0140. In Love – Out of Love / Cabina

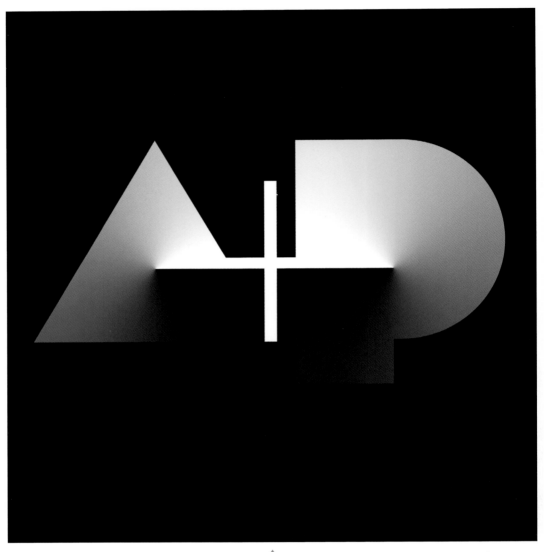

0141

ME TOO

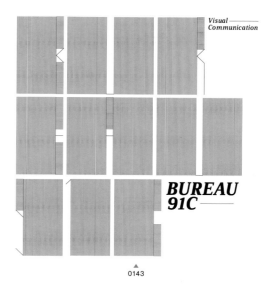

Visual Communication

BUREAU 91C

0142

0143

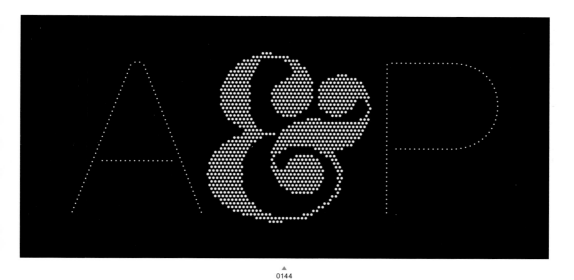

0144

---

142. Me Too / Cabina   **0143.** bureau 91c / HelloMe   **0144.** Accept & Proceed / The Luxury of Protest

0145

0146

0147

0148

0149

LAUREN MARKS

0150

LAUREN MARKS

0151

LAUREN MARKS

0152

LAUREN MARKS

0153

LAUREN MARKS

0154

LAUREN MARKS

0155

0145. Utopus / Tecnopop **0146.** Tech Mex Collective / Graphic Kitchen Studio **0147.** Falconer Chester Hall / Uniform
0148.–0149. Eno Krüger / Eno Krüger Design **0150.–0155.** Lauren Marks / TNOP Design

0156

0157

0158

0159

0160

0161

0162

0163

0164

MÉNDEZ FOTO

0165

0166

0167

---

156. Mira, Gerardo Maluje / Estudio González **0157.** Nobrand / Nobrand **0158.** Xinet / Pentagram **0159.** Matizmo, Jake Coventry / ntz creative **0160.** UrbanSilo, Jim Elliott / SectionSeven **0161.** Talega, Patricia Lascano / Estudio Garcia Balza **0162.** TuttiFrutti, atricia Lascano / Estudio Garcia Balza **0163.** Frakton / Projectgraphics **0164.** Fulô Estúdio / Fulô Estudio **0165.** Alfredo Méndez / studio González **0166.** Lya Zumblick / Lya Zumblick **0167.** De San Martín Design / ImagenHB

0168

0169

0170

0171

0172

0173

0174

0168. Renega / Dale Harris   0169. Monkey 01 / Glauco Diogenes Studio   0170. La Flama / La Flama   0171. Chilli Dog / Dale Harris
0172. SectionSeven / SectionSeven   0173. Accept & Proceed / USOTA   0174. Pyrochimps / Toastone, Amanzilla

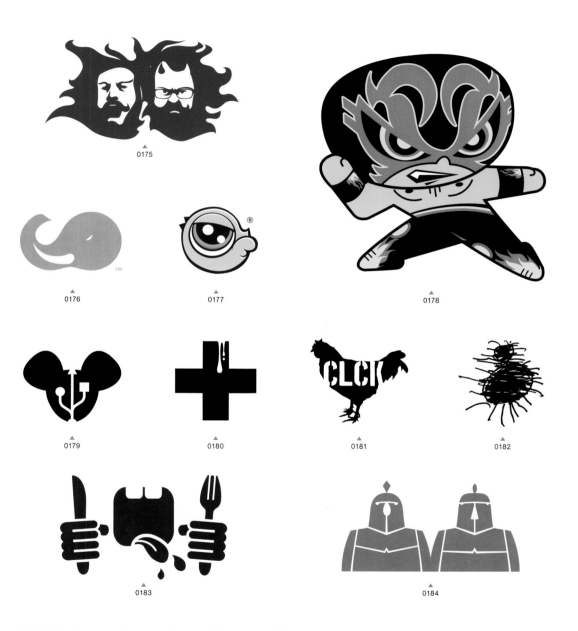

0175

0176

0177

0178

0179

0180

0181

0182

0183

0184

---

175. The boys / Attak **0176.** DS9 / TNOP Design **0177.** Dirb / Leo Vilas **0178.** Hijo de Fuego, PlasticPop / Escobas **0179.** USB Mouse / Attak **0180.** Seven Splat / Seven **0181.** Cluck Stencil, Cluck Design Collaborative / Listen Design **0182.** Adé Design / Helou Design **183.** WeEatDesign / WeEatDesign **0184.** Knights / Attak

0185

0186

0187

0188

0189

0190

0191

0192

0193

0194

0185. AB Rogers Design / Praline   **0186.** Estudio Infinito / Estudio Infinito   **0187.** Pixelway / Giovanni Bianco Studio 65   **0188.** Tangrama Design Studio / Tangrama   **0189.** FFAA, Felipe Francisco Aguirre / Juan Pablo Tredicce   **0190.** wg0055 / Ricardo Gimenes   **0191.** MC Dilo / Juan Pablo Tredicce   **0192.** Candy Productions / an agency called england   **0193.** Lush Industries / Dale Harris   **0194.** Va Va Voom, Silvina Moronta / NNSS Design

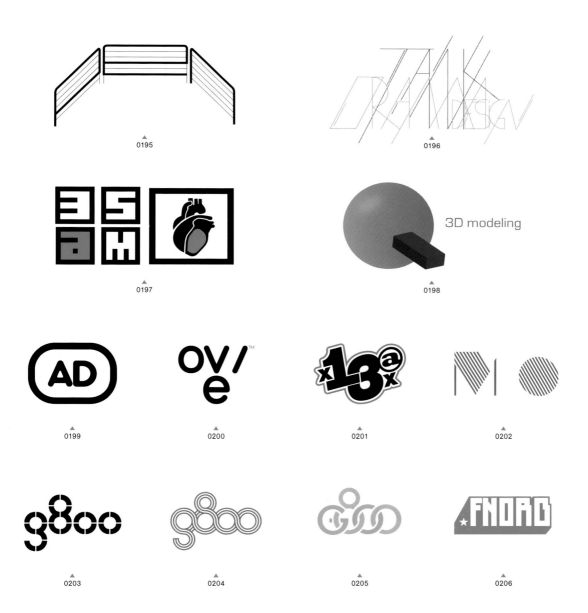

3D modeling

0195. Pen / BBH   **0196.** Tankorama Design / Ohyeah Studio   **0197.** 35AM Films / La Flama   **0198.** Q Studio / Branislav Design
0199. Another Digital / Giovanni Bianco Studio 65   **0200.** The Oculas Group / Hawaii Design   **0201.** x13Ax / xCOLITTx13Ax
0202. MO Creatives / Kasia Korczak and David Bennewith   **0203.–0205.** g800 / Apfel Zet   **0206.** FNORD / Permanent Unit

0207

LYNDON WADE

0208

casper. balslev

0209

 re-public

0210

NOBLANCO

0211

ANOTHER DIGITAL

0212

MATIZARFILMES

0213

the c42 collective®

0214

junge**schachtel**

0215

0216

QUADRA

0217

0207. Jaime Nuñez del Arco Studio / Nuñez del Arco **0208.** Lyndon Wade / Hello Monday **0209.** Casper Balslev / Hello Monday
0210. re-public / re-public **0211.** Noblanco / Noblanco **0212.** Another Digital / Giovanni Bianco Studio 65 **0213.** Matizar Filmes /
Dupla Design **0214.** The C42 Collective / Dale Harris **0215.** jungeschachtel / jungeschachtel **0216.** Lorena Duarte / Bercz
0217. Quadra, Patricia Lascano / Estudio Garcia Balza

KITA
VISUAL PLAYGROUND

0218

0219

0220

BANANEIRA
FILMES

0221

0222

0223

Miletina

0224

0225

0218. Nippon flowers / KITA **0219.** Divergente, INCINE / Diego Corrales **0220.** INCINE / Diego Corrales **0221.** Bananeira Filmes / Hardy Design **0222.** Word Jokey / Adrenalab **0223.** Little Fish Cards / Attitude Design **0224.** Phoenix, Irina Miletina / Ginter & Miletina **0225.** Morphos Studio / Eramos Tantos Studio

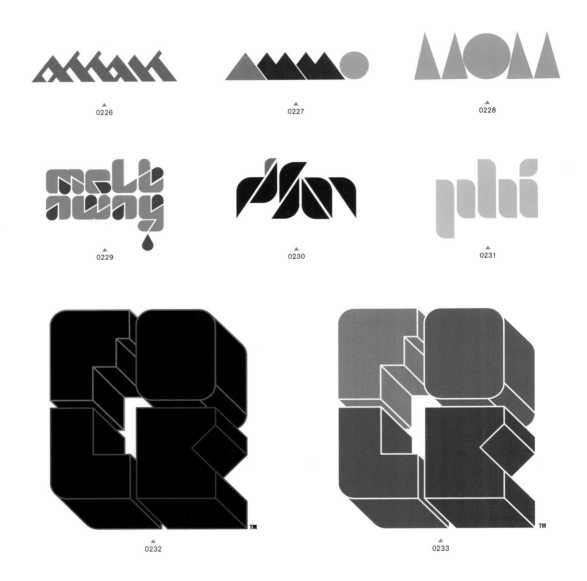

0226. Attak / Attak   **0227.** Ammo / Justin Harder   **0228.** MOM / Simone Inc.   **0229.** Melt Away / HelloMe   **0230.** Rison / HelloMe
0231. Phi / Apfel Zet   **0232.–0233.** Folk / Punga

0234

0235

0236

0237

ROSCA REALIZATEURS

0238

0239

0240

0234. Gravesend, Deadend Typeface / Chris Clarke **0235.** Slang / Slang **0236.** UML / Studio Makgill **0237.** Jaydee / Negro
0238. Rosca Realizateurs / Punga **0239.** Musae / Lya Zumblick **0240.** Paddington / Ohyeah Studio

0241

0242

0243

0241. Eno Krüger Design / Eno Krüger Design 0242. Permanent Unit / Permanent Unit 0243. Eno Krüger Design / Eno Krüger Design

0244

0245

0246

0247

0248

0244. 35AM Films / La Flama   0245. The Luxury of Protest / The Luxury of Protest   0246. Dale Harris / Dale Harris
0247. Art Design Studio / Art Design Studio   0248. Luciernaga, Firefly / Latinbrand

EVENTS & ENTERTAINMENT

CHAMPIONSHIPS, CONTESTS, EXHIBITIONS, FAIRS, FESTIVALS, SHOWS, THEATRE CO.

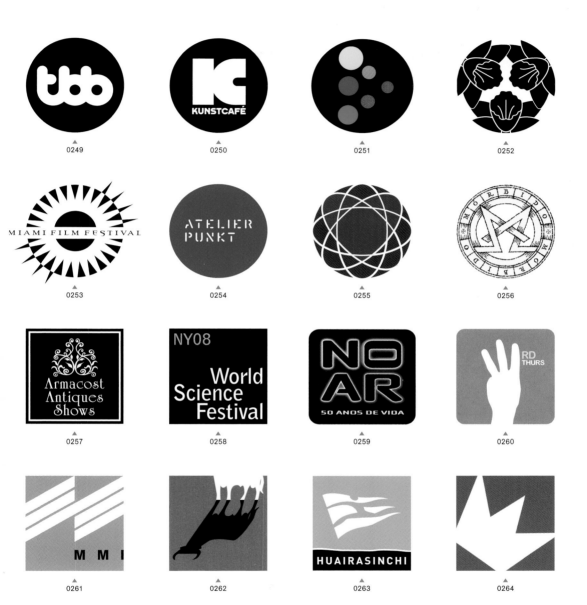

0249   0250   0251   0252

0253   0254   0255   0256

0257   0258   0259   0260

0261   0262   0263   0264

0249. The Big Beat / Falko Ohlmer   **0250.** Kunstcafé, Stichting bART / Attak   **0251.** Caracas Design, International Congress of Design / Juan Carlos Darias   **0252.** II CVK, Venezuelan Kendo Federation, FVK / Ariel Pintos   **0253.** Miami Film Festival / Elastic People   **0254.** Atelier Punkt, Melinda Pap / FEED   **0255.** Love Beat Boat / Krghettojuice   **0256.** Mórbido / Hula+Hula   **0257.** Armacost Antiques Shows / a+morph   **0258.** World Science Festival / Pentagram   **0259.** No Ar – 50 Anos de Vida, Mag+ Rede Cultural and Grupo RBS / 19 Design   **0260.** Third Thursda, Sticky Inc. / TNOP Design   **0261.** Messe München GmbH / Baumann & Baumann   **0262.** Salzburger Stier, SWR / Baumann & Baumann   **0263.** Huairasinchi, Proyecto Aventura / Latinbrand   **0264.** Kinder- und Jugendtheaterpreis, KJTZ / Apfel Zet

0265

0266

0267

0268

0269

0270

0271

0265. Reeperbahn Theater Hamburg / Firstflash X-media Labor   **0266.** Sexy Circus, Pleasure Room's / Kontra   **0267.** Young at Art / Paperjam Design   **0268.** La Yein Fonda, Neumann & Neumann Productions / Estudio González   **0269.** Fica Comigo Esta Noite, Chaim Produções / Arterial   **0270.** Follow Fluxus, Nassauischer Kunstverein Wiesbaden / 3Deluxe   **0271.** EVRU, Embassy of Spain in Abu Dhabi / area3

ENCUENTRO
INTERNACIONAL DE
COPRODUCCIÓN
DE DOCUMENTALES

0272

MiX

fil

0273　　0274　　0275

ROtA

NÓ

CRUEL

0276　　0277　　0278

CASA

MUCA
ecuador creative labs

0279　　0280

272. Doc Meeting Argentina, Planolatino / Bernardo+Celis　**0273.** MiX, Cia. de Dança Deborah Colker / Caótica　**0274.** Fil (Festival tercâmbio de Linguagens) / Laboratório Secreto　**0275.** 33-0, Wild Project / Nowhere　**0276.** Rota, Cia. de Dança Deborah Colker / aótica　**0277.** Nó, Cia. de Dança Deborah Colker / Caótica　**0278.** Cruel, Cia. de Dança Deborah Colker / Caótica
279. Casa, Cia. de Dança Deborah Colker / Caótica　**0280.** Muca, Ecuador Creative Labs / Nuñez del Arco

0282

0281

0283

0285   0286

0284   0287

0281. RB Speed Ride, Red Bull / Permanent Unit   **0282.** Road to the open, Orage / Permanent Unit   **0283.** As Pequenas Raposas, Oscar José Caótica   **0284.** Transalp Challenge / USOTA   **0285.** New School Picknick, Malua / Permanent Unit   **0286.** RB Bloc Buster, Red Bull / Permanent Unit   **0287.** The Mission, O'Neill Europe / DHM Graphic Design

0288

0289

0290

0291

---

288. Laranja Mecânica / Caótica **0289.** Coração Denunciador / Fulô Estudio **0290.** Multiplicidade / Caótica **0291.** Lab Project, Embassy of Spain in Abu Dhabi / area3

0292

0293

0294

0295

0296

0297

0292.–0294. Dinamo, Cia. de Dança Deborah Colker / Caótica **0295.–0297.** World Arts / VaryWell

0298

0299

0300

0301

0302

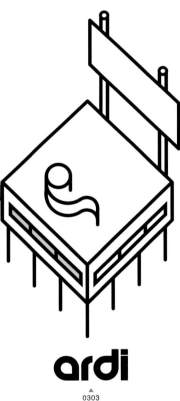

0303

0304

0305

298. if..., Cinéma du Parc / The Luxury of Protest   **0299.** Times Talks / Pentagram   **0300.** Angel Guido Art Project / ImagenHB
301. Twisted / eps51   **0302.** 100% Design / Pentagram   **0303.** Ardi, Sociedad Central de Arquitectos / ImagenHB
304. Wine Dine & All That Jazz, Covenant House / TAXI Toronto   **0305.** Nescafe Crave, Nescafe / Seven

0306

0307

0308

0309

0306. Contraditório, Fundação Athos Bulcão / Tecnopop   **0307.** Cinemaison, Consulado da França / Tecnopop
0308. Humor à Francesa, French Consulate in Brazil / Tecnopop   **0309.** Meumundo.com, Instituto Telemar / Vinte Zero Um Design

0310

0311

MÚLTIPLOS
projetos
culturais

0312

0313

310. Literaturas del Exilio, SEACEX / Bernardo+Celis **0311.** Skånes Dansteater / Anders Kavcic **0312.** Múltiplos Projetos Culturais,
Martha Pagy / Vinte Zero Um Design **0313.** The Big Art Project, Channel 4 / YES

0314

0315

0316

0317

0318

0319

0320

0314. Shifting Sites, Asia Art Archive / Milkxhake   **0315.** Andungen / Ohyeah Studio   **0316.** Shifting Sites, Asia Art Archive / Milkxhake   **0317.** October Contemporary / Milkxhake   **0318.** Beachdown Festival / Studio Makgill   **0319.** Shifting Sites, Asia Art Archive / Milkxhake   **0320.** Andersonville Arts Weekend, Andersonville Chamber of Commerce / estudiotres

DEN
GYLDNE'
PELS
NÅL

0321

THE
GOLDEN
FUR'
PIN

Shen
Wei
Dance
Arts

0322

● ● ● ● ●

deutscher
nachhaltigkeitspreis

0323

wild project

0324

NEW
YORK
CITY
BALLET

NEW YORK
CITY BALLET

NEWYORKCITYBALLET

0325

NYPH
08 New York
Photo Festival
May 14-18

0326

PREMIO
ALFAGUARA
1999

0327

---

321. The Golden Fur Pin, Kopenhagen Fur / re-public **0322.** Shen Wei Dance Arts / Nowhere **0323.** Deutscher Nachhaltigkeitspreis / Claus Koch **0324.** Wild Project / Nowhere **0325.** New York City Ballet / Pentagram **0326.** The New York Photography Festival 2008 / Pentagram **0327.** Alfaguara Prize / Graphic Kitchen Studio

0328. Time Brasil, Brazilian Olympic Committee / Soter Design **0329.** Semana Olímpica, Brazilian Olympic Committee / Soter Design **0330.** Rio 2016 – Candidate City, Brazilian Olympic Committee, *main logo* / Soter Design **0331.** Rio 2016 – Candidate City, Brazilian Olympic Committee, *development* / Soter Design **0332.** Pelé Station, Mag+ Rede Cultural and Prime Licensin, *main logo* / 19 Design **0333.–0336.** Pelé Station, Mag+ Rede Cultural and Prime Licensin, *development* / 19 Design

0337

0338

0339

337. Minto, Comvol 2002, *main logo* / Bernardo+Celis   **0338.** Minto, Comvol 2002, *development* / Bernardo+Celis   **0339.** Minto, Comvol 2002, *characters* / Bernardo+Celis

0340

0341

0342

0343

0344

0345

0346

0347

0348

0349

0350

0340. Galatasaray University Economics Days / 2FRESH   **0341.** Papier 07–Papier 08, AGAC / FEED   **0342.** Socialpest / DHM Graphic Design   **0343.** Companhia Suspensa / Osso Design   **0344.** Love and Money, British Council / Praline   **0345.** C & C, Bezalel Gallery / Oded Ezer   **0346.** Progressive Arts Network / Nowhere   **0347.** Late + Fuerte / NNSS Design + Ideas   **0348.** COP15 / re-public
0349. Pfalztheater Kaiserslautern / MAGMA Brand Design   **0350.** A Cuerda / Martino

0351

351. Exhibit A / The Killswitch Collective

0353

0352

0354

0355

0356

0357

0358

0352. Tiergarten Pforzheim / MAGMA Brand Design   **0353.** AIGA FRESH Talent / TNOP Design   **0354.** Ästhetiker Wängl Tängl / Permanent Unit   **0355.–0358.** AAUP Productions and Design Managers Meeting 2010, The University of Chicago Press / Lauren Nassef and Isaac Tobin

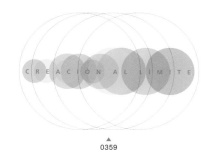

0359

0361

0360

0362

0363

0364

0365

359. Creación al Límite, Fundación Museos Nationales / Annella Armas   0360. Casulo Cultura / Osso Design   0361. Energy Plans, Provisions Library / Futurefarmers   0362. Surreal, Stichting bART / Attak   0363. Speak!, Stichting bART / Attak   0364. Dutch Masters, GEM Museum Contemporary Art / DHM Graphic Design   0365. Milkcrate Event Management Group / Liam Johnstone, Garus Booth

0366

0367

0368

0369

0370

0366. Ochoporojo, Cine Ochoymedio / Dema Werbeagentur   **0367.–0370.** Britspotting, Britspotting Film Festival 7 / upstruct berlin oslo

0371

0372

salonesregionales

0373

salonesregionales

0374

regionales

0375

71. Dingbats Brasil, Instituto de Artes Visuais / Bruno Porto   **0372.** Eduacion Biocentrica, Graciela Ficcardi / Boldrini & Ficcardi **73.–0375** 12 SRA, Ministerio de Cultura de Colombia / La Silueta Ediciones

0376

0377

0378

0379

0380

0381

0382

0383

0384

0385

0376. Grafik Parkour, Universidad del Desarrollo / Bercz   **0377.** Arcieri Della Merla / Adrenalab   **0378.** Taak / Adrenalab
0379. La Vache, GDFB / Attak   **0380.** Tony Fergo, Panama Grafico / Revolver   **0381.** The Little Bird Project, Daniel Arendt and Christian
Lindemann / Daniel Arendt   **0382.** Lobo Theater Corporation / Elastic People   **0383.** Golf Republic / Vladimir Sijerkovic
0384. Andersonville Chamber of Commerce / estudiotres   **0385.** Bloco dos Furtados / Caótica

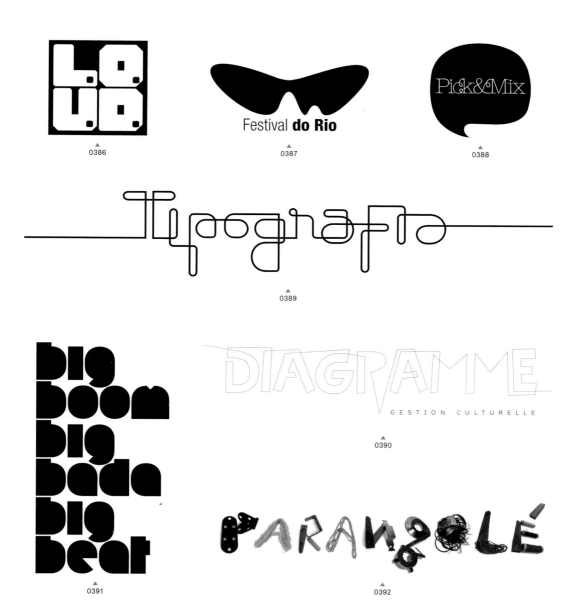

386. L.O.U.D., ISH / DBXL   0387. Rio Cine Festival, Festival do Rio / Vinte Zero Um Design   0388. Pick & Mix / Sockho
389. Tipografia, Utilitatio / Uselo   0390. Diagramme, Danielle Demers / Philippe Archontakis   0391. The Big Beat / Falko Ohlmer
392. Parangolé Awards, Secretaria das Culturas / Tecnopop

0393

0394

0395

0396

0397

0398

0399

0393. O'Neill Europe / DHM Graphic Design   **0394.** Highland Open, O'Neill Europe / DHM Graphic Design
0395.–0399. Coldwater Classic, O'Neill Europe / DHM Graphic Design

CIRCUIT DE SPA
FRANCORCHAMPS

0400

0401

0402

0403

0404

0405

0406

0407

0408

0400. Circuit de Spa Francorchamps / Hoet & Hoet   **0401.** Datamantes, Jebuke / Kontra   **0402.** Trama / Graphic Kitchen Studio
0403. France/Francia, Zaragoza 08, Commissariat Générale du Pavillon de la France / SIGN   **0404.** Cena Brasil Produções Culturais /
Felipe Taborda Design   **0405.** France/Francia, Zaragoza 08, Commissariat Générale du Pavillon de la France / SIGN   **0406.** AAAA,
Arte, Arquitectura, Antropologia y Autoritarismo", Universidad Central de Venezuela / Santiago Pol   **0407.** Kleines Haus, Ingolstadt Theatre /
hoch4   **0408.** NIU, Centro Metropolitano de Diseño / RDYA

FASHION & APPAREL

CLOTHING, EYEWEAR, FOOTWEAR, ACCESSORIES

0409

0410

0411

0412

0413

0414

0415

0416

0417

0418

409.–0418. Le Sucre Clothing / Falko Ohlmer

0419

0420

0421

0422

0423

0424

0425

0426

0427

0419. La Changa Wear / WeEatDesign   **0420.** Earth Crisis, Straightness / xCOLITTx13Ax   **0421.–0425.** Cheap Monday / Vår
0426. Loco-UK / Negro   **0427.** Black Icon Character, Sandpiper / Caótica

0428

0429

0430

0431

0432

0433

0434

0435

0436

0437

0438

0439

0440

0428. Happy Tails Grooming / Pepe Menéndez and Laura Llópiz **0429.** Banana Shield, Nike / Punga **0430.–0432.** Bad Bear Inc.,
USOTA Shirts / USOTA **0433.** Side Walk / São Paulo Criação **0434.** FIT / São Paulo Criação **0435.–0436.** Soul Circle / Eno Krüger Design
0437. My Gold School / Typozon Studio **0438.** Sweet Tooth Designs, Laurie Chapman / Typozon Studio **0439.–0440.** Le Sucre Clothing /
Falko Ohlmer

0441

0442

DONA COR

0443

no.mad agency

0444

0445

Charm

0446

0441. Nicola Dann / an agency called england   **0442.** Amulette, Johana Isaacs / Noblanco   **0443.** Dona Cor / Lya Zumblick
0444. no.mad agency / Apfel Zet   **0445.** Kooture / Ocular Ink   **0446.** Charm Perfum, Fragancias Nostrum / Bercz

▲
0447

▲
0448

▲
0449

▲
0450

▲
0451

▲
0452

▲
0453

▲
0454

447.–0450. Sweet Tooth Designs, Laurie Chapman, *development* / Typozon Studio 0451. Sweet Tooth Designs, Laurie Chapman, *main logo* / Typozon Studio 0452. Sweet Tooth Designs, Laurie Chapman, *development* / Typozon Studio 0453. Les Petits Cadeaux, Natural Beauty Basic Simone Inc. 0454. ION Essentials / 3Deluxe

0455

0456

0457

0458

0459

0460

0461

0462

0463

H·P·F,

0464

0465

0466

0455. Artist / Oscar Patzan Design　**0456.** Saudade / Oestudio　**0457.** Ossie Clark / SViDesign　**0458.** Totem / 6D　**0459.** Triton / Tempo Design　**0460.** Fakt / HelloMe　**0461.** Drops de Anis / Oestudio　**0462.** Zoomp / São Paulo Criação　**0463.** EGF, Eduard G. Fidel GmbH / MAGMA Brand Design　**0464.** H.P.F / Oestudio　**0465.** Picnic / Rock Instrument Bureau　**0466.** Bruuns Bazaar / Emenius Commercial Department, Kontrapunkt

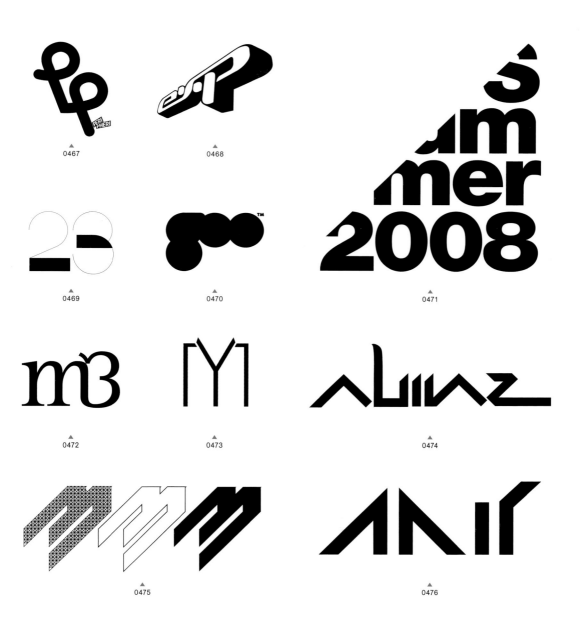

467. Peri Pheri / Jan Kallwejt 0468. Exp, Bob Experience / Eno Krüger Design 0469. 23, Neutral / HelloMe 0470. Goo / Clusta td. 0471. Le Sucre Clothing / Falko Ohlmer 0472. Mónica Borrero / Helou Design 0473. Yonca Moda / 2FRESH 0474. Crystallised, warovski / Muller 0475. Jessica McCormack / Hawaii Design 0476. A Night in Fashion / Stereo

0477

0478

0479

0480

0481

0482

0477.–0482. ION Essentials / 3Deluxe

0483

0484

0485

0486

0487

0488

0489

483. ION Essentials / 3Deluxe   **0484.** Melanie McLean Agency / Philippe Archontakis   **0485.** Country Club, Nike / Punga   **0486.** ION ssentials / 3Deluxe   **0487.** Cotton United / erde zwei   **0488.** ION Essentials / 3Deluxe   **0489.** Country Club, Nike / Punga

0490

0491

0492

0493

0494

0495

0490. Abandoned Clothing / Nalindesign **0491.** Mother Superior UK / Hello Vanilla **0492.** Rebel Rebel, Surda Clothing / Nuñez del Arco **0493.** Ästhetiker Wear / Permanent Unit **0494.** Okayplay / Christian Otto Studio **0495.** To Hell, Attakatoen / Attak

0496

0497

fukujìn

0498

Professional Skipping Rope

0499

0500

0501

final

0502

0503

---

496. Ninja Love, Invictus CFW / xCOLITTx13Ax **0497.** Fukujin / Vianet **0498.** Skipping Ropes / Toastone, Amanzilla **0499.** Osklen / omparsas **0500.** Jeans Dean, Johnny Velvet / Attak **0501.** Invictus CFW / xCOLITTx13Ax **0502.** Diabito Character / Caótica
503. Crazy Boys, Marcos Crisi / Boldrini & Ficcardi

0504

0505

0506

0507

I LCVE BLACKFIN
BLACKFIN THE LUXURY OF DIRT.
*HTTP://BLACKFIN.COM.AR

0508

PLEASE VISIT
BLACKFIN.COM.AR

0509

0510

PERIPHERI

0511

FASHION
FRINGE

0512

Thread.
The Ethical Line On Style

0513

RICARDO
PIÑEIRO

0514

appeal
DIVISION RICARDO PIÑEIRO

0515

0504. Vadum / Emenius Commercial Department   **0505.** Tunit, Adidas / Emenius Commercial Department, Kontrapunkt
0506. Estética Garbo / Paco Gálvez   **0507.–0510.** Blackfin, Trend Mill SA. / Negro   **0511.** Peri Pheri / Jan Kallwejt
0512. Fashion Fringe / Pentagram   **0513.** BBC Thread, BBC / MrBowlegs, Magnetic North   **0514.** Ricardo Piñeiro Modelos / Cabina
0515. Appeal, Ricardo Piñeiro Modelos / Cabina

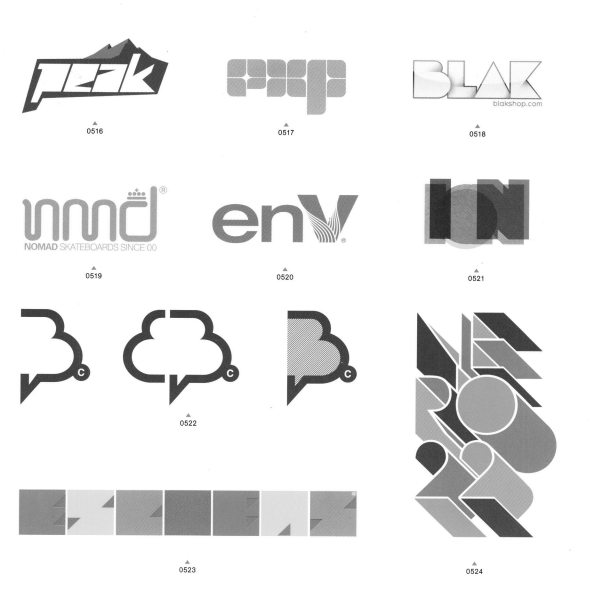

0516

0517

0518

0519

0520

0521

0522

0523

0524

516. Peak, Jan Rosenthal / HelloMe   0517. Exp, Be Phoenix / Eno Krüger Design   0518. Blak, Blakshop.com / Superexpresso
19. NMD, Nomad Skateboards / Medusateam   0520. enV, Bagby & Co. / TNOP Design   0521. ION Essentials / 3Deluxe   0522. Björkvin /
ello Monday   0523. Escobas / Escobas   0524. Nero22 / Falko Ohlmer

POZZI/LEI

0525

0526

0527

0528

0529

0530

0531

0532

0533

0534

0535

0525. Pozzilei / Giovanni Bianco Studio 65   **0526.** We Love Sneakers / LVL   **0527.** Fearless Clothing / Falko Ohlmer   **0528.** Triptico / Kontra   **0529.** Corazon Salomon, David Salomon / WeEatDesign   **0530.** Kavany, Bruno Assi / LVL   **0531.** Escendo / Anders Kavcic **0532.** Loco-UK / Negro   **0533.** Omino / São Paulo Criação   **0534.** Bsided / Sockho   **0535.** Missoni / Giovanni Bianco Studio 65

0536

0537

schmoove.

0538

soft gallery

0539

MARIA PINTO™

0540

DSQUARED²

0541

chris holzinger

0542

OSKLEN SURFING

0543

Discrete

0544

BRITISH COLONY

0545

BRITISH COLONY
MAXIME PERELMUTER

0546

MAXIME
PERELMUTER

0547

536.–0537. Scarab / eps51 0538. Schmoove / LVL 0539. Soft Gallery / Emenius Commercial Department 0540. Maria Pinto / TNOP ●esign 0541. Dsquared2 / Giovanni Bianco Studio 65 0542. Chris Holzinger / eps51 0543. Osklen / Comparsas 0544. Discrete Headwear ⌐Listen Design 0545.–0547. British Colony, Maxime Perelmuter / 6D

0548

0549

0550

0551

0552

0553

0548.–0553. Go!, Nike / Punga

0554

0555

0556

0557

0558

0559

0560

0561

0562

0563

---

554. Cowboy, Attakatoen / Attak **0555.** Father, Attakatoen / Attak **0556.** Puker, Attakatoen / Attak **0557.** Sweater, Attakatoen / Attak **0558.** Fist, Attakatoen / Attak **0559.** Heartgrenade, Attakatoen / Attak **0560.** Pitocatalán / Cabina **0561.** Bear Care / ustin Harder **0562.** Sai Baba, Nike / Hula+Hula **0563.** Caótica Pattern / Caótica

0564

0565

0566

0567

0568

0564. Rison Plane, Rison / HelloMe **0565.** Vilken Vom / Hello Monday **0566.** FilzFlash / Ducks Design Hamburg **0567.** Lisa Nuboer, Anita Korff / Faydherbe & De Vringer **0568.** Corazón de Melón / Hula+Hula

0569

0570

0571

0572

0573

0574

---

569. Ela Diseño y Moda / Helou Design **0570.** Premios de la Moda, Ivana Productions / shk.studio **0571.** Layali, Mint / Damián i Patrizio **0572.** Makite, Sociedad Minera Cerro Verde / Ideo Comunicadores **0573.** Coutours / RARE Design Associates 574. Charm Perfum, Fragancias Nostrum / Bercz

0575

0576

0578

0579

0580

MONICA VINADER

0577

BRUUNS BAZAAR

0581

COMPAÑIA DE COSTURA

0582

oxelo

0583

PIPERLIME

0584

0584

0585

0586

0575. Melissa Lo Jewellery / Studio Makgill   **0576.** Vande Falke / HelloMe   **0577.** Monica Vinader / David Standen, Frame   **0578.** Thimble Sourcing / Ideo Comunicadores   **0579.** Primondo, Karstadt Quelle AG / Claus Koch   **0580.** Tangerine Spa / WeEatDesign   **0581.** Bruuns Bazaar / Emenius Commercial Department, Kontrapunkt   **0582.** Compania de Costura, Mariana Chalulueu / Boldrini & Ficcardi   **0583.** Oxelo, Decathlon / Pentagram   **0584.** Piperlime, Gap, Inc. / Pentagram   **0585.** Suncoast, C&A / Oestudio   **0586.** Gilson Martins / RacoSchneider

0587

0588

0589

0590

0591

0592

0593

0594

587. Forey / Gaia 9 Studio   **0588.** Agrinia Jewelry / Tangrama   **0589.** Extra Fine Wool, The Woolmark Company / TAXI New York
590.–0592. Tuuli, Tudeboo / Hardy Design, Voltz   **0593.** Nido, Women Clothing, Art Gallery / Cabina   **0594.** Crush, Fashion Crush / owhere

INSTITUTIONS, GOVERNMENT & REGIONAL

ASSOCIATIONS, CHURCHES, CITIES, CLUBS, COLLEGES, COMMUNITIES, COUNTRIES, FOUNDATIONS, INSTITUTIONS, MUSEUMS, ORGANISATIONS, UNIVERSITIES, SCHOOLS

MML
MOBILE
MEDIA
LAB

MML
MOBILE
MEDIA
LAB

MML
MOBILE
MEDIA
LAB

MML
MOBILE
MEDIA
LAB

MML
MOBILE
MEDIA
LAB

MML
MOBILE
MEDIA
LAB

MML
MOBILE
MEDIA
LAB

MML
MOBILE
MEDIA
LAB

MML
MOBILE
MEDIA
LAB

MML
MOBILE
MEDIA
LAB

MML
MOBILE
MEDIA
LAB

MML
MOBILE
MEDIA
LAB

▲
0595

0595. Mobile Media Lab / FEED

0596

0597

0598

0599

0600

0601

0602

0603

0604

0605

0606

0607

0608

0609

0610

0611

0596. Subte, Metrovias / Shakespear Design   **0597.** Plus, Picture Licensing Universal System / Pentagram   **0598.** FVK, Venezuelan Kendo Federation / Ariel Pintos   **0599.** Asociación de Vecinos de Bello Monte / Juan Carlos Darias   **0600.** Staatstheater Nürnberg / Claus Koch
0601. NeoPolis / The Luxury of Protest   **0602.** Generations / Attak   **0603.** Window / KITA   **0604.** Maac, Banco Central del Ecuador / Studio Versus   **0605.** Stadthalle Schillerhöhe / Baumann & Baumann   **0606.** Seed / Dale Harris   **0607.** Details, Musashino Art University / Baumann & Baumann   **0608.** VDI / Claus Koch   **0609.** Württembergisches Landesmuseum Stuttgart / Baumann & Baumann
0610. The Philip Johnson Glass House, National Trust for Historic Preservation / Pentagram   **0611.** Art Institute of Chicago / Pentagram

0612

0613

0616

0614

0615

0619

0617

0618

0620

0621

12. Cynara, Adrepes / Amodesign   **0613.** Refugio Aboim Ascensao, Chama Inc. / Emiliano Rodriguez   **0614.** Garden for the Environment / turefarmers   **0615.** Quito World Flowers Capital, CMT, Quito Tourist Bureau / Belén Mena   **0616.** UCLA Arts, UCLA School of Arts and chitecture / Polychrome   **0617.** Boghossian Foundation / SIGN   **0618.** Distribuidora de Libros, CONAC (Consejo Nacional de la Cultura) / ntiago Pol   **0619.** BAIE (Barcelona Aeronautics & Space Association) / area3   **0620.** Victory Gardens 2008+, San Francisco Department for Environment / Futurefarmers   **0621.** Recycle Now / Momkai

0622. Hooli, Terve Eesti / Christoph Knoth   **0623.** Univida, Care / Latinbrand   **0624.** h(iv)eart, Terve Eesti / Christoph Knoth
0625. Anker Gemeente / DHM Graphic Design   **0626.** Sida+Violencia, Fundación para Estudio e Investigación de la Mujer /
Bernardo+Celis   **0627.** Observatorio de Asuntos de Genero, Amalia Aguilar / shk.studio   **0628.–0634.** Conamu, Goverment, *development* /
Latinbrand   **0635.** Conamu, Goverment, *main logo* / Latinbrand

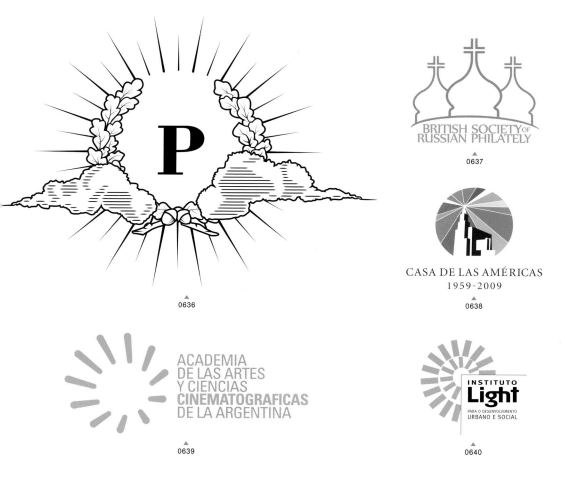

0636

BRITISH SOCIETY OF RUSSIAN PHILATELY

0637

CASA DE LAS AMÉRICAS
1959-2009

0638

ACADEMIA
DE LAS ARTES
Y CIENCIAS
CINEMATOGRAFICAS
DE LA ARGENTINA

0639

INSTITUTO
Light
PARA O DESENVOLVIMENTO
URBANO E SOCIAL

0640

Flatiron
23rd Street
Partnership

0641

PERSONA

0642

LUTHERAN STUDY BIBLE

0643

---

36. Plattform, Kunstwollen Association / Ronnie Fueglister, Martin Steocklin   **0637.** British Society of Russian Philately / Kent House
●nsulting Ltd.   **0638.** 50th Anniversary of Casa de las Américas / Pepe Menéndez   **0639.** Academia del Cine de la Argentina / Estudio Garcia
lza   **0640.** Light Institute of Urban and Social Development, Light Electric Distributer / eg.design   **0641.** Flatiron, 23rd Street Partnership /
■ntagram   **0642.** Persona, Banco Icatu / Interface Designers   **0643.** Luthern Study Bible, Augsburg Fortress / Spunk Design Machine

0644

0645

0646

0647

0648

0651

0649

0650

0644.–0651. Kohlekraft – Nein danke!, Greenpeace Media, Hamburg / USOTA

0652

0653

0654

0655

0656

0657

0658

0659

0660

0661

0662

0652.–0662. Oficina Desafio, Universidade de Campinas / Kiko Farkas, Máquina Estúdio

0663

0664

0665

0666

0667

0668

0669

0670

0671

0663.–0666. Codarts / 75B **0667.–0671.** Fundación Cultural de la Ciudad de México / Gabriela Rodríguez Studio

FH MAINZ

0672

GESTALTUNG
FH MAINZ

0673

WIRTSCHAFTS-
WISSENSCHAFTEN
FH MAINZ

0674

MUSEO
DE PALPA

0675

MUSEO
DE PALPA

0676

MUSEO
DE PALPA

0677

MUSEU
CASA DO
PONTAL

ARTE POPULAR BRASILEIRA

0678

MUSEU
CASA DO
PONTAL

ARTE POPULAR BRASILEIRA

0679

MUSEU
CASA DO
PONTAL

ARTE POPULAR BRASILEIRA

0680

CENTENÁRIO
PORTINARI
1903 | 2003
PROJETO PORTINARI

0681

CENTENÁRIO
PORTINARI
1903 | 2003
PROJETO PORTINARI

0682

CENTENÁRIO
PORTINARI
1903 | 2003
PROJETO PORTINARI

0683

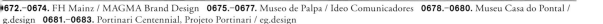

0672.–0674. FH Mainz / MAGMA Brand Design   **0675.–0677.** Museo de Palpa / Ideo Comunicadores   **0678.–0680.** Museu Casa do Pontal / g.design   **0681.–0683.** Portinari Centennial, Projeto Portinari / eg.design

0684

0685

0686

0687

0688

0689

0690

0691

0692

0693

0684. Museum für Film und Fernsehen / Pentagram **0685.** I teach NYC / Pentagram **0686.** Pont-Aven School of Contemporary Art / Pentagram **0687.** Cultura e Pensamento, Secretaria das Culturas / Tecnopop **0688.** Park Avenue Armory / Pentagram **0689.** The Drill Hall, Park Avenue Armory / Pentagram **0690.** VERDF, Voltear a Ver, A.C. / Gabriela Rodríguez Studio **0691.–0692.** New Orleans / Justin Harder **0693.** Mobile Experience Engine, Concordia University / FEED

The **Met**
ropolitan
Opera

0694

The **Met**ropolitan **Opera**

0695

The
Morgan
Library&
Museum

0696

**STAATLICHE
AKADEMIE DER
BILDENDEN KÜNSTE
STUTTGART**

0697

PRINCETON
UNIVERSITY
ART MUSEUM

0698

SAM SEATTLE ART MUSEUM

0699

arts LEWIS CENTER PRINCETON

0700

wpca
worldwide palliative
care alliance

0701

CU NY The City University of New York

0702

Columbia
Business
School

0703

Art
+Design
DMU

0704

0694.–0695. The Metropolitan Opera / Pentagram   **0696.** The Morgan Library & Museum / Pentagram   **0697.** Staatliche Akademie der
ildenden Künste Stuttgart / Apfel Zet   **0698.** Princeton University Art Museum / Pentagram   **0699.** Seattle Art Museum / Pentagram
700. Lewis Center for the Arts / Pentagram   **0701.** Worldwide Palliative Care Alliance / Pentagram   **0702.** City University of New York /
entagram   **0703.** Columbia Business School / Pentagram   **0704.** Art+Design DMU, De Montfort University / Un.titled

0705

0706

0707

0710

0708

0709

0711

0705.–0707. Inhotim Contemporary Art Center / Hardy Design, Voltz   **0708.** HallenSportBadBiberach, Stadtwerke Biberach GmbH / Baumann & Baumann   **0709.** Aysa, Agua y Saneamientos Argentinos / Estudio Garcia Balza   **0710.** Loddon Shire / Dale Harris
0711. CPFL Cultura / Gad' Branding & Design

▲
0712

▲
0713

▲
0714

DEUTSCHE
NATIONAL
BIBLIOTHEK

▲
0715

▲
0716

TO
RON
TO

▲
0717

GUAYAQUIL

▲
0718

Research
Centre
for Fashion
the Body
& Material
Cultures

▲
0719

K20 K21
KUNSTSAMMLUNG NORDRHEIN-WESTFALEN

▲
0720

▲
0721

---

712. Premio Luis Caballero, Instituto Distrital de Cultura y Turismo / Tangrama   **0713.** Launchpad, The Science Museum / Pentagram
714. Mali, Museo de Arte de Lima / Studioa   **0715.** Deutsche Nationalbibliothek / Claus Koch   **0716.** Rendez-vous Novembre 2007,
ille de Montréal / FEED   **0717.** Toronto Transit Comission, OCAD / Liam Johnstone   **0718.** Distrito de las artes, Fundación Distrito de las
rtes / Nuñez del Arco   **0719.** Research Center for Fashion the Body and..., University of Art / Praline   **0720.** K20 K21, Kunstsammlung NRW
Claus Koch   **0721.** ZOVAR, CIBG / Faydherbe & De Vringer

0722

0723

0724

0725

0726

0727

0728

0729

0730

0731

0732

0733

0734

0735

0722. Princeton University / Pentagram   **0723.** Gradara, Macramé / DOGO   **0724.** Boca, Club Atletico Boca Juniors / Shakespear Design   **0725.** Staatskanzlei NRW / Claus Koch   **0726.** San Diego Advertising Fund for Emergencies, SAFE / 9Myles   **0727.** Colégio Loyola / Hardy Design, Voltz   **0728.** Huevocherdo / Eramos Tantos Studio   **0729.** GD Football Club / Jan Kallwejt   **0730.** FC Makeni Juniors / Attak   **0731.** Hockey in the Hood / Zachary Richter, Oliver Munday, Jay Roop   **0732.** IANN / Anima   **0733.** American Society for Surgery of the Hand / 9Myles   **0734.** Fundación Boliviana para la Democracia Multipadari / Ernesto Azcuy   **0735.** Telecurso TEC, Fundação Roberto Marinho / eg.design

MINISTÉRIO DA SAÚDE

0736

CALIFORNIA
ACADEMY OF
SCIENCES

0737

0740

CNE
Corte Nacional Electoral
República de Bolivia

0738

kidsco
Personitas con sentido

0739

DISEÑADORES GRÁFICOS
B O L I V I A

0741

INSTITUTO
ESTUDIOS
GRÁFICOS
DE CHILE

0742

CALIFORNIA
COMMUNITY
FOUNDATION

0743

The Yorkshire Wolds

0744

---

36. Ministério da Saúde / Oz Design   **0737.** California Academy of Sciences / Pentagram   **0738.** Corte Nacional Electoral, Bolivia / Ernesto cuy   **0739.** Kidsco / GuaZa Studio   **0740.** San Isidro, Gobierno de Buenos Aires / Fileni & Fileni Design   **0741.** Diseñadores Gráficos Bolivia Machicao Design   **0742.** Instituto Estudios Gráficos de Chile, Asimpres / Larrea   **0743.** California Community Foundation / Geyrhalter esign   **0744.** The Yorkshire Wolds, Visit Hull & East Yorkshire / an agency called england

BICIVIA

0745

INSTITUTE OF MEDIA ENVIRONMENT
メディア環境研究所

0746

Buenos Aires IISI 40
ANNUAL CONFERENCE & MEETINGS

0747

the **victorian institute**
of **chemical science**

0748

Yale SCHOOL OF MANAGEMENT

0749

0750

0751

0752

0753

SARDEGNA

0754

musexum

0755

0745. Bicivia, Guayaquil City Hall / Anima   **0746.** ME, Hakuhodo DY Media Partners / A.C.O.   **0747.** International Iron and Steel Institute IISI 40, Techint Organization / Pump Diseño   **0748.** VICS Logo, Victorian Institute of Chemical Science / Dale Harris   **0749.** Yale School of Management / Pentagram   **0750.** Museo del Caribe, Mag+ Rede Cultural / 19 Design   **0751.** AAMAC, Contemporary Art Museum of Niteró Dupla Design   **0752.** Contemporary Jewish Museum / Pentagram   **0753.** VSBC, Association of Swiss Business Centres / Büro Ink **0754.** Sardegna / Pentagram   **0755.** Sex Museum / Esteban Salgado

0756

DETROIT
INSTITUTE
OF ARTS

0757

0758

0759

0760

0761

0762

0763

0764

0765

0766

0767

56.–0758. Detroit Institute of Arts / Pentagram **0759.** Argentina.Travel, Ministerio de Turismo de la Nación Argentina / Cabina
60. e3 Labs, Inc. / Essex Two **0761.** Sur Sud Sul, VSV / ImagenHB **0762.** b, byZOO Corporation / A.C.O. **0763.** World Music & Dance
entre / 75B **0764.** National Council of the Fauna / Graphic Kitchen Studio **0765.** Trole / Diego Corrales **0766.** Temaiken Foundation/
akespear Design **0767.** Mesa / Anima

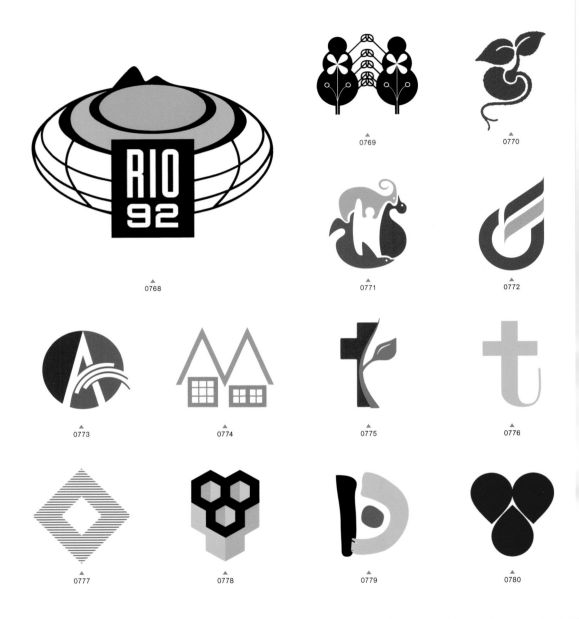

0768

0769

0770

0771

0772

0773

0774

0775

0776

0777

0778

0779

0780

0768. Rio 92, The City of Rio de Janeiro / eg.design **0769.** Garden for the Environment / Futurefarmers **0770.** New Growth, Greater Chicago Food Depository / Essex Two **0771.** Festa delle Oasi, WWF / Vertigo Design **0772.** Ero Kosova, Energy Regulatory Office / Projectgraphics **0773.** Asimpres / Larrea **0774.** Thomas Moran Trust / Pentagram **0775.** First Baptist Church of Paducah / Vladimir Sijerkovic **0776.** Tailor Missions / Pentagram **0777.** Artes Visuales / Felix Beltran **0778.** Colmena / Hula+Hula **0779.** Deutsches Zentrum Helou Design **0780.** Herzbluter / Forma

PATRIMOINE CULTUREL IMMATÉRIEL

0781

Jewish General Hospital

0782

NORSK
FORFATTERSENTRUM

0783

WPI World Premier International
Research Center Initiative

0784

Ohio
Environmental
Council

0785

SerCidadão

0786

HOCHTAUNUSKREIS

0787

OGLETHORPE
UNIVERSITY

0788

---

781. Patrimoine Culturel Immateriel, PCI / Oblicua   **0782.** Jewish General Hospital / TAXI Montreal   **0783.** Norsk Forfattersentrum /
>struct berlin oslo   **0784.** WPI, Japan Society for the Promotion of Science / A.C.O.   **0785.** Ohio Environmental Council, OEC /
Myles   **0786.** SerCidadão / RacoSchneider   **0787.** Hochtaunuskreis / Ginter & Miletina   **0788.** Oglethorpe University / Pentagram

0789

0790

0791

0792

0793

0794

0795

0796

0797

Design Leicestershire

0798

0799

0800

0789. CPVO (Community Plant Variety Office) / Hoet & Hoet **0790.** Copacabana Sagrado, Asociación Boliviana de Agencias de Viajes y Turis / Ernesto Azcuy **0791.** Sigedis / Hoet & Hoet **0792.** Cheese, Dairy Farmers of Canada / TAXI Toronto **0793.** ama (Art Moves Africa 1820eps51 **0794.** Mak, Mentorship System FEB / Pixelerate **0795.** IN, Instituto de Arte Contemporáneo de Cuenca / Helou Design **0796.** UIO, City Goverment / Latinbrand **0797.** Fisk, Fundacão Richard Hugh Fisk / Oz Design **0798.** Design Leicestershire / Un.titled **0799.** Get London Reading, Booktrust / KentLyons **0800.** John Charles Centre for Sport, Leeds City Council / an agency called england

0801

0802

0803

0804

0805

0806

0807

0808

0809

0810

iab.

0811

0812

0801. Vivantes / Pentagram 0802. Ancine / Vinte Zero Um Design 0803. Correos Chile, Chilean Government / Grupo Oxigeno 0804. SMN, Technical University Eindhoven / The Cre8ion.Lab 0805. bART, Stichting bART / Attak 0806. CCEBA, Centro Cultural de España en Buenos Aires / Bernardo+Celis 0807. DWP (Digital Water Pavilion), Zaragoza Municipality / studio FM milano 0808. Orlando Museum of Art / Push 0809. Museum of Arts and Design / Pentagram 0810. UC Riverside, University of California, Riverside / Pentagram 0811. The Internet Advertising Bureau / Pentagram 0812. ift, Leibniz Institute for Tropospherice Research / Christoph Knoth

0814

0813

0815

0816

0817

0818

0819

0820

0813. InSpira Performing Arts and Cultural Center / 3rd Edge Communications **0814.** MAC de Niterói, Contemporary Art Museum of Niterói / Dupla Design **0815.** Argentina Formidable, Argentinean Goverment / ImagenHB **0816.** Laranjeiras Clínica Perinatal / Interface Designers **0817.** Cornell Lab of Ornithology / Pentagram **0818.** Help Whale, Greenpeace / Nahon **0819.** Aves Uruguay, Gupeca / Marcos Larghero **0820.** Outward Bound Center for Peacebuilding / Pentagram

0821

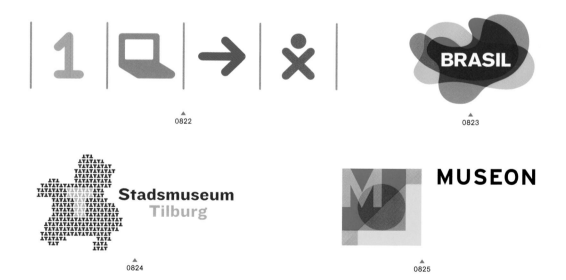
0822

0823

0824

0825

---

321. UCLA School of Theater, Film, and Television / Polychrome   **0822.** One Laptop per Child Foundation / Pentagram   **0823.** Marca Brasil, mbratur / Kiko Farkas, Máquina Estúdio   **0824.** Stadsmuseum Tilburg / Faydherbe & De Vringer   **0825.** Museon, Maarten Okkersen / ydherbe & De Vringer

0826

0827

0828

0829

0830

0831

0832

0826. HIV, International Planned Parethood Federation, IPPF / de.MO **0827.** TWS Ravensburg / Baumann & Baumann
0828. Emprendedor, Universidad Mayor / ImagenHB **0829.** Designprijs Rotterdam, Stichting Designprijs / 75B **0830.** CIVA,
Christians in the Visual Arts / asmallpercent **0831.** &c / Forma **0832.** College of Design, University of Minnesota College of Design /
Spunk Design Machine

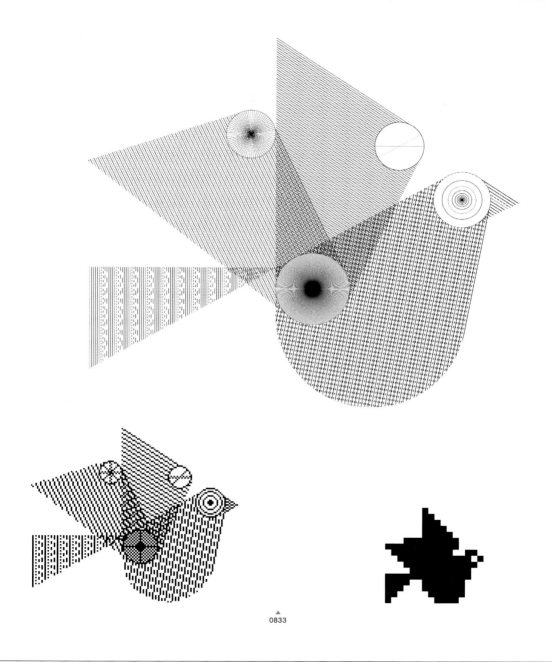

0833

833. Mobile Digital Commons Network / The Luxury of Protest

MEDIA

BOOKS, CAMPAIGNS, FILMS, MAGAZINES, NEWSPAPERS, PORTALS, PUBLISHERS, RADIO, TV, WEBSITES

0834

834. Neon Radio, Neon Magazine / Falko Ohlmer

0835

0836

0837

0838

0839

0840

0841

0842

0843

0844

0845

0846

0847

0848

0849

0850

0835. Cuerda Floja, Ediciones Vértigo / Sofia Saez Matos   **0836.** Reality Sandwich, Evolver / Nowhere   **0837.** 4FM / Hoet & Hoet
0838. The Guild Open Project / Illunatic   **0839.** Access Internet / Velesi   **0840.** Nike All Ball, RGA + Brandfields / Arterial   **0841.** Memory
Game / Ariel Pintos   **0842.** Flor Canibal Editorial / Fritz Torres   **0843.** I wanna be Paris' new best friend, MTV / The Killswitch
Collective   **0844.** Adrenalab Multimedia / Adrenalab   **0845.** Cool Guy / Justin Harder   **0846.** Cloud Magic / Justin Harder   **0847.** 24Seven
Vol 2, Image Comics / Muller   **0848.** The Criterion Collection / Pentagram   **0849.** Eclipse, The Criterion Collection / Pentagram   **0850.** IDN
Black & White / USOTA

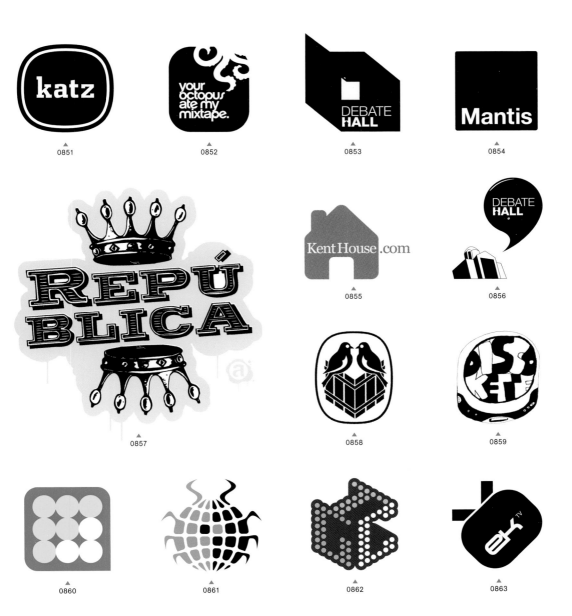

0851

0852

0853

0854

0857

0855

0856

0858

0859

0860

0861

0862

0863

0851. Katz Editores / Tholön Kunst   **0852.** Your octopus ate my mixtape / Dale Harris   **0853.** Debate Hall / VaryWell   **0854.** Mantis,
Editorial Diogenes / Boldrini & Ficcardi   **0855.** Kent House Consulting Ltd. / Kent House Consulting Ltd.   **0856.** Debate Hall /
VaryWell   **0857.** República, Rádio Atlântida / DEZ Propaganda   **0858.** Plotki / Apfel Zet   **0859.** Discokette / Nuñez del Arco
0860. De Ferrari / ImagenHB   **0861.** Global Roach / Logoholik   **0862.** TGC, The Games Company Worldwide GmbH / form one
0863. EK, Elektronica TV / Negro

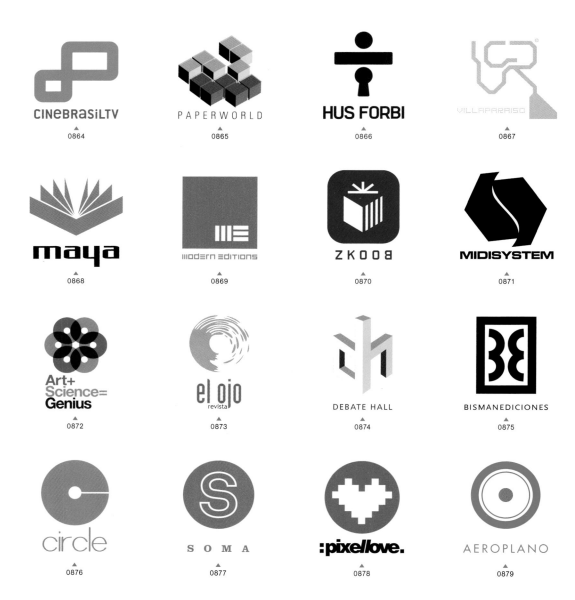

CINEBRASILTV
0864

PAPERWORLD
0865

HUS FORBI
0866

VILLAPARAISO
0867

maya
0868

modern editions
0869

ZKOOB
0870

MIDISYSTEM
0871

Art+
Science=
Genius
0872

el ojo
revista
0873

DEBATE HALL
0874

BISMANEDICIONES
0875

circle
0876

SOMA
0877

:pixellove.
0878

AEROPLANO
0879

0864. CINEBRASILTV / Vinte Zero Um Design   **0865.** Paperworld / RARE Design Associates   **0866.** Hus Forbi / Battin   **0867.** VCR Villaparaiso, La casa del cine / La fe ciega studio   **0868.** Maya ediciones / Azuca Ingenio gráfico   **0869.** Modern Editions, Rainer Behrens Modern Editions / Tilt Design Studio   **0870.** Zkoob, Soft Republic / ReStart Associates   **0871.** Midisystem / Sockho   **0872.** Genius, Channel 4 / YES   **0873.** El Ojo Magazine / Rodolfo Fuentes   **0874.** Debate Hall / VaryWell   **0875.** Bisman Ediciones / ImagenHB   **0876.** Circle Company / Eno Krüger Design   **0877.** Soma Productions Jacynthe Arsenault / Philippe Archontakis   **0878.** pixellove. / HelloMe   **0879.** Aeroplano / NNSS Design

0880

0881

0882

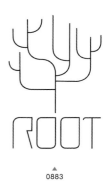

0883

0884

0885

0886

880. Comic Book Tattoo, Comic Book Publishing / Mr and Mrs M   0881. Platzhirsch, University of Art and Design Burg Gieb, Halle / hristoph Knoth   0882. Musa Enferma, Colectivo Elpaskin / Manifiesto 79   0883. Root Networks / Branislav Design   0884. Comic Book attoo, Comic Book Publishing / Mr and Mrs M   0885. Tinti, Black Ink / Toastone, Amanzilla   0886. Hear we Go, Mega Eins Verlag / pfel Zet

ediciones
cocolí

0887

ZEISIG™

0888

0889

THE**GAMES**COMPANY

0890

KHARMA

0891

MYRUNBASE

0892

VSONA

0893

fragmento**imán**

0894

zaeus®

0895

KS-CLUBBER

0896

ΛSUNTOIMPRESO

0897

CRITERIA

0898

0887. Ediciones Cocolí / Sofia Saez Matos   **0888.** Zeisig / HelloMe   **0889.** CCCP / Attak   **0890.** TGC, The Games Company / USOTA   **0891.** Kharma, SDC Films / Eramos Tantos Studio   **0892.** My Run Base / Firstflash X-media Labor   **0893.** Vsona / Geyrhalter Design   **0894.** Fragmento Imán Editores / Sofia Saez Matos   **0895.** Zaeus / Andrew Wilson Design   **0896.** KS-Clubber / Projectgraphics **0897.** Asunto Impreso Editores / ImagenHB   **0898.** Criteria C.A. / John Moore

0899

0900

0901

0902

0903

0904

0905

0906

0907

0908

0909

0899. Objectified, Gary Hustwit / Build   **0900.** In-forma, Escuela de Arquitectura de la Universidad de PR / Sofia Saez Matos   **0901.** Enfoques, BS, Colombia / Tangrama   **0902.** Andarilho, Cao Guimarães, Cinco em Ponto / Hardy Design, Voltz   **0903.** Arkade Magazine / Listen esign   **0904.** Capture / Clusta Ltd.   **0905.** Rip it Up, Satellite Media / Seven   **0906.** Riders Magazine, Hachette Rusconi Publisher / studio M milano   **0907.** LUFT / Branislav Design   **0908.** WFMU / alternatyves outc.   **0909.** Inflávio Magazine / Bruno Porto

0910

0911

0912

0913

0914

0915

0916

0917

0918

0919

0910. Ninja, *main logo* / Negro   **0911.–0917.** Ninja, *characters* / Negro   **0918.–0919.** Die Planung, A Terv / Anna Mándoki

0920

0921

0922

0923

0924

0920. El Clic, MTV Networks, *main logo* / Punga **0921.–0924.** El Clic, MTV Networks, *applications* / Punga

0925

0926

0927

0928

0929

0930

0931

0925.–0926. The N, MTV Networks / The Luxury of Protest   **0927.** Va Voom / Côme de Bouchony   **0928.** Las Vegas Magazine, Greenspun Media / Pentagram   **0929.** Ecléctica Magazine, *main logo* / Un.titled   **0930.–0931.** Ecléctica Magazine, *variations* / Un.titled

0933

0932

0934

0935

0936

0937

0938

0939

0940

932. Beat 98, Sistema Globo de Rádio / Tecnopop   **0933.** Lumiere / Oestudio   **0934.** Freshoops, Kevin Couliau / Eno Krüger Design
935. Casa da Palavra, Editora Casa da Palavra / Tecnopop   **0936.** Acessibilidade, [X] Brasil / Tecnopop   **0937.** Eyechat, AIM / Justin
rder   **0938.** Houyhnhnms.tv, Arroba Networks / Tea Time Studio, Joan Jimenez, Arroba Networks   **0939.** ESPN / Justin Harder
40. Twitter / Futurefarmers

0941

0942

0943

0944

0945

0946

0947

0948

0949

0941. Yups.tv / DOGO   **0942.** Logosvet / Logoholik   **0943.** WebVet / TNOP Design   **0944.** Sneakers, Reload / Attak   **0945.** Magazine Regards, CCLJ / SIGN   **0946.** Casaviva, Editorial Televisa / La fe ciega studio   **0947.** Monmiya, Shincho Press Co, Ltd. / Simone Inc. **0948.** Supertopic, Fabu / Büro Ink   **0949.** Urban Racer / WA007 Inc.

0950

0951

Onomatopee

0952

LA DISCUSIÓN

0953

MOMENTUM

0954

MANIFESTO
IDÉIA FORMA IMAGEM

0955

CINEMANÍA

0956

CLEARITY

0957

THEADVOCATE

0958

BACANAL

0959

50. Sixtynine Magazine, Edition Maku OG / Permanent Unit   **0951.** Gain Magazine, Freda Owusu, Info Plus / Chris Clarke
52. Onomatopee / Attak   **0953.** La Discusión / Bercz   **0954.** Momentum, Piraap / Attak   **0955.** Manifesto / Lya Zumblick
56. Cinemanía, Editorial Televisa / La fe ciega studio   **0957.** Clearity Magazine, Pearle Opticiens / DHM Graphic Design
58. The Advocate / Pentagram   **0959.** Bacanal, InfoMedia / Cabina

0960

0961

0962

0963

0964

0965

0960. Street a Porter / Attak   **0961.** Club TV / Fabrika de Typos   **0962.** Die Ludolfs, Discovery Networks Europe / Punga   **0963.** GPF, MTV Netherlands / DHM Graphic Design   **0964.** On Fuego Radio, Daddy Yankee / Elastic People   **0965.** Mixed Fight TV / Fabrika de Typos

0966

0967

0968

0969

0970

0971

0972

0973

0974

0975

0976

0977

66. Strange Detective Tales, Hungry Man Rio de Janeiro / Arterial   **0967.** El Patin / Hula+Hula   **0968.** Ready and Action TV /
natic   **0969.** Central Gráfica de Jornais, Grupo Vieira da Cunha / Planobase Design   **0970.** Urban Daddy / Nowhere   **0971.** Addicted to
awing, Plugzine / Milkxhake   **0972.** Evolver / Nowhere   **0973.** Debate Hall / VaryWell   **0974.** Chew it Over, Wrigleys / Stereo   **0975.** Cool
ands / Clusta Ltd.   **0976.** Trash Sudamerica / Negro   **0977.** Artline Films / Côme de Bouchony

0978

0979

0980

0981

0982

0983

0984

0985

0978. Encuesta Suple S!, Clarín / RDYA   **0979.** Canal 11 / Rodolfo Fuentes   **0980.** La Voix d'Assoli / Slang   **0981.** Gominola Creative Media
Superexpresso   **0982.** 27+1 / Caótica   **0983.** 647 / Nahon   **0984.** Mode, Studio Voice / Simone Inc.   **0985.** Slanted / USOTA

0986

0987

0988

0989

0990

0991

0992

0993

0994

86.–0994. Rock & Pop, Cie / Nahon

0995

0996

0997

0998

0999

1000

1001

1002

1003

1004

1005

1006

0995. Shado, *main logo* / Negro   **0996.–1000.** Shado, *variations* / Negro   **1001.** 2021 / Negro   **1002.** Ninja / Negro
1003. Odio / Negro   **1004.** Odic Force, Johnston Ayala / Pentagram   **1005.** Ojo / Negro   **1006.** The Forma Blog / Forma

1007

1008

1009

1010

1011

1012

Cinco años de **TrimarchiDG**
BODAS DE MADERA'S BOOK

1013

NinjaVisualsFire
DesignByJaydee™

1014

TV

1015

1016

1017

LOVE

1018

1007. Shado / Negro **1008.–1009.** Trash Sudamerica / Negro **1010.** Tenso, *variation* / Negro **1011.** Tenso, *main logo* / Negro
1012. Picnic Magazine / Eramos Tantos Studio **1013.** TMDG, TrimarchiDG / Negro **1014.** Ninja / Negro **1015.** EK, Elektronica TV /
Negro **1016.–1018.** Love / Negro

1019
1020
1021
1022
1023
1024
1025
1026

1019. Wonderland / de.MO **1020.** Made With Love / Nalindesign **1021.–1022.** City Hunters, Catmandu / Nahon **1023.** Big Magazine, *main logo* / Hula+Hula **1024.** Big Magazine, *development* / Hula+Hula **1025.** Fumaça Corp. / Osso Design **1026.** Whight On, Reload / Attak

1027

1028

1029

1030

1031

---

027. V-Radio, Vereniging Veronica / Momkai   **1028.** Cadena de favores, Win TV / Nahon   **1029.** Rock, File / xCOLITTx13Ax
030. Talento de Barrio, El Cartel Records / Elastic People   **1031.** Where you are heart?, Argos productions, Telemundo Miami /
Graphic Kitchen Studio

gyldendal business debate

1032

1033

DEBATE HALL

1034

1035

1036

1037

IVANA   PRODUCTIONS

1038

1039

1040

1041

1032. Gyldendal Business Debate, Gyldendal Publications / EHA Studio   **1033.** Big Boom Media / Geyrhalter Design   **1034.** Debate Hall / VaryWell   **1035.** Thinkbox / KentLyons   **1036.** weplaythis / Fatuus   **1037.** Jexbo / The Killswitch Collective   **1038.** Ivana Production / shk.studio   **1039.** 5411 Interactive / NNSS Design   **1040.** George Mélès, Embajada de Francia en Argentina / Estudio Garcia Balza **1041.** Relate / re-public

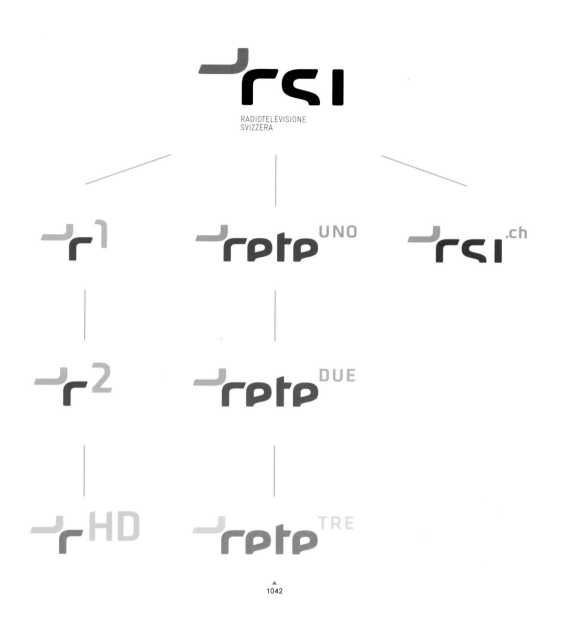

042. RSI, Radio Televisionne Svizzeria / Simon Mayer, Falko Ohlmer

MUSIC

ARTISTS, BANDS, CONCERTS, DJs, MUSIC FESTIVALS, MUSIC WEBSITES, RECORD LABELS

1043

1044

1045

1046

043. Revolution Miami, Grooveman / xCOLITTx13Ax   1044. Rock en Seine / Sockho   1045. Revelation Generation Music Festival /
d Edge Communications   1046. Disko404 / Permanent Unit

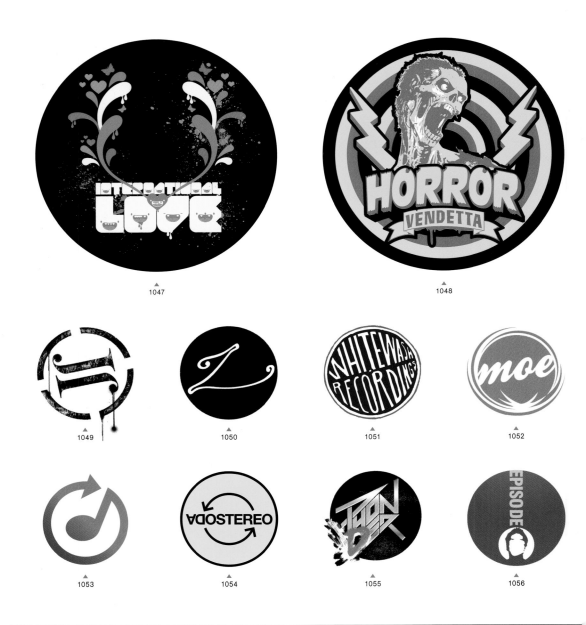

1047

1048

1049

1050

1051

1052

1053

1054

1055

1056

1047. International Love, Pop Art / xCOLITTx13Ax **1048.** Horor Vendetta, MR T records / xCOLITTx13Ax **1049.** Jaleo, Ricky Martin Enterprise / Elastic People **1050.** Zouk Recordings, Armada Music / DBXL **1051.** Whitewash Recordings / Dreamer **1052.** Moe / Illunatic **1053.** Nayatune / Logoholik **1054.** Soda Stereo / Alejandro Ros **1055.** PhonDER, Razer Records / Falko Ohlmer **1056.** Episode / Projectgraphics

1057

1058

1059

1060

1061

1062

1063

1064

57. Kopfnicker Records / Toastone, Amanzilla **1058.** Mijk Van Dijk, Primavera Sound / area3 **1059.** Troy Pierce, Electrosonic / a3 **1060.** Sounds Red / Justin Harder **1061.** Remedy Festival / Dale Harris **1062.–1063.** 80s Dance Night, LB Events / DBXL 64. Madonna Confessions on a Dance Floor, Madonna / Giovanni Bianco Studio 65

1065

1066

1067

1068

1069

1070

1071

1072

1065. BWA BWA Album, Ines / Eno Krüger Design   **1066.** Ines / Eno Krüger Design   **1067.** Eurockeénes de Belfort 2005 / Sockho
1068. Plena Records, Ana Perez / shk.studio   **1069.** Daddy Yankee, El Cartel / Elastic People   **1070.** Negra Li / Arterial   **1071.** Dead Sexy /
Sockho   **1072.** Le Touareg, Sesam Music / Eno Krüger Design

1074

1073

1075

1076

1077

1078

1079

1073. ParkLive Music Festival Brockwell Park / David Standen, AMP Associates   **1074.** Olga Tañon / Elastic People   **1075.** Caribbean Connection, Machete / Elastic People   **1076.** Foundation of Electronic Music Aarhus / Applied Projects   **1077.** Bipolar, Warner Music Mexico / Elastic People   **1078.** Triband / MAGMA Brand Design   **1079.** Le Cube Festival 2008 / Sockho

275

1080.

1081.

1082.

1083.

1084.

1080. Schaltkreis GbR / HelloMe   **1081.** Deep Black Heart, The Sicarios Of Rock & Roll / WeEatDesign   **1082.** Mutantes, Pierre Lapointe, Productions 3PM / FEED   **1083.** Bass Walk / xCOLITTx13Ax   **1084.** Federico Aubele Panamericana, ESL Music / Tea Time Studio

1085

1086

1087

1088

1089

085. Tropical Handgun / Caótica   **1086.** Fidel, X El Cambio Records / xCOLITTx13Ax   **1087.** Herzflattern, Radio Suu / HelloMe
088. Em Casa / Caótica   **1089.** Big J / phla

1090. Mind the Gap, Monopol Records, *main logo* / KITA   1091.–1096. Mind the Gap, Monopol Records, *variations* / KITA

MODERN GUILT

1097

97. Beck Modern Guilt, Interscope Records / Hugo & Marie

1098

1099

1100

R CK IS DEAD

1101

1102

the supahip

1103

1104

KATABASIS

1105

1098. Amsterdamse Popprijs 2008, GRAP Foundation / DBXL   **1099.** Unisono, Cerati / Alejandro Ros   **1100.** The Mooncats / MrBowlegs   **1101.** Rock is Dead / Sockho   **1102.** The Cassettes / Nuñez del Arco   **1103.** The Supahip, Big Radio Records / Dreamer **1104.** Clinch, X El Cambio Records / xCOLITTx13Ax   **1105.** Katabasis / MrBowlegs

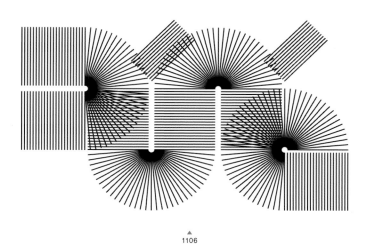

1106

1107

1108

MYAH

1109

ᐱ▙ᖇᖇᖕ

1110

REEK

1111

LNKP

1112

DIVIDE

1113

MANÁ

1114

1106. Dúné / Applied Projects   **1107.** Black Guayaba, Machete Music / Elastic People   **1108.** Loft Disco / Helou Design   **1109.** Myah / ·inter & Miletina   **1110.** Pheek / HelloMe   **1111.** REEK / FEED   **1112.** LinkUp, Foundation of Electronic Music Aarhus / Applied Projects ·13. Divide / MrBowlegs   **1114.** MANÁ / Elastic People

1115

1116

1117

1118

1119

1120

1121

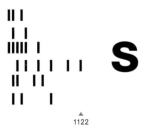

1122

1123

1115. SEM Label, *main logo* / Büro Ink   **1116.–1123.** SEM Label, *variations* / Büro Ink

1124

1125

1126

1127

1128

1129

1130

RICKYMARTIN
MTV:UNPLUGGED

1131

THE SECRET MACHINES

1132

FALOU GUN

1133

semtexgirls

1134

PURE GROOVE

1135

24. Mauricio Valladares / Arterial   1125. Pippa Drysdale, Glowbug Records / Dreamer   1126. The Green Kingdom, Michael Cottone /
ro Ink   1127. Concord Music Group / Polychrome   1128. Ricky Martin, Black & White Tour 2007, Sony BMG / Elastic People
29. Clubland / Alejandro Ros   1130. Dalles, Fanboy Records / Falko Ohlmer   1131. Ricky Martin, MTV Unplugged, Sony BMG /
astic People   1132. The Secret Machines, Warner / Nowhere   1133. Falou Gun, Koci / Eno Krüger Design   1134. Semtex Girls, Madonna /
ovanni Bianco Studio 65   1135. Pure Groove / No Days Off

1136

1137

1138

1139

1140

1141

1142

1143

1136.–1137. Adriane, Skull Records / Falko Ohlmer **1138.** Hembras y bandidas, Luis Trochón / Rodolfo Fuentes **1139.** Cutles / Forma
1140. Sex & Agriculture, Universal Music New Zealand / Seven **1141.** The Sicarios of Rock & Roll / WeEatDesign **1142.** Mandoza Family /
Tilt Design Studio **1143.** Plastik / Stereo

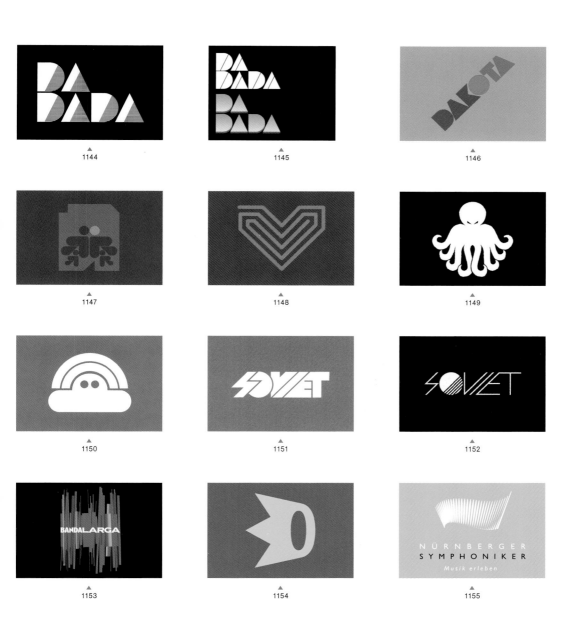

1144

1145

1146

1147

1148

1149

1150

1151

1152

1153

1154

1155

44.–1145. DaDaDa / Justin Harder 1146. Dakota / Justin Harder 1147. Dance Party / Justin Harder 1148. LoveMaze / Justin
rder 1149. Octopus / Justin Harder 1150. Saturday / Justin Harder 1151.–1152. Soviet / Justin Harder 1153. Banda Larga, Gege
oduções / Tecnopop 1154. Orquestral Imperial, Diversão & Arte / Tecnopop 1155. Nürnberger Symphoniker / Andrea Wong, Dievision

1156

1157

1158

1159

1160

1161

1162

1163

1164

1156. Taller Victor / Punga   **1157.** Kelly Key, Warner Music / Caótica   **1158.** Don Javor / Attak   **1159.** DMP rec / xCOLITTx13Ax
1160. Akin, DJ Quiet Force / Eno Krüger Design   **1161.** Fobia XX, Sony BMG / Hula+Hula   **1162.** Yellow Sound Lab / Sonar
1163. Please Pop, DJ Please / Eno Krüger Design   **1164.** Lux / Tilt Design Studio

1165

1166

1167

1168

1169

1170

1171

1172

1173

1174

1175

1176

1177

1178

1179

1180

65. Abradab / Jan Kallwejt   **1166.** 3 Pontas Brasil, 3 Pontas Music Publishing / 6D   **1167.** Sesc Rio.Som, SESC (Social Service of Commerce Brazil) / Vinte Zero Um Design   **1168.** Schallschnelle / Hafenbraut   **1169.** TNTY JNM, Columbia Music Entertainment, INC. / none Inc.   **1170.** Beyond Oblivion / Elastic People   **1171.** Love Hz Studios / Dreamer   **1172.** Audiolife, Inhance Media Inc. / Geyrhalter esign   **1173.** Muzik School / Oded Ezer Typography   **1174.** Opus Sound / D.Workz Interactive   **1175.** Deviate Records, Francesco Pagano / ghettojuice   **1176.** DJ Sounds, Pioneer pro DJ / Clusta Ltd.   **1177.** DJ Eleven / Jan Kallwejt   **1178.** PerVers / Jan Kallwejt   **1179.** VogelFrei / elloMe   **1180.** Uppercuts / Côme de Bouchony

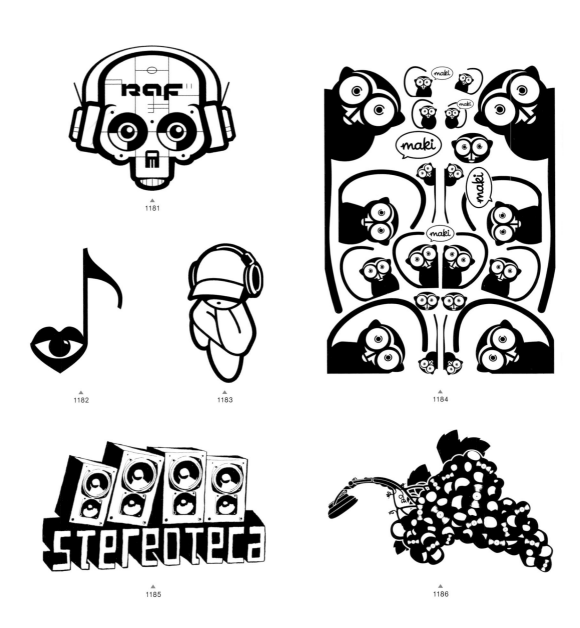

1181

1182

1183

1184

1185

1186

1181. RAF-Skull, Tonquelle / USOTA **1182.** Theater, Oper und Orchester GmbH Halle Competition / Christoph Knoth **1183.** Low Life / xCOLITTx13Ax **1184.** Club Maki / xhoch4 **1185.** Stereoteca, Casulo Cultura & Mercado Moderno / Osso Design **1186.** Addicted Online Eno Krüger Design

1187

1188

1189

1190

7. La Quinta Estación, Sony BMG, *main logo* / Hula+Hula   **1188.–1190.** La Quinta Estación, Sony BMG, *development* / Hula+Hula

1191

1192

1193

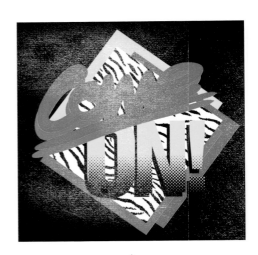

1194

1191.–1194. PhonDER, Razer Records / Falko Ohlmer

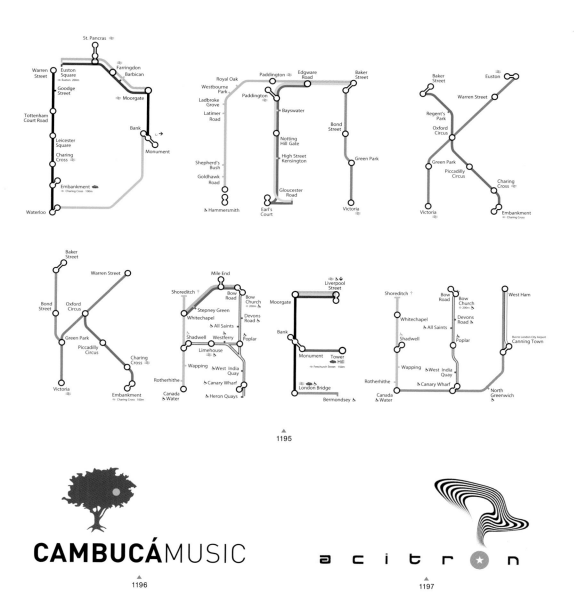

1195

CAMBUCÁMUSIC

1196

acitron

1197

95. Going Underground, DMX Krew, Edward Upton / Yuri Suzuki   **1196.** Cambucá Music / 6D   **1197.** Acitron / Eramos Tantos Studio

RETAILERS & FOOD OUTLETS

BARS, CAFÉS, MARKETS, SHOPPING MALLS, RESTAURANTS, STORES

CAPE ANN FARMERS' MARKET

▲
1198

CAPE ANN FARMERS' MARKET

▲
1199

CAPE ANN FARMERS' MARKET

1200

CAPE ANN FARMERS' MARKET

1201

CAPE ANN FARMERS' MARKET

▲
1202

CAPE ANN FARMERS' MARKET

▲
1203

---

98. Cape Ann Farmers' Market, *variation* / asmallpercent **1199.** Cape Ann Farmers' Market, *main logo* / asmallpercent
00.–1203. Cape Ann Farmers' Market, *application* / asmallpercent

1204.

1205.

1206.

1207.

1208.

1209.

1210.

1211.

1212.

1213.

1214.

1215.

1216.

1204. Skincare, Sainsbury's / Pentagram   **1205.** The Lonely Poet, Beannchor Ltd. / Paperjam Design   **1206.** Dolce / Helou Design
1207. DeporFan / Pump Diseño   **1208.** Petit Pois / Interface Designers   **1209.** S, Suite / HelloMe   **1210.** Fernando Jaeger / Soter Design
1211. Royal / Giovanni Bianco Studio 65   **1212.** Le Cycle Brainstorming, GB Investissements / Eno Krüger Design   **1213.** Burnside GmbH /
Christian Otto Studio   **1214.** A4 Bar / HelloMe   **1215.** Bindi, RECGM / Eno Krüger Design   **1216.** Q Design Store / Cuartopiso

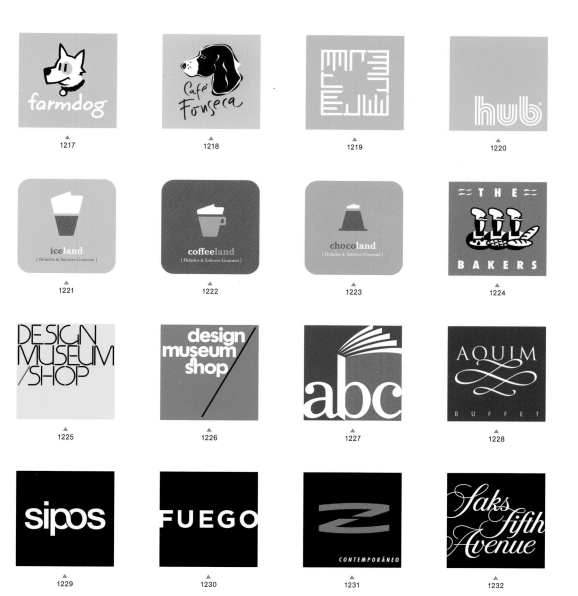

1217

1218

1219

1220

1221

1222

1223

1224

1225

1226

1227

1228

1229

1230

1231

1232

17. Farmdog / Dale Harris   **1218.** Café Fonseca, Cadas Abranches / Interface Designers   **1219.** T's Ethiopian and Asian Cuisine / Spunk sign Machine   **1220.** Hub / Stereo   **1221.–1223.** Iceland / ImagenHB   **1224.** The Bakers / eg.design   **1225.–1226.** Design Museum Shop / ild   **1227.** abc Bookstore / Helou Design   **1228.** Aquim / Interface Designers   **1229.** Sipos / Studio41 Designers   **1230.** Fuego North nerica / Pentagram   **1231.** Z Contemporâneo / Interface Designers   **1232.** Saks Fifth Avenue / Pentagram

1233

JAVINO
wine bar · restaurant

1234

ARABIA

1235

CALINOR
CHOCOLATERIE · CONFISERIE

1236

JERSEY

1237

SVERRE SÆTRE
OSLO

1238

ALKALĀ
CAFE / GALERIA

1239

1233. Fasan Afghanische Spezialitäten / 3Deluxe **1234.** Javino Restaurant / Boldrini & Ficcardi **1235.** Arabia Restaurant / São Paulo Criação **1236.** Calinor NV / Chilli Design & Multimedia **1237.** Jersey Café / Falko Ohlmer **1238.** Sverre Sætre / upstruct berlin oslo **1239.** Alkalá Café Galería / Helou Design

1240

1241

1242

1243

1244

1245

1246

1240. Jaipur, RECGM / Eno Krüger Design 1241. Istocna Cuda, Miracles from East / Vladimir Sijerkovic 1242. Vereda Tropical, Hilton Colón Hotel / Azuca Ingenio gráfico 1243. Orion / Ginter & Miletina 1244. Habibis Lounge Cafe / Revolver 1245. T's Ethiopian and Asian Cuisine / Spunk Design Machine 1246. Bollywood Masala / Dale Harris

1247. Yellow Deli, *main logo* / Hello Monday   1248.–1255. Yellow Deli, *variations* / Hello Monday

1256

1257

1258

1259

1260

1261

1262

1263

56. Glam Pet, *main logo* / Hula+Hula   **1257.–1263.** Glam Pet, *development* / Hula+Hula

Mallard

▲
1265

Mallard

▲
1264

Mallard

▲
1266

Mallard

▲
1267

Mallard

▲
1268

Mallard

▲
1269

▲
1270

▲
1271

▲
1272

1264.–1269. Mallard Tea Rooms / Brahm   **1270.** Café Amor Perfecto, *main logo* / Tangrama **1271.–1272.** Café Amor Perfecto, *variations* / Tangrama

1273

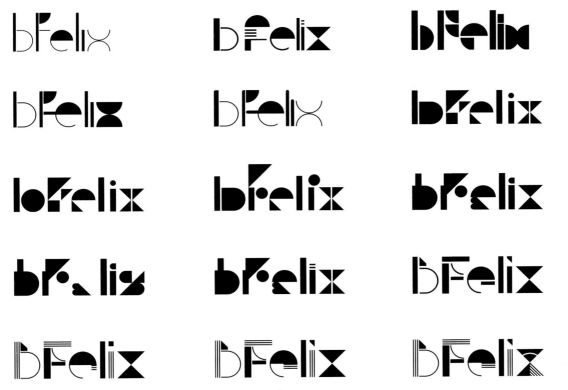

1274

---

73. BFelix, *main logo* / gardens&co.   **1274.** BFelix, *development* / gardens&co.

1275.

1276.

1277.

1278.

1279.

1280.

1281.

1282.

1283.

1284.

1285.

1286.

1287.

1288.

1289.

1275. Sun India, Interbaires S.A. / ImagenHB **1276.** Dianthus / ImagenHB **1277.** Aqua Magica, Grupo Riofisa / Fileni & Fileni Design **1278.** Howdy / Justin Harder **1279.** Caféserie GmbH / BKWA **1280.** Speicherhafen Interieur & Lifestyle e.V. / BKWA **1281.** Kato Cafe, Dario Tinelli / Boldrini & Ficcardi **1282.** La Aldea Sandwichs / Boldrini & Ficcardi **1283.–1285.** Piaf, Provisión Integral Negro **1286.** Heart Cream / Justin Harder **1287.** B&B / Justin Harder **1288.** Sushi Tech / Justin Harder **1289.** Robo Tussin / Justin Harde

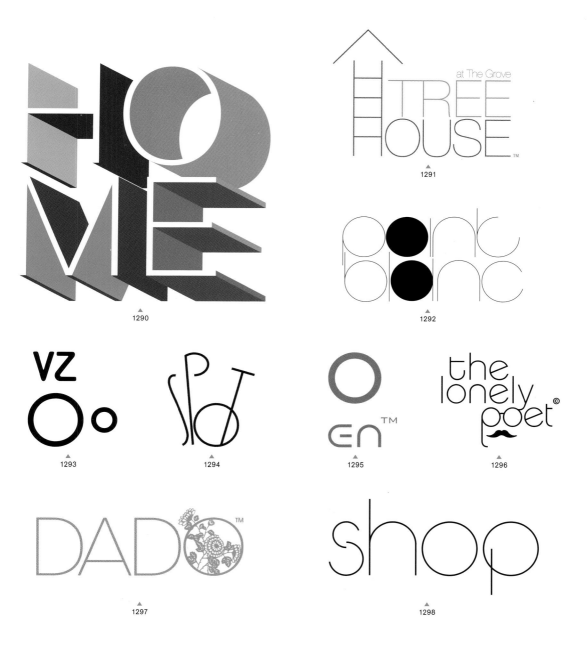

1290

1291

1292

1293

1294

1295

1296

1297

1298

---

90. Home, Palacio de las Telas / Hello Vanilla   **1291.** Tree House, ShakeFX / Damián Di Patrizio   **1292.** Point Blanc / HelloMe
93. VZ Producciones / Bernardo+Celis   **1294.** Spot / São Paulo Criação   **1295.** EN, Japanese Cuisine Restaurant / Knowledge+
96. The Lonely Poet, Beannchor Ltd. / Paperjam Design   **1297.** Dado / 802   **1298.** Design Museum Shop / Build

1299

1300

1301

1302

1303

1304

1305

1306

1307

1308

1299. Emerald City Press / Pentagram **1300.** Tepper Wine / Boldrini & Ficcardi **1301.** Janelle / gardens&co. **1302.** Apeteco / Boldrini & Ficcardi **1303.** Green Canteen, Blum Enterprises / Pentagram **1304.** Paninoteca / Henriquez Lara Estudio **1305.** Maki / Anima **1306.** Kero Kone / Ligia Santiago **1307.** 00 (Zero Zero) / Muti Randolph **1308.** 69 / Muti Randolph

1309

1310

1311

1312

1313

1314

1315

1316

1317

1318

09. CafeSiete, *main logo* / Helou Design   **1310.–1315.** CafeSiete, *development* / Helou Design   **1316.** Al Dente, *main logo* / Henriquez Lara
udio   **1317.–1318.** Al Dente, *development* / Henriquez Lara Estudio

1319

1320

PATAGONIA AGRESTE

1321

SANS-SOUCI

RESTÓ BAR

1322

1319. Weinstube Wagrain / redfloor designbuero   **1320.** Maximiliano / NNSS Design   **1321.** Patagonia Agreste / NNSS Design
1322. Sans-Souci / Boldrini & Ficcardi

VENDÔME
BAR + LOUNGE

▲
1323

janelle
Precious Essential Oils

▲
1324

GUSTO™
ITALIAN BUFFET

▲
1325

bleekr
N.Y.CUPCAKES

▲
1326

SNOG™
Pure Frozen Yogurt

▲
1327

LE PIANO
KITCHEN TOOLS

▲
1328

zoe

▲
1329

flores

▲
1330

guest

▲
1331

4food

▲
1332

Shop

▲
1333

PIAF
PROVISIÓN INTEGRAL

▲
1334

23. Vendome / Studio Output   **1324.** Janelle / gardens&co.   **1325.** Gusto / hotmonkey design   **1326.** Bleekr! / Estudio González
27. SNOG / ico Design   **1328.** Le Piano / SIGN   **1329.** Zoe Bar Restaurant / Helou Design   **1330.** Flores / Studio Output
31. Guest Catering / Eno Krüger Design   **1332.** 4Food, Imagineer / Elastic People   **1333.** Design Museum Shop / Build
34. Piaf, Provisión Integral / Negro

1335

1336

1339

1337

1338

1340

1341

1342

1335. GreenGenes / estudiotres **1336.** Panoramic, Beetham Organization / Uniform **1337.** Batuka, Prolacsa / GuaZa Studio
1338. Arroz Trillo, Arrocera San Francisco / GuaZa Studio **1339.** Akelarre Cafe / Helou Design **1340.–1341.** Almacén del paraiso /
Bernardita Brancoli **1342.** Books & Dreams Bookstore / Eduardo Chang

Belinda Café & Deli

1343

The Wheatsheaf

1344

1345

---

43. Belinda Cafe, Vizora / Fileni & Fileni Design   **1344.** The Wheatsheaf / Stereo   **1345.** T's Ethiopian and Asian Cuisine / Spunk Design achine

1346.

1347.

1348.

1349.

1350.

1351.

1352.

1353.

1354.

1355.

1356.

1357.

1346. Herbario / Cuartopiso   **1347.** Coldin Gastronomía / Frontespizio   **1348.** Marché 27 / FEED   **1349.** Mall Center, Grupo Parque Arauco Fileni & Fileni Design   **1350.** points24 / Forma   **1351.** The Burger Concept, MINT / Damián Di Patrizio   **1352.** Bombom, Sweet Dreams / Fulô Estudio   **1353.** Eisblume / Toastone, Amanzilla   **1354.** Ecomercado / Vinte Zero Um Design   **1355.** Sanity Drops, Lakosa / redfloor designbuero   **1356.** Green Park / Projectgraphics   **1357.** Design Museum Shop / Build

shrimp farm

▲
1358

dressipe

▲
1359

▲
1360

▲
1361

Corporation

AJINDA INDIGENOUS COSMETICS

▲
1362

▲
1363

FINE/TRA

caffe'

▲
1364

▲
1365

58. Shrimp Farm / Revolver **1359.** Dressipe / entz creative **1360.** Beauty Planet, Xoko / 802 **1361.** Holzkopf / HelloMe **1362.** Aurum
orporation / Kontra **1363.** Ajinda / The Cre8ion.Lab **1364.** Finestra Pizzaria / Estudio Infinito **1365.** Sette Chiese Caffè / Krghettojuice

ASPEN *Bistrot*

1366

NOZ MOSCADA

culinária

1367

DAMIEN MERCIER

CHOCOLATIER BELGE

1368

B L A C K
D I A M O N D

1369

KINGFISH

1370

israeliWine

OF THE MONTH CLUB

1371

MAGNÆTRURIA

1372

LondonSupply

1373

RÉGALIS

1374

TECHNOBUY

1375

KITCHENCAFé

1376

provacenter

professional video audio

1377

1366. Aspen Bistrot, Arcadia Urbanismo / DEZ Propaganda **1367.** Noz Moscada / Interface Designers **1368.** Damien Mercier / Pozo Marcic Ensamble **1369.** Black Diamond, Office48 / Simone Inc. **1370.** Kingfish Restaurant / EHA Studio **1371.** Israeli Wines / ImagenHB **1372.** Magnaetruria Srl / Studio41 Designers **1373.** London Supply / ImagenHB **1374.** Régalis / NNSS Design **1375.** TechnoBuy / Helou Design **1376.** Kitchen Café / eg.design **1377.** Prova Center / Projectgraphics

HANDCRAFTS◉DESIGND
MEXICO

1378

koken-op-maat

1379

THE VAULTS

1380

VIBRATIONS™

1381

Q Design Store

1382

The co-operative

1383

cioccolato

1384

tacksales

1385

DEPORFAN

1386

tecnova

1387

saloon

1388

GRIZZLY®

1389

1378. Handcrafts Design / Oblicua   **1379.** Koken op Maat / Faydherbe & De Vringer   **1380.** The Vaults, The Salubrious Bar Company / lusta Ltd.   **1381.** Vibrations / 802   **1382.** Q Design Store / Cuartopiso   **1383.** The Co-operative / Pentagram   **1384.** Cioccolato, Oem Value ternational / 1828   **1385.** Tacksales Ltd. / entz creative   **1386.** DeporFan / Pump Diseño   **1387.** Tecnova, Micro / Cabina   **1388.** Saloon Cafe aniel Lussier / Philippe Archontakis   **1389.** Grizzly / HelloMe

1390. menü / HelloMe   **1391.** Escucha / Studio Output   **1392.** Design Museum Shop / Build   **1393.–1394.** qba / The Luxury of Protest
1395. Ego Café & Bookshop / Oded Ezer Typography   **1396.** La Zurda / Negro   **1397.** Rootys, Mirrorball Leisure / Clusta Ltd.

PAIR
INGS

1398

1399

1400

PAIR
INGS

1401

URBAN
PANTRY

1402

STEMS
& ROOTS

1403

STEMS
& ROOTS

1404

98. Pairings Restaurant + Wine Bar, *main logo* / Spunk Design Machine   **1399.–1404.** Pairings Restaurant + Wine Bar, *development* /
unk Design Machine

VUDU
princess

1406

1407

1405

RdclGrl.

1408

1409

1410

1405. La Diablita Cantina / Henriquez Lara Estudio 1406. Vudu Princess / Boldrini & Ficcardi 1407. Maria / Attak 1408. Radical Girl, Mystic Productions / shk.studio 1409.–1410. Red Head Lounge / shk.studio

1411

1412

1413

Luckyfish

1414

1415

tagtraum.

1416

SCIENTIFIQUE

1417

1418

1419

1420

1421

1422

---

1. Boris the Cat / Caótica   **1412.** The Lonely Poet, Beannchor Ltd. / Paperjam Design   **1413.** 3 Monos / ImagenHB   **1414.** Luckyfish, ovative Dining Goup / Pentagram   **1415.** Mr. Fish Grill / São Paulo Criação   **1416.** Tagtraum / HelloMe   **1417.** Café Scientifique, Alliance nçaise / Helou Design   **1418.** BLVD / Latinbrand   **1419.** Café del Río / Helou Design   **1420.** Arabia Delivery, Arabia Restaurant / São Paulo ação   **1421.** Maya Java Café / Fritz Torres   **1422.** Mylius-Erichsen Bryghus / Battin, Hegnet

SERVICE & BUSINESS

BANKING, CATERING, CONSULTING, HOTELS, INSURANCE, LOGISTIC, TELECOMMUNICATION, TRANSPORTATION, PRINTING SERVICE, SPAS, YOGA STUDIOS

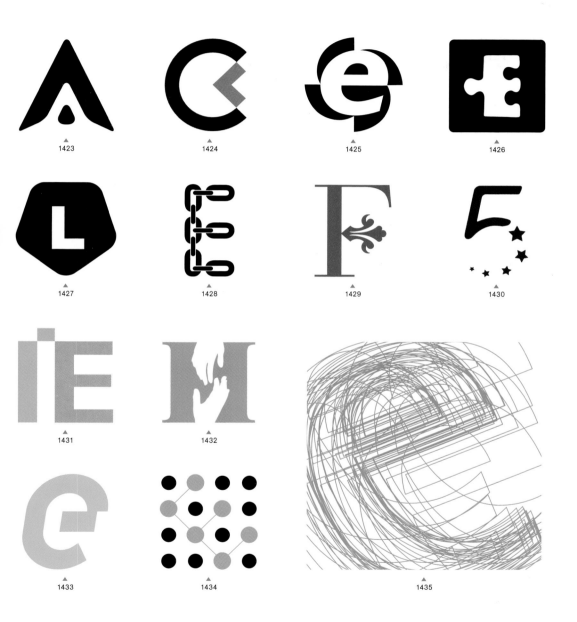

1423

1424

1425

1426

1427

1428

1429

1430

1431

1432

1433

1434

1435

23. AAmerican Financial Group Inc. / estudiotres **1424.** InCite, Inc. / Essex Two **1425.** Enigma, *development* / Latinbrand **1426.** Enigma, *in logo* / Latinbrand **1427.** Latingráfica / Tholön Kunst **1428.** Enigma, *development* / Latinbrand **1429.** Faena Hotel + Universe / olön Kunst **1430.** Five Cool Rooms Buenos Aires / 1828 **1431.** Jack in a Box, Icon Impact / KITA **1432.** Helping Hand Rewards, Inc. / sex Two **1433.** Etapatelecom, Etapa Cuenca / Helou Design **1434.** Enigma, *development* / Latinbrand **1435.** Else Club Moskow / umann & Baumann

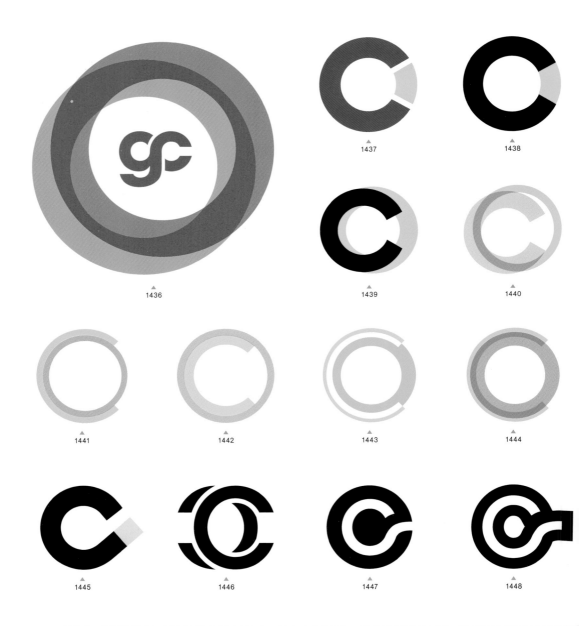

1436. Gema Carbajosa / Falko Ohlmer   1437. Classilio, *main logo* / Cheval de Troie   1438.–1445. Classilio, *development* / Cheval de Troie   1446.–1448. Cedar Realty Co. / estudiotres

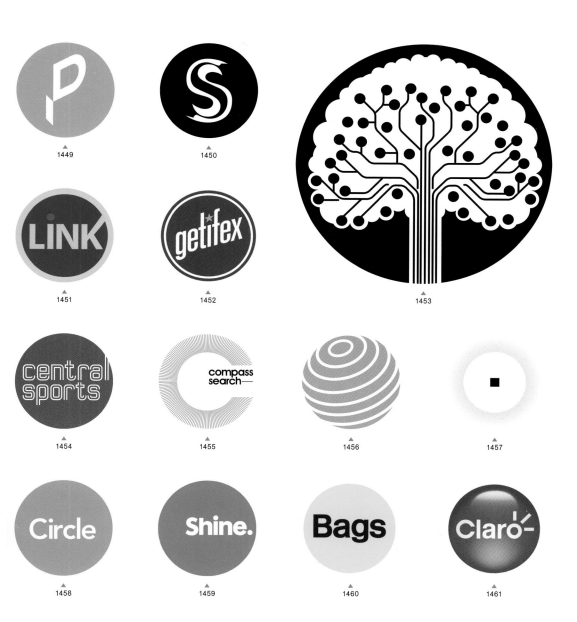

1449

1450

1451

1452

1453

1454

1455

1456

1457

1458

1459

1460

1461

9. Distribuidora del Parque / Pump Diseño **1450.** Spagna, Cristal / Studio41 Designers **1451.** Link, Red Link / Shakespear Design
2. Getifex / Apfel Zet **1453.** Digi Tree / Justin Harder **1454.** Central Sports / ICG **1455.** Compass Search / KentLyons
6. Finvesa / Pump Diseño **1457.** Robert Safdie / Versus **1458.** Circle, Participle / KentLyons **1459.** Shine / Studio Output
0. Bags / Push **1461.** Claro, Telecom America / Gad' Branding & Design

BiProduct
Recovery

City Hopper

Airports Group

1462

1463

1464

Biella Milano / Torino
Nord Ovest Italia Airport

1465

1466

JAVELIN

VERISTREAM

1467

1468

Innovative
Family
DentalHealth

conelsur
CONEXIÓN ELECTRICA DEL SUR

1469

1470

1462. Multired, Metro de Santiago, Chilean Government / Grupo Oxigeno   **1463.** BiProduct Recovery / ICG   **1464.** City Hopper /
ICG   **1465.** Biella, Blackpool International Airport / ICG   **1466.** Banco Solidario / Latinbrand   **1467.** Javelin, ZS Associates / The Killswitc
Collective   **1468.** Veristream, Infrasafe Inc. / Büro Ink   **1469.** Innovative Family Dental Health / Vladimir Sijerkovic   **1470.** Conelsur,
Transelec / Grupo Oxigeno

1471

1472

1473

1474

1475

1476

1477

1478

1479

1480

1481

1482

1471. Artvalley, Macramé / DOGO   **1472.** Finvesa / Pump Diseño   **1473.** i Lab Consulting / redfloor designbuero   **1474.** NuPress / Elastic People   **1475.** Spiralis / Oblicua   **1476.** Oranda Interim BV / Eva Lindeman   **1477.** Tenica / Ocular Ink   **1478.** Directenergy Website Hosting / Marshall & Marshall   **1479.** Joyco, Structural & Civil Engineering Consulting / Tangrama   **1480.** Imprenta Segura / Anima   **1481.** Towngas Telecom / gardens&co.   **1482.** MDGF (Advisors) Limited / Marshall & Marshall

NEW:IMMOMARKET

1483

ak sealogistik

1484

entreventos

1485

aura

1486

EnergiAustral

1487

HÁBITAT

1488

HELIODOR

1489

PALMAS 86

1490

contemporāneo

1491

mecanográfica

1492

VPAR

1493

KOMROWSKI

1494

1483. New immo marked / redfloor designbuero　**1484.** AK Sealogistk / redfloor designbuero　**1485.** Entreventos / Fulô Estudio **1486.** Aura, Grupo Icon / Escobas, Corazon diseño　**1487.** Energía Austral, Falconbridge / Grupo Oxigeno　**1488.** Bancaja / Estudio Mariscal　**1489.** Heliodor / Ginter & Miletina　**1490.** Télo, PV Inova / 6D　**1491.** Contemporâneo, Goldsztein / DEZ Propaganda **1492.** Mecanográfica / Diego Corrales　**1493.** VPAR, Red Group Ltd. / SViDesign　**1494.** Komrowski Group / form one

structures

1495

SIGHTS

1496

MicroPlace

1497

marbella amenities

1498

KUBIK

1499

Light

1500

DF Solutions

1501

qbase corp

1502

NEDERLANDSE
GRONDBEURS

1503

FACTORY
HOTEL

1504

boost
mobile™

1505

MASTER
ELECTRICIANS

1506

nirvana

1507

nordskak

1508

CONAH

1509

Praxis für
Osteopathie

1510

---

95. Structures Salon / multimediaHAAM   **1496.** Sights, Chama Inc. / Emiliano Rodriguez   **1497.** Microplace, eBay / ATTIK
98. MA, Marbella Resort & Spa / Grupo Oxigeno   **1499.** Kubik Modular / IAA   **1500.** Light / eg.design   **1501.** DF Solutions /
perjam Design   **1502.** Qbase / Geyrhalter Design   **1503.** Nederlandse Grondbeurs / The Cre8ion.Lab   **1504.** Factory Hotel, Deilmann
mbH & Co. KG / HelloMe, Jakob Schneider   **1505.** Boost Mobile / ATTIK   **1506.** Master Electricians / entz creative   **1507.** Nirvana /
uti Randolph   **1508.** Nordskak, Boris Beeli / Büro Ink   **1509.** Conah / Versus   **1510.** Osteopathie / Toastone, Amanzilla

LAHUEN-CO

1511

1512

1513

1514

1515

1516

1517

1511. Lahunco / ImagenHB **1512.** Wasatch Powder Clinics, *development* / Listen Design **1513.** Wasatch Powder Clinics, *main logo* / Listen Design **1514.** Wasatch Powder Clinics, *development* / Listen Design **1515.** Soultrips, SoulTraveler / Comparsas
1516. Porto Seguro Cia. de Seguros Gerais / Oz Design **1517.** Hotel Alpina / redfloor designbuero

 Gossler

1518

1519

 **alliacta**
technical consultants

1520

1521

 Grant Thornton

1522

1523

 OHLHABER
telekommunikation

1524

1525

---

18. Gossler / Ideograma Consultores, S.C.   **1519.** Artisan / Vik   **1520.** Alliacta Technical Consultants / Pure Communication
21. Transparenz Werkstatt, TUI Deutschland GmbH / Andrea Wong, Dievision   **1522.** Grant Thornton / Pentagram   **1523.** HM Assurantie
ixelerate   **1524.** Ohlhaber Telekommunikation / form one   **1525.** Launch Factory, Menzies Distribution / Gallusness

1526

1527

1528

1529

1530

1531

1532

1533

1534

1535

1536

1537

1538

1526. Aeromar S.A. / Helou Design   **1527.** IT Tours / Helou Design   **1528.** Andrew Duke Contracting / Oscar Patzan Design
1529. AndreaP Trading / RacoSchneider   **1530.** IF, Inmoforestal / Anima   **1531.** Terrabienes / Versus   **1532.** Capital Partners /
Pentagram   **1533.** Rocafuerte Seguros / Versus   **1534.** i Lab Consulting / redfloor designbuero   **1535.** The Dorchester / Pentagram
1536. 28 / Studio Output   **1537.** ESC / RARE Design Associates   **1538.** Interfacturas / ImagenHB

1539

1540

1541

1542

1543

1544

1545

1546

1547

1548

1549

1550

1551

1552

1553

539. Luisa Veiga / Arterial **1540.** Tulipandra / Graphic Kitchen Studio **1541.** St. Martin de Porres Foundation / Essex Two
542. EP, Eduardo Picon / Helou Design **1543.** Felix A. Schweikert Training & Consulting / Vladimir Sijerkovic **1544.** Impordisa /
elou Design **1545.** My Mobile Match, KPN / DHM Graphic Design **1546.** Marleen Breilmann / Tilt Design Studio, Marc Antosch
547. Taffera Builders, Robert Taffera / Pentagram **1548.** 4seasons, Dackkonzept 25 GmbH / KITA **1549.** Jack in a Box, Icon Impact /
ITA **1550.** Ulises Hotel / ImagenHB **1551.** SB, Sieglinde Baskut / Forma **1552.** Banco del Pacifico / Versus **1553.** La Poste,
e Post Group / SIGN

1554

1555

1556

1557

COBUS

1558

1559

Maginus

1560

esms

1561

ᴅᴇLOCATIE

1562

Ticon

1563

2ergo

1564

1565

1554. Glen, *development* / Carla Reinés Design   **1555.** Glen, *main logo* / Carla Reinés Design   **1556.** Sago Imports / Helou Design
1557. Omal / Clusta Ltd.   **1558.** Cobus Sistemas / Helou Design   **1559.** MMS / RARE Design Associates   **1560.** Maginus / Brahm
1561. ESMS, esmsystems.com / VaryWell   **1562.** De Locatie / Attak   **1563.** Ticon, UML / Studio Makgill   **1564.** 2ergo / Brahm
1565. Domo / Studioa

1566

1567

1568

---

66. Mojokite / Gazz   **1567.** Fios Group / Nobrand   **1568.** Orange Monkey Tours / Gazz

1569

1570

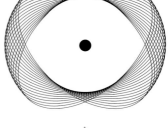

1571

1572

GASTRONOMIA
1573

GASTRONOMIA
1574

GASTRONOMIA
1575

GASTRONOMIA
1576

1569. Dynallia / Hoet & Hoet   **1570.** Royal Palm Hotels and Resorts / Gad' Branding & Design   **1571.** Belsim / Hoet & Hoet
1572. Centro de Oftalmologia, Dr. Jorge Tredicce / Juan Pablo Tredicce   **1573.–1576.** Green Tea / Arterial

1577

1578

7. Tierra Atacama, Hotel Tierra Atacama, *main logo* / Blanco Diseño   **1578.** Tierra Atacama, Hotel Tierra Atacama, *development* / nco Diseño

1579

1580

1581

1582

1583

1579.–1583. YogaStudio / Latinbrand

1584

1585

1586

1589

1587

1588

1590

84. EGO, Comunica / Damián Di Patrizio   **1585.** Moara, 22 DG / NNSS Design   **1586.** Dancer, Kristin Guttenberg, *development* /
morph   **1587.** Dancer, Kristin Guttenberg, *main logo* / a+morph   **1588.** Dancer, Kristin Guttenberg, *development* / a+morph
89. Fango / Simone Inc.   **1590.** Gema Carbajosa / Falko Ohlmer

1591

1592

CAPELLA
HOTELS & RESORTS

1593

ensemble℠
financial harmony

1594

SILKEWEGGEN™

1595

1596

VITRUM
HOTEL

1597

1598

1599

1591. Romano Autolinee / Krghettojuice   **1592.** Parktel / ImagenHB   **1593.** Capella Hotels & Resorts / Spunk Design Machine
1594. Ensemble Financial Planning / Spunk Design Machine   **1595.** Silke Weggen / Nalindesign   **1596.** ERB / Damián Di Patrizio
1597. Vitrum Hotel, NA Concepts / ImagenHB   **1598.** Camino Real / Art Design Studio   **1599.** Reliance Building Services / Tugba Güler

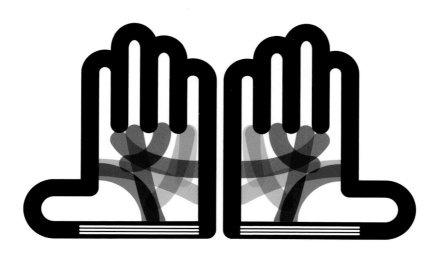

1600

1601

1602

1603

1604

1605

1606

0. Lectura de manos / ImagenHB   **1601.** Dreen Re-energy / Gad' Branding & Design   **1602.–1604.** Filmania / RacoSchneider
5. Scout, Virtual Advantage / Vectorform   **1606.** OHRA / DHM Graphic Design

1607

1608

PARK TAHOE
—— INN ——

1609

1610

IND IVIDUA L
S O LUTI O NS

1611

GALA
GYM

1612

1613

stokbroekx
stokbroekx&

1614

1615

1607. Crashstar, Kinotex / KITA **1608.** London Innovation, London Development Agency / KentLyons **1609.** Park Tahoe Inn / Geyrhalter Design **1610.** NEO, Catella - SimplyCty / SIGN **1611.** Individual Solutions / Pentagram **1612.** Gala Gym / Cabina **1613.** Bread & Butter Studio Output **1614.** Stokbroekx&Stokbroekx / Pure Communication **1615.** Allotment Business Tools / Paperjam Design

1616

1617

1618

1619

1620

1621

1622

1623

1624

1625

1626

1627

1628

1629

16. BDNA / Pentagram   **1617.** Land Investors / estudiotres   **1618.** Dolli Irigoyen / Alejandro Ros   **1619.** DF Solutions / Paperjam sign   **1620.** Retroflo / Brahm   **1621.** 21c Museum and Hotel / Pentagram   **1622.** Fulmer Landscape Design / 9Myles   **1623.** Tragon rporation / Pentagram   **1624.** Hunter House / Dale Harris   **1625.** Top Friseur / Larrea, Solé   **1626.** Customer Advocate Network / :hary Richter   **1627.** Tao Empreendimentos / 19 Design   **1628.** 15/40 Productions / Helou Design   **1629.** Sugar International / Seven

MISCELLANEOUS

BEVERAGE, ELECTRONICS, FOOD, SPORTS, TRANSPORT

1630

30. NADA Bike Spoke Cards, John Bielenberg, NADA Bike / Luke Williams

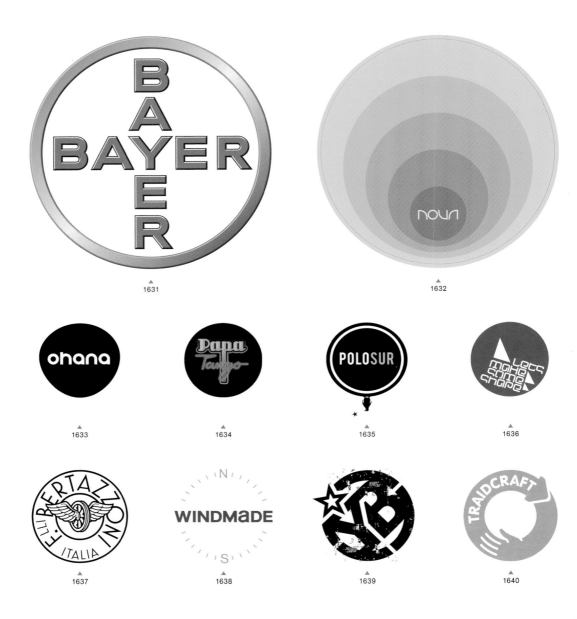

1631

1632

1633

1634

1635

1636

1637

1638

1639

1640

1631. Bayer AG / Claus Koch   **1632.** Nova / Muti Randolph   **1633.** Ohana, Microsoft / SectionSeven   **1634.** Papa Tango, GB Investissement / Eno Krüger Design   **1635.** Polo Sur, Les Yeux Wines / Boldrini & Ficcardi   **1636.** LMSS / Justin Harder   **1637.** Bertazzoni Spa / Pentagram   **1638.** Windmade, Nautiq Group / Estudio González   **1639.** North Kite and Kiteboard / 3Deluxe   **1640.** Traidcraft / Landor Associates

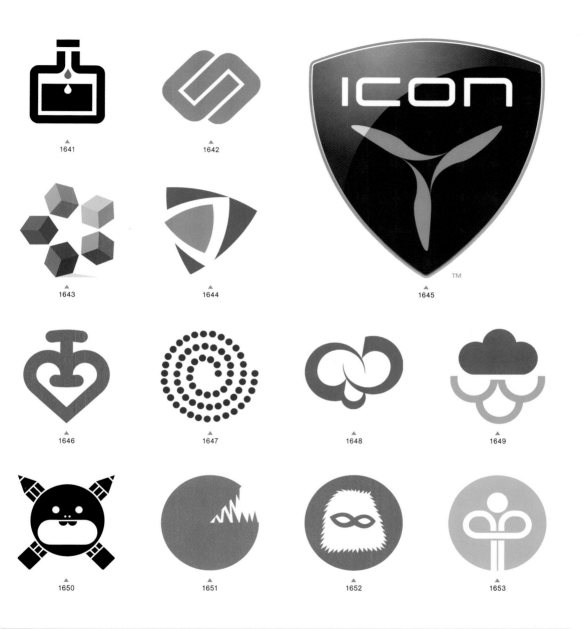

1641

1642

1643

1644

1645

1646

1647

1648

1649

1650

1651

1652

1653

41. Vampire Breathe / Justin Harder 1642. AIAS / Zachary Richter 1643. Five Blocks / Logoholik 1644. Mercandina / Helou
esign 1645. Icon Aircraft / ATTIK 1646. I Love / Versus 1647. Pilsbury Waves, Pisbury, Inc. / Essex Two 1648. Chris Diercks Surfboards
Myles 1649. Sleepy Cloud / Justin Harder 1650. *Various* / Negro 1651. Pacmen F.C. / Justin Harder 1652. Shades of Fur /
stin Harder 1653. CarPool / Justin Harder

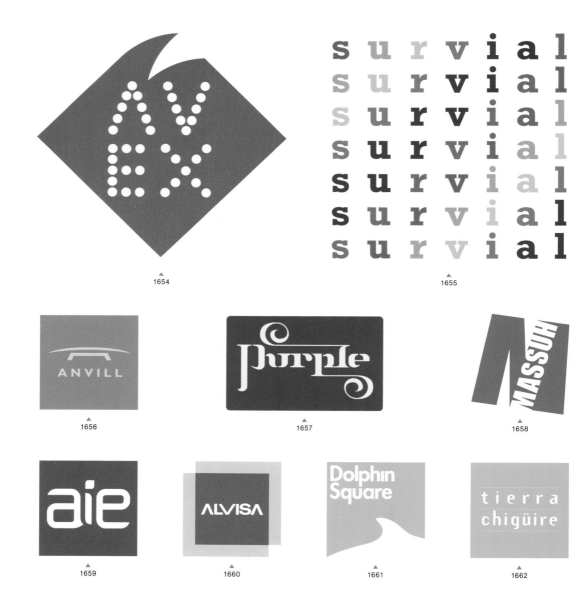

1654

1655

1656

1657

1658

1659

1660

1661

1662

1654. Avex / Shakespear Design   **1655.** Survial / Studioa   **1656.** Anvill / Dale Harris   **1657.** Purple, Kamel Najem / Eno Krüger Design
1658. Papelera Massuh / Shakespear Design   **1659.** Aie Construccion / Eduardo Chang   **1660.** Alvisa, Aluminio y Vidrio S.A. /
Helou Design   **1661.** Dolphin Square, Mantilla Limited / ico Design   **1662.** Tierra Chigüire / Annella Armas

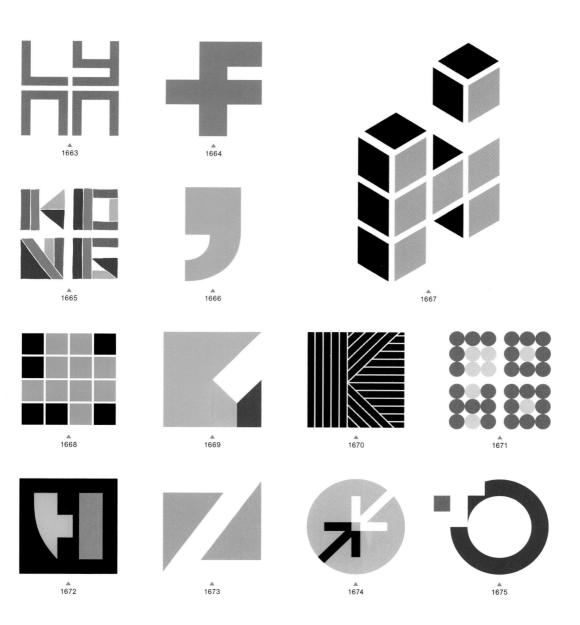

1663.

1664.

1665.

1666.

1667.

1668.

1669.

1670.

1671.

1672.

1673.

1674.

1675.

663. Lynn Management / Push   **1664.** Ferreyros / Studioa   **1665.** Kong / Hula+Hula   **1666.** Koma / Anima   **1667.** Harvey Inc. / Myles   **1668.** Somerset Partners / Pentagram   **1669.** Moblime Muebles / Helou Design   **1670.** Kanuhura, Sun Resorts / Pentagram **671.** Roho / ImagenHB   **1672.** Hormicreto / Helou Design   **1673.** Zeckendorf Development, LLC / Pentagram   **1674.** Almaty Financial istrict, Capital Partners / Pentagram   **1675.** Transoceanica / Versus

1676

1677

1678

1679

1680

1681

1682

1683

1684

1676. Harder Logo, *main logo* / <Justin Harder   **1677.** Radher / Justin Harder   **1678.** Harder Logo, *variation* / Justin Harder   **1679.** Bone Cres
/ Justin Harder   **1680.** Buckle Love / Justin Harder   **1681.** Harder Rock / Justin Harder   **1682.** Buddies / Justin Harder   **1683.** Micker /
Justin Harder   **1684.** Wall R Us / Justin Harder

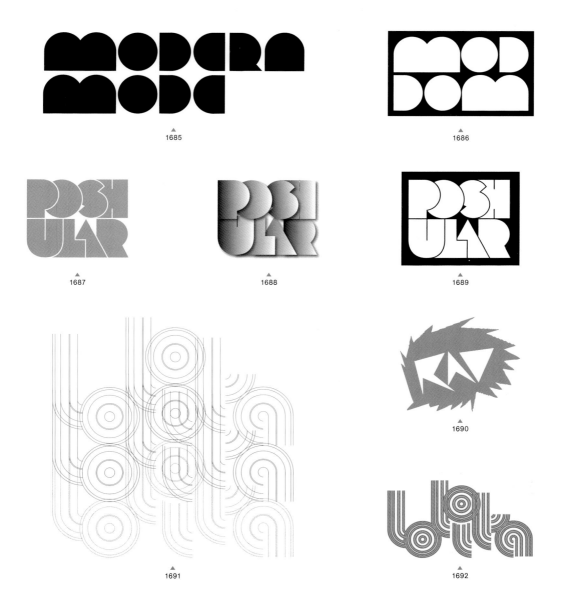

1685

1686

1687

1688

1689

1690

1691

1692

85. Modern Mode / Justin Harder   **1686.** Moddom / Justin Harder   **1687.–1689.** Poshular / Justin Harder
90. Rad / Justin Harder   **1691.–1692.** Lolita, Fanatic Snowboards / 3Deluxe

1693

1693. Arte Actual / Velesi

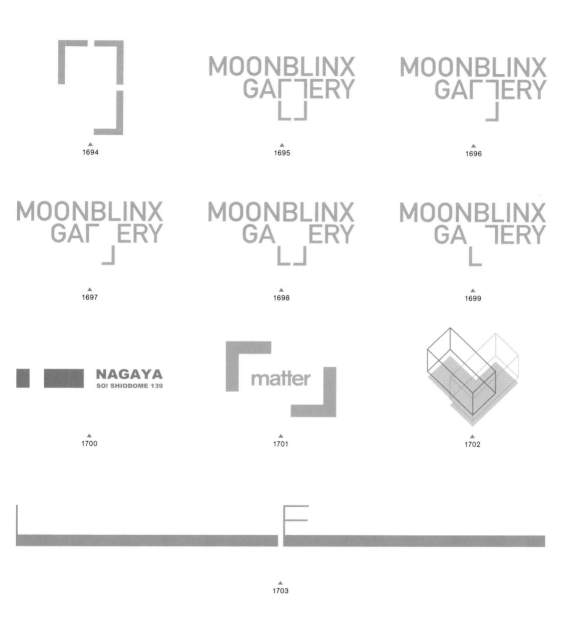

1694

1695

1696

1697

1698

1699

1700

1701

1702

1703

94. Moonblinx Gallery, *variation* / Büro Ink   1695. Moonblinx Gallery, *main logo* / Büro Ink   1696.–1699. Moonblinx Gallery, *variations* / ro Ink   1700. So! Nagaya / Knowledge+   1701. Matter, Fabric / Pentagram   1702. VarioBlock / Forma   1703. Laguna Escondida, source / Cabina

1704

1705

1706

1707

1704. MO, "por qué los cuadros se cuelgan?", Mónica Otero / Cabina   **1705.–1706.** Copenhagen Construction Company / EHA Studio
1707. LMSS / Justin Harder

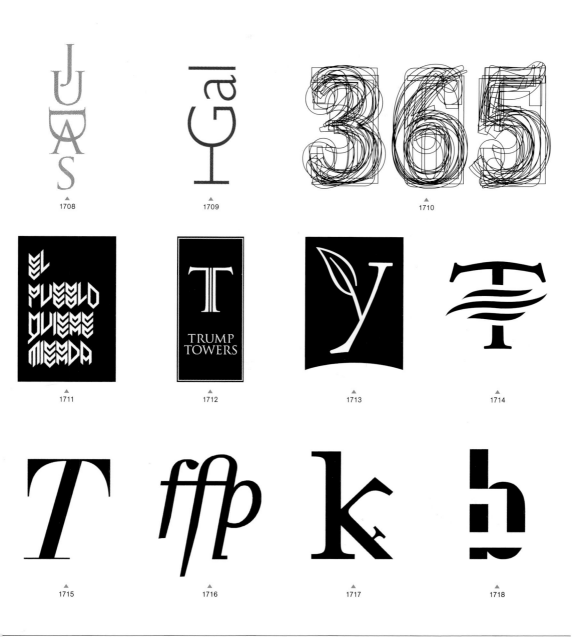

1708

1709

1710

1711

1712

1713

1714

1715

1716

1717

1718

08. Judas, Bodega Sottano / Boldrini & Ficcardi   **1709.** Gal / Pentagram   **1710.** Calender 365 / Pentagram   **1711.** Morboman, orbo Industries / Oswaldo Terreros   **1712.** Trump Towers / Elastic People   **1713.** Alpayura Reforestation / Velesi   **1714.** Trivento T / ldrini & Ficcardi   **1715.** Le Touessrok, Sun Resorts / Pentagram   **1716.** Five Franklin Place / Pentagram   **1717.** Kirkstall Forge, ommercial Estates Group / Brahm   **1718.** Building One at Atlantic Yards, Forest City Ratner Companies / Pentagram

VILLA LA ANGOSTURA - NEUQUEN

△
1719

ideas

△
1720

△
1721

nsfmlir ®

△
1722

ploce.

△
1723

iLamp ™

△
1724

UNLTD

△
1725

flux ™

△
1726

meos.

△
1727

uni×n.

△
1728

Norton ™

△
1729

writa.

△
1730

1719.–1722. *Various* / Negro **1723.** Place / Clusta Ltd. **1724.** iLamp, Adesso / Bluelounge Design **1725.** Fanatic Snowboards / 3Deluxe **1726.** *Various* / Negro **1727.** Meos, Agenda / Un.titled **1728.** Fanatic Snowboards / 3Deluxe **1729.** Norton, Symantec / Pentagram **1730.** writa., Fastline Ltd. / HelloMe

1731

1732

1733

1734

1735

1736

1737

1738

31. Ponsonby Quarter, Valencia Holdings / Seven   **1732.–1735.** *Various* / Negro   **1736.** Metalier / Seven   **1737.** North Kiteboarding / Deluxe   **1738.** Urbane, Autex / Seven

1739

1740

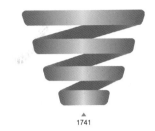
1741

1742

1743

1744

1745

1746

1747

1748

1749

1739. TB / Sockho **1740.** Valbona, Bodega Augusto Pulenta / Boldrini & Ficcardi **1741.** Ventus Medical / Pentagram **1742.** Simplecraft Fabrication / Listen Design **1743.–1747.** *Various* / Negro **1748.** Konk Tractors / Caótica **1749.** Ceri Hand Gallery / Uniform

1750

1751

1752

1753

1754

1755

1756

1757

1758

1759

THE NIGGA IS BLACK

1760

---

750. Morboman, Morbo Industries / Oswaldo Terreros **1751.–1752.** *Various* / Negro **1753.** RMX / Sockho **1754.–1760.** *Various* / Negro

1762

1763

1761

1764

1765

1766

1767

1768

1769

1770

1771

1761.–1762. *Various* / Falko Ohlmer   **1763.** Passion People / 3Deluxe   **1764.** Pirate Boy / Attak   **1765.** Pirate Girl / Attak   **1766.** *Various* / Falko Ohlmer   **1767.** *Various* / Sockho   **1768.** *Various* / Negro   **1769.** Stripes / Justin Harder   **1770.** Panos, Fake Roadsigns / Sockho   **1771.** Mercado / Escobas

1772

1773

1774

1775

1776

1772. Passion People / 3Deluxe   **1773.** Morboman, Morbo Industries / Oswaldo Terreros   **1774.** LMSS / Justin Harder   **1775.** Urban Soldierz / Medusateam   **1776.** Pyrochimps Meets H9 / Toastone, Amanzilla

1777

1778

1779

1780

1781

1782

1783

1784

1785

1786

1777. North Kiteboarding / 3Deluxe   **1778.** Fanatic Snowboards / 3Deluxe **1779.** Lolita, Fanatic Snowboards / 3Deluxe   **1780.** Smile, Club Air / Simone Inc.   **1781.–1782.** Dreu, North Kiteboarding, *variations* / 3Deluxe   **1783.** Slash, North Kiteboarding / 3Deluxe   **1784.** Rebel, North Kiteboarding / 3Deluxe   **1785.** North, North Kiteboarding / 3Deluxe   **1786.** Vegas, North Kiteboarding / 3Deluxe

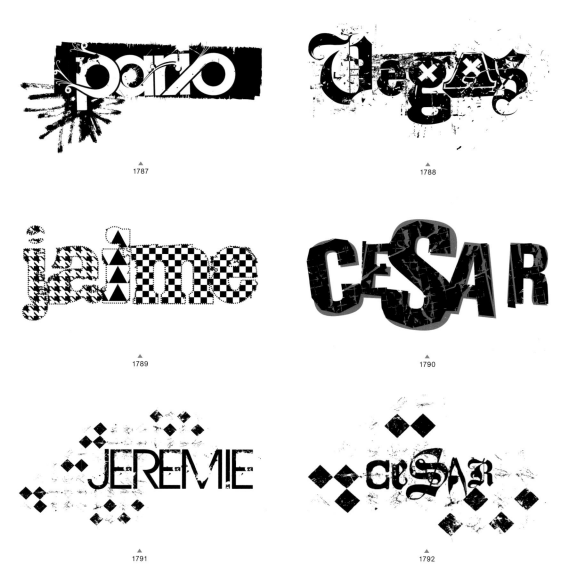

1787

1788

1789

1790

1791

1792

87. Pario, North Kiteboarding / 3Deluxe **1788.** Vegas, North Kiteboarding / 3Deluxe **1789.** Jaime, North Kiteboarding / 3Deluxe **90.** Cesar, North Kiteboarding / 3Deluxe **1791.** Jaime, North Kiteboarding / 3Deluxe **1792.** Cesar, North Kiteboarding / 3Deluxe

1793

1794

1795

1796

1797

1798

1793. Alkimia Wineart / Belén Mena **1794.** Paris, North Kiteboarding / 3Deluxe **1795.** Terroir Alliance / Belén Mena **1796.** Raforker Developments / Edward McMullin **1797.** Roots, Growing Real Estate / KITA **1798.** Vine to Vintage Trail / Dale Harris

1800

FAMILIA DEL RIO ELORZA
BODEGA & VIÑEDOS

1801

1799

PIEDEMONTE
BODEGAS

1802

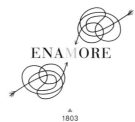

ENAMORE

1803

ALBANTA

1804

ZOLO

1805

1806

BRESSIA

1807

AVANTI

1808

---

99. Eloquent Rooster, Facundo Gallo / NNSS Design **1800.** Domados Wines / Boldrini & Ficcardi **1801.** Familia Del Rio Elorza / Boldrini Ficcardi **1802.** Piedemonte / Boldrini & Ficcardi **1803.** Enamore, Renacer Winery / Boldrini & Ficcardi **1804.** Albanta Wines of Spain / oldrini & Ficcardi **1805.** Zolo, Bodega Tapiz / Boldrini & Ficcardi **1806.** Llama, Bodega Belasco de Baquedano / Boldrini & Ficcardi **07.** Walter Bressia / Boldrini & Ficcardi **1808.** Avanti, Borbore Winery / Boldrini & Ficcardi

1809

Archisesto

1810

VIAGEN

1811

truvia

1812

dropbox

1813

exofrut

1814

1815

POBEDA
GALLERY

1816

œrlikon

1817

MARTIAN
RANCH & VINEYARD

1818

NEWPORT
LOFTS VON WELT

1819

Galerie
L.J.Beaubourg

1820

1809. Acqua Condominium / Ariel Pintos **1810.** Archisesto / Logoholik **1811.** Viagen / Pentagram **1812.** Truvia / Pentagram
1813. Dropbox, Monkeehouse / Studio Output **1814.** Exofrut / Anima **1815.–1816.** Pobeda Gallery / Praline **1817.** Oerlikon /
Claus Koch **1818.** Martian Ranch & Vineyard / Geyrhalter Design **1819.** Newport, Justus Grosse Projektentwicklung GmbH / BKWA
1820. Galerie L.J. Beaubourg / eps51

SAL VISTA
CAPE VERDE

▲
1821

STADTVILLEN
AM WERDERSEE

▲
1822

PEPPLERS GARTEN
Exklusiv leben

▲
1823

SAL VISTA
CAPE VERDE

▲
1824

sugarcoat
go stick it!

▲
1825

TABLESHIELD
BY MATRIX

▲
1826

Cerro Verde

▲
1827

OPENCANDY

▲
1828

CIVIC PUMP

▲
1829

School Gallery
Paris

▲
1830

ILIRIA MINING
CORPORATION

▲
1831

MACHINERY
DEVELOPMENTS

▲
1832

21. Sal Vista, IPC Properties / ICG   1822. Stadtvillen am Werdersee, Justus Grosse Projektentwicklung GmbH / BKWA   1823. Pepplers
rten, Justus Grosse Projektentwicklung GmbH / BKWA   1824. Sal Vista, IPC Properties / ICG   1825. Sugarcoat Designer Vinyl Decals /
ınk Design Machine   1826. Tableshield, Matrix Carpets / ICG   1827. Sociedad Minera Cerro Verde / Ideo Comunicadores
28. OpenCandy / Dale Harris   1829. Civic Pump, Southern Exposure Gallery / Futurefarmers   1830. School Gallery Paris /
me de Bouchony   1831. Iliria Mining Corporation / Projectgraphics   1832. Machinery Developments / Seven

1833

1834

1835

1836

1837

1838

1839

1840

1841

1842

1833. La Jolla Commons, Hines / 9Myles   **1834.** Laboratorios Avanti / Paco Gálvez   **1835.** Microspray / NNSS Design   **1836.** Armonea / Ho & Hoet   **1837.** Tmiint / Logoholik   **1838.** MillerCoors / Pentagram   **1839.** Modus Operandi / Philippe Archontakis   **1840.** Grupo Cornelio Brennand / Gad' Branding & Design   **1841.** Pravina / Vik   **1842.** Sheffield / Seven

1843

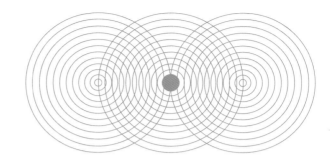

1844

Quieto

1845

1846

1847

1848

1849

1850

1851

43. Gramon / ImagenHB   **1844.** VMS / Pentagram   **1845.** Quieto, Bodega Montequieto / Boldrini & Ficcardi   **1846.** Golden / Gad'
anding & Design   **1847.** Subzero, Vodka SI&SI / Branislav Design   **1848.** Oneo, Grupo Domos / Ideograma Consultores, S.C.
49. Avondale, Autex / Seven   **1850.** Distillery Zhumir / Velesi   **1851.** Cleopatra / Hafenbraut for SiteSeeing

BLACK JACK

1852

PEACE MAKER

1853

1854

1855

1857

1856

1852. Black Jack, Fixie Inc. / MAGMA Brand Design   **1853.** Peace Maker, Fixie Inc. / MAGMA Brand Design   **1854.** Pure Blood, Fixie Inc. MAGMA Brand Design   **1855.** Betty Leeds, Fixie Inc. / MAGMA Brand Design   **1856.** Fixie Inc., *main logo* / MAGMA Brand Design **1857.** Tsingtao Beer, Halewood International / an agency called england

1858

1859

1860

1861

1862

1863

1864

1865

1866

1867

1868

1869

58. Atomium / SIGN 1859. Dubai Invest / Pure Communication 1860. Domo Guaymallen, VSV / ImagenHB 1861. Allseating / TAXI ronto 1862. Burgwardt Construction / Shakespear Design 1863. Antico D'Arte, Occidental Bolivia / Machicao Design 1864. Oncupan diator / Tugba Güler 1865. Various / Negro 1866. Eco Trade / Projectgraphics 1867. Parquet Nobre / Oestudio 1868. Madero Walk, zora / Fileni & Fileni Design 1869. Madero Office, Raghsa / Shakespear Design

1870

1871

1872

1873

1874

1875

1876

1877

1870. Impulse Energy Drink / Fritz Torres   **1871.** Passion People / 3Deluxe   **1872.** Lion / Ginter & Miletina   **1873.** Iori Hotel / Tea Time Studio   **1874.** Cibots Invaders, Red Magic / PO!   **1875.** Splash Toys Inc. / Essex Two   **1876.** Bond voor dieren / DHM Graphic Design **1877.** Basic Beaver / xhoch4

B A S E   M K
▲
1878

MOLYMET
▲
1879

aemedsa®
▲
1880

Wellsford
Estate
▲
1881

Hestia™
HEATING PRODUCTS
▲
1882

TIERGARTEN CARRÉE
Work · Life · Balance
▲
1883

BANANA BAY
V I L L A G E
▲
1884

MANGO GROVE
V I L L A G E
▲
1885

PARAISO®
— PROPERTIES —
▲
1886

B R U X A 9
▲
1887

GRAJAGAN
SURF RESORT
▲
1888

Alice ❤ Bruno
▲
1889

---

8. BASE MK / Pentagram   **1879.** Molymet, Molibdenos y Metales S.A. / Estudio González   **1880.** Aemedsa, Comunica / Damián Di rizio   **1881.** Wellsford Estate / Dale Harris   **1882.** Hestia Heating Products / Franke+Fiorella   **1883.** Tiergarten Carrée / Daniel ndt   **1884.** Banana BAY / Revolver   **1885.** Mango Grove / Revolver   **1886.** Paradise / Oestudio   **1887.** Bruxa 9 / Oestudio
8. Grajagan Surf Resort / Camisa 10 Propaganda   **1889.** Alice & Bruno / Amodesign

1890

1891

1892

1893

1890. *Various* / Falko Ohlmer   **1891.** Kong / Hula+Hula   **1892.** BIC Plastics / Escobas   **1893.** Beach City Builders / 9Myles

DOMOGUAYMALLEN

1894

TSN-COMEX   INVECØM

1895   1896

WONDERLAND™   Simplecraft

1897   1898

1899

1894. Domo Guaymallen, VSV / ImagenHB   **1895.** Tsn-ComEx, Tesin SRL / 1828   **1896.** Invecom / Bernardo+Celis   **1897.** Wonderland, Ministry of Sound / Studio Output   **1898.** Simplecraft Fabrication / Listen Design   **1899.** Nueveochenta Gallery / Tangrama

LOGOS

12345

00 **1307**
2ergo **1564**
3 Monos **1413**
3 Pontas Brasil **1166**
4FM **0837**
4Food **1332**
4seasons **1548**
12 SRA **0375**
15/40 Productions **1628**
21c Museum & Hotel **1621**
23 **0469**
24Seven Vol 2 **0847**
27+1 **0982**
28 **1536**
33-0 **0275**
35AM Films **0197, 0244**
50th Anniversary of
Casa de las Américas **0638**
69 **1308**
80s Dance Night
1062–1063
100% Design **0302**
647 **0983**
2021 **1001**
5411 Interactive **1039**
&c **0831**

A

A2 Studio **0094**
A4 Bar **1214**

AAAA **0406**
AAMAC **0751**
AAmerican Financial
Group Inc. **1423**
AAUP Productions
and Design Managers
Meeting 2010 **0355–0358**
Abandoned Clothing **0490**
abc Bookstore **1227**
Abradab **1165**
AB Rogers Design **0185**
Academia del Cine
de la Argentina **0639**
Accept & Proceed **0141,
0144, 0173**
Access Internet **0839**
Acessibilidade **0936**
Acitron **1197**
Acqua
Condominium **1809**
A Cuerda **0350**
Addicted Online **1186**
Addicted to Drawing **0971**
Adé Design **0182**
Adrenalab Multimedia
0844
Adriane **1136–1137**
Aemedsa **1880**
Aeromar S.A. **1526**
Aeroplano **0879**
Agrinia Jewelry **0588**

Agustín Zuluaga Olarte
0137
Aha! **0063**
AIAS **1642**
Aie Construccion **1659**
AIGA FRESH Talent **0353**
Ajinda **1363**
Akelarre Cafe **1339**
Akin **1160**
AK Sealogistk **1484**
Albanta Wines of Spain
1804
Al Dente **1316–1318**
Alfaguara Prize **0327**
Alfredo Méndez **0165**
Alice & Bruno **1889**
Alkalá Café Galería **1239**
Alkimia Wineart **1793**
Alliacta Technical
Consultants **1520**
Allotment Business Tools
1615
Allseating **1861**
Almacén del paraiso
1340–1341
Almaty Financial District
1674
Alpayura Reforestation
1713
Alvisa **1660**
ama **0793**

Ambigram **0116**
American Society for
Surgery of the Hand **0733**
Ammo **0227**
Amsterdamse Popprijs
2008 **1098**
Amulette **0442**
Ancine **0802**
Andarilho **0902**
Andersonville Arts
Weekend **0320**
Andersonville Chamber
of Commerce **0384**
AndreaP Trading **1529**
Andrew Duke Contracting
1528
Andungen **0315**
Angel Guido Art Project
0300
A Night in Fashion **0476**
Animal Days **0001**
Anker Gemeente **0625**
Another Digital **0199, 0212**
Antico D'Arte **1863**
Antje Klein **0075**
Anvill **1656**
A Penguin **0059**
Apeteco **1302**
Appeal **0515**
Aqua Magica **1277**
Aquim **1228**

Arabia Delivery **1420**
Arabia Restaurant **1235**
Archisesto **1810**
Arcieri Della Merla **0377**
Ardi **0303**
area3 **0106**
Argentina Formidable **0815**
Argentina.Travel **0759**
Arkade Magazine **0903**
Armacost Antiques Shows
0257
Armonea **1836**
Arquimia Architecture
0027
Arroz Trillo **1338**
Ars Thanea **0097**
Art+Design DMU **0704**
Art Design Studio **0247**
Arte Actual **1693**
Artes Visuales **0777**
Art Institute of Chicago
0611
Artisan **1519**
Artist **0455**
Artist House Holding **0125**
Artline Films **0977**
Artvalley **1471**
Asimpres **0773**
Asociación de Vecinos
de Bello Monte **0599**
Aspen Bistrot **1366**

As Pequenas Raposas **028[**
Ästhetiker Wängl Tängl
0354
Ästhetiker Wear **0493**
Asunto Impreso Editores
0897
Atelier Punkt **0254**
Atomium **1858**
Attak **0226**
Audiolife **1172**
Aura **1486**
Aurum Corporation **136[**
Automatica **0117**
Avanti **1808**
Aves Uruguay **0819**
Avex **1654**
Avondale **1849**
AV Produções **0012**
Aysa **0709**

B

b **0762**
Bacanal **0959**
Bad Bear Inc. **0430–0432**
Bags **1460**
BAIE **0619**
Banana BAY **1884**
Banana Shield **0429**
Bananeira Filmes **0221**
Bancaja **1488**
Banco del Pacifico **1552**

nco Solidario **1466**
nda Larga **1153**
RT **0805**
SE MK **1878**
sic Beaver **1877**
ss **1083**
tuka **1337**
yer AG **1631**
cB **1287**
C Thread **0513**
)NA **1616**
ach City Builders **1893**
achdown Festival **0318**
ar Care **0561**
at 98 **0932**
autiful Decay **0109–0110**
auty Planet **1360**
ck Modern Guilt **1097**
linda Cafe **1343**
sim **1571**
rtazzoni Spa **1637**
ty Leeds **1855**
yond Oblivion **1170**
elix **1273–1274**
civia **0745**
C Plastics **1892**
ella **1465**
g Boom Media **1033**
J **1089**
g Magazine **1023–1024**
ndi **1215**
polar **1077**
Product Recovery **1463**
sman Ediciones **0875**
rkvin **0522**
ack Diamond **1369**
ackfin **0507–0510**
ack Guayaba **1107**
ack Icon Character **0427**
ack Jack **1852**
ak **0518**
eekr! **1326**
oco dos Furtados **0385**
uelounge Design **0122**
VD **1418**
oca **0724**
ghossian Foundation
17
llywood Masala **1246**
mbom **1352**
nd voor dieren **1876**
ne Crest **1679**
oks & Dreams
okstore **1342**
ost Mobile **1505**
ris the Cat **1411**
ead & Butter **1613**
itish Colony **0545–0547**
itish Society of Russian
ailately **0637**
itspotting **0367–0370**
uuns Bazaar **0466, 0581**

Bruxa 9 **1887**
Bsided **0534**
Buckle Love **1680**
Buddies **1682**
Building One at Atlantic
Yards **1718**
Bunch **0139**
bureau 91c **0143**
Burgwardt Construction
1862
Burnside GmbH **1213**
Büro Ink **0030**
BWA BWA Album **1065**

C

Cadena de favores **1028**
Café Amor Perfecto
1270–1272
Café del Río **1419**
Café Fonseca **1218**
Café Scientifique **1417**
Caféserie GmbH **1279**
CafeSiete **1309–1315**
Calender 365 **1710**
California Academy
of Sciences **0737**
California Community
Foundation **0743**
Calinor NV **1236**
Cambucá Music **1196**
Camino Real **1598**
Camisa 10 Propaganda
0060
Canal 11 **0979**
Candy Productions **0192**
Caótica Pattern **0563**
Cape Ann Farmers' Market
1198–1203
Capella Hotels & Resorts
1593
Capital Partners **1532**
Capture **0904**
Caracas Design **0251**
Caribbean Connection
1075
CarPool **1653**
Casa **0279**
Casa da Palavra **0935**
Casaviva **0946**
Casper Balslev **0048, 0209**
Casulo Cultura **0360**
Caus Bambu **0056**
C & C **0345**
CCCP **0889**
CCEBA **0806**
Cedar Realty Co.
1446–1448
Cena Brasil Produções
Central Gráfica de Jornais
0969
Central Sports **1454**

Centro de Oftalmologia
1572
Ceri Hand Gallery **1749**
Cesar **1790, 1792**
Charm Perfum **0446, 0574**
Cheap Monday **0421–0425**
Cheese **0792**
Chew it Over **0974**
Chilli Dog **0171**
Chokolat **0073**
Chris Diercks Surfboards
1648
Chris Holzinger **0542**
Christian Otto Studio **0006**
Cibots Invaders **1874**
CIC **0113**
CINEBRASILTV **0864**
Cinemaison **0307**
Cinemanía **0956**
Cinimod Studio **0114**
Cioccolato **1384**
Circle **1458**
Circle Company **0876**
Circuit de Spa
Francorchamps **0400**
Circular 15 **0003**
City Hopper **1464**
City Hunters **1021–1022**
City University
of New York **0702**
CIVA **0830**
Civic Pump **1829**
Claro **1461**
Classilio **1437–1445**
Claudia Mahecha Design
0108
Clearity Magazine **0957**
Cleopatra **1851**
Clinch **1104**
Cloud Magic **0846**
Clubland **1129**
Club Maki **1184**
Club TV **0961**
Cluck Stencil **0181**
Cobus Sistemas **1558**
Codarts **0663–0666**
Coldin Gastronomía **1347**
Coldwater **0395–0399**
Colectivo Xpositivo **0081**
Colégio Loyola **0727**
College of Design **0832**
Colmena **0778**
Columbia Business School
0703
Comic Book Tattoo **0880,
0884**
Companhia Suspensa **0343**
Compania de Costura **0582**
Compass Search **1455**
Conah **1509**
Conamu **0628–0635**
Concord Music **1127**

Conelsur **1470**
Contemporâneo **1491**
Contemporary Jewish
Museum **0752**
Contraditório **0306**
Cool Brands **0975**
Cool Guy **0845**
COP15 **0348**
Copacabana Sagrado **0790**
Copenhagen Construction
Company **1705–1706**
Coração Denunciador
0289
Corazón de Melón **0568**
Corazon Salomon **0529**
Cornell Lab of Ornithology
0817
Correos Chile **0803**
Corte Nacional Electoral
0738
Cotton United **0487**
Country Club **0485, 0489**
Coutours **0573**
Cowboy **0554**
CPFL Cultura **0711**
CPVO **0789**
Craftsmen **0033**
Crashstar **1607**
Crazy Boys **0503**
Creación al Límite **0359**
Criteria C.A. **0898**
Cruel **0278**
Crush **0594**
Crystallised **0474**
Cuerda Floja **0835**
Cultura e Pensamento **0687**
Customer Advocate
Network **1626**
Cutles **1139**
Cynara **0612**

D

DaDaDa **1144–1145**
Daddy Yankee **1069**
Dado **1297**
Dakota **1146**
Dale Harris **0246**
Dalles **1130**
Damien Mercier **1368**
Dance Party **1147**
Dancer **1586–1588**
Datamantes **0401**
Dead Sexy **1071**
Debate Hall **0853, 0856,
0874, 1034, 0973**
Debriefing **0090**
Deep Black Heart **1081**
De Ferrari **0860**
De Locatie **1562**
Departement Interactive
Services **0072**
DeporFan **1207, 1386**

De San Martín Design
0167
Design Deluxe **0107**
Design Leicestershire **0798**
Design Museum Shop
**1225–1226, 1298, 1333,
1357, 1392**
Designprijs Rotterdam
0829
Design x Space **0107**
Details **0607**
Detroit Institute of Arts
0756–0758
Deutsche
Nationalbibliothek **0715**
Deutscher
Nachhaltigkeitspreis **0323**
Deutsches Zentrum **0779**
Deviate Records **1175**
DF Solutions **1501, 1619**
Diabito Character **0502**
Diagramme **0390**
Diana Cabeza **0017**
Dianthus **1276**
Die Ludolfs **0962**
Die Planung **0918–0919**
Digi Tree **1453**
Dinamo **0292–0294**
Dingbats Brasil **0371**
Dirb **0177**
Directenergy Website
Hosting **1478**
Discokette **0859**
Discrete Headwear **0544**
Diseñadores Gráficos
Bolivia **0741**
Disko404 **1046**
Distillery Zhumir **1850**
Distribuidora de Libros
0618
Distribuidora del Parque
1449
Distrito de las artes **0718**
Divergente **0219**
Divide **1113**
DJ Eleven **1177**
DJ Sounds **1176**
DMP rec **1159**
Doc Meeting Argentina
0272
Dolce **1206**
Dolli Irigoyen **1618**
Dolphin Square **1661**
Domados Wines **1800**
Domo **1565**
Domo Guaymallen **1860,
1894**
Dona Cor **0443**
Don Javor **1158**
Dreen Re-energy **1601**
Drei Groschen Studio **0005**
Dressipe **1359**

Dreu **1781–1782**
Dropbox **1813**
Drops de Anis **0461**
DS9 **0005**
Dsquared2 **0541**
Dubai Invest **1859**
Dúné **1106**
Dutch Masters **0364**
DWP **0807**
Dynallia **1569**

E

e3 Labs **0760**
Earth Crisis **0420**
East Photographic **0061**
Ecléctica Magazine
0929–0931
Eclipse **0849**
Ecomercado **1354**
Ecopartner **0119**
Eco Trade **1866**
Ediciones Cocolí **0887**
Eduacion Biocentrica **0372**
EGF **0463**
EGO **1584**
Ego Café & Bookshop
1395
Ein Anna Dans **0130**
Eisblume **1353**
EK **0863, 1015**
Ela Diseño y Moda **0569**
El Clic **0920–0924**
El Ojo Magazine **0873**
Eloquent Rooster **1799**
El Patin **0967**
Else Club Moskow **1435**
Em Casa **1088**
Emerald City Press **1299**
Emprendedor **0828**
EN **1295**
Enamore **1803**
Encuesta Suple S! **0978**
Energía Austral **1487**
Energy Plans **0361**
Enfoques **0901**
Enigma **1425–1426, 1428,
1434**
Eno Krüger **0148–0149,
0241, 0243**
Ensemble Financial
Planning **1594**
Entreventos **1485**
enV **0520**
EP **1542**
Episode **1056**
Eramos Tantos **0007**
ERB **1596**
Ero Kosova **0772**
ESC **1537**
Escendo **0531**
Escobas **0032, 0523**
Escucha **1391**

ESMS **1561**
Espace N **0079**
ESPN **0939**
Estética Garbo **0506**
Estúdio Infinito **0186**
Estudio Rosellini **0025**
Estúdios Mega **0124**
Etapatelecom **1433**
Eurockeénes
de Belfort 2005 **1067**
Evolver **0972**
EVRU **0271**
Exhibit A **0351**
Exofrut **1814**
Exp **0468**
Extra Fine Wool **0589**
Eyechat **0937**

F
Factory Hotel **1504**
Faena Hotel **1429**
Fakt **0460**
Falconer Chester Hall **0147**
Falou Gun **1133**
Familia Del Rio Elorza
1801
Fanatic Snowboards
**1725, 1728,
1778**
Fango **1589**
Farmdog **1217**
Fasan **1233**
Fashion Fringe **0512**
Father **0555**
Fatuus **0147**
FC Makeni Juniors **0730**
Fearless Clothing **0527**
Federico Aubele
Panamericana **1084**
Felix A. Schweikert
Training & Consulting
1543
Fernando Jaeger **1210**
Ferreyros **1664**
Festa delle Oasi **0771**
FFAA **0189**
FH Mainz **0672–0674**
Fica Comigo Esta Noite
0269
Fidel **1086**
Fil **0274**
Filmania **1602–1604**
FilzFlash **0566**
Finestra Pizzaria **1364**
Finvesa **1456, 1472**
Fios Group **1567**
First Baptist Church
of Paducah **0775**
Firsteight **0093**
Fisk **0797**
Fist **0558**
FIT **0434**

Five Blocks **1643**
Five Cool Rooms
Buenos Aires **1430**
Five Franklin Place **1716**
Five Point O **0050**
Fixie Inc. **1856**
Flatiron **0641**
Flor Canibal Editorial **0842**
Flores **1330**
FNORD **0206**
Fobia XX **1161**
Fold **0206**
Folk **0232–0233**
Follow Fluxus **0270**
Forey **0587**
Formlos **0065**
Foundation of Electronic
Music Aarhus **1076**
Fragmento Imán Editores
0894
Frakton **0163**
France/Francia **0403, 0405**
Freshoops **0934**
Fuego North America **1230**
Fukujin **0497**
Fulmer Landscape Design
1622
Fulô Estúdio **0164**
Fumaça Corp. **1025**
Fundación Boliviana para
la Democracia Multipadari
0734
Fundación Cultural
de la Ciudad de México
0667–0671
Furograma Architects **0115**
Futatsu **0045**
FVK **0598**

G
g800 **0011, 0203–0205**
Gain Magazine **0951**
Gal **1709**
Gala Gym **1612**
Galatasaray University
Economics Days **0340**
Galerie L.J. Beaubourg
1820
Garden for the
Environment **0614**
GD Football Club **0729**
Gema Carbajosa **1436,
1590**
Generations **0602**
Genius **0872**
George Mélès **1040**
Getifex **1452**
Get London Reading **0799**
Gilson Martins **0586**
Glam Pet **1256–1263**
Glen **1554–1555**
Global Roach **0861**

Go! **0548–0553**
Going Underground **1195**
Golden **1846**
Golf Republic **0383**
Gominola Creative Media
0981
Goo **0470**
Gossler **1518**
GPF **0963**
GRACOM **0016**
Gradara **0723**
Grafik Parkour **0376**
Grajagan Surf Resort **1888**
Gramon **1843**
Grant Thornton **1522**
Gravesend **0234**
Green Canteen **1303**
GreenGenes **1335**
Green Park **1356**
Greensky Films **0074**
Green Tea **1573–1576**
Green Volcano Software
0095
Grizzly **1389**
Grundfaktor **0077**
Grupo Cornelio Brennand
1840
Guest Catering **1331**
Gusto **1325**
Gyldendal Business Debate
1032

H
Habibis Lounge Cafe **1244**
Half **0067**
HallenSportBadBiberach
0708
Handcrafts Design **1378**
Happy Tails Grooming
0428
Harder Logo **1676, 1678**
Harder Rock **1681**
Harvey Inc. **1667**
Heart Cream **1286**
Heartgrenade **0559**
Hear we Go **0886**
Heliodor **1489**
Hello Monday **0037–0044**
Hello Vanilla **0008**
Helping Hand Rewards
1432
Help Whale **0818**
Hembras y bandidas **1138**
Herbario **1346**
Herzbluter **0780**
Herzflattern **1087**
Hestia Heating Products
1882
Highland Open **0394**
Hijo de Fuego **0178**
HIV **0826**
h(iv)eart **0624**

HM Assurantie **1523**
Hochtaunuskreis **0787**
Hockey in the Hood **0731**
Holzkopf **1361**
Home **1290**
Hooli **0622**
Hormicreto **1672**
Horor Vendetta **1048**
Hotel Alpina **1517**
Houyhnhnms.tv **0938**
Howdy **1278**
H.P.F **0464**
Huairasinchi **0263**
Hub **1220**
Huevocherdo **0728**
Humor à Francesa **0308**
Hunter House **1624**
Hus Forbi **0866**

I
IANN **0732**
Iceland **1221–1223**
Icon Aircraft **1645**
Idea Espacios **0009**
IDN Black & White **0850**
if... **0298**
IF **1530**
ift **0812**
II CVK **0252**
i Lab Consulting **1473,
1534**
iLamp **1724**
Iliria Mining Corporation
1831
Illunatic **0087**
I Love **1646**
I love xhoch4 **0127**
ImagenHB **0057**
Impordisa **1544**
Imprenta Segura **1480**
Impulse Energy Drink
1870
IN **0795**
INCINE **0057**
InCite **1424**
Individual Solutions **1611**
Ines **1066**
Inflávio Magazine **0909**
In-forma **0900**
Inhotim Contemporary
Art Center **0705–0707**
In Love – Out of Love
0140
Innovative Family Dental
Health **1469**
InSpira Performing Arts
and Cultural Center **0813**
Instituto Estudios
Gráficos de Chile **0742**
Interfacturas **1538**
Intermedia Creative Group
0002

International Iron and Steel
Institute's IISI 40 **0747**
International Love **1047**
Invecom **1896**
Invictus CFW **0501**
ION Essentials **0454,
0477–0482, 0483, 0486,
0488, 0521, 0477–0482**
Iori Hotel **1873**
Israeli Wines **1371**
Istocna Cuda **1241**
I teach NYC **0685**
IT Tours **1527**
Ivana Production **1038**
I wanna be Paris'
new best friend **0843**

J
Jack in a Box **1431, 1549**
Jaime **1789, 1791**
Jaime Nuñez del Arco
Studio **0207**
Jaipur **1240**
Jaleo **1049**
Janelle **1301, 1324**
Javelin **1467**
Javino Restaurant **1234**
Jaydee **0102, 0105, 0237**
Jeans Dean **0500**
Jeremy Levine **0034**
Jersey Café **1237**
Jessica McCormack **0475**
Jewish General Hospital
0782
Jexbo **1037**
JMW Architecture **0026**
John Charles Centre
for Sport **0800**
Joyco **1479**
Judas **1708**
jungeschachtel **0215**

K
K20 K21 **0720**
Kanuhura **1670**
Katabasis **1105**
Kato Cafe **1281**
Katz Editores **0851**
Kavany **0530**
Keenpixel **0091**
Kelly Key **1157**
Kent House
Consulting Ltd. **0855**
Kero Kone **1306**
Kharma **0891**
Kidsco **0739**
Kinder- und
Jugendtheaterpreis **0264**
King Emperor **0052**
Kingfish Restaurant **1370**
Kirkstall Forge **1717**
Kitchen Café **1376**

Kiu Enviromental Design
0128
Kleines Haus **0407**
KMDG Crew **0029**
Knights **0184**
Kohlekraft – Nein danke!
0644–0651
Koken op Maat **1379**
Koma **1666**
Komrowski Group **1494**
Kong **1665, 1891**
Konk Tractors **1748**
Kontra **0104**
Kooture **0445**
Kopfnicker Records **1057**
KS-Clubber **0896**
Kubik Modular **1499**
Kunstcafé **0250**

L
La Aldea Sandwichs **1282**
Laboratorios Avanti **1834**
Lab Project **0291**
La Changa Wear **0419**
La Diablita Cantina **1405**
La Discusión **0953**
La Flama **0170**
Laguna Escondida **1703**
Lahunco **1511**
La Jolla Commons **1833**
Landia **0020**
Land Investors **1617**
La Negrita **0028**
La Poste **1553**
La Quinta Estación **1187**
Laranja Mecânica **0288**
Laranjeiras Clínica
Perinatal **0816**
Las Vegas Magazine **0928**
Late + Fuerte **0347**
Lategan Media Group **012**
Latingráfica **1427**
Launch Factory **1525**
Launchpad **0713**
Lauren Marks **0150–0155**
La Vache **0379**
La Voix d'Assoli **0980**
Layali **0571**
La Yein Fonda **0268**
La Zurda **1396**
Lectura de manos **1600**
Le Cube Festival 2008
1079
Le Cycle Brainstorming
1212
Le Piano **1328**
Les Petits Cadeaux **0453**
Le Sucre Clothing
**0409–0418, 0439–0440,
0471**
Le Touareg **1072**
Le Touessrok **1715**

wis Center for the Arts
00
ght 1500
ght Institute of Urban
d Social Development
40
nk 1451
nkUp 1112
on 1872
sa Nuboer 0567
teraturas del Exilio 0310
ttle Fish Cards 0223
ama 1806
1SS 1636, 1707, 1774
ading 0101
bo Theater Corporation
82
co-UK 0426, 0532
ddon Shire 0710
ft Disco 1108
gosvet 0942
lita 1691-1692, 1779
ndon Innovation 1608
ndon Supply 1373
osefilms 0098
rena Duarte 0216
ve 1016-1018
ve and Money 0344
ve Beat Boat 0255
ve Hz Studios 1171
veMaze 1148
w Life 1183
ciernaga 0248
ckyfish 1414
JFT 0907
isa Veiga 1539
imiere 0933
sh Industries 0193
thern Study Bible 0643
ux 1164
VL 0014
va Zumblick 0166
yndon Wade 0208
nn Management 1663

M
A 1498
aac 0604
AC de Niterói 0814
achinery Developments
832
adero Office 1869
adero Walk 1868
ade With Love 1020
adonna Confessions
n a Dance Floor 1064
lagazine Regards 0945
laginus 1560
lagnaetruria Srl 1372
ak 0794
aki 1305

Makite 0572
Mali 0714
Mallard Tea Rooms
1264-1269
Mall Center 1349
Maltha 0066
MANÁ 1114
Mandoza Family 1142
Mango Grove 1885
Manifesto 0955
Mantis 0854
Marca Brasil 0823
Marché 27 1348
Maria 1407
Maria Pinto 0540
Marland Consultoria
& Design 0055
Marleen Breilmann 1546
Martian Ranch & Vineyard
1818
Master Electricians 1506
Matizmo 0159
MatrizB 0015, 0080
Matter 1701
Mauricio Valladares 1124
Maximiliano 1320
Maya ediciones 0868
Maya Java Café 1421
MC Dilo 0191
MDGF 1482
ME 0746
Mecanográfica 1492
Melanie McLean Agency
0484
Melissa Lo Jewellery 0575
Melt Away 0229
Memory Game 0841
menü 1390
Meos 1727
Mercado 1771
Mercandina 1644
Mesa 0767
Messe München GmbH
0261
Metalier 1736
Me Too 0142
Metro Ferreiro 0123
Meumundo.com 0309
Miami Film Festival 0253
Micker 1683
Microplace 1497
Microspray 1835
Midisystem 0871
Miguel Ángel Aragonés
Studio 0126
Mijk Van Dijk 1058
Milkcrate Event
Management Group 0365
MillerCoors 1838
Mind the Gap 1090-1096
Ministério da Saúde 0736
Minto 0337-0339

Mira 0156
Missoni 0535
MiX 0273
Mixed Fight TV 0965
MMS 1559
MO 1704
Moara 1585
Mobile Digital Commons
Network 0833
Mobile Experience Engine
0693
Mobile Media Lab 0595
Moblime Muebles 1669
MO Creatives 0202
Modani 0096
Moddom 1686
Mode 0984
Modern Editions 0869
Modern Mode 1685
Modus Operandi 1839
Moe 1052
Mojokite 1566
Molekül 0035
Molymet 1879
MOM 0228
Momentum 0954
Mónica Borrero 0472
Monica Vinader 0577
Monkey 01 0169
Monmiya 0947
Moonblinx Gallery
1694-1699
Mórbido 0256
Morboman 1711, 1750,
1773
Morphos Studio 0225
Mother Superior UK 0491
Mr. Fish Grill 1415
Muca 0280
Multiplicidade 0290
Múltiplos Projetos
Culturais 0312
Multired 1462
Musae 0239
Musa Enferma 0882
Museo del Caribe 0750
Museo de Palpa 0675-0677
Museon 0825
Museu Casa do Pontal
0678-0680
Museum für Film
und Fernsehen 0684
Museum of Arts
and Design 0809
Mutantes 1082
Muzik School 1173
Myah 1109
My Gold School 0437
Mylius-Erichsen Bryghus
1422
My Mobile Match 1545
My Run Base 0892

N
NADA Bike Spoke Cards
1630
Nalindesign 0133
National Council
of the Fauna 0764
Nayatune 1053
Nederlandse Grondbeurs
1503
Negra Li 1070
NEO 1610
Neon Radio 0834
NeoPolis 0601
Nero22 0524
Nescafe Crave 0305
New Growth 0770
New immo marked 1483
New Orleans 0691-0692
Newport 1819
New School Picknick 0285
New York City Ballet 0325
Nicola Dann 0441
Nido 0593
Nike All Ball 0840
Ninja 0910-0917, 1002,
1014
Ninja Love 0496
Nippon Boy 0018
Nippon flowers 0218
Nirvana 1507
NIU 0408
NMD 0519
Nó 0277
No Ar – 50 Anos de Vida
0259
Noblanco 0211
Nobrand 0157
no.mad agency 0444
Non 0023
Nordskak 1508
Normal 0103
Norsk Forfattersentrum
0783
North 1785
North Kite and Kiteboard
1639
North Kiteboarding 1737,
1777
Norton 1729
Nova 1632
Noz Moscada 1367
Nueveochenta Gallery 1899
NuPress 1474
Nürnberger Symphoniker
1155

O
Objectified 0899
Oblicua 0089
Observatorio de Asuntos
de Genero 0627
Ochoporojo 0366

October Contemporary
0317
Octopus 1149
Odic Force 1004
Odio 1003
Oerlikon 1817
Oficina Desafio 0652-0662
Oglethorpe University
0788
Ohana 1633
Ohio Environmental
Council 0785
Ohlhaber
Telekommunikation 1524
OHRA 1606
Ojo 1005
Okayplay 0494
Olga Tañon 1074
Omal 1557
Omino 0533
Oncupan Radiator 1864
O'Neill Europe 0393
One Laptop per Child
Foundation 0822
Oneo 1848
On Fuego Radio 0964
Onomatopee 0952
OpenCandy 1828
Opus Sound 1174
Oranda Interim BV 1476
Orange Monkey Tours
1568
Orion 1243
Orlando Museum of Art
0808
Orquestral Imperial 1154
Osklen 0499, 0543
Ossie Clark 0457
Osteopathie 1510
Outward Bound Center
for Peacebuilding 0820
Owar 0068
Oxelo 0583

P
Pablo Vintimilla 0022
Pacmen F.C. 1651
Paddington 0240
Pairings Restaurant
and Wine Bar 1398-1404
Paninoteca 1304
Panoramic 1336
Panos 1770
Papa Tango 1634
Papelera Massuh 1658
Paperworld 0865
Papier 07–Papier 08 0341
Paradise 1886
Parangolé Awards 0392
Pario 1787
Paris 1794
Park Avenue Armory 0688

ParkLive Music Festival
Brockwell Park 1073
Park Tahoe Inn 1609
Parktel 1592
Parquet Nobre 1867
Passion People 1763, 1772,
1871
Patagonia Agreste 1321
Patrimoine Culturel
Immateriel 0781
Peace Maker 1853
Peak 0516
Pelé Station 0332-0336
Pen 0195
Pepplers Garten 1823
Peri Pheri 0467, 0511
Permanent Unit 0121, 0242
Persona 0642
PerVers 1178
Petit Pois 1208
Pfalztheater Kaiserslautern
0349
Pheek 1110
Phi 0051, 0231
Phoenix 0224
PhonDER 1055, 1191-1194
Photographic Interiors
0082
Piaf 1283-1285, 1334
Pick & Mix 0388
Picnic 0465
Picnic Magazine 1012
Piedemonte 1802
Pilsbury Waves 1647
Pink Elephants Inc. 0120
Piperlime 0584
Pippa Drysdale 1125
Pirate Boy 1764
Pirate Girl 1765
Pitocatalán 0560
pixellove 0878
Pixelway 0187
Place 1723
Plastik 1143
Plattform 0636
Platzhirsch 0881
Please Pop 1163
Plena Records 1068
Plotki 0858
Plus 0597
Pluto Project
Spaces 0064
Pobeda Gallery 1815-1816
Point Blanc 1292
points24 1350
Polo Sur 1635
Pon a Punto tu Casa 0054
Ponsonby Quarter 1731
Pont-Aven School
of Contemporary Art 0686
Portinari Centennial
0681-0683

Porto Seguro Cia.
de Seguros Gerais **1516**
Poshular **1689**
Pozzilei **0525**
Pravina **1841**
Premio Luis Caballero **0712**
Premios de la Moda **0570**
Primegate **0078**
Primondo **0579**
Princeton University **0722**
Princeton University
Art Museum **0698**
Progressive Arts Network
0346
Project Album **0086**
Projectgraphics **0046**
Propaga **0088**
Prova Center **1377**
Proyecto Demo **0062**
Puker **0556**
Pure Blood **1854**
Pure Groove **1135**
Purple **1657**
Pyrochimps **0174**
Pyrochimps Meets H9
1776

Q

qba **1393.–1394**
Qbase **1502**
Q Design Store **1216, 1382**
Q Studio **0198**
Quadra **0217**
Quieto **1845**
Quito World Flowers
Capital **0615**

R

Rad **1690**
Radher **1677**
Radical Girl **1408**
Raforker Developments
1796
RAF-Skull **1181**
Rana **0100**
RB Bloc Buster **0286**
RB Speed Ride **0281**
Ready and Action TV **0968**
Reaktor **0024**
Reality Sandwich **0836**
Rebel **1784**
Rebel Rebel **0492**
Recycle Now **0621**
Red Head Lounge
1409–1410
REEK **1111**
Reeperbahn Theater
Hamburg **0265**
Refugio Aboim Ascensao
0613
Régalis **1374**
Relate **1041**

Reliance Building **1599**
Remedy Festival **1061**
Rendez-vous Novembre
2007 **0716**
Renega **0168**
re-public **0210**
República **0857**
Research Center
for Fashion the Body
and... **0719**
ReStart Associates **0134**
Retroflo **1620**
Revelation Generation
Music Festival **1045**
Revolution Miami **1043**
Ricardo Piñeiro Modelos
0514
Ricky Martin **1128, 1131**
Riders Magazine **0906**
Rio 92 **0768**
Rio 2016 – Candidate City
0330–0331
Rio Cine Festival **0387**
Rip it Up **0905**
Rison **0230**
Rison Plane **0564**
RMX **1753**
Road to the open **0282**
Robert Safdie **1457**
Robo Tussin **1289**
Rocafuerte Seguros **1533**
Rock **1029**
Rock en Seine **1044**
Rock is Dead **1101**
Rock & Pop **0986–0994**
Roho **1671**
Romano Autolinee **1591**
Ronda **0010**
Ronin Recruitment **0031**
Root Networks **0883**
Roots **1797**
Rootys **1397**
Rosca Realizateurs **0238**
Rota **0276**
Royal **1211**
Royal Palm Hotels
and Resorts **1570**
RSI **1042**

S

S **1209**
Sago Imports **1556**
Sai Baba **0562**
Saks Fifth Avenue **1232**
Saloon Cafe Daniel Lussier
1388
Sal Vista **1821, 1824**
Salzburger Stier **0262**
San Diego Advertising
Fund for Emergencies **0726**
San Isidro **0740**
Sanity Drops **1355**

Sans-Souci **1322**
Sardegna **0754**
Saturday **1150**
Saudade **0456**
SB **1551**
Scarab **0536–0537**
Schallschnelle **1168**
Schaltkreis GbR **1080**
Schmoove **0538**
School Gallery Paris **1830**
Scout **1605**
Seattle Art Museum **0699**
SectionSeven **0053, 0172**
Seed **0606**
Semana Olímpica **0329**
SEM Label **1115–1123**
Semtex Girls **1134**
SerCidadão **0786**
Sesc Rio.Som **1167**
Sette Chiese Caffè **1365**
Seven Splat **0180**
Sex & Agriculture **1140**
Sex Museum **0755**
Sexy Circus **0266**
Shades of Fur **1652**
Shado **0995–1000, 1007**
Sheffield **1842**
Shen Wei Dance Arts **0322**
Shifting Sites **0314, 0316,
0319**
Shine **1459**
Shrimp Farm **1058**
Sida+Violencia **0626**
Side Walk **0433**
Sigedis **0791**
Sights **1496**
Silke Weggen **1595**
Simplecraft Fabrication
1742, 1898
Sipos **1229**
Sixtynine Magazine **0950**
Skånes Dansteater **0311**
Skincare **1204**
Skipping Ropes **0498**
Slang **0235**
Slanted **0985**
Slash **1783**
Sleepy Cloud **1649**
Smile **1780**
SMN **0804**
Sneakers **0944**
SNOG **1327**
Socialpest **0342**
Sociedad Minera Cerro
Verde **1827**
Soda Stereo **1054**
Soft Gallery **0539**
Soma Productions Jacynthe
Arsenault **0877**
Somerset Partners **1668**
So! Nagaya **1700**
Soul Circle **0435–0436**

Soultrips **1515**
Sounds Red **1060**
Soviet **1151–1152**
Spagna **1450**
SpeachSquare **0058**
Speak! **0363**
Speicherhafen Interieur
& Lifestyle **1280**
Spiralis **1475**
Splash Toys Inc. **1875**
Spot **1294**
Staatliche Akademie der
Bildenden Künste Stuttgart
0697
Staatskanzlei NRW **0725**
Staatstheater Nürnberg
0600
Stadsmuseum Tilburg **0824**
Stadthalle Schillerhöhe
0605
Stadtvillen am Werdersee
1822
Stereoteca **1185**
St. Martin de Porres
Foundation **1541**
Stokbroekx&Stokbroekx
1614
Strange Detective Tales
0966
Street a Porter **0960**
Stripes **1769**
Structures Salon **1495**
Studio-A **0131**
Studio Jefrë **0036**
Subte **0596**
Subzero **1847**
Sugarcoat Designer Vinyl
Decals **1825**
Sugar International **1629**
Suncoast **0585**
Sun India **1275**
Supertopic **0948**
Surreal **0362**
Sur Sud Sul **0761**
Survial **1655**
Sushi Tech **1288**
Sverre Sætre **1238**
Sweater **0557**
Sweet Tooth Designs **0438,
0447–0450, 0451–0452**
Swirl **0099**

T

Taak **0378**
Tableshield **1826**
Tacksales Ltd. **1385**
Taffera Builders **1547**
Tagtraum **1416**
Tailor Missions **0776**
Talega **0161**
Talento de Barrio **1030**
Taller Victor **1156**

Tangerine Spa **0580**
Tangrama Design Studio
0188
Tankorama Design **0196**
Tao Empreendimentos
1627
Taylor Design Studio **0084**
TB **1739**
td designs **0076**
Tech Mex Collective **0146**
TechnoBuy **1375**
Tecnova **1387**
Telecurso TEC **0735**
Télo **1490**
Temaiken Foundation **0766**
Tenica **1477**
Tenso **1010–1011**
Tepper Wine **1300**
Terrabienes **1531**
Terra Firme Produtora
0138
Terroir Alliance **1795**
TGC **0862, 0890**
The Advocate **0958**
Theater **1182**
The Bakers **1224**
The Big Art Project **0313**
The Big Beat **0249–0391**
The boys **0175**
The Burger Concept **1351**
The C42 Collective **0214**
The Cassettes **1102**
The Co-operative **1383**
The Criterion Collection
0848
The Dorchester **1535**
The Drill Hall **0689**
The Forma Blog **1006**
The Golden Fur Pin **0321**
The Green Kingdom **1126**
The Guild Open Project
0838
The Internet Advertising
Bureau **0811**
The Little Bird Project
0381
The Lonely Poet **1205,
1296, 1412**
The Luxury of Protest **0245**
The Metropolitan Opera
0694–0695
The Mission **0287**
The Mooncats **1100**
The Morgan Library
& Museum **0696**
The N **0925–0926**
The New York
Photography Festival 2008
0326
The Oculas Group **0200**
The Philip Johnson
Glass House **0610**

The Secret Machines **113**
The Sicarios of
Rock & Roll **1141**
The Supahip **1103**
The Vaults **1380**
The Wheatsheaf **1344**
The Yorkshire Wolds **074**
Thimble Sourcing **0578**
Thinkbox **1035**
Third Thursda **0260**
Thomas Moran Trust **077**
Ticon **1563**
Tiergarten Carrée **1883**
Tiergarten Pforzheim **035**
Tierra Atacama **1577–157**
Tierra Chigüire **1662**
Time Brasil **0328**
Times Talks **0299**
Tinti **0885**
Tipografia **0389**
Tipos **0047**
TMDG **1013**
Tmiint **1837**
TNOP Design **0069**
TNTY JNM **1169**
To Hell **0495**
Tommy Chandler
Photography **0083**
Tony Fergo **0380**
Top Friseur **1625**
Toronto Transit Commissio
0717
Torres Fotografía **0013**
Totem **0458**
Towngas Telecom **1481**
Tragon Corporation **1623**
Traidcraft **1640**
Trama **0402**
Transalp Challenge **0284**
Transoceanica **1675**
Transparenz Werkstatt **152**
Trash Sudamerica
1008–1009, 0976
Tree House **1291**
Tre Uker **0111**
Triband **1078**
Triple L. **0049**
Triptico **0528**
Triton **0459**
Trivento **1714**
Trole **0765**
Tropical Handgun **1085**
Troy Pierce **1059**
Trump Towers **1712**
Truvia **1812**
T's Ethiopian and Asian
Cuisine **1219, 1245, 1345**
Tsingtao Beer **1857**
Tsn-ComEx **1895**
Tulipandra **1540**
Tunit **0505**
TuttiFrutti **0162**

uli 0590–0592
risted 0301
ritter 0940
o Worlds 0004
VS Ravensburg 0827

CLA 0821
CLA Arts 0616
C Riverside 0810
O 0796
ses Hotel 1550
ML 0236
ion 0070
isono 1099
ivida 0623
percuts 1180
ban Daddy 0970
ane 1738
ban Racer 0949
banSilo 0160
ban Soldierz 1775
B Mouse 0179
OTA 2007 0132
opus 0145

dum 0504
bona 1740
mpire Breathe 1641
nde Falke 0576
ioBlock 1702
rious – Falko Ohlmer
61–1762, 1766, 1890
rious – Negro 1650,
9–1722, 1726,
32–1735, 1743–1747,
51–1752, 1754–1760,
68, 1865
rious – Sockho 1767
ryWell 0092
Va Voom 0194
Voom 0927
CR Villaparaiso 0867
DI 0608
gas 1786, 1788
ndome 1323
ntus Medical 1741
RDF 0690
reda Tropical 1242
ristream 1468
agen 1811
orations 1381
CS Logo 0748
ctory Gardens 2008+
20
ken Vom 0565
ne to Vintage Trail 1798
rum Hotel 1597
va Architecture 0112
antes 0801
MS 1844

VogelFrei 1179
Voodoo 0118
VPAR 1493
V-Radio 1027
VSBC 0753
Vsona 0893
Vudu Princess 1406
VZ Producciones 1293

W

Wall R Us 1684
Walter Bressia 1807
Wasatch Powder Clinics
1512–1514
WebVet 0943
WeEatDesign 0183
Weinstube Wagrain 1319
Wellsford Estate 1881
We Love Sneakers 0526
weplaythis 1036
WFMU 0908
wg0055 0190
Where you are
heart? 1031
Whight On 1026
Whitewash Recordings
1051
Wild Project 0324
Windmade 1638
Window 0603
Windpassinger Architekten
0135
Wine Dine & All That Jazz
0304
Wonderland 1019, 1897
Wood Productions 0085
Word Jokey 0222
World Arts 0295–0297
World Music
& Dance Centre 0763
World Science Festival
0258
Worldwide Palliative
Care Alliance 0701
WPI 0784
writa. 1730
Württembergisches
Landesmuseum Stuttgart
0609

X

x13Ax 0201
Xinet 0158

Y

Yale School
of Management 0749
Yellow Deli 1247–1255
Yellow Sound Lab 1162
YogaStudio 1579–1583
Yonca Moda 0473
Young at Art 0267

Your octopus
ate my mixtape 0852
Yups.tv 0941

Z

Zaeus 0895
Z Contemporâneo 1231
Zeckendorf Development
1673
Zeisig 0888
Zkoob 0870
Zoe Bar Restaurant 1329
Zolo 1805
Zoomp 0462
Zouk Recordings 1050
ZOVAR 0721

STUDIOS

2FRESH
Turkey
http://2fresh.com
0340, 0473

3Deluxe
Germany
www.3deluxe.de
0270, 0454, 0477–0482,
0483, 0486, 0488, 0521,
1233, 1639, 1691–1692,
1725, 1728, 1737, 1763,
1772, 1777–1779,
1781–1782, 1783–1786,
1787–1792, 1794, 1871

**3rd Edge
Communications**
USA
www.3rdedge.com
0813, 1045

6D
Brazil
www.6d.com.br
0458, 0545–0547,
1166, 1196, 1490

9Myles
USA
www.9myles.com
0726, 0733, 0785,
1622, 1648, 1667,
1833, 1893

19 Design
Brazil
www.19design.com.br
0259,0332, 0336,
0750, 1627

75B
The Netherlands
0663–0666, 0763, 0829

802
Sweden
www.802.com
1297, 1360, 1381

1828
Argentina
www.1828buenosaires.com
1384, 1430, 1895

A.C.O.
Japan
http://aco-tokyo.com
0125, 0746, 0762, 0784

Adrenalab
Italy
www.adrenalab.com
0222,0377–0378, 0844

Alejandro Ros
Argentina
http://alejandroros.com.ar
1054, 1099, 1129, 1618

**alternatyves
outc.**
Belgium
http://
alternatyvesoutc.com
0908

Amodesign
Portugal
http://amodesign.net
0612, 1889

a+morph
Germany
http://a-morph.de
175, 335

**an agency
called england**
United Kingdom
www.englandagency.com
0192, 0441, 0744,
0800, 1857

Anders Kavcic
Sweden
http://cubical.se
0078, 0311, 0531

Andrea Wong
Germany
http://andreawong.de
1155, 1521

**Andrew Wilson
Design**
USA
http://
andrewwilsondesign.com
0895

Anima
Ecuador
0054, 0732, 0745,
0767, 1305, 1480, 1530,
1666, 1814

Anna Mándoki
Germany/Hungary
www.annamandoki.com
0918–0919

Annella Armas
Venezuela
0359, 1662

Apfel Zet
Germany
www.apfelzet.de
0011, 0051, 0203–0205,
0231, 0264, 0444, 0697,
0858, 0886, 1452

Applied Projects
Denmark
http://applied.dk
1076, 1106, 1112

area3
Spain
http://area3.net
0106, 0271, 0291, 0619,
1058–1059

Ariel Pintos
Venezuela
www.arielpintos.com
0252, 0598, 0841, 1809

Ars Thanea
Poland
www.arsthanea.com
0097

Arterial
Brazil
www.arterial.tv
0269, 0840, 0966, 1070,
1124, 1539, 1573–1576

asmallpercent
USA
http://asmallpercent.com
0830, 1198–1203

Attak
The Netherlands
http://attakweb.com
0033, 0059, 0175, 0179,
0184, 0226, 0250,
0362–0363, 0379, 0495,
0500, 0554–0559, 0602,
0730, 0805, 0889, 0944,

0954, 0960, 1026, 1158,
1407, 1562, 1764–1765

ATTIK
USA
www.attik.com
1497, 1505, 1645

Attitude Design
United Kingdom
www.attitudedesign.co.uk
0223

**Azuca Ingenio
Gráfico**
Ecuador
www.azucaingenio.com
0868, 1242

Battin
Denmark
0866, 1422

Baumann & Baumann
Germany
http://
baumannandbaumann.com
0261–0262, 0605, 0607,
0609, 0708, 0827, 1435

BBH
United Kingdom
http://
bartleboglehegarty.com
0118, 0195

lén Mena
ador
w.belenmena.com
5, 1793, 1795

rcz
le
w.bercz.net
6, 0376, 0446,
4, 0953

rnardita Brancoli
le
0–1341

rnardo+Celis
entina
p://bernardocelis.com
2, 0310, 0337–0339,
6, 0806, 1293, 1896

WA
rmany
p://bkwa.de
9–1280

nco Diseño
le
w.blancodiseno.cl
7–1578

uelounge Design
A
p://bluelounge.com
2, 1724

ldrini & Ficcardi
entina
w.bfweb.com.ar
2, 0503, 0582, 0582,
4, 1281–1282, 1300,
1, 1322, 1406, 1635,
8, 1714, 1740,
0–1808, 1845

ahm
ited Kingdom
p://brahm.com
4–1269, 1560, 1717

anislav Design
venia
w.branislavdesign.com
7, 0198, 0883,
7, 1847

uno Porto
azil
p://brunoporto.com
1, 0909

ild
ited Kingdom
p://wearebuild.com
9, 1225–1226, 1298,
3, 1357, 1392

ro Ink
rmany
p://bueroink.com

Cabina
Argentina
www.espaciocabina.com.ar
0090, 0140, 0142,
0514–0515, 0560, 0593,
0759, 0959, 1387, 1612,
1703, 1704

**Camisa 10
Propaganda**
Brazil
http://
c10propaganda.com.br
0060, 1888

Caótica
Brazil
www.caotica.com.br
0107, 0273, 0276–0279,
0283, 0288, 0290,
0292–0294, 0385, 0427,
0502, 0563, 0982, 1085,
1088, 1157, 1411, 1748

Carla Reinés Design
Brazil
www.fiodesign.com.br
1554–1555

Cheval de Troie
France
http://chevaldetroie.net
1437–1445

**Chilli Design
& Multimedia**
Belgium
http://chilli.be
1236

Chris Clarke
United Kingdom
http://chris-clarke.co.uk
0234, 0951

Christian Otto Studio
http://christianotto.com
0006, 0084, 0494, 1213

Christoph Knoth
Germany
http://knothen.de
0622, 0624, 0812,
0881, 1182

Claus Koch
Germany
www.clauskoch.de
1182, 0579, 0600,
0608, 0715, 0720, 0725,
1631, 1817

Clusta Ltd.
United Kingdom
http://clusta.com
0108, 0470, 0904, 0975,

1176, 1380, 1397,
1557, 1723

Côme de Bouchony
France
http://
comedebouchony.com
0139, 0927, 0977,
1180, 1830

Comparsas
Brazil
http://comparsas.com.br
0056, 0499, 0543, 1515

Cuartopiso
Colombia
www.cuartopiso.com
0137, 1216, 1346, 1382

Dale Harris
Australia
http://daleharris.com
0168, 0171, 0193, 0214,
0246, 0606, 0710, 0748,
0852, 1061, 1217, 1246,
1624, 1656, 1798,
1828, 1881

Damián Di Patrizio
Argentina
www.22-10-78.com
0028, 0049, 0571, 1291,
1351, 1584, 1596, 1880

Daniel Arendt
Germany
http://danielgrafik.de
0381, 1883

David Criado
Bolivia
0247, 1598

David Standen
United Kingdom
www.davidstanden.com
0577, 1073

DBXL
The Netherlands
www.dbxl.nl
0386, 1050, 1062–1063,
1098

Dema Werbeagentur
Germany
www.dema.de
0366

de.MO
USA
http://de-mo.org
0826, 1019

Dez Propaganda
Brazil
www.
dezpropaganda.com.br
0857, 1366, 1491

DHM Graphic Design
The Netherlands
http://dhmdesign.nl
0029, 0287, 0342, 0364,
0393–0399, 0625, 0957,
0963, 1545, 1606, 1876

Diego Corrales
Ecuador
0219–0220, 0765, 1492

DOGO
Argentina
http://undogo.com
0723, 0941, 1471

Dreamer
Australia
http://
dreamer-productions.com
1051, 1103, 1125, 1171

Ducks Design
Germany
www.ducksdesign.de
0566

Dupla Design
Brazil
www.dupladesign.com.br
0213, 0751, 0814

D.Workz Interactive
USA
www.dworkz.com
1174

Eduardo Chang
Costa Rica
www.eduardochang.sv.tc
1342, 1659

Edward McMullin
Ireland
www.edwardmcmullin.com
1796

eg.design
Brazil
www.egdesign.com.br
0640, 0678–0683, 0735,
0768, 1224, 1376, 1500

Ego Grafik
Germany
0001, 0035

Elastic People
USA
www.elasticpeople.com
0253, 0382, 0382, 1030,
1049, 1069, 1074, 1075,
1077, 1107, 1114, 1128,
1131, 1170, 1332, 1474, 1712

**Emenius Commercial
Department**
www.andreasemenius.com
0466, 0504, 0505, 0539,
0581

EHA Studio
Denmark
http://eha.dk
1032, 1370, 1705–1706

Emiliano Rodriguez
Argentina
http://
emilianorodriguez.com.ar
0613, 1496

Eno Krüger Design
France
www.enokuger.com
0148–0149, 0241, 0243,
0435–0436, 0468, 0517,
0876, 0934, 1065, 1066,
1072, 1133, 1160, 1163,
1186, 1212, 1215, 1240,
1331, 1634, 1657

entz creative
Singapore
www.entzcreative.com
0076, 0159, 1359, 1385,
1506

eps51
Germany
www.eps51.de
0113, 0301, 0536–0537,
0542, 0793, 1820

Eramos Tantos
Mexico
www.eramostantos.com.mx
0007, 0225, 0728, 0891,
1012, 1197

erde zwei
Germany
www.erdezwei.de
0487

Ernesto Azcuy
Bolivia
0734, 0738, 0790

Escobas
Mexico
www.escobas.com.mx
0032, 0081, 0178, 0523,
1486–1487, 1771, 1892

Essex Two
USA
www.sx2.com
0760, 0770, 1424, 1432,
1541, 1647, 1875

**Esteban Salgado/
Velesi**
Ecuador
www.velesi.com
0755, 0839, 1693,
1713, 1850

Estudio Garcia Balza
Argentina
www.garciabalza.com.ar

0010, 0161, 0162, 0217,
0639, 0709, 1040

Estudio González
Chile
www.estudiogonzalez.cl
0062, 0068, 0085,
0156, 0165, 0268, 1326,
1638, 1879

Estudio Infinito
Brazil
http://
estudioinfinito.com.br
0186, 1364

Estudio Mariscal
Spain
www.mariscal.com
1488

estudiotres
USA
www.estudiotres.com
0320, 0384, 1335, 1423,
1446–1448, 1617

Eva Lindeman
The Netherlands
www.evalindeman.com
0064, 1476

Fabrika de Typos
Brazil
0055, 0961, 0965

Falko Ohlmer
Germany
www.falko-ohlmer.com
0074, 0093, 0249, 0391,
0409–0418, 0439–0440,
0471, 0524, 0527, 0834,
1042, 1055, 1130,
1136–1137, 1191–1194,
1237, 1436, 1590,
1761–1762, 1766, 1890

Fatuus
Germany
www.fatuus.de
0021, 0024, 1036

**Faydherbe/
De Vringer**
The Netherlands
www.ben-wout.nl
0567, 0721, 0824, 0825,
1379

FEED
Canada
www.studiofeed.ca
0071, 0079, 0254, 0341,
0595, 0693, 0716, 1082,
1111, 1348

Felipe Taborda
Brazil
www.felipetaborda.com.br
0404

Felix Beltran
Mexico
0016, 0047, 0777

Fileni & Fileni
Argentina
www.filenifileni.com
0740, 1277, 1343, 1349,
1868

**Firstflash X-media
Labor**
Germany
www.firstflash.net
0265, 0892

Forma
Austria
http://for.ma
0065, 0780, 0831,
1006, 1139, 1350, 1551,
1702

form one
Germany
www.form-one.de
0862, 1494, 1524

Franke+Fiorella
USA
www.frankefiorella.com
1882

Fritz Torres
México
0002, 0842, 1421, 1870

Frontespizio
Mexico
www.frontespizio.com.mx
0126, 1347

Fulô Estudio
Brazil
0164, 0289, 1352, 1485

Futurefarmers
USA
www.futurefarmers.com
0361, 0614, 0620, 0769,
0940, 1829

Gabriela Rodríguez
Mexico
http://
gabrielarodriguez.com.mx
0667–0671, 0690

**GAD'
Branding & Design**
Brazil
www.gad.com.br
0711, 1461, 1570, 1601,
1840, 1846

Gaia 9 Studio
United Kingdom
www.gaia9studio.com
0587

Gallusness
United Kingdom
www.gallusness.com
1525

gardens&co.
www.gardens-co.com
1273–1274, 1301,
1324, 1481

Garus Booth
Canada
www.bythebooth.com
0365

Gazz
The Netherlands
www.gazz.nl
1566, 1568

**Geyrhalter
Design**
USA
www.geyrhalter.com
0743, 0893, 1033, 1172,
1502, 1609, 1818

Ginter & Miletina
Germany
http://alexginter.de
http://miletina.de
0224, 0787, 1109, 1243,
1489, 1872

**Giovanni Bianco/
Studio 65**
USA
www.giovannibianco.com
0187, 0199, 0212,
0525, 0535, 0541, 1064,
1134, 1211

Glauco Diogenes
Brazil
www.
glaucodiogenes.com.br
0169

Graphic Kitchen
Mexico
www.cocinagrafica.com
0146, 0327, 0402, 0764,
1031, 1540

Grupo Oxigeno
Chile
www.grupoxigeno.cl
0803, 1462, 1470, 1487,
1498

GuaZa Studio
El Salvador
www.guazastudio.com
0128, 0739, 1337–1338

Hafenbraut
Germany
www.hafenbraut.de
0075, 1168, 1851

Hardy Design
Brazil
www.hardydesign.com.br
0221, 0590–0592,
0705–0707, 0727,
0902

Hawaii Design
United Kingdom
www.hawaiidesign.co.uk
0031, 0200, 0475

HelloMe
Germany
www.tillwiedeck.com
0005, 0058, 0143,
0229–0230, 0460, 0469,
0516, 0564, 0576, 0878,
0888, 1080, 1087,
1110, 1179, 1209, 1214,
1292, 1361, 1389, 1390,
1416, 1504, 1730

Hello Monday
Denmark
www.hellomonday.net
0037–0044, 0048, 0208,
0209, 0522, 0565,
1247–1255

Hello Vanilla
United Kingdom
www.hellovanilla.co.uk
0008, 0491, 1290

Helou Design
Ecuador
www.heloudesign.com
0009, 0022, 0120, 0182,
0472, 0569, 0779, 0795,
1108, 1206, 1227, 1239,
1309–1315, 1329, 1339,
1375, 1417, 1419, 1433,
1526–1527, 1542, 1544,
1556, 1558, 1628, 1644,
1660, 1669, 1672

Henriquez Lara
Mexico
www.henriquezlara.com
1304, 1316–1318, 1405

Hoet & Hoet
Belgium
www.hoet-hoet.eu
0400, 0789, 0791, 0837,
1569, 1571, 1836

**hotmonkey
design**
United Kingdom
www.
hotmonkeydesign.com
1325

Hugo & Marie
USA
www.hugoandmarie.com
0141, 1097

Hula+Hula
Mexico
www.hulahula.com.mx
0256, 0562, 0568, 0778,
0967, 1023, 1024, 1161,
1187–1190, 1256–1263,
1665, 1891

IAA
Australia
www.iamabsolut.com
1499

ICG
United Kingdom
www.icgonline.co.uk
1454, 1463–1465, 1821,
1824, 1826

ico Design
United Kingdom
www.icodesign.co.uk
1327, 1661

Ideo Comunicadores
Peru
www.ideo.com.pe
0572, 0578, 0675–0677,
1827

**Ideograma
Consultores S.C.**
Mexico
www.ideograma.com
1518, 1848

il2d
Poland
www.il2d.com
0050, 0086

Illunatic
Germany
www.illunatic.de
0087, 0838, 0968, 1052

ImagenHB
Argentina
www.imagenhb.com
0017, 0025, 0057, 0123,
0167, 0300, 0303, 0761,
0815, 0828, 0860, 0875,
0897, 1221–1223, 1275,
1276, 1371, 1373, 1413,
1511, 1538, 1550, 1592,
1597, 1600, 1671, 1843,
1860, 1894

Interface Designers
Brazil
http://
interfacedesigners.com.br
0012, 0642, 0816, 1208,
1218, 1228, 1231, 1367

Jan Kallwejt
Poland
http://kallwejt.com
0467, 0511, 0729, 1165,
1177–1178

John Moore
Venezuela
www.johnmoore.com.ve
0898

Juan Carlos Darias
Venezuela
0251, 0599

**Juan Pablo
Tredicce**
Argentina
0189, 0191, 1572

jungeschachtel
Germany
www.jungeschachtel.de
0215

Justin Harder
USA
www.justinharder.la
0023, 0227, 0561,
0691–0692, 0845, 0846,
0937, 0939, 1060,
1144–1152, 1278,
1286–1289, 1453, 1636,
1641, 1649, 1651–1653,
1676–1684, 1685–1690,
1707, 1769, 1774

Kasia Korczak
Belgium
http://
korczak-vereecken.com
0202

Kent House
United Kingdom
www.kenthouse.com
0637, 0855

KentLyons
United Kingdom
www.kentlyons.com
0799, 1035, 1455, 1458,
1608

Kiko Farkas
Brazil
www.kikofarkas.com.br
0652–0662, 0823

King Emperor
Belgium/UK
http://kingemperor.net
0052

KITA
Germany
www.kita-berlin.com
0004, 0018, 0218, 0603,
1090–1096, 1431,
1548–1549, 1607, 1797

Knowledge+
Japan
www.knowledge-plus.jp
1295, 1700

Kontra
Colombia
www.kontra.ws
0104, 0266, 0401,
0528, 1362

Kontrapunkt
Denmark
www.kontrapunkt.dk
0466, 0505, 0581

Krghettojuice
Italy
www.krghettojuice.com
0255, 1175, 1365, 1591

**Laboratório
Secreto**
Brazil
http://
laboratoriosecreto.com
0274

La fe ciega studio
Mexico
www.lafeciega.com
0867, 0946, 0956

La Flama
Mexico
www.laflama.com
0170, 0197, 0244

Landor Associates
United Kingdom
www.landor.com
1640

Larrea
Chile
www.larrea.cl
0742, 0773, 1625

La Silueta
Colombia
www.lasilueta.com
193

Latinbrand
Ecuador
www.latin-brand.com
0248, 0263, 0623,
0628–0635, 0796, 1418,
1425–1426, 1428, 1434,
1466, 1579–1583

**Lauren Nassef
& Isaac Tobin**
USA
0355–0358

Leo Vilas
Brazil
0177

Liam Johnstone
Canada
www.liamjohnstone.com
0365, 0717

ia Santiago
azil
6

ten Design
A
w.listendesign.com
3, 0181, 0544, 0903,
2–1514, 1742, 1898

goholik
A
w.logoholik.com
1, 0942, 1053, 1643,
0, 1837

ke Williams
A
w.lukeluke luke.com
0

L
nce
w.level-art.com
4, 0099, 0526, 0530,
8

a Zumblick
azil
w.lyazumblick.com
6, 0239, 0443, 0955

achicao Design
livia
w.machicaodesign.com
1, 1863

agma
and Design
rmany
p://
gmabranddesign.de
9, 0352, 0463,
2–0674, 1078,
2–1856

nifiesto 79
lombia
p://visualgore.tv
2

rcos Larghero
uguay
9

aria Loor
A
w.marialoor.com
9

arshall & Marshall
nce
w.2marshalls.net
8, 1482

artino
gentina
w.martinoweb.com.ar
7, 0115, 0350

Martin Steocklin
Switzerland
0636

Medusateam
Spain
www.medusateam.com
0519, 1775

Milkxhake
Hong Kong
www.milkxhake.org
0314, 0316–0317, 0319,
0971

Momkai
The Netherlands
www.momkai.nl
0621, 1027

Mr and Mrs M
United Kingdom
www.mrandmrsm.com
0880, 0884

MrBowlegs
United Kingdom
www.mrbowlegs.co.uk
0513, 1100, 1105, 1113

Muller
United Kingdom
www.hellomuller.com
0474, 0847

multimediaHAAM
USA
www.multimediahaam.com
1495

Muti Randolph
Brazil
www.muti.cx
1307–1308, 1507, 1632

Nahon
Argentina
www.nahon.com.ar
0818, 0983, 0986–0994,
1021–1022, 1028

Nalindesign
Germany
www.nalindesign.com
0133, 0490, 1020, 1595

Negro
Argentina
www.negronouveau.com
0102–0103, 0105, 0237,
0426, 0507–0510, 0532,
0863, 0910–0917, 0976,
0995–1003, 1005,
1007–1011, 1013–1018,
1283–1285, 1334, 1396,
1650, 1719–1722, 1726,
1732–1735, 1743–1747,
1751–1752, 1754–1760,
1768, 1865

NNSS
Design + Ideas
Argentina
www.nnss.com.ar
0194, 0347, 0879, 1039,
1320–1321, 1374, 1585,
1799, 1835

Noblanco
Colombia
www.noblanco.com
0211, 0442

Nobrand
Lebanon
www.nobrand.name
0157, 1567

No Days Off
United Kingdom
www.nodaysoff.com
0061, 1135

Nowhere
USA
www.nowherenyc.com
0275, 0322, 0324,
0346, 0594, 0836, 0970,
0972, 1132

Nuñez del Arco
Ecuador
http://
nunezdelarco.blogspot.com
0207, 0280, 0492, 0718,
0859, 1102

Oblicua
Mexico
www.oblicua.com.mx
0089, 0781, 1378, 1475

Ocular Ink
USA
www.ocularink.com
0077, 0091, 0095, 1477

Oded Ezer
Israel
www.odedezer.com
0345, 1173, 1395

Oestudio
Brazil
www.oestudio.com.br
0456, 0461, 0464,
0585, 0933, 1867,
1886–1887

Ohyeah Studio
Norway
www.ohyeahstudio.no
0109–0111, 0130, 0196,
0240, 0315

Oscar Patzan
Canada
www.oscarpatzan.com
0455, 1528

Osso Design
Brazil
www.osso.com.br
0343, 0360, 1025, 1185

Oswaldo Terreros
Ecuador
www.oswaldoterreros.com
1711, 1750, 1773

Oz Design
Brazil
www.ozdesign.com.br
0736, 0797, 1516

Paco Gálvez
Mexico
0506, 1834

Paperjam Design
North Ireland
www.paperjamdesign.com
0267, 1205, 1296, 1412,
1501, 1615, 1619

Pentagram
Worldwide
www.pentagram.com
www.pentagram.co.uk
0003, 0116, 0158, 0258,
0299, 0302, 0325–0326,
0512, 0583–0584, 0597,
0610–0611, 0641,
0684–0686, 0688–0689,
0694–0696, 0698–0703,
0713, 0722, 0737, 0749,
0752, 0754, 0756–0758,
0774, 0776, 0788,
0801, 0809–0810, 0817,
0820, 0822, 0848–0849,
0928, 0958, 1004, 1204,
1230, 1232, 1299, 1303,
1383, 1414, 1522, 1532,
1535, 1547, 1611,
1616, 1621, 1623, 1637,
1668, 1670, 1673–1674,
1701, 1709–1710,
1715–1716, 1718, 1729,
1741, 1838, 1838,
1844, 1878

Pepe Menéndez
Cuba
0428, 0638

Permanent Unit
Austria
www.permanent-unit.com
0121, 0206, 0242,
0281–0282, 0285–0286,
0354, 0493, 0950, 1046

Philippe
Archontakis
Canada
http://
philippearchontakis.com
0072, 0390, 0484, 0877,
1388, 1839

phla
Austria
www.phla.at
1089

Pixelerate
The Netherlands
www.pixelerate.nl
0026, 0794, 1523

Planobase Design
Brazil
0969

PO!
Patricio Oliver
Argentina
www.patriciooliver.com.ar
1874

Polychrome
USA
www.polychrome.com
0616, 0821, 1127

Pozo Marcic
Ensamble
Chile
www.ensamble.cl
1368

Praline
United Kingdom
www.designbypraline.com
0185, 0344, 0719,
1815–1816

Projectgraphics
Kosova
www.projectgraphics.net
0046, 0094, 0163,
0772, 0896, 1056, 1356,
1377, 1831, 1866

Pump Diseño
Argentina
www.pumpd.com.ar
0747, 1207, 1386, 1449,
1456, 1472

Punga
Argentina
www.punga.tv
0232–0233, 0238,
0429, 0485, 0489,
0548–0553, 0920–0924,
0962, 1156

Pure
Communication
Belgium
www.
pure-communication.be
0063, 1520, 1614, 1859

Push
USA
www.pushhere.com
0036, 0808, 1460, 1663

RacoSchneider
Brazil
www.racoschneider.com
0015, 0080, 0586, 0786,
1529, 1602–1604

RARE Design
Associates
United Kingdom
www.wearerare.com
0573, 0865, 1537, 1559

RDYA
Argentina
www.rdya.com
0408, 0978

redfloor
Austria
www.redfloor.at
1319, 1355, 1473,
1483–1484, 1517, 1534

re-public
Denmark
www.re-public.com
0210, 0321, 0348, 1041

ReStart Associates
Hong Kong
www.restart-associates.com
0134, 0136, 0870

Revolver
Panama
www.elrevolver.com
0380, 1244, 1358,
1884–1885

Ricardo Gimenes
Brazil
www.ricardogimenes.com
0190

Rock Instrument
Bureau
Argentina
www.mailrock.com.ar
0020, 0465

Rodolfo Fuentes
Uruguay
www.rodolfofuentes.com
0873, 0979, 1138

Ronnie Fueglister
Swtizerland
0636

Santiago Pol
Venezuela
0406, 0618

São Paulo Criação
Brazil
http://
saopaulocriacao.com.br
0433–0434, 0462, 0533,
1235, 1294, 1415–1420

SectionSeven
USA
www.sectionseven.com
0034, 0053, 0160, 0172,
1633

Seven
New Zealand
www.seven.co.nz
0180, 0305, 0905, 1140,
1629, 1731, 1736, 1738,
1832, 1842, 1849

**Shakespear
Design**
Argentina
www.shakespearweb.com
0596, 0724, 0766, 1451,
1654, 1658, 1862, 1869

shk.studio
Panama
http://
shk-studio.blogspot.com
0570, 0627, 1038, 1068,
1408–1410

SIGN*
Belgium
www.designbysign.com
0403, 0405, 0617, 0945,
1328, 1553, 1610, 1858

Simone Inc.
Japan
www.simone.co.jp
0228, 0453, 0947, 0984,
1169, 1369, 1589, 1780

Slang
Germany
www.slanginternational.org
0235, 0980

Sockho
France
www.sockho.com
0388, 0534, 0871, 1044,
1067, 1071, 1079, 1101,
1739, 1753, 1767, 1770

Sofia Saez Matos
Puerto Rico
0835, 0887, 0894, 0900

Sonar
USA
http://
sonarproductions.com
1162

Soter Design
Brazil
www.soterdesign.com.br
0328–0331, 1210

**Spunk Design
Machine**
USA
www.spkdm.com

0643, 0832, 1219, 1245,
1345, 1398–1404,
1593–1594, 1825

Stereo
United Kingdom
www.hellostereo.co.uk
0476, 0974, 1143,
1220, 1344

Studio41 Designers
Italy
www.studio41.it
0066, 1229, 1372, 1450

Studioa
Peru
www.studioa.com.pe
0714, 1565, 1655, 1664

studio FM milano
Italy
www.studiofmmilano.it
0807, 0909

Studio Makgill
United Kingdom
www.studiomakgill.com
0114, 0236, 0318, 0575,
1563

Studio Output
United Kingdom
www.studio-output.com
0082, 0098, 1323, 1330,
1391, 1459, 1536, 1613,
1813, 1897

Versus
Ecuador
www.versus.com.ec
0604

Superexpresso
Spain
www.superexpresso.com
0518, 0981

SViDesign
United Kingdom
www.svidesign.com
0457, 1493

Tangrama
Colombia
www.tangramagrafica.com
0188, 0588, 0712, 0901,
1270–1272, 1479, 1899

TAXI
Canada
www.taxi.ca
0073, 0129, 0304, 0782,
0792, 1861

TAXI New York
USA
www.taxi-nyc.com
0589

Tea Time Studio
Spain
www.teatimestudio.com
0938, 1084, 1873

Tecnopop
Brazil
www.tecnopop.com.br
0117, 0145, 0306–0308,
0392, 0687, 0932,
0935–0936, 1153–1154

Tempo Design
Brazil
www.tempodesign.com.br
0138, 0459

The Cre8ion.Lab
The Netherlands
http://cre8ion.com
0804, 1363, 1503

**The Killswitch
Collective**
USA
http://
killswitchcollective.com
0351, 0843, 1037, 1467

**The Luxury
of Protest**
United Kingdom
http://
theluxuryofprotest.com
0144, 0245, 0298, 0601,
0833, 0925–0926,
1393–1394

Tholön Kunst
Argentina
www.tholon.com
0013, 0851, 1427, 1429

**Tilt Design
Studio**
Germany
www.tiltdesignstudio.com
0869, 1142, 1164, 1546

TNOP Design
USA
www.tnop.com
0045, 0069, 0150–0155,
0176, 0260, 0353, 0520,
0540, 0943

**Toastone
& Amanzilla**
Switzerland
www.toastone.com
0174, 0498, 0885, 1057,
1353, 1510, 1776

Tugba Güler
Turkey
http://
tugbaguler.blogspot.com
1599, 1864

Typozon Studio
Colombia
www.typozon.com
0101, 0437–0438,
0447–0452

Uniform
United Kingdom
www.uniform.net
0147, 1336, 1749

Un.titled
United Kingdom
www.un.titled.co.uk
0704, 0798, 0929–0931,
1727

upstruct berlin oslo
Norway/Germany
www.upstruct.com
0367–0370, 0783, 1238

Uselo
Chile
www.uselo.cl
0070, 0088, 0100, 0389

USOTA
Germany
http://
unitedstatesoftheart.com
0132, 0173, 0284,
0430–0432, 0644–0651,
0850, 0890, 0985, 1181

Vår
Sweden
www.vaar.se
0421–0425

VaryWell
USA
www.varywell.com
0092, 0295–0297, 0853,
0856, 0874, 0973, 1034,
1561

Vectorform
USA
www.vectorform.com
1605

Versus
Ecuador
www.versus.com.ec
1457, 1509, 1531, 1533,
1552, 1646, 1675

Vertigo Design
Italy
0771

Vianet
Italy
0497

Vik
USA
www.v-i-k.com
1519, 1841

Vinte Zero Um Design
Brazil
www.vintezeroum.com
0124, 0309, 0312, 0387,
0802, 0864, 1167, 1354

Vladimir Sijerkovic
Serbia
http://
vladimirsijerkovic.com
0096, 0383, 0775, 1241,
1469, 1543

WA007 Inc.
USA
www.wa007.com
0949

WeEatDesign
Mexico
www.weeatdesign.com
0131, 0183, 0419, 0529,
0580, 1081, 1141

xCOLITTx
Argentina
http://www.xcolittx.com.ar
0201, 0420, 0496, 0501,
1029, 1043, 1047–1048,
1083, 1086, 1104, 1159,
1183

xhoch4
Germany
www.xhoch4.de
0127, 0135, 0407, 1184,
1877

YES
United Kingdom
www.yesstudio.co.uk
0313, 0872

Yuri Suzuki
Japan
1195

Zachary Richter
USA
0731, 1626, 1642

Zappness
Belgium
www.zappness.net
0112

THANKS

…e challenge of making a second volume …any book is usually greater than doing …e first. The bars had already been raised …th the volume 1 of Logo Design, but …e wanted to make this second volume …en better. As we said before, to produce …ook like this, it is nearly impossible …thout the help and hard work of a lot …people – people I was glad to have …ound me all the time. And I would …ve to start with Daniel Siciliano Bretas, …y right hand in all my publications.

…st to start with some figures, we col-…orated with over 300 design offices …orldwide this time, from Berlin to New …rk, from Buenos Aires to Tokyo. We …d to go through more than 10.000 …fferent logos and judge carefully which …es would give our readers the most joy …d knowledge. Not the easiest of tasks.

With Daniel also working in the office, we both had the support of people from across many countries that would send us materials and revise texts, write cases and coordinate material delivery, send recommendations and research infor-mation. From among all these people I would like to start by thanking our contributors to the case studies, because their work will definitely give design-ers and all other professionals an insight into how things work when we design (or redesign) a logo. This section has been the strength of this publication.

My next big thanks goes to all the design-ers and design offices that submitted work and spent their time on enriching the publication. They are the ones that work tirelessly to make this world a more beautiful one. We communicated via thousands of emails, and many of them we now know personally, nevertheless you can be sure that we value every single bit of effort you have put into this.

Once more, Stefan Klatte has been our right hand man on the production front, always making things easier for us and finding solutions to make the book more beautiful, and Jutta Hendricks for the great job on the texts. Moreover, Andy Disl has given us his unwavering support with enhancing the design he created.

I hope you will find this book not just inspiring, but also a useful guide to go through once in a while.

Julius Wiedemann

IMPRINT

© 2009 TASCHEN GmbH
Hohenzollernring 53, D-50672 Köln
www.taschen.com

To stay informed about upcoming TASCHEN titles, please
request our magazine at www.taschen.com/magazine or write to
TASCHEN, Hohenzollernring 53, D-50672 Cologne, Germany,
contact@taschen.com, Fax: +49-221-254919. We will be happy
to send you a free copy of our magazine which is filled with
information about all of our books.

Design: Sense/Net, Andy Disl and Birgit Eichwede, Cologne
& Daniel Siciliano Brêtas
Layout: Daniel Siciliano Brêtas
Design Assistant: Wahideh Abdolvahab
Production: Stefan Klatte

Editor: Julius Wiedemann
Editorial Coordination: Daniel Siciliano Brêtas & Jutta Hendricks

English Revision: Chris Allen
French Translation: Martine Joulia (Equipo de Edición)
German Translation: Daniela Thoma (Equipo de Edición)

Printed in China
ISBN: 978-3-8365-0942-8

TASCHEN is not responsible when web addresses cannot be reached,
if they are offline or can be viewed just with plug-ins.

Barnsley College

Learning Centre